# SUNLIGHT AT MIDNIGHT

# SUNLIGHT
## at
# MIDNIGHT

*St. Petersburg
and the Rise of
Modern Russia*

## W. Bruce Lincoln

THE PERSEUS PRESS
A Member of the Perseus Books Group

The Perseus Press
A Member of the Perseus Books Group

Originally published in the United States by Basic Books 2001

Designed by Elizabeth Lahey
Typeset in Adobe Caslon 11 on 14

Printed and bound in Great Britain.

A CIP catalogue record for this book is available from the British Library

ISBN 1-903985-00-5

# CONTENTS

# $\mathcal{A}$CKNOWLEDGMENTS

St. Petersburg was Bruce Lincoln's first port of entry into Russia in 1964, and he returned to it often, sometimes for extended periods. In the city's rich historical archives, libraries, and museums he discovered much that sustained him as a scholar and a writer, but it was St. Petersburg itself that stirred his imagination. Somehow, the old imperial city with its shadows and light seemed to reflect his own conflicting attitudes about Russia and its past. Perhaps it is fitting, then, that he turned to it in this his twelfth and final book.

Many friends, colleagues, and institutions helped to make this book possible, and Bruce would have wanted to acknowledge everyone to whom he felt indebted. But time did not permit him to see his finished manuscript through production, so it comes to me to express my appreciation to the people who contributed to the creation of this book, especially those who assisted in the process of publication. In particular, Christine Worobec and Sam Ramer have generously given encouragement and advice on matters beyond my expertise. Marc Raeff, whose insights on Russian history never ceased to stimulate Bruce's thinking, has warmly extended his friendship. Lee Congdon, Jack Kollmann, Jerrold Zar, James Norris, Curt Richardson, and Fred Kitterle have all come forward to help in various ways.

Without the efforts of Mary Himmelberger, *Sunlight at Midnight* would not be so richly illustrated with historical images. While in St. Petersburg, Mary collected most of the photographs and engravings for this book and put together the captions. Special thanks are due also to the staff of the Slavic Reference Service at the University of Illinois Library, especially to Helen Sullivan and Jan Adamczyk, who, in researching queries large and small, have generously given their time and resources.

No book is published without the help of many people. Don Fehr, executive editor at Basic Books, contributed to the development of *Sunlight at Midnight* at all stages, and I am grateful for his editorial guidance and for the good work of his staff. To the man who "discovered" Bruce more than twenty years ago and played a vital role in his career—Robert Gottlieb, his literary agent—I owe lasting appreciation. Although I am unable to name everyone to whom a debt is owed, I wish to thank all who have graciously contributed to the making of this book.

*Mary Lincoln*
*November 2000*

# PROLOGUE

C LIMATE, COMFORT, AND CONVENIENCE were not what Russia's
Tsar Peter the Great had in mind when he decided to build a
new capital in the muddy marshes of the Neva River delta. The site he
chose stood in a remote northwest corner of his realm and was still
claimed by the Swedes, with whom Russia was in the midst of a long and
bruising war. Barely five hundred miles below the Arctic Circle and easily
submerged by the tides that flowed upriver from the Gulf of Finland, the
region saw snow as early as September and as late as May. Its foul
weather, bad water, and low-lying, sodden soil made it triply unattractive.
Yet in the imagination of the larger-than-life Tsar of All the Russias, the
place he named Sankt Pieter Burkh in the spring of 1703 had the mak-
ings of a "paradise."[1] His successors would call it St. Petersburg, Petrograd, and Leningrad. But to the generations of men and women who
watched picturesque canals and stately palaces rise from its fever-ridden
swamps, Peter's city would be forever known as "Piter," the Dutch version
of the name of the sovereign whose will had brought it into being.

Fascinated by the manner in which the Dutch had drawn wealth and
power from the sea, Peter wanted Russia to become a seafaring nation like
Holland. St. Petersburg's greatest attraction therefore lay in its nearness to
the sea lanes of Europe, from which the Russians could acquire the means

I

to escape from the backwardness that made them so vulnerable to their enemies. Peter knew that it would take decades to "borrow" from the West all the new weapons, technology, and ways of looking at the world that his nation needed, for Russia had not yet embraced the modern ways of thinking that had made Europeans of the sixteenth and seventeenth centuries so daring and adventurous. Thanks to the instruments of modern naval science, ship captains from the West had discovered new continents and circumnavigated the globe, while Russia at the time of Peter's birth in 1672 was not very different from what it had been when Ivan the Terrible had mounted its throne almost 150 years earlier. Russians continued to be superstitious, afraid of change, and wedded to traditions that bound them closely to the past. Only in the lands east of the Urals, where a handful of adventurers had begun to reach toward the Pacific at the end of the sixteenth century, had there been any concerted effort to break those bonds. But the numbers who had shared in the "conquest" of Siberia were minuscule at best. Although the Russians reached the Pacific before 1650, the men and women who had dared to challenge the Siberian wilderness still numbered far fewer than five thousand half a century later.

Progress—the force that modernized the lives of Europeans in the sixteenth and seventeenth centuries—was not a concept that most Russians living at the time of Peter's birth understood. Scientific inquiry and rational thought—the new ways of thinking about the present and future that had transformed Europe—still remained foreign to all but a handful of Peter's subjects, and most of them continued to place greater value on thoughts about the hereafter than on concerns for the here-and-now. People whose everyday language could express neither the idea of progress nor a sense of efficiency still confused miracles with the achievements of modern technology. Most Russians still thought that the earth stood at the center of the universe, and that the hand of God shaped their daily lives. To their way of thinking, famines, plagues, floods, and any sort of personal misfortune all stemmed from forces that lay beyond the realm of human comprehension. That the power of science could harness the forces of nature in the service of human masters was not yet something in which they could bring themselves to believe.

To modernize Russia, Peter had to change all this. Russia needed science and technology. Its armies needed the instruments of modern warfare, and its statesmen needed the forms of knowledge that were shrinking the Europeans' physical world and broadening their intellectual horizons.

Superstition had to be set aside, knowledge raised higher than belief, and the power of human intelligence put ahead of divine guidance in shaping the contours of daily life. If Russia was not to be overwhelmed by the West it needed to become its equal, but at the end of the seventeenth century Russia had no factories or armories, no modern army or navy, no modern institutions of government and finance, and no modern art, literature, or music, all of which the West enjoyed in abundance. Because the wealth and power required to shape the nation's destiny lay in the hands of Russia's Tsar alone, all these shortcomings would have to be dealt with from above. Surrounded by the traditions and conservative values that had molded Russian life for centuries, only the sovereign who sat in the Kremlin could take the lead in setting Russia on the path taken by the West.

From a distance of more than three hundred years, we cannot tell whether Peter the Great consciously plotted his course or sensed it instinctively, but his vision of building a modern imperial capital on marshlands that had defied human habitation encompassed all these things. The rise of St. Petersburg was designed to show that the power of the human mind could triumph over the forces of nature, and that Russia was as much a part of the modern world as any other nation. From the moment he overthrew his half-sister's regency in 1689, Russia's first modern Tsar therefore worked most of all to modernize the ways of thinking of people who had few inklings about his larger purpose. If Russians were to stand among the people of Europe, they had to look beyond their borders and to enter the larger, dynamic world to which their rivals belonged.

In urging the Russians to embrace the ways of the modern West, Peter the Great did not ask them to become Frenchmen, Dutchmen, Englishmen, or Germans. That his nation needed to borrow much from Europe he was very certain. But once the Russians had regained the strength they had lost by being cut off for so long from the modern world, Peter looked for them to "show their ass to the West" and to chart the political course that their nation's unique position astride the continents of Europe and Asia demanded.[2] In the meantime, he spoke of making his new capital at St. Petersburg a "window" through which technology and new ideas could flow. St. Petersburg was to mark the way for Russia to become modern by creating a physical environment that could be maintained only by broader and deeper contact with the West.

Like Russia itself, Peter's new capital became a place of startling and enduring contrasts. Bathed in sunlight at midnight in the summer, it brooded in darkness at noon in the winter, and its canals, which called so quickly to mind the more temperate settings of Amsterdam and Venice, froze for at least four months every year. Nature and geography placed St. Petersburg several times closer to London and Paris than to Russia's far-off Siberian lands, but the new city quickly became the political and cultural center of an empire that stretched across more than fifteen time zones onto three continents. A European-style capital of an Asiatic nation whose people at first distrusted the new world it portrayed, St. Petersburg eventually became a living model of what Russia wanted to become, and the Russians embraced everything it represented. Not since the days of Rome has a city stood so completely for the realm it ruled. Especially for that reason, a "biography" of St. Petersburg inevitably must become also a history of modern Russia.

To be the subject of a biography, a city has to have a soul, and the soul of St. Petersburg is as complex as the contrasts that shape its character. More than any other city, St. Petersburg is a blend of conflicting and contrasting images that must be distilled with caution if its inner nature is not to evaporate. For almost two hundred years, virtually every Russian writer of note has struggled to blend autumnal fogs, summer fantasies, and wintry frosts with heritages of Amsterdam, Venice, Paris, and Rome to reveal the soul of Peter's city. Yet no one—not even Dostoevskii or the great modern poet Anna Akhmatova—has ever managed to extract St. Petersburg's soul directly from the surreal, romantic, symbolist, and realist elements that make up its past and present, for the soul of St. Petersburg is more than a combination of poetic elements and natural phenomena. It is the collective spirit of all the human souls that built Peter's city—loved it, hated it, lived in it, and died for it—in the course of three hundred years. Nowhere is the collective spirit of St. Petersburg more evident than in the Piskarevskoe Cemetery on the outskirts of the city, where a score of burial mounds holding the remains of nearly half a million men, women, and children who perished in the Nazi siege of Leningrad combine peacefully in death those who were once the stern and stubborn people of a city that refused to die.

The nine hundred days of the Nazi siege represent only one of the many chapters in the story of St. Petersburg that dramatize the forces that have shaped Russia's past and present. This is the city that could never have come into being had not superhuman will and Russian fortitude overcome the forces of nature, and its biography shows how the vital processes of borrowing, assimilation, transformation, and creation have molded a nation's history in modern times. Russian writers are fond of pointing out that St. Petersburg is at one and the same time Russia and not Russia and that, as the mystical and mysterious point at which Europe becomes Russia and Russia becomes Europe, it represents both the best of Russia's efforts to borrow from the West and a vision of what Russia can become. Yet, what it meant to be Russian and European was not always clear to the men and women who followed in Peter's footsteps, for the forces of emotion, culture, and politics changed Petersburgers and their world. What remains indisputable, however, is that Russia and Europe have been firmly linked since the time of Peter the Great. And the point at which they have been joined—whether as friend or foe, cultural allies or intellectual antagonists—has always been St. Petersburg.

Russia's ever-changing relationship to Europe therefore lies at the heart of St. Petersburg's biography and the story of the nation for which it served as a "window to the West." Clearly the city is European in its structure and design, but the imperial vision it came to represent embraced much more than one backward nation's effort to change its course. As a state of mind and a way of thinking that loses meaning in any other place, St. Petersburg continues to represent a subtle psychological force that at times has rivaled the power of the "Russian idea" itself. Posing the question "Whither St. Petersburg?" inevitably asks where Russia is going and how it is going to get there. For that reason alone the city has stood at the center of some of its artists' greatest works. From the death of Peter the Great in 1725 until the present day, writers, painters, composers, and thinkers all have had to confront the meaning of St. Petersburg. Did its existence mean that Russia was fated to follow the path of Europe? Or did St. Petersburg stand for a vision that embraced a whole that was greater than the sum of Russia and Europe together?

Confusion about what St. Petersburg meant and where Russia was headed led the nineteenth-century novelist and playwright Nikolai Gogol to exclaim that Peter's capital was a city of specters in which "everything's an illusion, everything's a dream, everything's not what it seems."[3] In Gogol's St. Petersburg, people lose sight of what it means to be Russian at the same time as they fail to become truly European. Fedor Dostoevskii shared that view, and so did most of the avant-garde painters and poets who lived through the city's sudden transformation from imperial capital to Soviet metropolis between 1900 and 1920. To the early twentieth-century poet-novelist Andrei Belyi, St. Petersburg on the eve of World War I seemed to be an "un-Russian-but-nonetheless-capital city" whose "ashy and indistinct" images represented a vision of "tragic imperialism" that had turned away from the native roots that could have made Russia greater than any of its rivals. As twentieth-century Russians searched for ways to reunite their nation with that abandoned heritage, Lenin sought to bind the Bolsheviks' all-powerful state to its impoverished masses by means of a European ideology that once again drew Russia back to the West.

Supported by the creations of novelists, painters, and poets, some historians have searched for the meaning of St. Petersburg's past and present in the never-ending struggle between Europe and Asia. Others have hoped to find it in the conflict between the achievements of the human personality and the power of the city's faceless masses. From either perspective, St. Petersburg has provided a sense of direction and a vision of hope that has had meaning for all of Russia. For the story of St. Petersburg's—and Russia's—past reflects the never-ending historical dilemmas faced by a tormented and tragic nation. Over the past three hundred years, St. Petersburg and Russia both have stood at the brink of disaster more than once, and both have gained strength and a stronger sense of purpose from those encounters.

Reminiscent of the public structures that once towered over Imperial Rome, the huge government buildings that housed Russia's Ruling Senate, Guards regiments, and a dozen or more ministries in St. Petersburg projected a vision of imperial invincibility across Eurasia. The city held the nation's greatest cathedral, its tallest and largest buildings, and its most fearsome prison. Its avenues were the broadest and its shops the grandest. And nowhere in Russia were the streets better paved or the carriages and their passengers more elegant. In St. Petersburg the grandees of Russia lived in palaces fit for the kings and queens of other countries. Theirs was a city of power and wealth, the likes of which could be matched by few capitals anywhere on earth.

The authority that flowed from St. Petersburg did not always equal the intimidating images of the city's power and wealth. Its instruments were the hordes of scribes who dealt with Russia's affairs in mindless, mechanical ways that eventually undermined the effectiveness of the men who tried to rule a far-flung empire from one of its westernmost corners. Yet, even as that empire began to bend beneath the weight of its inert bureaucracy, St. Petersburg continued to project a sense of power that remained a part of its image until at least the Revolution of 1917. Because Russians continued to see anything that linked them with their capital as a means of touching the authority that flowed from the emperor, St. Petersburg continued to attract people from all parts of the empire.

Being in St. Petersburg thus meant living in the shadow of some of the most intimidating expressions of power that the modern world has ever seen, but it also meant that the many men and women who made up the city's legions of workers, servants, soldiers, and clerks had very limited prospects. Often obliged to live from hand to mouth in slums that stood only a short distance from the grand buildings in which they served the powerful and famous, most Petersburgers could never even dream of touching the power that radiated from the city in which they spent their lives. Remaining forever beyond their reach, the power and glory of Imperial Russia therefore seemed even greater to the city's lesser folk than it really was.

Described by an early visitor as "a heap of villages linked together like some plantation in the West Indies,"[4] St. Petersburg became one of Europe's most beautiful cities. By 1800 it called to mind Venice, Amsterdam, and Paris, yet it conveyed a mystique that none of them ever matched. Perhaps this came from the unique images that its pink, turquoise, green, red, and yellow stuccoed palaces projected against the northern sky. Or perhaps it stemmed from the indisputably feminine quality that female sovereigns imparted to it during the three quarters of a century after the death of Peter the Great. The empresses Anna, Elizabeth, and Catherine the Great all left their marks on St. Petersburg during the six and a half decades in which they reigned. The exuberant baroque of the Winter Palace, the restrained classical beauty of the Marble Palace, and the enduring elegance of the Tauride Palace all had their beginnings on the drawing boards of builders whose talents these empresses recognized and encouraged.

As the nation that Peter the Great had raised from medieval backwardness took its place among the Great Powers of Europe, St. Petersburg set the tone for an entire empire. Manor houses built in the Petersburg style dotted the countryside of European Russia at the end of the eighteenth century, and buildings that would have fitted easily along the city's elegant avenues and embankments began to appear in faraway Tobolsk and Irkutsk not long after that. By 1850, huge imperial-style structures towered over wooden cottages in scores of out-of-the-way places, while thousands of provincials struggled to reproduce what they imagined to be St. Petersburg's style of life in their homes and social relationships. In cities and towns that were home to Estonians, Chechens, Uzbeks, and Mongols, the grandeur of Imperial St. Petersburg left indelible footprints to mark the march of Russian power across Eurasia. Looked at from the West, the city continued to be the window through which Europe saw Russia. Viewed from the East, it showed the Russians how the ways of Europe could become an important part of their lives.

Even more than in the cities of Europe, poverty lived side by side with grandeur in Imperial St. Petersburg. Barely half a mile from the elegant Nevskii Prospekt stood the Haymarket, around which the poorest of the poor sold rags, scraps of firewood, and stolen goods, but every quarter of the city housed its share of the carters, cleaners, and humble clerks who made up the ranks of St. Petersburg's less than fortunate. Set apart in terms of wealth and living standard, these people nonetheless crossed the paths of the city's upper classes at almost every step, for even in the best parts of St. Petersburg, the downtrodden and disdained shared courtyards with the rich and famous. Generals, statesmen, petty bureaucrats, seamstresses, cobblers, and ladies of the night often called the same building home. The common practice of renting cramped rear rooms in St. Petersburg's larger buildings to the working poor while the well-to-do lived in the spacious, high-ceilinged splendor of apartments that looked out on the street made that inevitable.

St. Petersburg's rich and poor lived side by side until the Industrial Revolution began to draw its lower classes to factories in the suburbs. The great Russian industrialists Putilov and Obukhov had their factories there, and so did the foreigners Siemens, Thornton, and McCormick. By the time St. Petersburg's name was changed to Petrograd at the beginning of World War I, a ring of factory smokestacks and workers' slums surrounded its center. And, as these proletarian suburbs tightened their grip on the city's core, relations between rich and poor turned sour. With its people struggling to bear the burden of a war that was beyond their strength, the stage was set for the European-style class revolution that Russia had previously been spared. In less than a week in February 1917, the working men and women of Petrograd made their city the cradle of the revolution that launched Russia on its three-quarter-century experiment with the brave new world of Communism.

Soon to be renamed Leningrad in honor of the Revolution's creator, St. Petersburg languished as Russia's political center from the moment the Bolsheviks moved their capital to Moscow in 1918. As the city of the poet Anna Akhmatova and the composer Sergei Prokofiev, it became the place to which those Russians who opposed the Bolsheviks' dictatorship gravitated, and it continued to flourish as a center of intellectual and cultural life throughout the 1920s and 1930s. At the end of 1925, the brilliant young Imagist poet Sergei Esenin came to Leningrad to commit suicide after his ill-starred marriage to Isadora Duncan broke apart and he realized that Russia's new masters would no longer let him write as he pleased. Five years later, the great Bolshevik poet Vladimir Maiakovskii ended his life in a dramatic attempt to proclaim that there was no longer any hope that the Revolution would set art free. The moral force of the city that had served so long as Russia's window onto the future remained even as Stalin's dictatorship tightened its grip. Moscow—Asiatic, anti-Western, heavy-handed, vulgar, oppressive, and provincial—now ruled the Russian land as it had in the days of Ivan the Terrible, but Leningrad remained the imperial city that represented Russia's greatness to the rest of the world.

Not until the mid-1930s did the shadow of Moscow, the city from which Stalin continued to direct his ongoing war against the Russians, begin to darken Leningraders' sense of the future. Rebuilt in part to reflect the brave new world it had been chosen to represent, Moscow grew into the world's first socialist capital while Leningrad became a living museum of a way of life and a political vision that Russia's socialist leaders wanted their people to forget. Yet, if Stalin and his minions sought to turn the Russians away from Leningrad, the moral and intellectual authority it had represented since the days of Peter the Great drew others toward it. Remembering its past as the point at which Russia and Europe met, the leaders of Nazi Germany made the city a key objective when their armies invaded Russia in 1941. For Hitler and his generals the capture of Russia's "window to the West" ranked in importance with seizing the grainfields of Ukraine, the oilfields of the Caucasus, and the Soviet capital itself. For nine hundred days the armies of Nazi Germany lay siege to Leningrad. And, as had happened so often in years gone by, the eyes of Russia again turned to the city of Peter the Great.

While German bombs and shells rained upon them between 1941 and 1944, Leningrad's people stood firm, even though deaths far outnumbered births among them for three long years. "There is no good news," a friend of the famed poet Olga Berggolts wrote when the siege seemed to be at its worst. "No good news yet. But we will wait. We will fight."[5] Leningraders burned books for heat, melted snow for drinking water, ate vermin, and starved. "Zhenia died 28 December at 12:30 in the morning, 1941," the eleven-year-old Tania Savicheva wrote in her diary during the siege's first winter. "Grandmother died 25 January . . . 1942," she added a month later. "Leka died 17 March . . . Uncle Vasia died 13 April . . . Uncle Lesha, 10 May . . . Mama, 13 May, 7:30 a.m. 1942 . . . All have died," she wrote in her last entry.[6] At Leningrad's Piskarevskoe Cemetery, the living buried their dead in massive hecatombs that each held the remains of twenty to twenty-five thousand people. But the city stood, and this greatest of Soviet Russia's "hero cities" became a living monument to the fighting spirit of the nation it once had ruled. Poets and propagandists alike saw in Leningrad the renewed power of the Russian spirit and promised that so long as their nation continued to give birth to men and women such as those who had withstood the Nazi siege it would always be strong.

Whether St. Petersburg reigned as an imperial capital, languished as the fading second city of the Soviet Union, or faced the devastation of the Nazis' siege, a magical force drew the Russians to it. "We provincials somehow turn our steps toward Petersburg," the novelist Mikhail Saltykov-Shchedrin explained in the middle of the nineteenth century. "It's as if Petersburg with its name, its streets, its fog, rain, and snow could solve life's problems or shed new light on them."[7] Memories of St. Petersburg's streets, palaces, and magical White Nights filled the works of Dostoevskii, Rimskii-Korsakov, and Shostakovich, and some of the most powerful lines that the poets Pushkin, Aleksandr Blok, Akhmatova, and Joseph Brodsky ever wrote reflected its grandeur and power. As the great bronze horseman that Catherine the Great had dedicated to Peter's memory in 1782 cast its shadow across the work of these poets and many others, it posed the same questions Russians had been asking for centuries. Had their first emperor made their country rear back (as the statue's pose implied), or had he caused it to leap forward (as the horse and rider seemed about to do)? The answer to those questions seemed to hold the key to St. Petersburg's—and Russia's—vision of progress, the West, and the future.

For men and women living at any time between the reign of Peter the Great and the present day, St. Petersburg has been a psychological force, an intellectual vision, and a way of life against which everything else in Russia has been measured. This does not mean that the city has always been loved and admired by all. But it does mean that no Russian during the past three centuries has been able to set aside the idea of St. Petersburg. Neither Gogol nor Dostoevskii could embrace their own double images of the city's past, present, and future without reservation, and neither could many others who sought to understand its place in Russia's history. Could the bronze horseman overcome the vision of the swamp whence it had sprung? And could human will continue to make up for the burden of Russian tradition and the gifts that Nature had failed to endow? No matter how Russians chose to answer those questions, the fact remained that St. Petersburg demanded recognition, even from those who sought the true meaning of Russia elsewhere. Even the Bolsheviks, who dedicated nearly three-quarters of a century to making Moscow the socialist city of the future, had to confront the hard realization that Leningrad—whose citizens had withstood the worst that Nazi Germany could inflict—represented the psychological inner strength that had sustained the Russians in their darkest hour.

At different times in its history, St. Petersburg has portrayed power, heroism, and fortitude. It has encompassed all the things that the Russians are, and much of what they hope to become. It is the city of Peter and Catherine the Great, and the final resting place of Mikhail Kutuzov, the field marshal who led Russia to victory against Napoleon. The great ballerina Anna Pavlova and her fabled partner Vatslav Nizhinskii (Nijinsky) once danced across the stage of its Imperial Mariinskii Theater, and Sergei Diagilev, the impresario who brought the Russian ballet to Paris at the beginning of the twentieth century, organized the Ballets Russes there, too. Apart from the years he spent in Siberia's prisons, Dostoevskii lived most of his adult life in St. Petersburg, as did the composers Glinka, Borodin, and Rimskii-Korsakov. The chemist Dmitrii Mendeleev created his periodic table of elements in St. Petersburg. Ivan Pavlov worked there on the studies of conditioned reflexes that won him the Nobel Prize for Medicine in 1904. And in its back streets and alleys, the teenaged Joseph Brodsky, destined to become America's only foreign-born poet-laureate, rummaged through garbage cans to find the books that shaped his self-education.

To every Russian, St. Petersburg was and is a city of superlatives. The ethereal White Nights that blossom around its summer solstice create a legendary aura of romance, and no other place in Russia moves the hearts of poets so deeply. Russians insist that the beauty of St. Petersburg's canals rivals that of Venice's, and that its Neva River surpasses the grandeur of the Thames and the romance of the Seine. The dome of the city's huge St. Isaac's Cathedral is only slightly smaller than St. Peter's in Rome and St. Paul's in London. And the 1,054-room Winter Palace, with a grand staircase of the whitest Carrara marble, a ballroom larger than the one at Versailles, and art treasures that rival those of the Louvre and the Vatican, has few equals anywhere on earth.

In tsarist times, St. Petersburg boasted a level of wealth that dazzled the imagination, and the balls and dinners that highlighted its social season wove the fabric for countless legends. Peter Karl Fabergé located his main shop in the city's center because there was no clientele anywhere else in Europe that could support his work so generously, but his presence did nothing to lessen the prosperity of half a dozen other jewelers whose creations rivaled his own. For in Russia in the year 1900 there was no shortage of men and women who could pay more for an Easter egg than a mansion would have cost in Paris or New York. Aristocratic St. Petersburg continued to value conspicuous consumption, even as the poverty of its lower classes became more desperate. Skilled workers in St. Petersburg's mills could not earn the price of such an egg in several lifetimes, yet little was done to ease their burdens or better the conditions under which they lived. Concerned to perpetuate the power that their predecessors had bequeathed, the Romanovs paid little attention to the wretched lives that most Petersburgers—and, for that matter, most Russians—had to endure. The images of suffering that formed the inner fabric of Dostoevskii's novels reflected a reality that grew more stark and threatening as the Revolution of 1917 approached.

Blended with images of poverty, suffering, and heroism on a monumental scale, opulence, raw political power, and artistic brilliance make up the historical persona of St. Petersburg. Its biography is first and foremost a tale of men and women struggling against the awesome forces of Nature and repression to create the stunning triumphs in politics, culture, and science that make up its three-hundred-year history. Factories and slums are therefore as important to St. Petersburg's story, as are palaces and parade grounds. Revolutionaries must take the stage alongside tsars. And builders, soldiers, and statesmen must share pride of place with poets and composers. St. Petersburg's biography cannot be told without reference to the many lesser human events that give meaning to its past and present, and the comings and goings of those common folk whose labor filled its marshes, drained its swamps, built its palaces and cathedrals, ran its machines, and defended it against its enemies deserve their proper place as well.

Looked at in the broadest historical terms, St. Petersburg's past, present, and future continue to stand at the center of a centuries-long conversation that the Russians have carried on among themselves about what their nation is and what it needs to become. In the past, this conversation has been about Russia and Europe, Russia and Asia, Russia and empire, Russia and salvation, Russia's suffering as a key to its redemption, Russia and apocalypse, and Russia and revolution. Recently, its focus has shifted back to where it was in the time of Peter the Great—to what St. Petersburg means in the context of where Russia is headed. The latter part of that equation is still unclear, but a number of powerful truths remain unchanged. For many Russians, St. Petersburg continues to be a dramatic symbol of the fact that Russia still has "only one door to Europe."[8] Many now believe that that door opens upon Russia's future, just as it did in the days of Peter the Great.

Will St. Petersburg and the Russians again embrace foreign ways as they did three hundred years ago and return to the mainstream of the European culture and politics of which Peter the Great made them a part? Or, will they "borrow" only the essentials needed to regain their strength, and then—in Peter's memorable phrase—"show their ass to the West"? Those questions confront every statesman and every thoughtful citizen as the twenty-first century begins. And the answers inevitably will help to shape the course of world politics in the years that lie ahead.

Petersburgers still believe that, so long as the great bronze statue of Peter the Great continues to rear above the Neva River, their city and nation will find ways to prosper. "The bronze horseman," as the poet Pushkin wrote, "gallops still," but his direction is less clear now than at almost any other time in St. Petersburg's history. "Where will you plant your hooves? And on whom?" Pushkin asked of Peter's bronze steed in those long-ago days when Russia had just defeated Napoleon and seemed to be the most powerful nation in Europe.[9] That question still lies at the heart of Russia's destiny. Perhaps by telling St. Petersburg's story, this book can point the way to an answer.

Part 1

PART I

*Window
on the West
(1703–1796)*

# THE BUILDERS

*F*ROM THE SOUTHERN TIP OF LAKE LADOGA, the largest lake in all of Europe, the Neva River flows forty-one miles west to the sea. As it nears the Finnish Gulf, its fast-moving currents divide into more than a dozen branches, the twistings and turnings of which have carved out an intricate archipelago from the low-lying marshes around them. At the beginning of the eighteenth century these islands numbered over a hundred, but today there are only forty-four, the narrow streams and channels between them having been filled in as a city took shape. None of these islands have any topographical irregularities. There are no hills or outcroppings as in Paris, Athens, Florence, or Rome. No point on the delta stands more than thirty feet above the sea.[1]

In years gone by, the Finns, Swedes, and Russians who claimed these scrub-covered lands gave them such names as the Isle of Brushwood, the Isle of Birches, the Isle of Stones, and the Isle of Goats. A sandy, elongated oval less than half a mile long and a fifth of a mile wide, the Isle of Hares is one of the smallest of the Neva's islands, and it splits the river's channel near its northern bank. Over the centuries, this island served as a refuge for fishermen seeking shelter while mending their nets, but a permanent settlement never took root. Never, that is, until May 16, 1703, when a detachment of Russian soldiers under the command of Peter the Great's lifelong friend General Aleksandr Menshikov set in place the first wooden palisades for a large hexagonal fort whose guns would bar the river to enemy ships. The city that would take shape on the islands around this fort would be the product of Tsar Peter's vision, but he was not there to see its beginnings. Only six weeks after Menshikov's men had set the first palisades in place, laid out the rough outlines of the fort, and built the first crude shelters did Peter finally join them. On that day, June 29, the Orthodox feast day of Saints Peter and Paul, he named the settlement Sankt Pieter Burkh in honor of his patron saint.

The residents of Sankt Pieter Burkh soon Russified its Dutch-sounding name into St. Petersburg, and Menshikov's fort, later enlarged to enclose all of Hare Island within its sixty-foot-thick masonry walls, would become the Fortress of Saints Peter and Paul. Until the Revolution of 1917, this formidable structure would protect Peter's city, and from its center would rise St. Petersburg's first great cathedral, in which each of Russia's emperors and empresses would be laid to rest. Scarcely a stone's throw away, St. Petersburg's first political prison lay deep within the foundations of the fortress bastions themselves. Here Dostoevskii would languish in 1849, as would hundreds of others who, in the half-century that followed, struggled against autocracy in the name of freedom. To the dungeons of this dank, gray hulk the statesmen who inherited the floundering government of Russia after the Revolution of February 1917 would send Nicholas II's advisers and confidants, only to be sent there in their turn by Lenin's vengeful Bolsheviks a few months later. Set on a single island too small to leave room for a palace or a main street, the Fortress of Saints Peter and Paul nonetheless enclosed two of the most fundamental secular and ecclesiastical instruments on which the power of Russia's sovereigns depended.

In less than a century after its founding, the city that had been built on the Neva's marshes began to glow with a mysterious charm that fascinated Russians and foreigners alike. By 1790, the brackish streams of the Neva delta had become picture-perfect canals faced with carefully cut embankments of red Finnish granite. Elegant palaces, government offices, and townhouses stood upon the very lands that once had shifted so easily beneath the river's capricious currents, and avenues wider than the Champs Elysées stretched from the river's edge to the city's suburbs. "The view of Petersburg delights us less by what it is than by the idea of what it will be," a German visitor wrote just ten years before the city celebrated its hundredth birthday. "Berlin," he added, "may vie with it . . . in regard to its beautiful symmetry, but Petersburg has more grand possibilities."[2]

To discover all the dimensions of those possibilities required time and foresight. Still struggling to bring his vision of St. Petersburg into focus, Peter the Great vacillated about where its hub ought to be. By the time he officially named it Russia's capital in 1712, he had already experimented with centering his city on Kotlin Island (site of the present-day Kronstadt naval base), some twelve miles downstream from Hare Island and well out into the shallows of the Finnish Gulf. When Kotlin Island had proved unsatisfactory, Peter turned to Vasilevskii Island, which like the Fortress of Saints Peter and Paul stood along the Neva's northern bank. Larger and more accessible than Kotlin Island, which was separated from the mainland by more than a mile of water, Vasilevskii Island still suffered from low-lying topography that brought the stormy waters of the Finnish Gulf over its banks every spring and fall. Peter himself would never abandon his dream of building Russia's capital on land that was protected by water on every side. But in the end, St. Petersburg would find its natural center on the islands that the narrow Fontanka and Moika rivers had cut from the Neva's southern bank and on the mainland just beyond. Here in little more than a century after Peter's death his successors would build the Winter Palace, the General Staff Headquarters, the Admiralty, the Imperial Ruling Senate, the Holy Synod, and St. Isaac's Cathedral—all the institutional edifices from which Russian power could be projected across Eurasia and around the globe.

The marshlands from which Peter's relentless will shaped Sankt Pieter Burkh have been part of Russia's story for nearly a thousand years. In the tenth century, these were claimed by the great commercial entrepôt of Novgorod, the only true republic in the long and turbulent history of the Russian land, and in the year 1240, Novgorod's legendary Prince Aleksandr Nevskii defeated Sweden's armies not far from where Peter's city was to stand. During the next century, Prince Aleksandr's descendants waged at least twenty campaigns against the Swedes, Germans, and Lithuanians, but the land itself remained poor, able to sustain only a few fishing villages, some trading posts, and a handful of farmers. Had farmland and fish been their only attractions, the processes of history would have passed the marshes of the Neva delta by. But other forces were at work, for the Neva River formed a part of a vital water route that had connected Europe and the Near East since at least the middle of the ninth century.

What drew the Russians and their enemies to this northernmost point on the fabled river road that flowed "from the Varangians to the Greeks" was trade. Starting in the ninth century, the chance to exchange goods with the Near and Middle East had drawn the princes and merchants of northern Europe to the Neva's mouth, and the struggle to control that trade accounted for the battles that the armies of Novgorod, Sweden, and the Teutonic Knights had fought to retain the lands through which it flowed. After relinquishing the Neva delta to the Swedes in the fourteenth century, the Russians returned briefly in the sixteenth, when Ivan the Terrible began his ill-fated drive to gain a foothold on the Baltic. Then, the Swedes regained their grip and built the fortress of Nyenskans less than three miles upriver from Hare Island. Nyenskans had been Menshikov's first objective in the spring of 1703. Only after he had driven the Swedes from it could he begin to lay the foundations for St. Petersburg on Hare Island.[3]

Even with the Swedes pushed aside, Peter's choice of the Neva River delta as the place to build Russia's "window on the West" violated almost every principle by which the sites for cities are usually chosen. It had no reliable source of fresh water, and the soil around it was too barren to grow the crops needed to feed its people. For nearly five months of the year from November through March, the Neva was usually frozen, and history would show that the islands and marshlands at its mouth suffered serious floods almost every year.[4] Timber for all but the smallest and rudest buildings had to be cut in the hinterland and floated downstream, and material for foundations and paving proved so hard to come by that the city's eighteenth-century governors levied a tax payable only in stones on every wagon and ship that arrived. Virtually every foot of land reclaimed from the marshes on which St. Petersburg was built had to be filled with oaken piles sixteen feet long and driven their full length into the ground. No other capital city in Europe had to overcome so many obstacles. St. Petersburg's beginnings had no counterpart anywhere in the modern West.[5]

Every year, Peter ordered between ten and thirty thousand serfs, prisoners of war, and common criminals to be marched to the Neva delta to drain marshes, drive piles, and build St. Petersburg's first buildings. These men worked with the crudest tools under conditions that killed them by the thousands. Some dug dirt with their hands and carried it away in containers made from their shirts and coats, while others hacked at the swampy ground with roughly made picks and wooden shovels. Cholera and giardiasis threatened everyone who entered the region, and the bad water that caused those ailments has condemned St. Petersburg's residents to endure those sicknesses ever since.[6] "It would be difficult to find in the annals of military history any battle that claimed more lives than the number of workers who died in [the building of] St. Petersburg," the historian Kliuchevskii wrote at the end of the nineteenth century. For the men who built Russia's new capital, he concluded, the new city "turned out to be nothing but a huge graveyard."[7]

That first summer, encampments of forced laborers sprang up on several of the Neva delta's low-lying islands, only to be washed away by floods that left their residents unprotected in the wind and mud. "We have terrible weather coming in from the sea and it floods the bivouacs of my troops," a worried officer wrote to Peter that August. In an ominous postscript, he added: "The natives around here say that at this time of year this place is always flooded."[8] A visiting French physician reported that the Neva and its tributaries had "joined together to form one great sea, on the surface of which the city seemed to float" during one such flood,[9] and the Tsar himself once nearly drowned when rising waters submerged the newly built Nevskii Prospekt, the main avenue of the city. Scientific records kept since those early days show that the Neva's waters have risen more than five feet above flood stage on 260 occasions. Despite predictable floods, the city continued to stand. "His will was Fate," the poet Pushkin wrote a century later in remembering how Peter the Great had ordered St. Petersburg to rise from the Neva's swamps.[10] And nothing, it seemed, could shake his resolve to make it into a "paradise."[11] St. Petersburg was to be Russia's New Constantinople, New Rome, and New Zion. In Peter's own words, it became the "promised land," "God's Heaven," a "sacred place" established by imperial decree on "holy Russian land."[12]

What impelled Peter to start building a new capital on a swamp still ruled by his enemy the King of Sweden remains something of a mystery, even now. When the young Tsar seized the throne in 1689, Moscow had been Russia's capital for the better part of two hundred years and its prince had dominated Russian politics for a century longer than that. Moscow's rulers led Russia's feuding princes when they defeated the Mongols in 1380 and then gathered their separate domains into a kingdom that stretched from the frontiers of Poland to the shores of the Pacific. Fifteenth-century

Russians revered Moscow as the Third Rome—the final hope for the salvation of all humankind—and their rulers and churchmen insisted that the purity of their Orthodox faith set Russia above all its rivals. As the capital of Holy Russia, pious medieval Moscow continued to seem as sufficient unto itself in the seventeenth century as it had in the fifteenth. Peter's plan to build a new capital in one of his kingdom's remotest corners therefore challenged all the prejudices, beliefs, and hopes that had shaped Russians' destinies for hundreds of years.

An extraordinary six-foot-nine-inch giant who sensed that his country either must become part of the modern world or be overwhelmed by it, Peter drove Russia forward from his first day on its throne to the last. To those Dutch and English merchants who once had demanded a foothold on his nation's lands, he offered alliances, not submission, and against the sovereigns of Sweden and the Ottoman Empire who had claimed spoils from Russia in earlier times he marched as a dangerous foe. In a single generation, Peter gave his country a victorious army, a new way of life, and a capital created in the image of what he wanted it to become. As the window he opened to the West, St. Petersburg became the nerve center of a mighty modern empire that covered fifteen time zones and a sixth of the earth's surface at the same time as it remained an eternal reminder of the forces that had shaped its founder's idea of the future.

The vision that Peter brought to St. Petersburg stemmed from a turbulent youth, during which he had gravitated to Moscow's Foreign Quarter and learned at first hand the secrets of mathematics, modern weapons, and ships that could sail into the wind. As a royal jack-of-all-trades, he was fascinated by the lives of Moscow's Europeans, and took that infatuation with him on the Grand Embassy of Russians he led to the West in 1697. There, he saw men and women living more grandly than any of his subjects, and he witnessed the many ways in which modern technology made Europeans' lives easier and more comfortable. He could not stay away from Europe's museums, hospitals, shipyards, and cannon foundries, and he was enthralled by the elegantly designed urban buildings in which his hosts lived and worked. Everything Peter saw during his first trip to the West helped him create an eclectic image of what Russia might become, and that was the vision he brought to the first rough huts he helped Menshikov and his soldiers put together on the sodden marshes of the Neva delta in 1703 and 1704.

When Peter formally transferred his residence from Moscow to St. Petersburg in 1710, the outlines of his new capital had begun to emerge. Although designed to be approached from the sea, the new city's structure was best seen when arriving from the hinterland along the Neva river-highway that traders had used nearly a thousand years before. As it moved toward the infant city's eastern limits, the river shifted course from west to north, and then turned sharply west again before dividing into the branches that formed the delta's main islands to the north of its main channel. Just before reaching the log defenses that would one day become the Fortress of Saints Peter and Paul, the Greater Nevka branched off to the right, and then the Lesser and Middle Nevka both broke off from it further on. The first two defined the island that became the Petersburg Quarter, in which Peter himself had already settled to oversee his builders' progress. A little further down the Neva, the Little Neva flowed off to the right, leaving the land that stood between it and the main current to form Vasilevskii Island. These were the islands upon which Peter intended to center his new capital to make it safe from attacks by land or sea. But the Russian mainland lay along the Neva's southern bank, and it was there that the forces of history and nature had determined that the center of St. Petersburg's political and aristocratic life eventually would take shape. Even by the time Peter died in January 1725, the focus of St. Petersburg had already begun to shift away from the islands he loved so much.

The Petersburg Quarter already boasted a hundred and fifty substantial dwellings when Peter moved Russia's capital to St. Petersburg in 1712. Its center was Trinity Square, around which the wooden Trinity Cathedral, the Government Printing Office, and St. Petersburg's first hospital had been built. Nearby stood the main city market, recently rebuilt after fire had destroyed it in 1710, its huge courtyard surrounded on three sides by a rough two-story wooden building that housed its hundreds of shops and stalls. Here St. Petersburgers could buy foreign luxuries before moving on to the "Glutton's Market" that offered such home-grown necessities as lentils, peas, bacon, and flour for sale just a few blocks away. Somewhat nearer to the quarter's center, St. Petersburg's Tatar Market flourished, even in those early days, as an outlet for used and stolen goods. In years to come, it would become the city's famous flea market, to which knowledgeable collectors thronged on Thursday mornings to buy antiques and rare paintings that had made their way to Russia in the baggage of well-heeled but not always well-educated noble travelers.[13]

Built of square-hewn logs that were painted to resemble brick, the Tsar's own quarters stood beneath a huge lime tree not far from Trinity Square. At times, Peter worked on the building himself and even made some of the furniture that filled its three smallish rooms. Other times, he and his friends gathered at St. Petersburg's first tavern, ostentatiously named the Triumphal Osteria of the Four Frigates, which an enterprising German had built nearby. There, they drank the Tsar's favorite vodka laced with cayenne pepper, laughed, cursed, and ate the naval rations of salt beef and hard biscuits of which Peter was especially fond. Late at night, they would make their way home through streets whose names told the tale of the first men Peter had brought to settle there: Dvorianskaia (nobles') Street, Ruzheinaia (armorers') Street, Pushkarnaia (cannon makers') Street, and Monetnaia (coin minters') Street all reflected the Tsar's resolve to bring the things he thought most important to St. Petersburg. Because war lay at the core of his plan to modernize Russia, he expected St. Petersburg to become a producer of armaments as well as a bastion of defense. Only then could the city play its proper part as the capital of the empire that fate had given the Romanovs to rule.

Although it contained St. Petersburg's first buildings, the Petersburg Quarter did not become the center of the city, even though Peter himself had chosen to live there. Just to the west, Vasilevskii Island had already been laid out in regular streets called "lines" that would be intersected at right angles by canals to create precisely shaped building lots on which Peter wanted the center of his capital to be built. Transformed into a watery checkerboard, Vasilevskii Island was to become (according to Peter's vision) a model of his cherished Amsterdam, with each of its buildings fronting on a canal that would make sail-driven boats the main form of transportation. Here, the Tsar's plan failed. The first canals were too narrow and quickly silted up. A sixth sense seemed to turn St. Petersburg away from Vasilevskii and Petersburg Islands toward the slightly higher land and more convenient access to the hinterland that the Neva's opposite bank offered.

Because no bridges linked any of the islands on which St. Petersburg took shape, all of its daily life gravitated toward the river. This was precisely what Peter had intended from the very first, for he had hoped to make St. Petersburg's dwellers into the sailors his nation had always lacked. The Neva and its branches thus became the avenues along which workers, aristocrats, soldiers, statesmen, and diplomats all had to make their way in roughly made boats that sometimes broke apart as they struggled against the wind, crippled by the Tsar's prohibition against using oars. Such accidents claimed the lives of one Polish ambassador, several prominent army officers, and even one of Peter's attending physicians in St. Petersburg's early days, when floods sometimes cut the islands off from the mainland for days and weeks at a time.

Once St. Petersburg had formally been named Russia's capital, Peter ordered hundreds of merchants and traders, two thousand artisans, and a thousand of Russia's leading aristocrats to move there "with their entire families and everyone who lives in the same household with them."[14] To make the city grow quickly, the impatient Tsar earmarked nearly five percent of his state budget for new government buildings, and he chose his friend and confidant Prince Aleksandr Menshikov to become St. Petersburg's first Governor General. Probably the most powerful man in Russia after Peter himself, Menshikov lived far more extravagantly than his master, and it would be he, not Peter, who would set the standards by which the aristocratic residences of Russia's capital would be measured for the next quarter of a century or more. In years to come, some would call St. Petersburg a "city of palaces," while others remembered it as a "city of barracks."[15] Both images had their beginnings under Menshikov and Peter, who brought aristocrats and soldiers to the city in large numbers the moment it began to take shape.

Begun by the Italian architect Giovanni Fontana, whose designs were supplemented by half a dozen other builders before it was finished in 1721, Menshikov's urban palace occupied nearly a sixth of Vasilevskii Island's main embankment. Rising from an elaborate landing pier at the river's edge, and with extensive gardens that reached far back toward the island's center, the building blended the vivacious features of an Italian baroque palazzo with more austere classical influences from France, and it contained every luxury that could be had in St. Petersburg at the time. Its outside walls were salmon pink highlighted by white, and its roof was made from flat iron plates painted a brilliant red. Fashionable Delft tiles covered the interior walls and some of the ceilings in several rooms, while its parquet floors featured an extravagant blend of exotic woods. Foreigners and Russians alike called Menshikov's palace the "largest and finest in all of St. Petersburg,"[16] although some were heard to wonder if some of its furnishings had not been stolen from Polish castles. Peter himself often used it for diplomatic receptions, his own being far too small.

Elegance and extravagance conspicuously displayed in a rural setting were the obvious hallmarks of the country palace that Menshikov planned twenty-five miles away at Oranienbaum while his St. Petersburg palace was being built. An aristocrat's refuge from the diseases that plagued the city in the summer, the Oranienbaum Palace was easily the most opulent of its day, and it gave the Russians their first glimpse of how grand buildings would be used to define the capital's suburbs in the century ahead. "The palace is built on a hill from which there is a splendid view," wrote Friedrich Wilhelm von Bergholtz, a general in Peter's army who had gone back to his native Germany only to return in the entourage of the Duke of Holstein in 1721. "The rooms," he added, "are small but beautiful, and decorated with marvelous paintings and furniture."[17] Before the palace spread the Finnish Gulf, the gateway to the sea lanes that led to the Western world from which its designers had drawn their inspiration, and from the Grand Hall visitors could see Kotlin Island, upon which the first line of St. Petersburg's defenses had been built. The ill-fated Emperor Peter III would commission the Italian Antonio Rinaldi to build a smaller palace in the gardens of Oranienbaum, and Catherine the Great would add to his assignment by ordering a Chinese palace and a Sliding Hill Pavilion along which she and her court rode on sleds in winter and small four-wheeled carts in summer.[18]

When Peter the Great's father had built a wooden palace in the Moscow suburb of Kolomenskoe to please his young and "modern" second wife in 1670, a handful of secular paintings, mirrors, and European furnishings had led the leading writer of the day to call it the eighth wonder of the world.[19] Now, half a century later, such a statement seemed quaint, for Peter the Great, Menshikov, and their allies had moved Russia into a world in which progress and luxury were measured in grander terms. By the early 1720s, clothing, manners, furnishings, and entertainments in St. Petersburg all reflected the excesses of baroque Europe. The Summer Garden for which Peter set aside space on the Neva River's southern waterfront as soon as the ground thawed in the spring of 1704 reflected all those new and modern tastes.

The French architect Jean-Baptiste Alexandre Le Blond, who had worked closely with André Le Nôtre in designing Louis XIV's gardens at Versailles before being hired by Peter's agents to work in St. Petersburg, insisted that "groves make the chief beauty of a garden," and that "fountains and water are [its] soul." Peter therefore ordered limes and elms from Kiev, oaks from Moscow, fruit trees from the lands of the Volga, and cypresses from the south for his Summer Garden. He sent agents to Hamburg for chestnuts, ordered tulips from Holland, and collected roses, lilacs, sweet peas, and carnations in Russia and abroad. He installed rare birds in aviaries shaped like pagodas and left blue monkeys to chatter nearby in decorative cages. Alabaster arbors imported from Venice decorated cleverly built grottoes, and there were conservatories that sheltered orange and lemon trees against the fierce winter winds. Fifty marble fountains that took the form of cascades, spouting dolphins, and gushing horses added to the display in keeping with Le Blond's dictum that a garden without water "appears dull and melancholy."[20]

Eventually, the Summer Garden grew to cover more than thirty-five acres of walks shaded by lime trees, along which nestled nearly a hundred antique Italian marble statues. Catherine the Great thought it all a monument to bad taste and took pains to rebuild it in the less formal English style after a flood uprooted many of its trees in 1777. But the Empress Elizabeth loved every one of its excesses, and so did many of her contemporaries. In the nineteenth century, the Summer Garden became the place to which Petersburgers went on holidays and summer evenings to parade their new fashions and be seen in the right company. At its front gate, one of Russia's first terrorists tried to kill the Emperor Alexander II in 1866.

By bringing all the elements of European upper-class leisure into play on the sodden Neva marshes, the Summer Garden formed the perfect setting for the small Summer Palace that Peter commissioned in 1710 to show the city's forcibly transported aristocrats what he had in mind when he told them to build residences that befitted their station. Typical of Peter's tastes, the palace was designed on a modest scale, with only fourteen rooms that he shared with his consort, the future empress Catherine I. Peter's rooms showed his pragmatism and fascination with technology, with one actually being given over to the lathes and machinery with which he loved to work in his leisure hours. Elsewhere, elegantly woven fabrics highlighted by mirrors covered the interior walls, and parquet floors featured carefully cut designs of contrasting woods. The stoves—still Russian in design, for the Europeans had not yet matched the Russians' ability to provide heat in winter—were inset with the same Delft tiles that had won favor in England's American colonies and in every part of northern Europe. And the first system of water pipes anywhere in the city brought water to the palace kitchen. Now restored to show the way it had been in Peter's time, the Summer Palace remains one of the few places in St. Petersburg where one can actually feel Peter's presence. Here a sense of Russia's first emperor still fills the air.

Twenty-nine carved stone reliefs set in the Summer Palace's outside walls celebrated Peter's victories in his continuing war with Sweden and made it into a secular monument to Russia's imperial triumphs. To twenty-first-century viewers, these reliefs seem hardly more than minor decorations, but to Russians of Peter's time they represented a monumental shift in the balance between Church, State, and the values of modern life. For just as the Summer Palace's modern design and conveniences served notice that the days of dark interiors and cloistered women would never return, so its secular artistic commemorations of military triumphs made it clear that Russia's Tsar had made its Church permanently subordinate to the State. The days in which Tsars built churches to celebrate battles thought to have been won with the help of God had, for the time being, passed into history. Only when the Russians had grown comfortable with the trappings of empire and modernity would the practice be revived.

The influences that shaped Peter's plans for St. Petersburg came from the impressions he gathered on several journeys to the West, but he required professional architects to give his ideas form and substance.[21] From the beginning, he relied most of all on Domenico Trezzini, a thirty-three-year-old Italian-Swiss architect and engineer from the town of Lugano, whose builders had played a part in shaping baroque architecture all across southern Germany and northern Italy. As one of the first European builders to reach Russia at the beginning of the eighteenth century, Trezzini had brought with him several years of experience as a fortifications engineer in Copenhagen, where he had learned to build on the marshy subsoils that parts of Denmark's capital and St. Petersburg had in common. Trezzini gave secular form to Peter's still unfocused architectural visions, and he used them to begin St. Petersburg's transformation from a collage of rough huts into the city that eventually became the Venice of Europe's north.

Setting aside the exuberance of his native Italian baroque, Trezzini drew his vision from the Protestant style of northern Europe with which he had worked before coming to seek his fortune in Russia. He designed fortifications, cathedrals, palaces, government buildings, and a monastery, all in the more rigid, restrained style of the north, and he prepared a series of master plans for several types of private dwellings that transformed Peter's infatuation with Amsterdam into model designs. These he made into the antithesis of the rough wooden buildings he had seen in Moscow and the towns through which he had passed on his journey to Russia in the spring of 1704, for it was clear that he and his master intended to set Russia's past aside on every level of urban life.

If it had not been evident before, Trezzini's work in St. Petersburg made it clear that Peter's new capital was to be everything Moscow was not. Moscow was the city of Russia's past, its eyes upon Asia and its people fearful of all that Peter the Great and his new city represented. Moscow stood for Orthodox piety, for the old way of doing things, and for the time when Russians had bowed to the Church that had dominated their lives. The onion domes of Moscow's churches shaped its identity, and even the Kremlin reflected the power of the Church, not that of the State. By contrast, Trezzini's vision of St. Petersburg emphasized all the precision and regularity that sprawling Moscow could never claim. Here the focus was on the West—on Paris, Amsterdam, and Rome—where secular power held the Church in check. Nowhere in Peter's new capital would any structure representing the Church ever overshadow one belonging to the State. Even the soaring spire of the Cathedral of Saints Peter and Paul would be set firmly in the center of the fortress that defended the city and served as one of its main political prisons until the Revolution of 1917.[22]

Trezzini's work in Russia began just a month or two after he arrived. After testing him with several lesser assignments, in the spring of 1706 Peter commissioned him to enlarge the Peter and Paul Fortress and then to build in its center the Cathedral of Saints Peter and Paul, which would dramatize how thoroughly Russia had turned from Byzantium to the West. But the fortress and cathedral represented only the first two of many buildings on which Trezzini worked during the next thirty years. Using designs that the Swiss-German architect Georg-Johann Mattarnowy had drawn up, he built Peter's Second Winter Palace on the Neva River embankment and then turned to the far end of Nevskii Prospekt, where the Emperor wanted him to erect a monastery in memory of the princely Saint Aleksandr Nevskii. As always, Trezzini worked in the symmetrical style of the northern baroque that stood so many centuries apart from the traditional fortress monasteries that surrounded Moscow. While medieval Moscow had been the city of a thousand churches, the architecture of St. Petersburg would always emphasize the firm temporal power of autocrats who ruled lands that stretched from Poland to Alaska.

When Peter the Great died at the beginning of 1725, St. Petersburg boasted nineteen churches and cathedrals, fourteen imperial palaces and residences, a dozen government buildings, five major warehouses and covered markets, two theaters, a military hospital, an almshouse, the Admiralty, the Peter and Paul Fortress, and six thousand lesser buildings. Reluctantly, Russia's greatest lords and ladies now made their homes in St. Petersburg, and so did the foreign merchants, traders, and artisans who supplied their wants and needs. Diplomats, artists, and hundreds of other enterprising Europeans who saw the rise of Russia's new capital as a way to win fame or fortune had come to Peter's city, too. So had the army of favor seekers and influence peddlers that would be a part of its social and political landscape ever after.[23]

By 1725, St. Petersburg's upper classes were beginning to enjoy elegance and conspicuous consumption on a scale their ancestors had never imagined, and because all of them required housing appropriate to their station, they clamored for the services of any architect who could build in the style of Europe. All the builders of Petrine St. Petersburg were Europeans who had enjoyed varying degrees of fame before they had come to Russia. Among the most famous were Le Blond and Andreas Schlüter, who had served for a time as an architect and sculptor at the Prussian court. Niccolò Michetti, Georg-Johann Mattarnowy, and Johann Friedrick Braunstein all worked and died in St. Petersburg before 1725, while Trezzini, Gottfried Schädel, and young Bartolomeo Rastrelli carried their work into the reigns of Peter's successors. Each worked in the European style, and little if anything in their work reflected the influences that had shaped Russia's building styles in the centuries that had gone before.

Visitors to St. Petersburg in the mid-1720s were as amazed at what these European architects and their Russian patrons had created as they were impressed by the speed with which they had worked. Holstein's Wilhelm Friedrich von Bergholtz thought the city "so changed" in 1721 from what it had been four years earlier that he claimed to "scarcely recognize it." Von Bergholtz was entranced by the soaring 394-foot Germanic Protestant spire of Trezzini's cathedral, "covered in brightly gilded copper plates which look extraordinarily fine in the sunlight," that rose high above the heavy walls of the Peter and Paul Fortress and boasted an observation deck from which visitors could view the city.[24] Just a year before, a clock and carillon had been installed in Trezzini's tower, and the very next year the indefatigable Italian began the 400-yard-long building that would house the offices of the restructured central government that Peter had created a few years before.

Buildings in various stages of completion—a sure sign that St. Petersburg was growing in many places at once—seemed to be everywhere. The

Nevskii Prospekt, now three miles long and fully paved in stone by Swedish prisoners of war, had been finished during von Bergholtz's absence, and he described it as "a more wonderful sight than any I have ever beheld anywhere." At one end of the avenue stood the "huge and beautiful building" of the Admiralty.[25] At the other, the walls of Trezzini's Aleksandr Nevskii Monastery rose against the backdrop of the Neva River. In between, the palaces and townhouses of the nobility were taking shape. Even then, St. Petersburg was becoming what it would be forever after: a city of huge monuments built on a massive scale.

And yet, as so often happens in Russia, this facade of progress masked serious flaws. Often used by St. Petersburg's impatient builders to save time, the uncured frames and siding of the city's many wooden buildings warped as they dried, while brick walls that had been laid in the dead of winter heaved and split apart. Fires continued to destroy large parts of the city, and flooding continued to wash away newly built streets and buildings almost every spring and fall. Worst of all, many of St. Petersburg's reluctant residents despised its bad climate and resented its high cost of living. To the Hanoverian diplomat Friedrich Weber it seemed in 1714 that "a man could live at Moscow for one-third of what it will cost him at St. Petersburg," and that estimate did not take into account the expense of building palaces and townhouses in a place where the price of building materials was as inflated as all of life's everyday necessities.[26]

Russia's lords and ladies needed a constant supply of ready cash to live in St. Petersburg. In a society where Siberian sable pelts still served as substitutes for gold and silver coin, chronically cash-starved aristocrats begged for relief from the new capital's high costs. Again and again, nobles assigned to live in St. Petersburg asked for permission to return to Moscow, if not permanently then at least for a few months. But Peter turned a deaf ear to their pleas, and so did his wife and successor, the Empress Catherine I. Then, almost overnight, the politics of Russia changed. Catherine's early death in 1727 brought to the throne Peter's thirteen-year-old grandson, Peter II, who moved the capital back to Moscow the very next year. Moscow recalled a past that Russia now seemed destined to forget, but many reluctant St. Petersburgers gladly returned to the homes in which their ancestors had lived and prayed. In 1728, these men and women breathed a collective sigh of relief and hoped that the capricious torrents of modernization that had poured upon them for almost forty years would somehow lose their force in the maze of Moscow's crooked streets.

As Russia's political center shifted back to its old capital, St. Petersburg fell upon hard times, and the shoddy construction that had accounted for its rapid growth now contributed to its further decay. An Englishwoman who visited for a few weeks at the beginning of 1730 found parts of it nearly empty, and she carried away a firm impression that Peter's fading capital ranked a very poor second to Moscow.[27] What kept the city alive during those dark days was trade. So long as Russia's aristocrats demanded those luxury goods they had come to enjoy during Peter the Great's time, the ships of England and Holland could be counted upon to bring ever-growing quantities of European wines, fine foods, and fashions to them by way of St. Petersburg.[28]

When Peter II suddenly died of smallpox at the beginning of 1730, many more goods were passing through St. Petersburg's docks and warehouses than they had when his reign had begun. Determined to pull her enemies away from their long-standing base of economic and political strength in Moscow, Russia's new empress, Anna Ivanovna, sought to use the city's growing economic strength to good advantage by moving her court and capital back to the banks of the Neva in 1732. Almost overnight, the frantic building that had been cut short a few years earlier began anew, and St. Petersburg became Russia's "window on the West" once again. Until the Revolution of 1917, the city would remain an ever-changing vision of what its rulers hoped Imperial Russia would become and a portal through which Europeans could enter Russia.

With the return of the capital to St. Petersburg, the first modern Russian builders laid the foundations for what has been called "an independent national school [that] paved the way for the flowering of Russian architecture in the middle of the eighteenth century."[29] As the first native architects to leave their imprint on the city, Petr Eropkin, Ivan Korobov, and Mikhail Zemtsov broke the monopoly that foreigners had enjoyed in the time of Peter the Great, and each left a mark that reflected his own special vision of how Russia related to the West. The oldest of the three, Zemtsov had become one of Trezzini's first pupils in 1709, and he had won enough fame in Peter's time to be put in charge of expanding the Summer Garden and completing the parks around the imperial summer palace at Peterhof in the early 1720s. As the leading foreign architects of the Petrine era died or returned to the West, he went on to design several churches and complete the Kunstkammer, the first institution of higher learning anywhere in Russia. Zemtsov's work defined St. Petersburg's style during the decade after Trezzini died in 1734. Then, the brilliant young Italian Bartolomeo Rastrelli began to overshadow him.[30]

Some fourteen years younger than Zemtsov, Ivan Korobov became one of the first Russians to study architecture in the West. Returning home not long after Peter II mounted the throne, he accepted the young emperor's appointment as chief architect of the Admiralty, only to be left behind when the court and government returned to Moscow a few months later. During Peter's short reign, Korobov did little more than design a few minor churches in St. Petersburg, and it was not until Anna returned to the city that he began to work on the larger projects for which his foreign studies had prepared him. In the 1730s, Korobov built the tower and spire that transformed St. Petersburg's sprawling Admiralty building into one of the city's most enduring landmarks, but history remembers him most of all for working with Zemtsov and the city planner Petr Eropkin to create the plan that would shape Russia's capital for the rest of its history.[31]

Reasons of geography and convenience drew the center of St. Petersburg toward the Admiralty Island, which was separated from the mainland only by the narrow Moika River. Peter the Great had worked against that tendency by insisting that such key buildings as the Kunstkammer, Menshikov's Palace, and Trezzini's Twelve Administrative Colleges, which housed Russia's new central government, all be built on Vasilevskii Island, and he had allowed a tangle of wooden houses and shops to be built around the Admiralty in an effort to downplay the importance of that part of the Neva's south bank. But the return of the capital to St. Petersburg had made people think differently about its development, and in the early 1730s, Anna and her counselors decided to let the city grow according to its natural inclinations. Realizing that their decision would eventually make it necessary to raze hundreds of huts and shops, they worried about the danger of popular discontent until, in 1736 and 1737, two terrible fires destroyed two-thirds of the 520 wooden buildings that had stood in the way of realizing their new vision.[32] Now, with a chance to give St. Petersburg a new focus, they worked with a sureness that established the city's shape for all time to come.

In the summer of 1737, Anna established the St. Petersburg Construction Commission and placed its work entirely in the hands of Russians. Together with Eropkin, whose studies of architecture and city planning in Rome had made him deeply aware of how Renaissance architects had used radial streets to give that city shape and focus, Korobov and Zemtsov decided to extend three grand avenues outward from the Admiralty in the shape of a huge crow's foot that reached all the way from the Neva embankment to the suburbs. Symbolically, the power of Church and State flowed along each of these thoroughfares, with Voznesenskii Prospekt and Gorokhovaia Street ending at the barracks of the Izmailovskii and Semenovskii Imperial Guards while the Nevskii Prospekt came to an end at the Aleksandr Nevskii Monastery.[33]

As an early expression of the imperial vision that would culminate in the gigantic architectural creations of Carlo Rossi in the next century, the Empress Anna's Russian builders planned to link St. Petersburg's three main arteries by a network of semicircular streets and canals on which the city's most elegant and expensive private residences were soon to be built.[34] Their efforts transformed Russia's capital into a "masterpiece of Baroque urbanism," with a unique beauty and spatial integrity that even the most insensitive Soviet builders never managed to erase.[35] If ever there was a time when St. Petersburg inevitably became the city we know today, it was at this point in the reign of Anna, the Empress whom history has so often remembered unfairly as a paragon of crudity and bad taste.

In order to make certain that St. Petersburg's new center would belong mainly to aristocrats and high officials, Eropkin, Zemtsov, and Korobov insisted that only stone or brick buildings could be built in the Admiralty Quarter after the fires of 1737. But before their grand design could take shape, Eropkin went to the gallows for being an unwitting accessory in a plot against his Empress, and Zemtsov died of natural causes just three years afterwards. Anna's death in the fall of 1740 left Russia in the hands of her squabbling German favorites for more than a year, and it was not until Peter the Great's daughter Elizabeth seized the throne in late 1741 that St. Petersburg could begin to acquire the brilliance that the Construction Commission's planners had foreseen. Between 1741 and 1761, it would be the genius of one single-minded Italian that would create the buildings that endowed St. Petersburg with the first elements of imperial grandeur.

While the Empress Elizabeth sat on Russia's throne, Bartolomeo Francesco Rastrelli shaped St. Petersburg into an architectural jewel that reflected all the frivolity of her age.[36] Born just a few months after his sculptor father, Carlo, had migrated from Florence to Paris, Rastrelli had grown up in the dynamic world of art and patronage that had swirled around the court of Louis XIV until the death of the Sun King in 1715 deprived France's artists of their greatest patron. Rather than join a legion of artists struggling to find new backers in the West, the Rastrellis set out for St. Petersburg, where the demand for men who could paint, draw, design, and carve all but guaranteed them work. From the moment the pair arrived, the elder Rastrelli was flooded with commissions. Russians still remember him as the sculptor whose full-length likeness of the Empress Anna blended "blowsy flamboyance" and "portly vulgarity" into a bronze portrait of imposing majesty,[37] but their appreciation for his modest talent as an architect has long since faded from mind and sight.

In those days, the wealth of Russia's sovereigns and aristocrats offered any artist willing to trade the comforts of the West for the rigors of daily life and politics in St. Petersburg a hopeful future. Of the artists who came during the next two centuries, many found success, and a few won true acclaim for works they might never have been able to create had they stayed in the West. Carlo's son stood near the forefront of this immortal handful, for just as Bernini had changed the face of seventeenth-century Rome with sculptures, fountains, and buildings that gave full meaning to the term "baroque," so Bartolomeo Rastrelli would define the character of Elizabethan St. Petersburg. More than a score of the city's most notable buildings would one day bear the stamp of his genius, and many more would reflect the spell he cast upon an entire generation of builders. No other architect ever did more to shape the character of a city. Nor was the work of any other builder ever better suited to realizing the dreams of the sovereign who employed him.

To St. Petersburg in the spring of 1716, the sixteen-year-old Bartolomeo Rastrelli brought a Parisian artistic education, an Italian heritage, and a subtle, supple mind that quickly embraced the new world into which fate had cast him. Predominantly influenced by the baroque, he soon tempered his memories of Rome and Versailles with a sense of the Eurasian past that flowed from the ancient churches and monasteries that had caught his attention during his earliest travels in Russia. Eventually, he blended his impressions of East and West by adding Russian highlights to the European style that dominated his work, but how and where he learned his trade still remains a mystery. As so often happens in exploring Russia's past, the scattered documents that have survived almost three hundred years of turmoil give us only tantalizing glimpses into what really happened and why. We do not know if Bartolomeo Rastrelli ever returned to study in the West. Nor do we know how he made contact with the influences that ultimately defined his work.

One of the few things we know for certain about Rastrelli's first steps as an architect is that he had barely turned twenty-one when Prince Dmitrii Kantemir engaged him to build a mansion on the Millionnaia, the new avenue of elegant structures that ran parallel to the Neva Embankment from the Winter Palace Square to Tsaritsyn Meadow (later called the Field of Mars). Aside from building a large wooden model for an imperial suburban palace at Strelna, he had not a single architectural accomplishment to his credit, and it seems that the young builder's first commission stemmed more from the city's acute shortage of architects than from any precocious display of talent on his part. Certainly the results of Bartolomeo Rastrelli's first venture into the trade that would make him famous showed hardly a hint of the brilliance that marked his later work. Probably for that reason, his biographers continue to believe that his disappointment with the uninspired form of Kantemir's palace led him to further study in Europe, even though no documentary record has ever been found to show that he returned to the lands of his birth.

The next documents on Rastrelli's life date from 1730 and show him working with his father to construct palaces for the Empress Anna in Moscow and St. Petersburg. Although none of the records indicates whether father or son took the lead in directing these projects, it seems clear that the Empress's favor had settled upon the son by the time she moved her court back to St. Petersburg in 1732. Almost immediately, she commissioned him to enlarge and redecorate the Winter Palace in time for her forty-first birthday in January 1734, and she placed at his disposal the colossal sum of two hundred thousand rubles, which represented the equivalent of a year's taxes collected from a quarter of a million serfs.

With less than two years in which to work, Rastrelli paid little attention to the Winter Palace's already lumpy facade and concentrated instead on turning its grand staircase, great hall, theater, and apartments of state into a series of artistic triumphs. Shining stone columns, sparkling mirrors, paintings, and marble sculptures added new brilliance to the palace's two hundred-odd rooms and gave the Russians their first hint of the masterpieces Rastrelli would create in years to come. For Anna's birthday celebration, he filled the palace's new 180-foot-long Great Hall with orange trees and myrtles his gardeners had brought to full flower in the midst of the northern winter. "The beauty, fragrance, and warmth of this new-formed grove, when you saw nothing but ice and snow through the windows, looked like enchantment," a visiting Englishwoman wrote to a friend. "The walks and trees filled with beaux and belles . . . made me fancy myself in Fairy-land," she went on. "Shakespeare's *Midsummer Night's Dream* was in my head all evening."[38]

For the rest of Anna's reign and into the first years of Elizabeth's, Rastrelli contended with architects who enjoyed favor that equaled or exceeded his own. Now on the threshold of middle age, he had reached the line that divides men of talent from artists of genius, but he had to wait until the reign of Elizabeth was well under way before he managed to cross it. The first years of Elizabeth's reign, in fact, saw Zemtsov gain particular favor at Rastrelli's expense, for it was he who won the commissions to design the triumphal arches for Elizabeth's coronation and to draft plans for building the Empress's new Anichkov Palace. But when Zemtsov's death in 1743 left his Russian followers without a leader, Rastrelli's star soared. During the next decade, Elizabeth's many commissions made him the preeminent architect in Russia's capital. The city's greatest magnates competed for his services. By 1760, the Vorontsovs, Stroganovs, Bestuzhevs, and Razumovskiis all had moved into palaces that Rastrelli had designed.[39]

Nothing reflected the tone of Russia's Elizabethan Age more emphatically than St. Petersburg's changing face, and no one played a greater part in bringing that about than Rastrelli. First and foremost, he shared Elizabeth's inclination to replace the stolid Germanic tastes of Anna's time with a flamboyant exuberance that would give Russia's capital a new tone. The festivals and celebrations he arranged left Elizabeth's courtiers breathless with amazement, and he built palaces and churches whose interiors fairly blazed with gold-leaf rococo decorations. Rastrelli painted the stucco coverings of his elaborately decorated buildings in almost every shade of the rainbow so as to highlight their silhouettes against the fanciful cloud formations that so often filled St. Petersburg's northern sky, and he especially favored turquoise with trimmings of white and gold to highlight massed columns and baroque statuary. As he blended the influences of East and West into an exuberant Russian baroque that surpassed the sum of its sources, he flooded his interiors with light and used a profusion of mirrors to reflect it upon the silk-covered walls and parquet floors that his Empress adored. Thanks to Rastrelli, the Russians at last ended their forty-year infatuation with the styles of Holland, Germany, and Scandinavia and turned instead to the elegance of Versailles and the exuberance of Venice and Rome.

By the time Rastrelli completed St. Petersburg's "third" Summer Palace
in the spring of 1744, he had cast aside some of the inhibitions that had restrained his work in earlier times. Set in a stunning aquatic frame formed by
the intersection of the Fontanka and the Moika, this new palace was designed to celebrate the sunlit nights of the city's far northern summer. Ac-
centuated by the elegant fountain-filled gardens that spread out beyond its
southern facade, Rastrelli's creation radiated an aura of enchantment, especially during the White Nights, when the ethereal light of the midnight sun
bathed its pink wooden walls and a thousand candles lit its Grand Hall
with a special glow. Until the Emperor Paul I razed it to make room for the
gloomy Mikhailovskii Castle in which he was assassinated in 1801, the
Summer Palace shone as the first of the many creations with which Rastrelli staked his claim to preeminence as the builder of mid-eighteenth-
century St. Petersburg. To Russians and Europeans alike, it seemed so like a
fantasy come true that it became one of the city's best-loved landmarks.[40]

Rastrelli's next two commissions took him into St. Petersburg's suburbs,
where, following the example of Menshikov's architects at Oranienbaum,
he replaced two modest royal summer residences with a pair of splendid
baroque palaces. As a monument to Peter the Great, whose secular revolution had paved the way for Elizabeth's reign, Rastrelli's palace at Peterhof
became an Italian's homage to the spirit of Old Russia at the same time as
it celebrated the arrival of the Western ideas and tastes that had brought
St. Petersburg to life. The Peterhof Palace stretched for nearly a thousand
feet, and its gardens, in which fountains and an immense cascade flowed
with water that had been piped through a twenty-four-mile system of
canals and underground pipelines, overshadowed even those at Versailles.
The gilded onion-shaped cupolas that rose from the pavilions at each of
the palace's ends evoked memories of eras long past and gave the first hint
of how Rastrelli intended to reinterpret the heritage of Old Russia in
baroque form. Yet, despite its grandeur and extravagance, the Peterhof
Palace still showed traces of artistic caution. Like the Elizabethan era in
which they took shape, Rastrelli's later works would reflect an unfettered
exuberance that would make them completely unique.

Thirty-five miles away from Peterhof and fifteen miles to the south of
St. Petersburg, Rastrelli turned his attention in 1751 to a heavily wooded
plateau that rose abruptly from the surrounding lowlands. Here, where his
Empress's parents had built a small rural retreat at Tsarskoe Selo, he created the Catherine Palace (named for Catherine I) that bubbled with the

gaiety Elizabeth so adored. Working according to Rastrelli's instructions, the Italian painters Giuseppe Valeriani and Antonio Peresinotti painted the entire eight-thousand-square-foot ceiling of the palace's Great Hall with allegorical scenes portraying Russia enjoying the bounties of civilization, and nothing in Europe could equal the Amber Room in which Elizabeth entertained special guests at birthday parties and intimate receptions. Festooned with gilded capitals, pilasters, and statues to set off its yellow walls and bright white columns, the 978-foot-long palace stood as the first unrestrained triumph of Russia's baroque.[41] In years to come, Catherine the Great's preference for neoclassical simplicity would lead her to condemn it as an example of inexcusably bad taste, but Russia's Elizabethans greeted it as a stunning display of imperial wealth that proclaimed their nation's new greatness in Europe. With the help of thousands of masons, master carpenters, sculptors, plasterers, and painters who had worked for the better part of a decade, Rastrelli had brought into being an artistic vision of unprecedented dimensions that he would transpose into the very center of Russia's capital. That vision—defined by an extravagant display of baroque statuary and massed columns—would personify the spirit of the reign of the Empress he served.

As the Empress Elizabeth crossed the threshold of middle age and deepened her devotion to the Russian Church in the late 1740s, she started to think of building St. Petersburg's first convent, perhaps as a sanctuary in which she herself might seek refuge in her final years.[42] Drawing heavily upon the Kremlin's fifteenth-century Dormition Cathedral and Novgorod's even older Cathedral of St. Sofiia, Rastrelli in 1749 drafted a plan for the Smolnyi Cathedral and Convent that would blend the building styles of Old Russia with the baroque designs of the West. Neither he nor Elizabeth would live to see his vision fully translated into brick and stone. The cathedral's interior would not be finished until the 1830s (and then in a very different style from what either patron or architect had envisioned), and the bell tower intended to rise five hundred feet would never be started because even the enthusiastic Elizabeth could not afford the cost. Nonetheless, the Smolnyi Cathedral became for a time St. Petersburg's most beautiful church, even with its interior unfinished. Giacomo Quarenghi, the Roman architect who served Catherine the Great and shared her distaste for the baroque, used to remove his hat every time he passed Rastrelli's cathedral and exclaim (so people said), "Now there is a *real* cathedral!"[43]

Together with its connected chapels, convent buildings, and outer walls, the soaring Smolnyi Cathedral called vividly to mind the great fortified monasteries that had defended Russia in earlier times. It had taken two thousand soldiers more than a year to drive home the fifty thousand pilings needed to make the land firm enough to support its weight, and its turquoise walls, white columns, and gilded three-hundred-foot-high dome proclaimed that modern Russia continued to pray to its Orthodox God, even if its sovereign and people now walked resolutely in the footsteps of Europe. Here was Orthodoxy brought into the eighteenth century without altering any of the intense belief that had shaped the Russians' faith in earlier times. The rationalism, materialism, and secular power that Peter the Great had brought to Russia from the West all seemed diminished in the shadow of Rastrelli's monument to God.

Fate and the Empress Elizabeth decreed that Rastrelli's career in St. Petersburg should end at the Winter Palace, exactly where it had begun. Now well into middle age, architect and Empress each entered the second half of the eighteenth century in search of an enterprise that would give greater meaning and focus to their final years, and both found it in the task of rebuilding the Winter Palace that Rastrelli had designed for the Empress Anna twenty years before. Destined to survive into the present as St. Petersburg's great Hermitage Museum, this "fourth" Winter Palace that Rastrelli built for Elizabeth in the 1750s has always remained his greatest tribute to the Elizabethan Age. Rastrelli brought to the Winter Palace—the culmination of his life's work and vision—all the experience he had gained from a quarter-century of building for Russia's empresses and aristocrats. As the final word in his flamboyant interpretation of his age, the Winter Palace became perhaps the most stunning eighteenth-century architectural creation in Russia and certainly one of the last great baroque buildings to take shape anywhere in the world.

To raze and rebuild the Winter Palace, Elizabeth placed at Rastrelli's disposal all the revenues that her government collected from its taxes on salt and liquor for all of 1754, the year he began to work. Yet even that sum of nearly 900,000 rubles could not support Rastrelli's vision. Each of the palace's windows cost more than one of its construction workers could earn in a decade, and the rococo interior doors each cost three times that amount. By the time Elizabeth's successor, Peter III, moved into the Winter Palace in 1762, its price had exceeded two and a half million rubles, which the aging Empress had demanded her counselors provide even though Russia was in the midst of an expensive foreign war. At times, they could not do her bidding. In the last year of Elizabeth's life, the Imperial Treasury could not produce the 380,000 rubles Rastrelli needed to complete the private apartments into which the Empress was hoping to move the following spring.[44]

Before demolishing his "third" Winter Palace to make way for the "fourth," Rastrelli built for Elizabeth a one-story temporary wooden residence on the Nevskii Prospekt between the Moika River and Morskaia Street. Finished in seven short months in 1755, this became her final home while she waited impatiently for the completion of the masterpiece she would never live to see. In the flimsy "wooden Winter Palace," where she lived in fear of being burned alive in her bed by one of the fires that still swept through the city, Elizabeth turned ugly and old, with horribly swollen legs that kept her from traveling or even from walking from one part of her palace to the other. Yet, even the thousands of workmen Rastrelli ordered to labor year round could not outrun the ravages of time. On Christmas Day, 1761, Elizabeth died at the age of fifty-two, a good three and a half months before the palace that was to have been her final accomplishment could be finished.

The Winter Palace that became the ultimate monument to Russia's Elizabethan Age stretched for nearly five hundred feet along the Neva River embankment and enclosed almost a quarter of a million square feet of ground. It had 1,054 rooms and several times that many windows. Two hundred and fifty columns ornamented its facades and nearly two hundred statues and ornamental vases decorated the balustrades above them. Intricate parquet floors, gilded rococo carvings of plaster and wood, and all the other flamboyant excesses of the baroque marked every room of Rastrelli's creation. Its Jordan Staircase, so-named because Russia's tsars came down it to attend the blessing of the frozen Neva's waters on the Feast of the Epiphany each year, expressed his vision best of all.[45] "More grandiosely than any of his predecessors or contemporaries," a commentator once concluded, Rastrelli had succeeded in making "as imperceptible as possible the transition from the life of the stage to the life of the world" that had been so much a part of the Russian court during the reign of an Empress who preferred masquerade balls to all other forms of entertainment.[46]

Before the end of Elizabeth's reign, St. Petersburg had become Russia's capital in a much larger sense than in Peter the Great's time. Palaces built by Rastrelli and his favorite Russian pupil, Savva Chevakinskii, gave the city an aura of aristocratic elegance, while the great public buildings created by the Russian followers of Peter's foreign architects emphasized its importance as the center of a new empire. Peter's dream of centering his city on the low-lying lands of Vasilevskii Island had been decisively set aside by the plans that Eropkin, Korobov, and Zemtsov had drawn up in the 1730s, and St. Petersburg now occupied nine of the Neva delta's main islands, plus the mainland on its southern bank. By the middle of the eighteenth century, no one of any consequence lived on Vasilevskii Island. Even the grandiose palace in which Menshikov had once held court had been converted into a boarding school for the First Cadet Corps, which the empresses Anna and Elizabeth had created to transform a select handful of Russia's young lords into full-fledged courtiers.[47]

Although the Twelve Colleges of Peter the Great still occupied the quarter-mile-long building that Trezzini had designed for them near Menshikov's Palace in the 1720s, Vasilevskii Island had become mainly the center of St. Petersburg's trade and commerce by the middle of the eighteenth century. The Commodity Exchange was there, and so were the trading arcades through which millions of rubles' worth of goods passed every year. Yet, except for these and a few other brick and stone buildings that lined its Neva River embankment, the island upon which Peter had dreamed of centering his capital in a manner reminiscent of Amsterdam and Venice now displayed few hints of the grandeur its founder had envisioned. Its houses were still mainly built of wood, and the lands on its northern side remained wild, in sharp contrast to the embankments of the Neva, Moika, and Fontanka that were lined with elegant palaces and townhouses.[48]

In 1727, St. Petersburg's first pontoon bridge linked Vasilevskii Island with the mainland during the months when the Neva was free of ice, and another made it possible to cross to the island of the Petersburg Quarter, which stood behind the Fortress of Saints Peter and Paul. A third pontoon bridge connected the same island to the mainland on the Neva's northern shore, but all three of these had to be removed the moment the ice started to form. By contrast, ten permanent bridges spanned the Moika and the Fontanka in what had become St. Petersburg's true center, and these made it possible to follow the three main avenues that Anna's planners had laid out all the way to the suburbs.[49]

St. Petersburg by 1760 had nearly two hundred named streets and a population of almost a hundred thousand. Viewed from the perspective of the Winter Palace, the arc-shaped course of the Fontanka River had by that time become a dividing line that separated aristocrats, merchants, tradesmen, and government officials from the day laborers, carters, shipyard workers, and street sellers who lived beyond it.[50] Yet the separation of the city's menial workers from their social betters was by no means so rigid as these first lower-class settlements implied. The thousands of serfs who performed all the tasks connected with aristocratic daily life continued to live in the households of their masters, and it was not unusual for noble households in mid-eighteenth-century St. Petersburg to boast staffs that numbered between fifty and two hundred.[51] With no space to call their own, these bonded servants had less than even the least fortunate of the city's draymen and peddlers. Relegated to odd corners in the households in which they served, they slept on stairwell landings and in out-of-the-way nooks and doorways. In doing so, they set the precedent for mixing rich and poor in the same parts of the city that would prevail until the twentieth century.

Afoot, on horseback, and in carriages, everything and everyone began to gravitate to St. Petersburg's Nevskii Prospekt as the eighteenth century passed its midpoint. The number of horses clearly announced the rank and station of whoever rode behind them, with generals, their counterparts in the civil service, and their wives being drawn by equipages of six, while colonels, majors, collegiate and court councilors, and collegiate assessors were allowed only four. Junior officers, lesser officials, and their wives had to settle for conveyances drawn by one or two horses, while the vast majority of the city's inhabitants went about their business on foot. Some of St. Petersburg's finest shops, its main theater, the Stroganov and Anichkov palaces, and a score of other notable buildings would one day line this central avenue, which (Russians noted with pride) was fully twice the breadth of Oxford Street in London and as wide as the Champs Elysées. In years to come St. Petersburg's jewelers' row would lead into the Nevskii Prospekt, and the House of Fabergé would be located just a stone's throw beyond it. Cathedrals, the main building of the city government, and at the beginning of the twentieth century even the Singer Sewing Machine Company's main Russian office all stood on the Nevskii Prospekt, along with Eliseev's and Filippov's, the city's two most elegant confectioneries.

Soldiers, aristocrats, honest workmen, civil servants, peddlers, and thieves all mingled on the Nevskii Prospekt, and so did men and women from every corner of the empire. No other city in Europe boasted such a rich mixture of races and nationalities, and European visitors were amazed at the variety of languages spoken in its salons and places of business. Visitors from the Near and Far East, the Americas, and Europe all came together on the Nevskii Prospekt, and the array of goods offered in its shops reflected all the diversity of South, East, and West. Eurasia's overland trade, which entered the Russian Empire at Kiakhta on the faraway Chinese frontier, brought fine silks, furs, spices, and tea—even the dried Chinese rhubarb root that middle- and upper-class Europeans so prized for purging their bowels—to the shops and trading arcades of the Nevskii Prospekt. From there they made their way to Europe, where the exotica of the East commanded even higher prices than in Russia. At the same time, European fashions, fabrics, and fine wines came to the shops on the Nevskii Prospekt from the West, all of them commanding premiums that status-conscious Russian aristocrats willingly paid.

With its array of people, shops, merchandise, and opportunities representing all of Russia in microcosm, it was perhaps no accident that virtually every great architect who worked in eighteenth- and nineteenth-century Russia claimed credit for at least one building located on or within sight of the Nevskii Prospekt. Rastrelli's genius was represented there by Elizabeth's "wooden" Winter Palace and the palace of the Stroganovs, while the Aleksandr Nevskii Monastery at its far end bore testimony to Trezzini's accomplishments. The Admiralty and the Anichkov Palace (before Rastrelli took on the task of completing it) owed their designs to Ivan Korobov and Mikhail Zemtsov, two of the first Russians to design buildings in the modern style. In years to come, Carlo Rossi would build several monumental imperial structures—the General Staff Headquarters, the Aleksandrinskii Theater, and the Mikhailovskii Palace—on or near the Nevskii Prospekt, and later on so did Andrei Voronikhin and Andreian Zakharov. With its wealth, great buildings, crowds, and excitement, the Nevskii Prospekt had become the spinal cord from which life in St. Petersburg drew much of its vitality by the middle of the eighteenth century. When Elizabeth died in 1761, what came and went on the Nevskii Prospekt was becoming the image of Russia itself.

How much that image still depended on the person of Russia's ruler became clear within months after Elizabeth passed from the scene. For nearly all of her reign, Rastrelli's vision of the baroque had defined the style and images of St. Petersburg, but the Emperor Peter III did not share his aunt's passion for building, and the Empress Catherine the

Great, who deposed him in 1762, had very different tastes. Within half a decade after Elizabeth's death both Rastrelli and the style in which he built had slipped completely out of favor. Russia's new Empress insisted on smoothing out all the curves and curlicues of the Italian's ebullient baroque and overlaying it with more elegant neoclassical features that reflected the grander imperial vision of which she wanted to make Russia a part. More emphatically than any sovereign before or since, Catherine insisted that Russia must be Western in culture and destiny, and she set out to make her adopted country the equal of Europe in ways that even Peter the Great had never foreseen. Her goal was to close the gap that still divided Russia from Europe and to erase the differences between them. Had she lived another fifteen years, she would have found the ultimate tribute to her success in an émigré Frenchman's statement that life in St. Petersburg seemed to him no different from that in Paris.[52]

The daughter of a petty German prince, the woman who would be remembered as Catherine the Great had come to Russia in 1744 to marry its future Emperor, Peter III. For the next eighteen years, she lived in the shadows of Elizabeth's court, disdained by both her husband and the Empress he had been chosen to succeed. Coveting the power that would allow her to rule Russia in her own right, Catherine appears to have driven her husband from the throne, for although her complicity in the plot that cost Peter III his life has never been proved, historians find it difficult to believe she was not deeply involved. Only Peter the Great himself rivaled Catherine in her talent for transforming people into her willing instruments. "Her brilliance blinded, her friendliness attracted, and her generosity attached," the poet Pushkin wrote a quarter of a century after she had died. "The very voluptuousness of this clever woman," he concluded with undisguised admiration, "confirmed her majesty."[53]

Although she had no legitimate claim to the throne she seized in the summer of 1762, Catherine would rule Russia for thirty-four years. Her imperial vision led her to tighten her grip on Siberia, reach out to Alaska and northern California, and play a leading role in dividing up the lands of Poland with Austria and Prussia. Even though her efforts to tighten the bonds that held millions of Russians in servitude sparked the greatest serf revolt in the nation's history, she continued to see herself as a philosopher on the throne, with a mission to bring prosperity and happiness to her people. At the same time, she became the most energetic builder her empire had ever seen. "The more you build, the more you want to build," she once confessed. "It's a sickness somewhat akin to being addicted to alcohol. Or maybe it's just a habit."[54] Catherine's energy and vision transformed the city that Peter the Great, Trezzini, Elizabeth, and Rastrelli had created into a grander, more elegant imperial capital. More than two hundred years after her death, St. Petersburg still remains more the city of Catherine the Great than of any other Russian ruler.

Begun just three years after she seized Russia's throne, the building that housed the Imperial Academy of Fine Arts illustrated the transformation of style and function that Catherine had in mind. Just a few steps downriver from the sprawling Menshikov Palace on the Vasilevskii Island Embankment, the Academy's main building blended the neoclassical designs of the Russian Aleksandr Kokorinov and the Frenchman Vallin de la Mothe into a work of true classical elegance. A huge rectangle that was 460 feet long and 410 feet deep, the building rivaled the Winter Palace in size and took more than fifty years to finish. With none of the elaborate ornamentation and exuberant design that Rastrelli had incorporated into the Winter Palace, the Academy of Fine Arts building spoke to the rationality of the Enlightenment and brought to St. Petersburg an imperial vision that drew more forcefully upon the heritage of Greece and Rome.[55]

By the early 1770s, the Neva River's main embankments had started to take on the form they have today. The Winter Palace and the Admiralty dominated the river's southern bank, while the Peter and Paul Fortress, the Kunstkammer, the Twelve Administrative Colleges, Menshikov's Palace, and the beginnings of the Academy of Fine Arts building filled the space on its northern side. Anxious to bring a full-blown capital city into being, Peter, Anna, and Elizabeth all had paid little attention to the river's edge itself, and for half a century it had been left as a muddy bank, its slippery expanses punctuated by wooden docks and ramshackle pilings. Catherine therefore encouraged St. Petersburg's builders to devise ways to bind nearly twenty-five miles of the city's waterfront to the buildings along it, an undertaking that, the Russian art historian Igor Grabar once explained, demanded "an artist who would not lose sight of the larger aesthetic goal, even for a single minute."[56] So often unerring in her ability to find genius in out-of-the-way places, Russia's Empress recognized the artist she needed in Georg Friedrich Velten, whose father had come from Danzig to serve as Peter the Great's "master cook." Along with the three grand avenues that Korobov, Eropkin, and Zemtsov had laid out from the Admiralty in the 1730s, Velten's granite embankments became a key feature in defining St. Petersburg's center.

Velten had begun his career in the 1750s as one of Rastrelli's apprentices, but he had been quick to remove all traces of his teacher's influence from his designs the moment Catherine came to the throne. Working under her benevolent gaze, he began facing St. Petersburg's Palace Embankment with red Finnish granite in 1764, punctuated it with carefully planned oval stairways that reached down to the river's surface, and placed between them several gracefully arched bridges to form gateways through which the Moika, Fontanka, and several small canals could flow into the Neva. While serving the very practical purpose of providing landing stages for the river traffic of a city that still lacked permanent bridges across the Neva's main current, Velten's designs framed St. Petersburg's riverfront in a way that the builders of eighteenth-century London and Paris never managed to match.[57]

When Velten's work on the Palace Embankment was well under way, Catherine highlighted it with new buildings, the most impressive of which was the Marble Palace. Built by the Italian architect Antonio Rinaldi, this was to be the Empress's gift to Grigorii Orlov, the handsome guardsman and lover who had directed the coup d'état that had put her on the throne. No other palace in eighteenth-century St. Petersburg could rival the Marble Palace's subtle restraint, and none stood more clearly as a triumph of the stonecutter's art. The simplicity of its neoclassical design and the cool elegance of its natural stone made it one of the city's most stunning monuments to the Catherine Age, and to this day it remains a reminder of the powerful impact that neoclassicism made when it first came to Russia.

Rinaldi had come to Russia in the 1750s, when Rastrelli's influence was at its peak, and in his early work he attempted to strike a balance between his own neoclassical preferences and Rastrelli's passion for the baroque. At first he worked mainly at Oranienbaum and became a favorite of Catherine and her soon-to-be-assassinated husband, both of whom commissioned him to build small country palaces that reflected their special preferences and tastes. Unlike his predecessors, Rinaldi preferred to work with natural stone, producing effects that could never be achieved by Rastrelli's method of overlaying brick walls with brightly painted stucco. Seeing that Rinaldi's buildings emphasized classical simplicity at the expense of baroque excess, Catherine recognized in his work (as she did in Velten's) a way to replace Rastrelli's flamboyance with more subtle, elegant forms.

Begun in 1768 and finished twenty years later, Rinaldi's Marble Palace embodied St. Petersburg's transition from baroque to neoclassical architectural styles.[58] It had none of the rococo cornucopias, seashells, and curlicues of which Rastrelli had been so fond, and there were few urns, statues, and ornate window surrounds that had been so much a part of the exteriors of the Catherine and Winter palaces. For the lower portions of the Marble Palace's outer walls, Rinaldi chose rough-cut red Finnish granite much like the stone Velten had used for his quays. He adorned the gray granite of the palace's two main stories with Corinthian pilasters of pink marble from Karelia, and he highlighted them with capitals and panels cut from newly discovered quarries of bluish-gray Siberian marble. Special battalions of workers had to travel more than a thousand miles to bring the Siberian stone from beyond the Urals, and master masons and stonecutters were brought from all over Russia to shape it and set it in place. The palace's main staircase blended the blues, grays, and whites of this natural stone, while the walls of its Marble Hall were an intricate study of subtly shaded grays, whites, blues, and greens set off by pink marble pilasters topped by gilded capitals. Taken together, these expressed a maturity and self-confidence that even Rastrelli's best buildings never achieved, and they appealed to the forces that moved the mind and spirit, rather than those that had stirred the emotions.

Of all the builders to work in Catherine's St. Petersburg, only Giacomo Quarenghi came close to gaining the undisputed preeminence that Rastrelli had enjoyed in the days of Elizabeth. A man whose features and style of dress had none of Rastrelli's elegance, Quarenghi wore simple military frock coats and cropped his hair short rather than powder it in the manner preferred by high society. Portrait painters portrayed him with heavy eyebrows that seemed knit in a perpetual frown, and his nose, "a great bluish bulb that Nature had stuck on his face where his nose should have been," one observer remembered, dominated his entire face and form.[59] Like his manner of dress, Quarenghi's work was devoid of frivolous ornamentation. Palladio's *Four Books* were for him the Gospel around which he shaped his work in Catherine the Great's St. Petersburg, but he drew upon any other influences that seemed relevant to whatever task came to hand. A critic once noted that his style, which blended the experiences of France, England, and Italy, was "irreproachably severe but no less picturesque than that of Rastrelli."[60] And like Rastrelli, Quarenghi imposed a vision on St. Petersburg that symbolized what Russia hoped to become.

After graduating from the Bergamo Academy in the early 1760s, Quarenghi had moved to Rome. With an eye, as he later said, to "pillaging the good wherever I could discover it," he had devoted more than a decade to studying the classical and Renaissance masterpieces of Italy, yet unlike so many of his lesser contemporaries he never allowed the principles that had shaped architecture in centuries past to dominate his life or work. "[My] studies and observations have made me adopt the principle that common sense and reason should not be the slaves of certain rules," he once explained, and he insisted that even though a "foundation of simplicity and antique grandeur" might be drawn from the ancients, their principles had to be modified to fit the time and place in which he worked. "Without paying attention . . . to local circumstances," he warned, "one will produce only mediocre things."[61] His overriding concern was to build in a style that was "antique without being archeological and grandiose yet human in scale."[62] As the epitome of Catherinian neoclassicism, his work between 1783 and 1817 paved the way for his successors to transform St. Petersburg into the imperial city that projected a vision of Russian power across all of Eurasia.

Quarenghi's commissions in St. Petersburg—a total of forty-five in the city and twenty-five in the suburbs—ranged from government buildings, aristocratic palaces, and townhouses to barracks, trading arcades, warehouses, and triumphal arches.[63] He began in 1781 by building the English Palace at Peterhof, and then quickly moved on to design the State Bank, the Imperial Academy of Sciences, and the Hermitage Theater, all before the 1780s came to an end. During the same decade he built a huge suburban palace for Count Aleksandr Bezborodko and followed that with an elegant palace for the Iusupov princes on the Moika Embankment. Still at work on the palace for the Iusupovs in the 1790s, he began another at Tsarskoe Selo for the future Emperor Alexander. The Sheremetievs, Gagarins, and Lanskois all engaged him during the 1780s and 1790s, as his ability to produce one building after another without ever seeming to stop won him Catherine's unrestrained praise. "The whole town is filled with his buildings," she crowed enthusiastically in one of her letters. "And they are all of the very best."[64]

At the beginning of the new century, Quarenghi went on to build the Smolnyi Institute for the Education of Young Women of Noble Birth and a riding school for the Imperial Horse Guards Regiment. Finally, to celebrate the victories of Russia's forces over the armies of Napoleon, he designed the Narva Gates, which called to mind the towering triumphal arches of ancient Rome as they greeted the Tsar's victorious soldiers on their return in 1815.[65] Now drawing confidently on the heritage of the Caesars, the Russians were beginning to transpose to their empire the full grandeur of Imperial Rome. In that, Imperial St. Petersburg owed its beginnings to Quarenghi, but its full flowering depended upon builders in whose ranks Russians would share pride of place with Europeans for the first time.

Even before Quarenghi's influence reached its peak, Russian architects had begun to play a larger part in St. Petersburg's design, and none more impressively than Ivan Starov. As one of the first Russians to work successfully in the neoclassical style that Catherine the Great preferred, Starov was the proud recipient of a gold medal from the Imperial Academy of Fine Arts, and he had devoted much of the 1760s to studying the same classical sources that Quarenghi used with such dramatic effect. In Russia, he had begun his career by designing neoclassical country mansions for several of Catherine's favorites. Then, in 1776, the Empress had chosen him to design the Trinity Cathedral, which was to become the centerpiece of Trezzini's Aleksandr Nevskii Monastery. At the age of thirty-one, Starov began to work on the first of the two buildings that would make him the best-known Russian architect of his age.[66] At the time, nothing in St. Petersburg rivaled his work. Nor did any other structures influence the development of the city's architecture more profoundly.

Intent upon creating an imperial vision that would reflect the tastes of the Empress he served, Starov modeled his cathedral on a Roman basilica. The Trinity Cathedral had none of Rastrelli's jubilant excesses but relied instead on clean lines and simple designs that spoke clearly for themselves. Its huge rotunda and great ribbed dome stood an age apart from the style of Russia's churches, and it contrasted sharply with the baroque towers of the cathedral that Rastrelli had built at nearby Smolnyi. No one could doubt the connections that the builders who now served Russia's autocrats wanted to make between the empire of the Romanovs and that of Rome's Caesars. By focusing the attention of St. Petersburg and Russia on the architecture of Imperial Rome, Starov's creation would become the architectural parent of a host of great public buildings that proclaimed the power of the Russian Empire across the length and breadth of Eurasia.

Completed in the year of Quarenghi's arrival in Russia, Starov's Trinity Cathedral signaled the arrival of full-blown neoclassicism in Russia. His greatest masterpiece followed just a few years later and was set in a corner of St. Petersburg that had been too isolated to receive earlier builders' serious attention. Acting again on Catherine's orders, Starov built the Tauride Palace on an empty grassy knoll that rose gradually from the river's edge where, by using a minimum of decoration to achieve a maximum of elegance, he worked on a scale that could have been used only in Russia to create one of the "wonders of Europe."[67] Some have called his Tauride Palace the "most significant of all Russian classical buildings."[68] All across the empire during the half-century after it was finished in 1789, aristocrats and country gentlemen reproduced this "poetry in columns"[69] in smaller versions that brought a sense of grandeur to isolated lands in which the values and visions of Old Russia still reigned supreme.

At the time of Catherine's death in 1796, the city to which Starov's and Quarenghi's buildings had given new elegance stood a world apart from the rude settlement Peter the Great founded on the Neva's hostile marshes. In less than a century, St. Petersburg's population had risen to more than two hundred thousand, and it spread onto eleven islands in the Neva delta. Instead of the many sprawling collections of wattle and daub cabins that Peter had left behind, St. Petersburg had become a city of stone, brick, and stucco.[70] Palaces and townhouses that bore the imprint of Rastrelli, Zemtsov, Rinaldi, Quarenghi, Starov, and their disciples lined the city's main streets and embankments. Sewers now ran beneath the main streets in St. Petersburg's central sections, and although they were still scarce in outlying sections, street lights shone brightly in its center. In terms of the services it offered, Russia's capital now rivaled the great metropolises of the West. It had become the Palmyra of the North, a gleaming architectural jewel in a part of Europe that had previously been distinguished mainly for its somber, Protestant style of building.

St. Petersburg now boasted artisans in the many thousands, and scores of factories produced the necessities and luxuries demanded by the new ways of life it had called into being. By the end of the eighteenth century, the city's first spinning and weaving mills, which a century later would give birth to the workers' movement that fanned the revolutionary flames in 1917, had taken shape. Leather and glass had their makers, too, but what struck late-eighteenth-century visitors most of all was the variety of luxuries St. Petersburg's artisans produced. By 1796, silks, tapestries, porcelains, bronzes, clocks, watches, carriages, and all manner of fine arts and jewelry were made in the city that Peter the Great had created. It had become a center of the arts and elegance, a place in which the cosmopolitan elite of Europe could feel at home and at ease.

Yet, no amount of native industry could meet the demand for goods and luxuries that Peter's transformation had stirred. Toward the end of Catherine's reign, silks and woolens valued in the millions of rubles, tens of thousands of looking glasses, hundreds of thousands of hogsheads of wine, books, crystal, dyes, and over sixty thousand copperplate engravings poured into St. Petersburg every year. These and life's necessities came to the city in hundreds of ox-drawn caravans and thousands of foreign ships to create a commerce valued at more than fifty million rubles every year.[71] St. Petersburg by 1796 had become a city of shops and arcades in which anything could be had for a price, and often in quantities that amazed European visitors. "The sale of these goods scarcely pays the freight," Heinrich Storch wrote of the huge quantities of oranges and lemons that arrived every spring. "A chest of four hundred lemons is usually had for two or three rubles," he added. "These delicious and wholesome fruits may therefore be enjoyed on the banks of the Neva in greater profusion and much cheaper than they can on the borders of the Seine."[72]

The merchants, artisans, and builders whose labor had transformed the Neva's marshes into Russia's sparkling northern capital in the space of a single century all served the city's aristocrats first and foremost. Whereas Peter the Great had focused on making his new capital into Russia's chief port and center of government, the lords and ladies who dominated the city's life after the Empress Anna returned the seat of government there in 1732 had defined its character in a very different way. From chronic complainers who had lamented Peter's demand that they move to the new capital and bear its high cost of living, these men and women quickly had become its chief consumers, who, by the early days of Catherine the Great's reign, were demanding every measure of luxury imaginable. So far had their expenditures outstripped their incomes by the 1770s that Catherine was obliged to establish special banks to extend them the credits needed to support their style of life.[73] Yet she did so willingly, for, as we shall see, Russia's capital had become a city that lived and moved according to the whims of its aristocrats.

TWO

# LORDS
# OF THE REALM

EVER SINCE MOSCOW ROSE TO RULE the Russian land in the fourteenth century, the Tsar's court stood in the way of progress. Here religion and tradition formed the bulwark of a society that took its bearings on the past and gave little thought to the future. Custom set women apart, forbade the painting of portraits, and demanded that beards be left uncut lest the wearer defile God's image. Like their parents and grandparents before them, the men and women of the Tsar's court felt certain that the world of their grandchildren would be no different from the one in which they lived and died, and they believed that things would continue to be done in the same way from one century to the next. They bowed before God and the Tsar in all things, and even the greatest lords called themselves the sovereign's most humble slaves. Few could read and write. Fewer still had any sense of the modern world that lay just a fortnight's journey to their west. Habit and superstition sustained them. Ritual and ceremony drawn from the empires of Byzantium and Genghis Khan still ruled their lives.

This was the world that Peter vowed to change through contact with the West, education, and a new capital. He imposed new attitudes and values upon those people whom tradition and the accident of birth had placed around him, and he broadened his circle of counselors to include men from different social backgrounds. Like the Tsars before him, he drew some of his intimates from such illustrious families as the Buturlins, Golitsyns, Romodanovskiis, and Sheremetievs, but he also added to their ranks merchants, priests, and serfs whose personal qualities attracted him. An Abyssinian prince (the grandfather of the famed poet Aleksandr Pushkin), whom bad luck had transformed into a Turkish slave before Peter's army captured him, rose to become a general in the Russian army, and despite the anti-Semitism that had plagued Russia for centuries, the Jewish shopkeeper Petr Shafirov became the sovereign's vice chancellor.

Many came from abroad to join Peter's entourage. A few like the Scots artillery expert General James Bruce actually were born in Russia, but most had left their homelands in search of their fortunes. That was true of the Scotsman Patrick Gordon and the Swiss mercenary Franz LeFort, not to mention the Germans Andrei Ostermann and Burkhard Münnich. "They came to him from different directions and all possible conditions," the historian Vasilii Kliuchevskii once wrote in describing the people around Peter the Great.[1] One had been a swineherd in Lithuania, another a house serf, and still another a cabin boy on a Portuguese ship. There were Royalist Scots Catholics who had fled the rising tide of Protestantism, and others whose biographies included shadows of a criminal past. Of Peter's closest (but illiterate) friend, the future field marshal, prince, and governor-general of St. Petersburg Aleksandr Menshikov, it was widely rumored that he had sold pies on the streets of Moscow in his youth.[2] And finally there was Catherine herself, the woman Peter married in 1711 and crowned Empress in 1724. Starting out as a peasant household servant in Livonia, Catherine had made her way through the beds of a Swedish dragoon, a Russian sergeant, Field Marshal Sheremetiev, and Menshikov before becoming Peter's mistress in 1704.

Peter set out to create new values for this diverse inner circle by attacking the rituals and customs of medieval Muscovy. He outlawed beards, demanded that his followers wear Western clothing, and replaced Orthodox religious symbols with pagan and military ones. In search of a clear imperial image, he became Russia's first reigning hero, who claimed greatness from his victories rather than embrace the piety that had been the mark of a true Tsar in earlier times. After being excluded for centuries, women now appeared at court, not as objects to be set apart but as participants in the life of modern Russia. Instead of piety and tenderness, wisdom, beauty, and modern civility became almost overnight the virtues for which the women of Russia were expected to strive. No longer did the holy Mother of God in her many forms express the essence of female perfection. Now the goddess Minerva dressed in a décolleté gown and wielding a sword became a model with which women were expected to identify.

To create the powerful secular images that buttressed Peter's imperial vision, his followers drew upon the rites of ancient Rome, not the rituals of Orthodox Byzantium. Poets and propagandists identified him with Mars, Hercules, and Alexander the Great, and feats of arms took precedence over prayer. Haughty triumph replaced pious humility, and practical achievements in the here-and-now claimed priority over deeds that would count in Heaven. As he built Russia's first navy, rode to war against his enemies, and laid the foundations for St. Petersburg, Peter the Great never allowed the Church to direct his daily life as his father and grandfather had done. War, conquest, and secular pleasures now shaped the values he pressed upon the Russians.[3]

Some of the first hints of how Peter intended to reshape life at Russia's court came around 1690, when he and his close friends formed the All-Mad, All-Jesting, All-Drunken Assembly. Organized in part as a parody of Old Muscovite symbols of piety and authority, the Assembly met throughout Peter's reign and featured grotesque carnivalesque activities that revolved around drunken orgies. Peter always found time to devote serious attention to its rituals and drafted detailed instructions for its meetings, even when such major crises as the revolt of Moscow's palace guards and early defeats in the war with Sweden demanded his attention. At various ceremonies, participants rode in carriages drawn by pigs, dogs, and goats. Sometimes they dressed in outlandish costumes and at others wore no clothes at all. Always, they mocked piety and tradition, and liquor flowed so freely that participants sometimes confessed to not remembering how they returned home at night.[4]

Amidst elaborately constructed ceremonies that ridiculed the values and institutions of medieval Muscovy, intoxication became a virtue and sobriety a sin, as men who would have been deemed unfit in earlier times staked their claims to high office. In this world of new ceremonies and visions, the building of St. Petersburg became the greatest and most elaborate ceremony of all, in which tens of thousands had to play their parts. Here in the huge drama of St. Petersburg's rise from swamp to national capital men fought barehanded against Nature as they and their sovereign struggled to show that brute strength and human will could surpass the power of prayer. Above them all, Peter stood triumphant. Here was the sovereign whose will had made possible feats that challenged those wrought by the heroes of ancient times.

Built on land conquered from a defeated enemy, St. Petersburg became the physical expression of Russia's new secular vision and the symbol of its new imperial triumphs. In St. Petersburg, Peter brought together foreigners and Russians who shared his view of what he wanted Russia to become, and he sought to blend these men and women of diverse backgrounds and cultures into the beginnings of an imperial court. Peter clearly intended for European manners, ceremonies, and his new belief in progress to transform Russian life, but few of the men and women he forced to move to St. Petersburg during the last two decades of his reign had any clear idea about how to shape the city and empire that would carry Russia into the future. All of them relied on foreign models to set the prevailing patterns for manners, fashions, and cuisine to show how St. Petersburg would be laid out, how its buildings would be designed, and how its people would behave. In an important sense, this emphasis on mimicking the West forced the Russians in Peter's circle to become foreigners too, for as adults they had to learn languages, manners, and ways of daily life that children usually absorbed by direct experience.[5]

Compiled from sources that ranged from the precepts of Erasmus to comments from the handful of Russians who had recently been abroad, *The Honorable Mirror of Youth* provided Russians with their first manual of etiquette in 1717. Combining moral precepts with rules for public behavior, this brief volume instructed St. Petersburg's aspiring courtiers and their ladies how to behave in polite society, how to use a knife and fork, and how to converse in public. Its pages spoke of "maidenly honor" as "a crown of virtue," urged aristocrats to speak foreign languages to prevent servants from eavesdropping, and sternly warned their readers that the path to ruin was wide and well-populated.[6] Yet, no single volume could offer instruction in the minutiae of daily life, nor put at ease men and women seeking to acquire social graces practiced in a society most of them had never seen. Published rules of etiquette had to be tempered with practical experience if the Russians were to reproduce the society of the West. To create a living, working model of the brave new society he wanted his courtiers and comrades to enter, Peter therefore needed to bring the social world of Europe directly to St. Petersburg.

On November 26, 1718, St. Petersburg's chief of police Anton Devier issued a decree calling upon a handful of leading aristocrats to hold special gatherings that would bring together the men and women of the capital. Devier himself had come to St. Petersburg as a cabin boy in a Portuguese ship, and his rise to high office had depended on his willingness to carry out Peter's will and bear his frequent abuse. Men who knew him remembered that he was "strict and quick in carrying out the tsar's orders," and that the mere mention of his name instilled fear in St. Petersburg's citizens.[7] Devier's orders therefore could never be taken lightly, not even when, as in this case, they applied to a scant two dozen households. Speaking with the authority of the Emperor himself, Devier decreed that St. Petersburg's great lords and ladies must open their homes to all "persons of rank, merchants of note, headmasters [by which were meant mainly ship-builders], persons employed in the chancery, and their wives and children," according to a publicly announced schedule. Hosts were to display a sign advertising the time and place of each "assembly," and guests were to be free to smoke, dance, engage in polite conversation, or play cards as they chose.[8]

So that each could demonstrate at first hand how European society worked in practice, a number of Europeans found themselves on Peter's list of assembly hosts. Under Peter's watchful eye, guests were expected to make a serious effort to be civil, and liquor did not flow as freely as it did at most Russian entertainments. With scores of European diplomats, army officers, and merchants in attendance, would-be Russian courtiers danced the minuet, bestowed flowers and compliments on the ladies they admired, and struggled to achieve that easy elegance that ruled polite society in the capitals of the West. Under the threat of Peter's fists if they misbehaved, St. Petersburg's ill-at-ease courtiers soon found their way. Talk of fashions and earthly pleasures replaced the prayers and the gross entertainments of Muscovite times, and European visitors began for the first time to measure Russian court life by Western standards rather than to dismiss it as Asiatic and barbaric as they had in days gone by.

As the men and women of St. Petersburg's court danced, dined, and chatted in the new European manner, Peter donned the Roman armor and laurel wreaths worn by the conquerors of old. He transformed the religious processions that had dominated life in medieval Moscow into tri-

umphal entries taken from the courts of Europe's absolute monarchs, and
he used military parades to emphasize the new status Russia had gained
among the nations of the West. In public celebrations, Peter now appeared as a conqueror whose prowess in war bound his people to the great
empires of human history, and St. Petersburg, as his prized creation, held
center stage. Courtiers became mirrors of the image that Peter himself
conveyed, and some truly reveled in the new freedoms he had brought to
Russia. "The fair sex are allowed all manner of freedom," one observer remarked. "They live in a perpetual round of pleasure and diversion, spending most part of their time in balls and entertainments."[9] To popularize
women as symbols of "love, beauty, and civilization," Peter ordered statues
of Venus and the virtues Justice, Mercy, and Truth to be set prominently
in St. Petersburg's Summer Garden and requested paintings of Minerva
and Venus to adorn the ceilings of the city's first palaces.[10] For the first
time in Russian history, women ceased to be what Moscow's patriarch
once had called "imperfect and subordinate beings," and entered fully into
the churning daily life of the court and its politics.[11]

Among Russia's women, none entered this new world with greater enthusiasm than Peter's consort and future empress Catherine. Catherine
often traveled with her husband on his campaigns, and she continued the
active life to which her lower-class origins had accustomed her even after
she became Empress. At court, she dressed in the latest European fashions and became a model of gaiety and charm to counteract the old-fash-
ioned Muscovite image of female piety. Dancing was her favorite pastime,
and fashions one of her chief concerns. Pages at her court strutted in bot-
tle-green uniforms trimmed with gold lace and faced in red as they served
guests in the European fashion. An orchestra played the works of modern
composers during her dinners, and her guests were treated to entertainments that led a visiting French dancing master to observe that "nowhere
in Europe do they dance the minuet with more grace than at the Petersburg Court."[12] Throughout Peter's reign and her own that followed,
Catherine helped to set the new model for civility and elegance that was
repeated at scores of assemblies, holiday celebrations, balls, and official
fetes as the life and culture of upper-class Russians moved closer to becoming a comfortable copy of European aristocratic life.

In 1721, the Treaty of Nystadt ended the Great Northern War between
Russia and Sweden and gave Russia full undisputed title to the land on
which St. Petersburg stood. That fall, the celebrations that followed the

treaty's signing showed how much the St. Petersburg court had been Euro-peanized, for the military parades and breathtaking fireworks displays all demonstrated Russia's affinity with the nations and political culture of the West. A thousand-gun artillery salute made it seem as if the Neva and the Fortress of Saints Peter and Paul "were covered in flame," one observer wrote,[13] and the fashions worn by Catherine and her ladies-in-waiting pre-sented a spectacle of brilliant colors and precious stones at the balls and dinners that followed. Russia had moved very far indeed from the great church processions with which its Tsar had greeted the end of its First Northern War with Poland some sixty years earlier. Now the Tsar had be-come the ruler of an empire who celebrated not his descent from the Chris-tian sovereigns of Byzantium but the lineage that bound him to ancient Rome. Proclaimed "the Great," Peter became the creator of modern Russia, and his new city the capital of an empire. From top to bottom, Russia was to be based on the principle that all Russians would serve the empire Peter had created. That principle applied especially to all in St. Petersburg, from the nobility who served in the army and the government down to those men and women who served the empire by serving the nobility.

Viewed from the Neva riverfront at the time of Peter's death, St. Peters-burg seemed already to have become a beautiful city, with a solid row of majestic buildings lining each bank. But behind that facade, the real St. Petersburg still remained, as one commentator wrote, "full of log cabins, kitchen gardens, cowsheds, and clutchy mud."[14] Cattle still grazed on Vasilevskii Island and in the region that would eventually become Dosto-evskii's unforgettable Haymarket. This was the St. Petersburg of the lower classes, of the tens of thousands of men, women, and children whose rea-son for being in the city was in some way to serve the nobility, the Tsar, and the state. Carters, water carriers, carpenters, soldiers, serfs, and shop-keepers filled the ranks of this ever-changing throng. Over time, their numbers would increase as the poverty of St. Petersburg's lower classes fed upon itself.

Most obvious among St. Petersburg's masses in 1725 was the city's gar-rison of 15,000 soldiers, for one out of every six Petersburgers in those days wore a uniform. In addition to four regiments of the regular army, these included the Semenovskii and Preobrazhenskii Imperial Guards regiments that were assigned permanently to the capital. Created by Peter the Great to replace the rebellious musketeers who had attempted to overthrow him at the beginning of his reign, these were Russia's finest and numbered about sixty-five hundred men.[15] In 1731, Anna would add the Izmailovskii and Horse Guards regiments to their numbers, and in the years to come Elizabeth and Catherine the Great would expand them further by creating the Grenadier Life Guards and the Chevalier Guards. Able to march to any part of the capital on short notice, these elite troops became a powerful political instrument in the hands of St. Petersburg's aristocrats. As self-proclaimed arbiters of the imperial succession, they and their officers took part in four "palace revolutions" between 1725 and 1762, another in 1801, and still another in 1825. Every autocrat had to win their support by granting new privileges to the lords who commanded them. Without the guards, no eighteenth-century sovereign could sit safely on Russia's throne.

Especially after Anna returned Russia's capital to St. Petersburg, one of the cherished privileges of the Russian nobility was to own property in the city. As the main holders of wealth, these men and women were St. Petersburg's chief consumers, and their growing demands attracted large numbers of merchants, craftsmen, and purveyors of services. St. Petersburg's great merchants, who numbered well over a thousand by the middle of the century, concentrated on large-scale trade and lived very similarly to the nobility, while the rest of the non-noble classes lived much more hand-to-mouth. More than three thousand hackney drivers and countless sellers of food hawked their wares and services on the city's streets, along with the carters, water carriers, and woodcutters who provided firewood and drinking water to St. Petersburg's residents. Several thousand craftsmen and artisans sold goods and services from small stalls and shops that were scattered all over the city, while many thousand more serfs came to spend the building season working for hire as carpenters, bricklayers, and painters before returning to their villages.[16] Many of these working folk lived in the rough wooden shacks and cottages that crammed the city's outskirts from the far banks of the Fontanka and Ligovskii Canal to the Okhta Quarter on the other side of the Neva. These slums remained untouched until the nineteenth century, when a shortage of land around the edges of St. Petersburg's center led nobles and wealthy merchants to begin to build townhouses along outlying streets and avenues.

If the mystique of St. Petersburg as Russia's window on the West and the center of imperial power drew people to it from every corner of the empire, it also attracted many Europeans. Germans, Dutch, and Swedes all lived in Peter's city, and so did Italians, Spaniards, and Portuguese. Virtually all of the senior officers in Russia's navy and more than half of the generals in its army were foreigners,[17] and a large number more were involved in foreign trade. Many of St. Petersburg's Germans were high officials who had entered Russia's service when Peter the Great annexed Sweden's Baltic provinces at the end of the Great Northern War, but there were also German professors at St. Petersburg's Imperial Academy of Sciences and German craftsmen who printed books, tailored clothing, built clocks, and made engravings. Russians placed particular store by the knowledge of Germans in medicine. By the middle of the century it had become all but a requirement for a physician to have a German name if he hoped to treat patients among St. Petersburg's rich and famous. At the same time, Frenchmen, Italians, and Spaniards supplied most of the growing body of foreign teachers who tutored the children of Russian aristocrats in the art of being courtiers. Some of the Swedes and Finns who had come to the city as prisoners of war and had made their peace with the Russians also became tutors.

Although by no means as numerous as the Germans, Swedes, or French, the English boasted the closest-knit community of all the foreigners in St. Petersburg, and their impact on the city's life in the eighteenth century was out of all proportion to their numbers. From somewhere around two hundred at the end of Peter's reign, St. Petersburg's English community grew to about fifteen hundred during the heyday of its influence in the 1780s and 1790s, and it continued to play a part in the city's life until the Bolshevik Revolution of 1917 broke it apart. Originally, the heart of the British community in St. Petersburg centered in the British Factory, an association of English merchants that had its headquarters in the Exchange and Warehouses building that Trezzini built on Vasilevskii Island between 1723 and 1735. Later, it moved across the Neva to the quay that stood just downriver from the Ruling Senate. This English Embankment (so named toward the end of Catherine the Great's reign) contained the Anglican Church—which remains to this day—and more than a score of impressive townhouses owned by St. Petersburg's most prosperous English merchants.

In houses along the English Embankment and in lesser buildings fronting on the street just behind it, St. Petersburg's English men and women gathered to worship, exchange visits, dine and dance at the English Inn, and to read books and newspapers from their homeland at the

Subscription Library. Although they learned Russian readily and mixed easily with Russians and other Europeans (as in "the most respectable and exclusive" English Club),[18] the English remained bound closely together by shared business interests and an overpowering sense of being British. In St. Petersburg, English residents could hire English valets, tutors, and governesses, as well as English barbers, grooms, and riding masters, and they studied, rode, and hunted together. In addition to dresses, haberdashery, and superbly made firearms from London, English books, hats, stockings, cloth, buttons, gloves, writing supplies, and toys could always be bought in St. Petersburg's English Shop, of which there were four branches by the end of the century. By Catherine the Great's time, the British community seemed to have become "a sort of transplanted City of London in miniature," with all the frivolities and peculiarities that shaped British life at home.[19] "In the houses of Britons settled here a competent idea may be formed of the English manner of living," a German observer once wrote. "Everything is English—even to the chimney fire. Here where wood is in such plenty," he added in amazement, "the Englishman fetches his coals from [England]."[20]

The common cause that brought and bound the English to St. Petersburg was trade. Trade was the lifeblood of the British Empire, and the English Industrial Revolution was dependent on raw materials from Russia. By the second half of the eighteenth century, more than 50 percent of Britain's imports of bar iron, 96 percent of its hemp, 90 percent of its tallow, 80 percent of its flax, and nearly 75 percent of its great masts all came from Russia. In exchange, the English brought woolens, linens, silks, cottons, French, Spanish, and Portuguese wines, cognac, and coffee from Europe, Asia, and the Americas to St. Petersburg.[21] Oranges and lemons came from Italy and Spain, and large loans for the Imperial Treasury from the bankers in London and their allies in Amsterdam. English fortunes made in the Russia trade played a part in shaping Russian foreign and domestic policy throughout the eighteenth century, and there is substantial evidence that its influence continued until the Revolutions of 1917.[22]

But most of all St. Petersburg's lords and ladies looked to the English for luxuries. "Whatever [the Russians] possess useful or estimable comes to them from England," one Cambridge don wrote after visiting St. Petersburg at the end of the century. "Books, maps, prints, furniture, clothing, hardware of all kinds, horses, carriages, hats, leather, medicine, almost every article of convenience, comfort, or luxury," he concluded proudly, "must be derived from England or it is of no estimation."[23] Ornate British clocks found enthusiastic buyers in Russia through dealers in St. Petersburg, and so did nautical and optical instruments that were thought to be of unsurpassable quality. And, finally, there was the exquisite porcelain made by the factory that the Englishman Francis Gardner established outside of Moscow in the 1760s. Gardner's firm made several table services for Catherine the Great that commemorated the imperial orders of St. George, St. Aleksandr Nevskii, St. Andrew, and the knights of St. Vladimir. In the hands of Gardner's descendants, the factory continued to produce fine porcelain in Russia until 1892.

As the collective experience of the British colony showed, European technology, trade, and the arts all helped to maintain St. Petersburg as Russia's window on the West. But Peter's city was Europe's window on Russia, too, and as Russia's role in the affairs of Europe increased Europeans' curiosity deepened. Spurred on by that same spirit of adventure that had driven their ancestors to discover new continents two centuries earlier, people from the West came to Russia in growing numbers after the middle of the eighteenth century. From St. Petersburg, they looked into Russia itself, and what they wrote about what they saw—or thought they saw—through Europe's window on Russia reflected in part the peculiarities of their own national character. The Germans tended to be most ready to confront Russia on its own terms, the French less so, and the English, as in all other parts of the world, focused mainly on the many ways in which the Russians and their capital diverged from their own cherished measures of civility and comfort. "I think it very much worth any curious man's while . . . to stay there three weeks or a month," an English traveler concluded not long after Anna had returned Russia's seat of government to St. Petersburg. "But after the curiosity is satisfied," he added, "I think one could amuse oneself better [elsewhere]."[24]

Although every European nation had its representatives among the men and women who explored St. Petersburg and Russia in the eighteenth century, the Germans and the English led the way. In the 1720s and 1730s, scholars from Central Europe took up appointments as professors at St. Petersburg's newly founded Imperial Academy of Sciences, and a few of these men carried out some of the most astounding explorations ever to be undertaken in Russia's history. Chief among them were the introspective twenty-eight-year-old Westphalian scholar Gerhardt Friedrich Müller and the twenty-two-year-old Württemberg physician

Johann Georg Gmelin, who spent more than a decade in Siberia record-ing its history, flora, fauna, and natural resources. Together they traveled more than twenty-three thousand miles, copied thousands of rare docu-ments, and discovered scores of new plants and forms of wildlife between the Urals and the Pacific. Müller recorded a wealth of information about Siberia's natives, their languages, history, and customs that Russia's own scholars would draw upon for the rest of the century, and Gmelin's mas-sive *Flora Sibirica* would remain a classic for even longer than that. But al-though Müller spent virtually all the last half of his life in St. Petersburg (Gmelin died much earlier) he did not maintain the close relationship with Europe that made the accounts of later travelers so popular in the West. Nor did his work on Siberia stir the imagination of Europeans in the way that later travelers' comments about St. Petersburg and European Russia would do.

During the reign of Catherine the Great, two other Germans pro-duced detailed accounts of life in St. Petersburg itself, and these still stand among the most reliable descriptions that we have of the city at the end of the eighteenth century. Heinrich Storch, who worked in the chancery of one of the Empress's closest advisers, and Johann Gottlieb Georgi, a professor at Russia's Academy of Sciences, both shared a love of detail and a fascination with Russia that enabled them to blend tech-nical statistics on climate, population, and trade with vivid descriptions of daily life. Artists, writers, statesmen, and ordinary people all had a place in their accounts, and so did commentaries on local fashions and manners. Storch's *Picture of Petersburg* (1792) and the *Description of the Russian Imperial Capital City of St. Petersburg* that Georgi published two years later both set a standard by which other studies of Russia's capital would be measured until well into the next century, and scholars still quote them today.[25] But there were other, more personalized portraits that appealed to the larger audience of literate eighteenth-century men and women who found pleasure in vicariously sharing in the adventures of their more daring countrymen. These accounts belonged most of all to the English, who visited St. Petersburg in ever growing numbers as the century wore on. Always, trade stood at the center of their concerns, but they added observations about local customs and daily life that provided their readers with a vivid sense of participation in the ventures that had taken them so far from home.

Profit and curiosity were powerful forces in sending the English to St. Petersburg in the eighteenth century, but so was a desire to reaffirm that English life and culture were superior to every other form of human existence. That thread ran through all the eighteenth-century British accounts of life in Russia and St. Petersburg, and it supplied their authors with the means to excuse or condemn whatever they found. "I am confident that most of the defects which appear in their national character, are in consequence of the Russian government," a thoughtful professor from the University of Glasgow wrote of the Russians in his *Anecdotes of the Russian Empire* in 1784. "How can they possess the spirit and elevation of sentiment which distinguish the natives of a free state," he asked his readers. "Treated with so much inhumanity, how can they be humane?"[26] Other British travelers embroidered on that theme in more strident tones as the Western world moved through the French Revolution and into the industrial age. "The same system of tyranny . . . has entirely extinguished every spark of liberality in the breasts of a people composed entirely of slaves," the tutor Edward Clarke concluded about the Russians he saw in St. Petersburg in 1810. "They are all, high and low, rich and poor, servile to superiors; haughty and cruel to their dependants; ignorant, superstitious, cunning, brutal, dirty, and mean."[27]

In proclaiming the superiority of British manners, morals, and character, such accounts often paid scant attention to what had been accomplished in St. Petersburg before Catherine the Great mounted the throne in 1762. Nor did they note some of the great transformations that made Russia's capital into a truly imperial city by the year 1800. In part because both Catherine and its residents began to regard Russia's capital as a true city rather than a center of government, it finally gained an aura of permanence that neither Peter, Anna, nor Elizabeth had ever managed to impart. Between 1762 and 1800, the log cabins, cowsheds, and muddy lanes of earlier times finally gave way in the city's interior to paved streets lined with buildings of stucco and brick. Street lighting appeared. The wolves disappeared from Vasilevskii Island and the mainland suburbs, and such public services as almshouses and hospitals became a part of the city's life. The vision of elegance, prosperity, and order that had been confined mainly to the Neva's embankments in earlier times spread further along the Nevskii Prospekt and the two sister avenues that the planners of the 1730s had laid out. Under the hand of a sovereign who wielded absolute and arbitrary power over a sixth of the earth's land mass, a city government of elected officials took shape.[28]

Everything about Russia's capital seemed to affirm that human will could conquer Nature. Russia's last reigning Empress has often been said to have inherited a capital made largely of wood and left behind one made of stone and brick. The main buildings in central St. Petersburg were constructed of masonry, but two-thirds of the city's buildings were still of wood at the end of the 1780s, although observers estimated that fewer than half of the Petersburgers still lived in them. Large, elegant, and solidly built, St. Petersburg's brick and stucco buildings gave a new sense of permanence to its center at the same time as Velten's granite embankments helped to make the Neva's frequent floods seem less fearsome. Between 1750 and 1788, the Neva burst its banks on no fewer than twenty-four occasions, but the great buildings that lined the capital's new streets and avenues seemed more than able to withstand the danger.[29] At the same time, permanent bridges over the Neva's branches and several pontoon bridges over its main current added to the feeling that the river could be mastered in time. Although still an obvious fact of life, the Neva no longer remained *the* factor in shaping St. Petersburg's day-to-day experience as it had been in Peter the Great's time.

As the river's significance in separating one part of the city from another diminished, artists' renditions began to narrow the space occupied by water and broaden that filled by land. Not so much the natural setting of the city but the ways in which human hands had altered it dominated their art, and they concentrated more on the details of daily life than ever before. Nowhere was that more evident than in the work of Benjamin Paterssen, a Swedish artist who settled in St. Petersburg in the 1780s and lived there until his death in 1815. Paterssen's vision of the city embraced markets, shops, street vendors, water carriers, aristocrats, their coachmen and footmen, soldiers, and peasants, in addition to portraying leisure entertainments, the ways in which boats were rigged and loaded, and many of the other tasks that occupied Petersburgers from dawn to dusk. Perhaps more than any other artist of his time, Paterssen created a chronicle of daily life that presented a collective portrait of Russia's capital as it moved from the eighteenth century into the nineteenth.[30]

Paterssen's work showed that life in St. Petersburg continued to move on water much as it did in Venice. But, also as in Venice, water had by the late eighteenth century become a means for tying the city's parts together rather than a force for keeping them apart. Water in Paterssen's paintings more often appeared as a backdrop against which the city lived its life rather than as an elemental force with which its residents and planners continually had to contend. Most of all, St. Petersburg acquired a comfortable and comforting sense of being Russia's capital during Catherine's reign as Russians and foreigners began to see it as an image of what their nation ought to become rather than a reminder of what it had failed to be. Russians now looked to St. Petersburg as a focus for their ambitions and their lives. Rather than an alien example of hostile foreign ways, it had become a symbol of success and a reminder of how Russia's future ought to look.

St. Petersburg's population reached one hundred thousand soon after 1750, and then doubled before the end of the century.[31] During Catherine's reign, it required about a quarter of a million tons of rye, wheat, and barley, over a hundred tons of fats and oils, ten thousand tons of salt, about ten million eggs, more than three-quarters of a million fish, nearly sixty thousand beef cattle, and almost five million liters of vodka to supply the city's twelve main markets every year. All of these products had to be shipped by oxcart and river barge from hundreds of miles away.[32] Drinking water continued to be supplied by St. Petersburg's many water carriers, who dipped it from the Neva River and delivered it to doorsteps throughout the city. Citing scientific studies claiming that the Neva's waters contained only the smallest amounts of foreign matter, contemporaries insisted that this was some of the purest water in Europe.[33] But eighteenth-century scientists could not see the microbes flowing from St. Petersburg's first sewers into its rivers, nor could they understand that such organisms could not be easily drained away by the Neva's current and the city's sodden soil. In addition to the bacteria that produced typhoid fever and cholera, the city's sewage carried microorganisms that caused giardiasis and other virulent intestinal ailments. These made St. Petersburg's water so unhealthy that even in the early twentieth century Baedeker's *Guide to Russia* still had to warn visitors to Russia's capital that "unboiled water should on no account be drunk."[34]

In the early days of St. Petersburg's history, public health was of little concern to the authorities because they expected large numbers of its lower classes to die as a matter of course. Catherine was the first Russian sovereign to take a different view and to insist on trying to control the spread of infectious diseases. There seemed to be little hope of stemming the waves of influenza, cholera, malaria, and diphtheria that washed across the empire every year, but the deadly scourge of smallpox offered a chance for Russia's Empress to launch one of the eighteenth century's most daring public health experiments. When a raging smallpox epidemic struck St. Petersburg in the spring of 1768, Catherine sent an urgent invitation to the English Quaker physician Thomas Dimsdale, who had perfected a method of using small amounts of matter taken from the pustules of recovering smallpox victims to inoculate others. Dimsdale claimed to have minimized many of the risks that had made earlier versions of that procedure dangerous, and Catherine therefore wanted him in St. Petersburg, where she hoped that his discoveries could be used to slow the spread of the disease.

Reaching Russia at the end of August, Dimsdale devoted several weeks to careful preparations and then successfully inoculated Catherine and her son Paul. When over a hundred courtiers and their families had been inoculated without serious consequences, the Empress ordered the first smallpox inoculation center to be set up in St. Petersburg.[35] Far ahead of anyone in the West, she thus launched one of the first campaigns anywhere in the world to inoculate people against an infectious disease. More than a century would pass before anyone else tried to match her effort.

Catherine's concern for public health in St. Petersburg reflected not only the worries of an enlightened sovereign but also the dramatic progress that science and learning had made in Russia's capital during the eighteenth century. Lacking any native scholars or scientists at the time of Peter the Great's death, St. Petersburg's Academy of Sciences had soon grown into an institution in which Russians and Europeans both pursued serious scientific study. There in the 1740s Mikhail Lomonosov had discovered the law of conservation of matter and energy a quarter of a century before Lavoisier in France, and then had gone on to develop a "corpuscular theory" that had anticipated by more than a century those molecular theories that now form the basis for modern chemistry. When Lomonosov left St. Petersburg in 1755 to establish Russia's first full-fledged university in Moscow, others took his place. Among those whose work had immediate practical value, Ivan Kulibin created some of the earliest designs for steamboats and produced a plan for bridging the 970-foot-wide Neva River with a single wooden span nearly a century before the development of structural cast iron.[36]

But if the Academy of Sciences had been virtually the only institution devoted to learning in St. Petersburg in 1725, the city boasted nearly fifty schools and almost seven thousand students when Catherine died seventy years later.[37] Students in Russia's capital studied to become gentlemen and gentlewomen, engineers, navigators, experts in mining, and officers in the imperial army and navy. Orphans learned trades, and would-be teachers were trained to teach. Future priests studied at the Aleksandr Nevskii Monastery's seminary, and the sons of merchants, tradesmen, and state officials acquired the special sorts of education their careers would require. Many of St. Petersburg's eighteenth-century students valued training more than education, but however they focused their interest, the time they spent in school deepened the level of civility in Russia's capital. The imperial court had become a center of proper manners and good taste by the middle of Catherine's reign, and literacy was no longer rare among the men and women who stood close to the throne. When commentators compared Russia's court with others in Europe, they no longer saw it as standing far behind the West.

St. Petersburg's fifty-odd schools showed that modern education was making strides in Russia. Education made it possible for science and the literary arts to flourish and for men and women of talent to express themselves more easily as individuals. In St. Petersburg, the eighteenth century saw the first Russian play, the first Russian novel, and a flood of Russian poetry as the men and women of the capital began to take pride in what they wrote and how they wrote it. Literary creations became a fine art in the St. Petersburg of Catherine the Great. While the first Empress Catherine had not even known how to sign her name until she began to rule Russia in 1725, her successor became Russia's leading patron of the arts and wrote more than a dozen plays herself.

Catherine the Great thought that science, education, and the arts had value for their own sake, but she also regarded them as useful tools for confronting important social and economic problems. For hundreds of years, most of Russia's peasants had been bound to the land, either as serfs or as bondsmen of the central government. Now, Catherine and her counselors had to ask how Russia could compete against the more modern nations of the West if its workforce continued to be made up of serfs. And could such people be expected to be as productive as those who worked in the fields and cities of Europe? The dramatic growth of cities in the West during the seventeenth and eighteenth centuries had showed that the forces of progress eventually would pull men and women from the countryside to the city, and that more slums and crime would follow them. How could Russia, with its limited wealth and backward economy, meet the challenges posed by a growing proletariat? Could the European scenario of progress even be played out in a country in which more than eight out of every ten men and women continued to be bound to the land?

The virtual disappearance of serfdom in the West seemed to argue that modernization required liberation. But Catherine and her advisers knew they dared not abolish servitude in Russia so long as the Imperial Treasury and more than a hundred thousand aristocrats depended upon it. Ways therefore had to be found to preserve serfdom for the present while making plans to abolish it in the future. To discuss these problems, Catherine founded St. Petersburg's Free Economic Society in 1765 and appointed her former lover Grigorii Orlov to be its president. Throughout the 1770s and 1780s, the Society provided a forum in which some of Russia's leading scholars and agronomists sought ways to balance the economic and social limitations of serfdom with the needs of progress.[38] As the eighteenth century moved ahead, these men also began to discuss how to provide for serfs whose masters sent them to work in the cities, especially in St. Petersburg. Peasant elders had always worked closely with masters and officials to supply a minimum of poor relief, food and shelter for orphans, and facilities for the sick in the countryside. But in St. Petersburg there were neither masters nor communities to care for those lower-class people who fell on hard times. The number of proletarians in St. Petersburg was increasing more than three times faster than in the country as a whole, not counting the forty thousand or so construction workers who came to the city every spring and left when the snow fell. Such people inevitably suffered a higher rate of injuries and disabilities than did the rest of the city's population. Meeting the needs of this growing working class required more money than St. Petersburg's coffers could provide.[39]

In response to the needs of the poor in her capital, Catherine built hospitals, schools for orphans and illegitimate children, a poor house, and homes for foundlings to supplement the efforts of private charities and the city government. The capital boasted ten hospitals and dispensaries for its lower classes by the end of Catherine's reign, but many more facilities were needed, and the government never responded adequately to that demand. As their numbers increased, the plight of St. Petersburg's lower classes grew worse, but it still would be more than a century before the miseries of urban life drove them to open revolt. In Catherine's time, observers explained this passivity in terms of national character. "The Russian, on the whole, is a cheerful being," Heinrich Storch wrote at the end of the century. "A happy volatility and a thoughtlessness peculiar to himself accompany him through life," he added. "[Even] the most penurious condition and the most toilsome labor leave him always some sensibility for enjoyment."[40]

According to the time of year and their circumstances, people amused themselves in various ways in eighteenth-century St. Petersburg. In the early days, there had been only the Triumphal Osteria of the Four Frigates, where Peter the Great and his companions gathered to drink, dine, and carouse, but by the mid-1730s the numbers of eating houses, taverns, and gaming houses began to grow. The lower classes used these places to escape the hovels in which they lived, and they often gathered during evenings and holidays to sing, dance, and drink in public. As in Russia's many peasant villages, singing played a part in many of St. Petersburg's amusements. "The postillions sing from the beginning of a stage to its end," wrote England's Reverend William Coxe after his visit to Russia's capital in the 1770s. "Soldiers sing during their march," he added, "and the . . . [peasants] sing amid the most laborious occupations. The public houses," he concluded, "re-echo with their carols."[41] Upper-class Petersburgers often paid peasant singers to entertain them during picnics and outings on the river. "In summer the Neva is covered with boats from which the songs [of these singers] resound," Storch explained. "On fine evenings [they] delight the ears of the solitary walkers on the quays . . . awakening in them mild sensations by their soft and plaintive tones."[42]

The White Nights that clustered around the summer solstice brought Petersburgers in droves to stroll the whole night through along their city's embankments and in its parks and gardens. This was a time of magic, when the sun never set, the antithesis to the long winter nights when the sun rose at ten-thirty and set before four. During the White Nights, life took on a different tone and meaning. Poets wrote of the Nevskii Prospekt during the White Nights, of the famed Bronze Horseman statue of Peter the Great, and of how the golden spires of the Admiralty and the Fortress Cathedral shone in the never fading twilight. This was a time when spring was just edging into summer and the world was turning green. It was a season of romance and special feelings, all intensified by the sure and certain knowledge that the summer's warmth and light would quickly fade.

When summer gave way to winter, St. Petersburgers took to the open air with even greater enthusiasm. Once the rivers froze, workmen built a number of sledding hills down which the people of St. Petersburg raced at high speeds. So popular were these soaring ice-covered scaffolds that the architect Antonio Rinaldi built one for Catherine and her court at Oranienbaum in St. Petersburg's more distant suburbs, and the ones that dotted the frozen surface of the Neva drew crowds on every winter Sunday and holiday. The amazed Reverend Coxe gave a detailed account of how Petersburgers slid down these steep inclines on small sledges that followed each other "with inconceivable rapidity," and pointed out that the chief danger consisted "in poising the sledge in its rapid descent down the inclined plane. If the pilot is not steady, but totters either through inadvertence or fear," Coxe warned, "he is liable to be overturned, and incurs no small risk of breaking his bones if not his neck." But Coxe clearly envied the exhilaration with which the Russians enjoyed this pastime. "I have frequently stood above an hour at the bottom of these ice-hills," he wrote, "but never had sufficient courage to try the experiment, as one failure might have proved fatal."[43]

William Richardson, who accompanied England's ambassador Lord Cathcart to Russia in the late 1760s, actually risked the ride that Coxe thought too dangerous. "The slide by which you go down is so steep as to be just not perpendicular," Richardson wrote to a friend. "You slide with such velocity," he added, "that for some seconds you cannot breathe."[44] While people waited their turns to climb to the top of sledding hills, skated, or raced along the frozen rivers in sleighs, huge bonfires blazed on the shore. All of St. Petersburg gathered around them to take the edge off the frost that sometimes fell to forty degrees below freezing. Yet while foreigners spoke of its dangers, the Russians thrived on the cold. Something about winter spurred the Russians to action, brought them to life, and gave them a sense of well-being that Europeans never managed to understand. Petersburgers found in winter a joy that no other season could equal.

Between winter and summer came the Russian holiday of *maslenitsa* or Shrovetide, the last festival before the beginning of Lent. Here St. Petersburg's lower classes flocked to the city's huge fair to be entertained by organ grinders and primitive versions of ferris wheels and carousels. At puppet theaters, everyone gathered to watch the performances of "Petrushka," a hapless puppet whose many misadventures delighted young and old, and elsewhere the crowd enjoyed the antics of dancing bears, jugglers, and fire eaters. Street vendors sold festive pancakes and

*Sledding hills on Tsaritsyn Meadow. (Courtesy of the Russian National Library, St. Petersburg)*

dispensed tea from steaming samovars, whose brass chimneys puffed smoke from the charcoal that heated them from within. There seemed no end to the fantasies that various performers created for their strolling audiences. Then, after six weeks of self-denial in Lent, Petersburgers celebrated Easter by reproducing the Shrovetide festivities in grander form, and with even more excitement. "All kinds of machines are set up in public squares, as the vulgar are remarkably fond of this diversion," one observer explained. "This is a joyful season for the populace," he added, "[and they] devote themselves without restraint to their national propensity to mirth."[45]

In contrast to the common folk, St. Petersburg's aristocrats entertained themselves in much the same ways as their counterparts in Western Europe. "The extent of civilization and the regular intercourse of nations," Storch sadly confessed, meant that the diversions of the upper classes had "become so much alike in all countries, that the account of them taken from one capital would nearly suit all others."[46] As in Europe's other cities, St. Petersburg by the middle of Catherine's reign boasted a Musical Club, an English Club, a Club for the Nobility, and a Merchants' Club, at which members dined and enjoyed various sorts of entertainments. Several literary circles had begun to draw members from the increasing numbers of men and women in the capital devoted to literature, and it was in that setting that a handful of educated Russians first confronted the ideas that were leading Western Europe toward the French Revolution. Such ideas first came into vogue in St. Petersburg during the 1770s, when Catherine herself urged Russia's courtiers to explore the ideas of the Enlightenment. To be sure, few of them took the writings of Voltaire, Diderot, Montesquieu, or Rousseau very seriously, and even fewer tried to shape new values around them. More quickly than most, Catherine realized that such radical views could pose a serious danger to the established order, and she cut short the debate she had begun. But the day would soon come when a handful of Petersburgers would begin to insist that the Social Contract and the Rights of Man had to have a place in Russia, too. Out of this small circle was born the radical intelligentsia that would challenge Russia's government until the autocracy finally collapsed in 1917.

For the much larger body of St. Petersburg aristocrats, who saw European ideas as little more than topics for polite dinner and salon conversation, entertainment revolved around elegant dinners, society balls, the theater, the opera, and the ballet. Around 1780, the city boasted four large theaters in addition to several private ones at which lords, ladies, and wealthy merchants gathered during the winter season. On the south bank of the Moika, the palace that Rastrelli had built for the wealthy Iusupovs in the 1750s contained a theater of its own in which serf actors performed the latest plays for the enjoyment of the masters and their friends, but the most dazzling theatrical performances of all were to be found at the opera, which drew enthusiastic crowds whenever it opened its doors.

Petersburgers had embraced the opera with true passion from the moment it appeared in their midst during Anna's reign, and by the 1770s its performances had become objects of amazement for Russians and Europeans alike. Catherine herself wrote several light operas and supported the writing of dozens more, and the results established a tradition to which the Russians still hold fast. "The magnificence of the performance far exceeded every thing I had ever beheld of this kind in Paris and other capital cities," an amazed Storch confessed after seeing a production of the grand opera *Oleg* in St. Petersburg's main theater. "The sumptuousness of the dresses, . . . the dazzling lustre of the pearls and diamonds, the armorial decorations, [and] the implements of war," he explained, "went far beyond even the boldest expectations." He was amazed to see on stage "romantic regions, sailing fleets, towns and the proud battlements of antique palaces."[47] Nowhere else in Europe were sets created with more ingenuity or used with such dramatic effect. Over the next two centuries, such stunning sets and scenes would become the Russians' forte as set designers arranged for mystical realms to be created on stage and for entire towns to go up in flames. In Soviet times, live horses would parade on stage for scenes in Borodin's *Prince Igor*, and Prokofiev's *War and Peace* would portray the heroic battle of Borodino before the audience's very eyes, always with the purpose of leaving viewers breathless and cheering for more.

For Russia's greatest aristocrats and best-connected foreigners, the imperial court itself served as a source of entertainment, for it was, in every sense, the most stunning masquerade to be found in all of St. Petersburg. Insisting that "the richness and splendor of the Russian Court surpassed description" because it retained so "many traces of Asiatic pomp blended with European refinement," England's Reverend Coxe thought that "the magnificence of other courts gave [only] a faint idea" of what one could find in Russia. "Amid the sumptuous articles which distinguish the Russian nobility, none perhaps is more calculated to strike a foreigner than the profusion of diamonds and other precious stones, which sparkle in every part of the dress," Coxe wrote. "Many of the nobility were almost covered with diamonds," he added after his first visit. "Their buttons, buckles, hilts of swords, and epaulets were set with diamonds; their hats were frequently embroidered . . . with several rows. A diamond star on the coat," he concluded in amazement, "was scarcely a distinction."[48]

Nor was the brilliance of the Russian court limited only to the gems worn by its courtiers and their ladies. Until the very last years of her reign, the Empress Elizabeth reveled in an unending procession of masquerades, gala balls, and celebrations, and these all played a part in the life of her court. When Rastrelli built her palaces, Elizabeth had insisted upon ballrooms of such vast dimensions that the grand salon in her Summer Palace in St. Petersburg was larger than the one at Versailles, and that at Tsarskoe Selo was larger still. On Elizabeth's orders, Rastrelli filled the gardens at Tsarskoe Selo and Peterhof with grottoes and pavilions that became a part of court celebrations, and he designed dazzling fireworks displays to celebrate the main events of his Empress's reign. Elizabeth's passion for changing gowns several times in the course of an evening's celebration set a tone of costly extravagance that others all too gladly followed. Diamonds, rubies, emeralds, cloth of gold and silver, and every sort of opulent display became almost commonplace at a court in which Russia's aristocrats competed continually for their Empress's attention.

But if Elizabeth reveled in extravagance, Catherine surpassed her in the blend of studied elegance and open-handed generosity with which she replaced her predecessor's impulsive exuberance. William Tooke, chaplain of the English church at St. Petersburg's Kronstadt naval base and a close friend of the Petersburg academician Johann Georgi, estimated that the annual expenses for the court midway through Catherine's reign amounted to a million and a half rubles every year. "About two hundred tables are spread [at court] twice a day," Tooke reported in the lengthy account of life in the Russian Empire he published not long after Catherine died.[49] "The waste at Court was carried to an inexpressible height," the amazed Englishman confided to his readers in a footnote. Everyone stole and everyone exaggerated the cost of each item purchased and every service rendered. "Twelve hundred candles were every day delivered to the guard, who never consumed one hundred," he wrote. Court records claimed that 145 tons of salt were consumed every month, and that dinner for the officer of the guard cost seventy rubles a day at a time when an average peasant family was struggling to pay taxes that amounted to less than a tenth of that sum a year.[50]

The cost of Catherine's court, which by the early 1790s included 2,336 grandees and their wives, was much higher than even Tooke dared to estimate. In 1781, the cost of maintaining the imperial court stood at something over four and a half million rubles, and by the last year of Catherine's reign it had risen to nearly eleven million.[51] The court celebrated nearly sixty major events every year, including formal balls to which as many as five thousand guests were invited for a single evening. The Empress lavished huge sums on these grand entertainments and encouraged her courtiers to do the same. Count Bezborodko, in whose chancellery Storch worked for a number of years, was known to have spent forty thousand rubles on a single evening's entertainment, and Catherine's long-time confidant Grigorii Potemkin was reputed to have spent much more than that.[52] "No Court was more splendid and festive than that of St. Petersburg," the ever present Storch wrote in recalling the time he had seen "streams and cascades rolling over various colored lamps [and] the leaves of the trees trembling in the glitter of millions of broken rays of light" at one of the celebrations Catherine staged in the gardens at Peterhof. "Amidst these miracles of fairy art," he confessed, "it is easy to transport oneself to the shores that border the Elysian fields. . . . The guests willingly resign themselves to the enchanting tumult," he concluded, "till the rising sun dispels the fascinating illusion, and the fiery sea of the over-night is suddenly metamorphosed into a miserable show of smoky lamps."[53]

But the costs of Catherine's court did not stop at entertainments, for her open-handedness to favorites fully matched her passion for pomp. No service went unrewarded, and no personal favor was ever left unpaid. In just the last few months of her life, the Empress gave 160,000 rubles to the mother and sisters of her grandson Konstantin Pavlovich's fiancée, and then bestowed jewelry worth 50,000 rubles on the young woman herself. When the couple married, she gave them the Marble Palace as a wedding gift, and just two months later granted one of her favorites a gift of 100,000 rubles. In earlier times, she had heaped gifts upon younger lovers. Upon Aleksandr Lanskoi, the twenty-three-year-old Horse Guards officer who was her lover in the early 1780s, she reportedly bestowed several million rubles. To another who held her affections for scarcely more than a year she gave huge estates in Belorussia and 130,000 rubles. A lover who eventually betrayed her with another woman received more than two thousand serfs, a large estate, and another 100,000 rubles in cash. And so it went. By the end of Catherine's reign, her court cost Russia nearly a seventh of its annual revenue.[54] That amounted to more than the yearly cost of running the entire Russian Empire.

If eighteenth-century St. Petersburg was a city of aristocrats, the tradesmen and artisans who supplied them, and the lower classes who served them, it was also the center of Russia's government. Peter the Great had found Russia saddled with a grossly inefficient central administration, whose overseers paid more attention to form than to substance and relied heavily on a few clerks whose main qualifications were merely that they knew how to read and write. Peter had therefore tried to modernize his empire's government in St. Petersburg and to create a modern bureaucracy that was capable of putting his vision of a new Russia into effect. From the beginning, an acute shortage of men who could read and write had slowed his efforts, and made it all but impossible to extend some of his plans into the provinces by ordinary means. Peter therefore relied on a handful of favorites, and as a result the number of officials who helped to rule the Russian Empire from St. Petersburg grew only slowly.

By the middle of the eighteenth century, Russia's entire central government had slightly more than eleven hundred officials, a number of whom were aristocrats with high positions at court. Probably half again that number worked in government offices as scribes whose horizons rarely reached beyond the offices in which they worked.[55] Army and naval officers, merchants, and courtiers all outnumbered government officials, and that single fact continued to set the tone of St. Petersburg life until well into the next century. Of the 130 most important buildings listed on city maps in 1800, only nine functioned as offices of the central government, while more than half were churches or had to do with the army and navy. Another quarter of the city's major buildings provided facilities for public services, schools, manufacturing, and commerce, and only during the first half of the nineteenth century did that balance begin to change. By then, the edifice that Trezzini had built in the late 1720s to house Peter's Twelve Administrative Colleges on Vasilevskii Island had been turned into the main quarters for St. Petersburg University, and the agencies of Russia's central government had begun to function from huge buildings scattered across all four Admiralty quarters and into areas beyond.

By the middle of the nineteenth century, the comparative handful of officials who had run Russia's central government at the time of Elizabeth's death had burgeoned into a veritable army of civil servants numbering more than thirty thousand.[56] St. Petersburg in 1850 thus would be very different from the city of 1750 or even 1800, as a clerical proletariat in search of cheap food and housing crowded into the central parts of the city. In contrast to the proletarian men and women who worked with their hands, these literate proletarians lived by the many rules and restraints imposed by government service, which dictated the values that shaped their view of the world around them. By the middle of the nineteenth century, regularity, precision, proper procedure, and order had begun to rule life in St. Petersburg in ways that none of its eighteenth-century monarchs had ever imagined, and the monolithic vision that those principles represented would be reflected in buildings all across the city. That would be true most of all in the Winter Palace, which, like the Romanovs themselves, became a feature of Russian life that was set apart from St. Petersburg and the rest of the empire.

The first clear hints of the Winter Palace's separation from the life of St. Petersburg came in the way the artist Andrei Martynov portrayed it and its Hermitage in 1822. "The facade wall formed by the Winter Palace . . . has no depth and hangs, as it were, in bright ether," one commentator wrote after seeing Martynov's work. "There is no sign," he added, "that an immense city stretches out for miles and miles beyond."[57] Separate and remote from all of Russia, the Winter Palace seemed surrounded by an immense emptiness. In that, it had become much like the post-Napoleonic Russian Empire itself: abstract, remote from its roots, and separated from the human forces that churned within it.

Yet the Winter Palace had not always been so remote, nor had Russia's eighteenth-century sovereigns ever intended for it to be. Theirs had been a vision that set the Winter Palace at St. Petersburg's very center so as to make it the focus of their empire's political and cultural life. As the residence of Russia's eighteenth-century autocrats, the Winter Palace symbolized the power of the empire itself and the role that the Romanovs had chosen to play in its life. Here, as living embodiments of Peter the Great's vision, the Romanovs made their main residence a symbol of everything they stood for. It was the center of political power, of modern manners and fashion, and of the artistic patronage that totally transformed Russia's artistic experience between 1700 and 1800. Peter's successors thus sought to make the Winter Palace a critical focal point for everything that happened in eighteenth-century Russia. Looking at how the Winter Palace figured into the lives of the people of St. Petersburg can reveal the ways the Romanovs worked to shape the contours of their world.

# THREE

# THE SHADOW
# OF THE
# WINTER PALACE

*M*ORE THAN IN ANY OTHER CITY in Europe, shadows have a place in the story of St. Petersburg. Heightened by the fogs that roll in from the sea, these shadows are part of the city's everyday life, changing the appearance of its buildings and even the shape of its streets. When the city is bathed in sunlight at midnight during the summer solstice, such shadows add a touch of romance, but they turn ominous when darkness begins to descend during midafternoon in the winter. Then, a building, a street scene, even a gathering of people that seems clear can become murky in an instant. Most Russian writers have commented on this phenomenon of shadows, and several have used it to shape their literary visions. Shadows highlight the short stories that Nikolai Gogol wrote about St. Petersburg in the 1830s, and they play an even greater part in the Symbolist novel, *Petersburg*, that Andrei Belyi wrote on the eve of World War I. When the poet Aleksandr Pushkin immortalized the shadow of Peter the Great as the great Bronze Horseman, he played upon a theme with which all Petersburgers are familiar. For anyone who has lived in Peter's city knows how heavily his shadow lies upon it. Perhaps that is why so many newlyweds still leave bouquets at the feet of the Bronze Horseman that overlooks the Neva from the city's Senate Square.

In the days when the Romanovs ruled Russia, the Winter Palace cast the longest and most complex of St. Petersburg's many shadows. No one could remain untouched by it, for this shadow represented the promise of success and the threat of punishment. Especially during the eighteenth century, when the imperial bureaucracy had not yet grown large enough to stand between Tsar and people, the shadow of the Winter Palace touched everyone and everything in Peter's city. The palaces of Europe's kings and queens never conjured up moods and meanings in the way the Winter Palace did. As the hub of the imperial court, one commentator explained, the Winter Palace was "the center from which the cultural life of the country radiated as far as its light could penetrate."[1] And, as the hub on which the Russian Empire turned, its political authority stretched from the Vistula River in Central Poland to Canada's Yukon and the coasts of Northern California.

Even more than the granite mass of the Peter and Paul Fortress that sits across the river from it, the Winter Palace dominates St. Petersburg's riverfront. Built by Bartolomeo Rastrelli between 1757 and 1762, it is a baroque extravaganza of ornamental vases, statues, and syncopated columns which, an observer once remarked, "creates an unexpected effect of motion."[2] Whether that is what Rastrelli intended we can never know for certain. But in none of his other palaces did he achieve the same effect, and nowhere else did he use the baroque's many ornamental features to the same advantage. Many have commented that the palace appears to be flying, an impression heightened by a number of artists, especially Vasilii Sadovnikov, who painted it on several occasions in the 1840s and 1850s. Although better known for his precisely engraved panoramas of the Nevskii Prospekt, Sadovnikov painted the Winter Palace in watercolors, and those enhanced the ethereal qualities with which Rastrelli had endowed it.

On the Winter Palace's Neva River side its stunning grand facade can be appreciated only from the opposite bank, nearly a fifth of a mile away. Across a square so large that fifty battalions of infantry can march in review at a single time, its southern facade faces the huge semicircular building that Carlo Rossi designed in the 1820s for the General Staff, Ministry of Finance, and Imperial Foreign Office. For tourists approaching from the Nevskii Prospekt, the massive arch with which Rossi divided his building forms a perfect frame, which like everything else in the vicinity is cast in gigantic proportions. Here, as in Russia itself, space has its own meaning. Not since the days of Imperial Rome has any state expressed so grand a vision on such a monumental scale.

From the main balcony of the Winter Palace, the Emperor Alexander I blessed the armies that defended Russia against Napoleon in 1812. And, from the same place a hundred and two years later, his great-grandson Nicholas II prayed with the people of St. Petersburg for guidance in the war that was to destroy the ruling dynasties of Russia, Austria, and Germany. From the Winter Palace, the Provisional Government's Prime Minister Aleksandr Kerenskii fled in a car belonging to the U.S. Ambassador in October 1917, just hours before squads of Bolshevik Red Guards took command of the city. Then, the Bolsheviks transformed the Winter Palace into the Hermitage, one of the world's greatest museums of art, in which the vast treasures of the Romanovs were merged with those confiscated from Russia's aristocrats and industrial barons. The rival of the Louvre and richer than the Vatican, the Hermitage contains some of the world's finest paintings and some of its rarest antiquities. In its collection, there are fifty major works by Rubens and nearly three dozen by Van Dyck. Its more than forty Rembrandts form the largest and best display of that artist's work to be found anywhere in the world, and its Spanish paintings are surpassed in quality only by those of the Museo del Prado, and perhaps the Louvre. Thanks to the efforts of the passionate merchant art collector Sergei Shchukin, whose collection the Bolsheviks confiscated, much of Matisse's early work is in the Hermitage. So are scores of paintings by such Italian Renaissance masters as Botticelli, Fra Angelico, Perugino, and Fra Filippo Lippi.

Every modern-day visitor finds the treasures of the Winter Palace overwhelming. Stone carvings of Egyptian and Assyrian deities, busts from Greece and Rome, fabulous gold from the Scythian burial mounds of South Russia, ancient vases cut from chalcedony, jade, lapis, and jasper, and tens of thousands of coins from the world's great civilizations all add to their diversity and richness, as does porcelain from the workshops of Meissen, Sèvres, and ancient China. Silver plate from the medieval masters of Augsburg and Nuremberg, gold from the workshops of Louis XIV's Paris, and jewelry from every place and time are all there, too, along with ancient swords and antique firearms that once belonged to the great captains of Russia and Europe. Burial mounds from the High Altai, the pyramids of Egypt, and the catacombs of ancient Rome all have yielded their treasures to the Winter Palace, and so have the great sovereigns and artists of China, Japan, and ancient India. The treasures seem endless.

There are emeralds the size of the nail on a man's thumb and baroque pearls that are larger than pigeon eggs, for Russia's rulers and aristocrats always bought the best, and the most, of everything they could find.

Just to the east of the Winter Palace stands the original Hermitage, the gallery in which the Romanovs displayed the best of their fabulous collection of art while they still sat on Russia's throne. Built by the French architect Vallin de la Mothe for Catherine the Great in 1765, this "little retreat," from which all but her inner circle of favorites were excluded, was connected to her private apartments by a unique flying bridge. "[It] is so situated that to go there and back from my room is just three thousand paces," she wrote to a friend. "There I walk about in the midst of a quantity of things that I love and delight in, and these winter walks are what keep me in health and on foot."[3] Later in her reign, Catherine opened parts of her Hermitage to the entire court and commissioned Quarenghi to model its theater on Palladio's Teatro Olimpico in Vicenza. In the next century the court architect Andrei Shtakenshneider remodeled parts of the Hermitage to resemble the Oriental salon described in Aleksandr Pushkin's poem *The Fountain of Bakhchisarai*. But whatever the setting, the treasures continued to hold center stage. Even at the end of the eighteenth century the Hermitage was well on its way to becoming one of the finest collections of art and precious objects to be found anywhere in the world.

A French *chargé* once reported of Catherine the Great that "figuring in the world is [her] passion."[4] To that end she posed as an enlightened practitioner of politics and a devoted patron of the arts, and she applied a great deal of Russia's resources to enhancing those images. For her expanding Hermitage Catherine therefore purchased art on a scale that no sovereign in the West could match, and its cost rarely seemed to enter into her calculations. She bought whatever her agents found whenever they found it, and at whatever price was asked, although she complained from time to time that she could ill afford what she paid. She began in 1762 with a collection of more than two hundred Old Masters (including three Rembrandts) that she bought from Johann Gotzkowski, a Berlin dealer who had initially planned to sell them to Frederick the Great. From that point, she went on to add paintings at the rate of dozens—sometimes hundreds—every year, and supplemented them with collections of rare coins and carved gems that numbered in the tens of thousands.

In 1766, Catherine bought for less than six thousand French francs Rembrandt's *Return of the Prodigal Son*, now thought by some to be the finest masterpiece in the Hermitage. Two years later, she paid 180,000

Dutch guilders for the famed collection of Count Heinrich von Brühl, who as Chancellor to Augustus III of Saxony had misappropriated large sums from his master's Treasury to buy treasures and art. By the time von Brühl's estate was put up for sale to pay his debts, his collection included four Rembrandt masterpieces and five more by Rubens, not to mention a series of highly prized landscapes by Jacob van Ruisdael, twenty-one paintings by Philips Wouvermans, Watteau's *Embarrassing Proposal*, and an early masterpiece from the easel of Caravaggio.[5]

Four years later, Catherine bought most of the collection of rare paintings and drawings that the French banker Pierre Crozat had assembled in Paris. "There are Raphaels, Guidos, Poussins, Schidones, Carlo Lottis, Van Dycks, Rembrandts, Wouvermans, Teniers, etc.," the *philosophe* Denis Diderot wrote to a friend after arranging for the Empress to buy it. "We sell our pictures and our statues in time of peace," he continued in amazement. "But Catherine buys them in time of war." For the five hundred paintings her agents chose from Crozat's collection, Russia's Empress paid 460,000 francs, and that, Diderot confided, was "not half its value."[6] Indeed, the eight Rembrandts, six Van Dycks, the *Holy Family* by Raphael, and three finished paintings by Rubens were probably worth that sum without taking into account any of the others.

Ruled by a passion that knew few limits, Catherine confessed that it was "not love of art but voracity" that drove her on.[7] Just three months after she bought the Crozat collection, she spent another 440,000 francs on fifty more masterpieces and then hurried to pay Madame Geoffrin, whose salon in Paris she much admired, the huge sum of 30,000 francs for a pair of paintings by Van Loo. She bought Sir Robert Walpole's famed collection from Houghton Hall including twenty works by Van Dyck, nineteen by Rubens, and another score by Titian, Murillo, Velázquez, Franz Hals, and Raphael. From the collection of the Chevalier Bardouin, she added more paintings by Rubens and Van Dyck, in addition to masterpieces by Correggio and Rembrandt. Using Diderot's friend, the well-born German courtier and publicist Melchior Grimm as her agent, she then acquired more paintings by Poussin, Titian, Veronese, and Raphael, not to mention several landscapes by Claude Lorrain. In 1771, she bought at auction in Amsterdam the entire collection of Gerrit Braancamp, only to lose it all when the ship to which it had been consigned sank off the coast of Finland. Proclaiming that "I am not an *amateur*, I am a glutton,"[8] Catherine then gathered up paintings by Murillo and Van Loo from the estate of Louis XV's secretary Louis Jean Guignot, and she soon added several more masterpieces from the Prince de Conti and Dezaillier d'Argenville. Two years before the French Revolution, she acquired the Duke of Orléans's entire collection of cameos and engraved gems in one avid swoop, while she continued to urge Grimm and her other agents to search for any treasures that might be pried loose from private collections anywhere else in Europe.

From the French artists Chardin and Vernet, Catherine implored Diderot and Grimm to request landscapes. She commissioned Jean-Antoine Houdon to carve marble statues of Voltaire and the goddess Diana, and from Sir Joshua Reynolds she purchased several of his most admired historical scenes. She ordered from the German artists Gunterberger and Reiffenstein copies of the frescoes that Raphael had painted at the Vatican, even though she was beginning to plead poverty more frequently. She swore to her friend Grimm that she would stop her purchases, even claiming to be "poor as a church mouse," and vowing "to buy nothing more, not a picture, nothing," regardless of how rare a treasure might be found. "I must pay my debts," she stated firmly. "I must save up money."[9] But then she bought more, or had her lovers buy more for her.

In 1765, Catherine purchased Diderot's library, allowed him to retain it until his death, and paid him an annual stipend for serving as its caretaker. At Voltaire's death thirteen years later, she paid his heirs 135,000 francs for his collection of seven thousand beautifully bound red morocco volumes and added them and their priceless annotations to the other treasures that continued to pour in. The quantity and variety of her purchases amazed even Catherine herself as her reign neared its end. "[My museum] at the Hermitage consists of pictures, the panels of Raphael, 38,000 books, four rooms filled with books and prints, 10,000 engraved gems, nearly 10,000 drawings," she wrote to Grimm in 1790. For her collection of cameos and intaglios, she had three magnificent mahogany chests made by the renowned German cabinetmaker David Roentgen, and when those became too small she added another five made in London by the master craftsman James Wyatt.[10]

Each and every one of Catherine's successors would add to her Hermitage collection. After having been given the famed Gonzaga cameo by the fallen Empress Josephine at the beginning of May 1814, Alexander I paid nearly a million francs for thirty-eight of the best paintings from her estate after her sudden death later that same month. These included four of Claude Lorrain's finest landscapes, Rembrandt's *Descent from the Cross*, and several more major paintings by Teniers. Just a few months later, Alexander added another sixty-seven major Spanish works from the collection of the London banker Coesvelt, and many more from booty that the armies of Napoleon had brought to the Louvre. Then Nicholas I acquired thirty paintings from France's Queen Hortense in 1829, and two years later added thirty-three more from the collection of Don Manuel Godoy. Nicholas had a passion for antique arms and armor, and his collection eventually became so large that he built a small castle to house it in the gardens at Tsarskoe Selo. But the art of the Hermitage continued to grow, even as Russia's nineteenth-century autocrats indulged their special whims and passions.

Including several masterpieces by Velázquez, a large collection of paintings that had belonged to the King of the Netherlands made its way to the Hermitage in 1836, and Alexander II added Raphael's precious *Madonna Connestabile* in 1880. In keeping with the Romanovs' tradition, Alexander III bought seventy-four paintings from a Moscow nobleman, including one of Pietro Perugino's best works, and Nicholas II added a Madonna painted by Leonardo da Vinci, plus an array of masterpieces by Filippino Lippi, Perugino, and El Greco.[11] After 1917, the Soviets added rare paintings confiscated from Russia's fallen aristocrats and industrialists, and then during World War II filled the museum's storerooms with treasures taken from the castles and palaces of Eastern Europe and Germany. As in the days of Catherine and her successors, they chose the best. Only true masterpieces from every historical period could be given a place in the Hermitage. This was truly the treasure house of an empire, and it changed the very meaning of the name given to it. Defined by the dictionary as "a secluded retreat," the Hermitage in St. Petersburg became one of the world's finest museums, and it cast its shadow upon the heart and soul of every lover of art on earth.

But the Winter Palace was more than a museum or a residence, and its shadow embraced politics as well as culture. While Russia's political center had been wherever the autocrat happened to be in the time of Peter the Great, Catherine set it firmly within the Winter Palace, from which her power touched every corner of Europe, most of Asia, and the northwestern parts of North America. From the Winter Palace she issued laws, declared war, made peace, and dispensed justice, and to it she invited ambassadors, great lords and ladies, and the commanders of Russia's armies.

Anyone and everyone whose presence Catherine desired had access to the Winter Palace, and it was among these men and women that she spread the ideas of the Enlightenment and debated how they would shape Russia's future. In the Winter Palace, Catherine wrote her famed *Nakaz* that set forth the principles on which she believed government and society should be based. Called "one of the most remarkable political treatises ever compiled and published by a reigning sovereign in modern times," the *Nakaz*, or instructions, was designed to guide the Legislative Commission that the Empress summoned for the purpose of drafting an enlightened code of laws for Russia in 1767.[12]

Kind to her friends and magnanimous to fallen foes who paid her tribute, Catherine sought to reign from the Winter Palace as an enlightened and generous sovereign. She installed her lover Stanislaw Poniatowski on Poland's throne and made the Tatar Khan of the Crimea her vassal, but she dealt severely with those who challenged her authority. For the Cossack chieftain Emelian Pugachev, who led a huge serf uprising against her in 1773–1774, Catherine reinstated the death penalty, and she condemned the Polish patriot Tadeusz Kosciuszko to prison as a spokesman of Jacobinism, a follower of Saint-Just, and a disciple of Robespierre. In the Winter Palace, Catherine received word in 1770 of Russia's victory over the Turks at the great naval battle at Chesme Gulf. There she received word of victory again in the Second Russo-Turkish War of 1787–1792, and of the three partitions of Poland that brought tens of thousands of square miles of territory and tens of millions of new subjects into her empire. From the audience chambers of the Winter Palace she made and broke the alliances that obliged Europe's monarchs to respect Russia as an equal, and she celebrated the triumphs of her one-time lover and long-time statesman Grigorii Potemkin as the colonizer of South Russia.

Catherine placed the Winter Palace at the center of the complex ceremonial rituals that eventually would set Russia's sovereigns apart from the people they ruled, and she surrounded these events with displays of wealth that no one in Russia could surpass. "It was in this large palace . . . [that the Empress Catherine] displayed through her long reign that magnificence and liberality which made her court the admiration of foreigners and obtained for her the just eulogisms of all literary travelers," Heinrich Storch wrote in the 1790s. "[The palace itself] occupies the space of a small town," he added in an effort to give his readers a sense of perspective, "[and its] situation . . . is truly majestic."[13] As the amazed William

Coxe observed soon after he arrived in St. Petersburg two decades earlier, "the richness and splendour of the Russian Court surpassed description."[14] Catherine arranged there the most elegant balls of the season and served the costliest dinners. "No Court ever exhibited such a brilliant and variegated spectacle," a French visitor remarked as her reign neared its end. Catherine, he added, in amazement, "dined on a throne raised in the midst of different tables. Crowned, and covered with gold and diamonds, her eyes carelessly wandered over the immense assembly, composed of persons of all nations, whom she seemed to behold at her feet."[15] Yet, some saw a less flattering image lurking in the darker shadows that were so much a part of Petersburg life. James Harris, first Lord Malmesburg and England's ambassador to Russia's capital in the late 1770s, looked beneath the court's brilliant veneer to find "one continued scene of intrigue, debauchery, iniquity, and corruption. . . . It is beyond the powers of my pen," he added in another context, "to describe a scene in which every passion that can affect the human mind bore a part, and which were by all actors concealed by the most masterly hypocrisy."[16]

Although the rituals of Russia's court would eventually separate the Romanovs from their subjects, Catherine moderated them enough to prevent her people from being set apart. The young daughter of one of her courtiers insisted that the Empress's very presence transformed any building into a temple that could "inspire that divine ecstasy and celestial joy that only the gods have the power to produce," for in Catherine she saw "Minerva, goddess of knowledge, the sciences, and the arts, Phoebus, god of light, and Hebe, the ornament of Empire."[17] That powerful mystique always surrounded Catherine's public appearances at the Winter Palace, where she shone as sovereign, mother, and goddess all rolled into one. "No one could be more imposing than the Empress at times of State," one of her ladies-in-waiting explained, but "no one could be greater, kinder, or more indulgent than she in her private circle."[18]

Reigning from the Winter Palace as an imperial "goddess of knowledge, the sciences, and the arts," Catherine lavished patronage and privileges on Russia's artists. In doing so, she continued on a grander scale the effort to modernize Russian culture that Peter the Great had begun when he had invited European artists to Russia and had sent the first Russian artists to study in the West. Peter had overseen the first great transformation in modern Russian art, when oil and pigment replaced the tempera and egg-yolk paints with which Muscovite artists had worked, and when

*Peter the Great*

*Peter's first house, built in 1703 on the northern bank of the Neva River.*
*(Courtesy of the Russian National Library, St. Petersburg)*

*A section of Aleksei Zubov's 1716 giant panorama of the Neva River's northern bank.*
*(Courtesy of the Russian National Library, St. Petersburg)*

*This 1753 panorama, from a drawing by Mikhail Makhaev, looks eastward along the Neva River from the Admiralty. The Peter and Paul Fortress (left) can be seen in the distance on the northern shore of the river, with the Winter Palace to the south. (Courtesy of the Russian National Library, St. Petersburg)*

*The Summer Garden. This 1833 engraving, from a drawing by Vasilii Sadovnikov, looks onto the palace of Peter I from one of the garden's interior walkways. (Courtesy of the Russian National Library, St. Petersburg)*

*Aleksandr Nevskii Monastery. (Courtesy of the Russian National Library, St. Petersburg)*

*Elizabeth I*

*Bartolomeo Rastrelli*

*Ivan Starov*

*Smolnyi Cathedral. (Photo courtesy of Jack Kollmann)*

*The Jordan Staircase, by Rastrelli, in the Winter Palace.*
*(Courtesy Central State Archive of Kino-Photo-Phono Documents, St. Petersburg.)*

*Catherine the Great*

*The Catherine Palace at Tsarskoe Selo, designed by Rastrelli, served as a summer retreat for the empress Elizabeth I. (Photo courtesy of Jack Kollmann)*

*The Winter Palace, built by Rastrelli for Elizabeth I, as seen from the Admiralty. (Courtesy of the Russian National Library, St. Petersburg)*

*Giacomo Quarenghi*

*This 1820s view of the Admiralty and St. Isaac's Cathedral from the southern bank of Vasilevskii Island depicts one of three pontoon bridges that spanned the Neva River in St. Petersburg's early days. (Courtesy of the Russian National Library, St. Petersburg)*

*Life along the Kriukov Canal, one of the many canals and rivers running along St. Petersburg's streets. The Cathedral of St. Nicholas, designed by Savva Chevakinskii, can be seen in the background. (Courtesy of the Russian National Library, St. Petersburg)*

*The Smolnyi Institute for Young Noblewomen, built by Giacomo Quarenghi, during the reign of Catherine the Great. (Courtesy of the Russian National Library, St. Petersburg)*

*The Marble Palace (right), designed by Antonio Rinaldi. (Courtesy of the Russian National Library, St. Petersburg)*

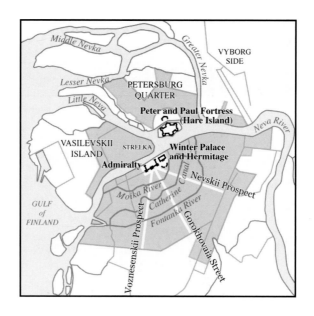

*St. Petersburg in 1801*

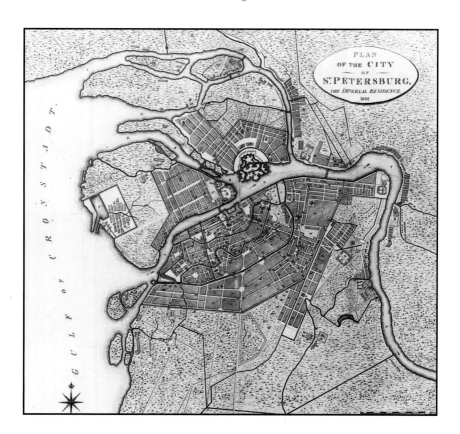

Russian artists began to portray their subjects in three dimensions instead of the stereotyped two-dimensional images of Muscovite times. Like so much else in Petrine Russia, the first instruments of this transformation had been Europeans, but by the middle of the eighteenth century the process had moved firmly into the hands of Russians, the greatest of whom was Dmitrii Levitskii.

After several years of modest success, Levitskii exploded on the Petersburg artistic scene in a single brilliant burst in 1770, when six of his portraits won glowing reviews at the Imperial Academy of Fine Arts' first public showing of its students' and teachers' works. A master at capturing the character of his subjects, Levitskii became the chronicler of St. Petersburg's aristocracy in the reign of Catherine the Great. And just as Sir Anthony Van Dyck's likenesses of England's lords and ladies projected the image of Charles I's court across the centuries, so Levitskii's portraits still reflect the self-image of St. Petersburg's high society during the Golden Age of its nobility.

Levitskii's portraits showed how far Russian art had come since the childhood of Peter the Great, when the handful of portraits painted in defiance of the Church's proscription against graven images more clearly resembled icons than depictions of real-life people. In a style that reflected the inspiration of Watteau, Levitskii painted several full-length portraits of Catherine the Great that ranked among the most majestic state portraits of his era, and his paintings of the grandees at court captured the essence of Catherinian Petersburg in ways no other artist ever matched. Between 1770 and 1800, virtually everyone who stood at Russia's social and political apex sat for Levitskii, and so did the men and women who shaped the city's arts and letters. Each of Levitskii's scores of portraits made it clear that the society of St. Petersburg now fit closely with that of Paris, Vienna, and London, and his shift to the simpler English manner on the eve of the French Revolution reflected the changing focus of Europe as a whole. Most of all, his art revealed the manner in which the Empress Catherine had given greater substance and sophistication to Peter the Great's vision and the way St. Petersburg life reflected that achievement.[19]

Like Levitskii, most Russian artists of the eighteenth century concentrated on portraiture, and their paintings captured the dramatic physical transformation that Peter the Great's new capital had brought to the Russians' way of life. From these paintings, we know how people looked, what fashions they wore, and how the complex world of physical objects that surrounded them had changed. Most noticeably, their images give us a clear sense that the men and women of Catherine's era were beginning to feel at ease in the world that had seemed so alien to their grandparents, and that the values that once had set Europeans and Russians apart had changed enough to bring them closer together. Yet, even as Petersburgers in the Age of Catherine the Great became more European, they also began to feel more certain of being Russian. For, although Peter the Great had rejected Russia's past as backward, Catherine, her courtiers, and a handful of scholars at St. Petersburg's Academy of Sciences decided to reclaim it in order to gain a better perspective on the present. Educated men and women now began to ask where Russia and the Russians had come from. To whom and to what influences did Russia owe its autocratic form of government? And how had Russia related to the West over the eight hundred years that had passed since its princes first embraced Christianity?

To discover what it meant to be Russian and where the Russians had come from meant tracing Russia's history back to the time when the ancestors of the Slavs had made their first contacts with the civilizations of Greece and Rome, to which present-day Europe owed its beginnings. Catherine and her contemporaries confronted that problem by arguing that Russians were in no way inferior to the West, and that for every phenomenon in Russia's history a parallel could be found in the experience of Europe. They also claimed that their nation's past embraced achievements that helped to define it as uniquely Russian.[20] But where precisely did St. Petersburg fit in? Remote from the centers around which Old Russia had developed, St. Petersburg had to be identified with Russia and not merely with the person of Peter the Great. At the same time, as the capital of the Russian Empire, it needed to be identified with the Rome of the Caesars, not, as Moscow once had been, with the Rome that had been a shifting center of the medieval Church.

While painting had played a part in defining the physical and cultural world of eighteenth-century Petersburgers, poetry and theater helped to link their city, Russia, and its monarch more closely to Rome and its classical deities. "The Russian state has spread out like ancient Rome," one poet exclaimed, while another insisted that Russia had "soared with greatness like Rome in its flourishing days."[21] "What more can Russia desire? Minerva is on her throne," an ode to Catherine's name day proclaimed. Masquerades portraying Catherine saving the Russians from despotism and the sins of drunkenness, prodigality, and deceit announced the advent in St. Petersburg of the Age of Gold. And Mikhail Kheraskov, whose *Rossiad* would one day make him eighteenth-century Russia's leading epic poet, promised that Catherine's laws would bring "truth triumphant and virtue rejoicing" to make Russia into a "flourishing Rome."[22]

To these accolades Catherine in the 1780s added the vision of a reborn Hellenic empire over which her second grandson would reign from Constantinople as the new Constantine. Poets now spoke of Russia as Achilles and of Turkey as Troy, while Catherine herself composed an opera that played on imperial themes. Set in tenth-century Byzantium, her *Early Reign of Oleg* featured Greek choruses calling forth images of ancient Greece and Rome while the pagan Russian Prince Oleg triumphed over Byzantium and tied its former brilliance to the future glory of Russia.[23] Mars, Minerva, Astraea, Themis—all gods and goddesses of the ancient world—appeared in Russians' paeans to Catherine, the "monarch surrounded by glory, love, and magnificence."[24] In the poetry of her day, Catherine became the mistress of an empire that recalled the glory of Rome. And, as her capital, St. Petersburg became the imperial city that bound Russia to it.

If the baroque architecture of the Empress Elizabeth's St. Petersburg had reflected Russia's new ties to the West, the neoclassical styles favored under Catherine the Great emphasized the parallels between Russia's capital and Rome. Rinaldi's Marble Palace, the Academy of Fine Arts designed by Kokorinov and Vallin de la Mothe, and Quarenghi's Academy of Sciences all called to mind the greatness of an empire whose artists had made elegance and simplicity their stock in trade. The "poetry of columns" that Starov incorporated into his designs for the Tauride Palace especially reminded contemporaries of the manner in which the ancients had blended wealth and elegance. "Its distinction is its ancient elegant taste," one poet concluded. "It is simple but majestic."[25] That marked the whole tone of St. Petersburg in the age of Catherine the Great, when all the arts combined to impose a vision of imperial brilliance and authority upon a city and empire that had not even existed a scant three-quarters of a century before. Unlike London, Paris, or Vienna, the center of St. Petersburg had few back streets or alleys. By the end of the eighteenth century, it still followed the bold pattern laid down by Anna's planners in the 1730s, which relegated slums to its outskirts in order to concentrate a sense of grandeur in its center.

To reign from St. Petersburg as mistress of an empire descended from ancient Rome, Catherine needed to connect Peter's capital with Russia's history and herself to Peter the Great. Bound to Peter as a niece and a daughter, the empresses Anna and Elizabeth had not felt the need to stress their ties to Russia's first imperial sovereign, but Catherine, as a princess from an obscure corner of Germany, needed to link herself and her reign to the founder of the Russian Empire. Seeking all the more to reign in Peter's image and establish her claim as the second "great" Russian sovereign of the century, she commissioned an immense bronze statue of Peter the Great as her special tribute to the founder of the Russian Empire and its first imperial city, to be unveiled on the hundred-year anniversary of Peter's accession to Russia's throne, August 7, 1782. More than sixteen years in the making, the statue would represent the Russians' first decisive effort to determine what the transformations wrought by Peter actually meant and what the man who had opened their "window to the West" had really stood for. Perhaps most important, it represented an attempt to relate the introspective Muscovite vision that Peter had cast aside to the more closely connected outside world of which once-isolated Russia had so dramatically become a part.

The debate about how Peter the Great ought to be represented in bronze or stone had raged in St. Petersburg since at least the 1740s, when men and women still confused by having leaped so quickly from the medieval world into the modern had insisted that any likeness of their Emperor ought to be set above an "edifice" filled with allegorical figures representing the many virtues he had embraced. Wisdom, truth, justice, courage, firmness, and daring all had to be remembered. So, too, did the great Emperor's sure-sighted political vision and his dedication to the well-being of Russia's people. Along with several other members of the Imperial Academy of Sciences, the great poet-scientist Mikhail Lomonosov envisioned such a statue as having a cluster of greater and lesser allegorical figures—a whole "arsenal of allegories" as a critic later remarked—that would create a symbolic and emblematic setting above which Russia's first emperor could stand in triumph.[26] To Russians living in the 1750s and 1760s, the person of Peter the Great—"so fearsome to his enemies, yet a father to his people" in Lomonosov's carefully crafted words—still loomed so much larger than life that no single image seemed capable of bringing it into focus.[27] To them, Peter had been father, defender, teacher, and avenger—an awe-inspiring colossus who towered above them all.

Because Catherine despised allegory in any form, she sought an artist who could reach beyond the constraints of time and place that continued to bind Russians so closely to Peter's person. She therefore turned to the French sculptor Etienne-Maurice Falconet in the summer of 1766, largely because he had spoken of a "larger plan" that could rise above the cluttered allegorical combinations that earlier sculptors had imagined. The true meaning of Peter the Great's life and accomplishment, Falconet explained, must emerge "from within" the sculpture itself, not from figures clustered at its base. Confident that this vision embraced the very qualities she sought, Catherine offered Falconet an annual salary of 25,000 French francs, comfortable accommodations, and whatever provisions he might require for himself and his assistants if he would come to St. Petersburg and create the monument he had in mind. After agreeing to complete the commission in eight years, Falconet and his eighteen-year-old assistant Marie-Anne Collot set out for the city whose very existence proclaimed that Peter had once wielded the power to move the forces of man and nature in ways that few rulers had done at any time or place.[28]

Falconet reached St. Petersburg just a fortnight after his fiftieth birthday, in the middle of October 1766. He would not see his native Paris again until after he had turned sixty-two, and by that time his many disputes with the Russians would have soured him so thoroughly that he never returned to see his masterpiece once it had been set into place. Obliged to deal with Lieutenant-General Ivan Betskoi, whom Catherine had put in charge of Russia's newly founded Imperial Academy of Fine Arts, the sculptor found himself on a collision course with a man of narrow imagination almost from the beginning.[29] A man who thought more like a high official than an artist, Betskoi could not imagine Falconet's statue in the larger context of which Peter and his new capital had become a part, and he struggled at every turn to contain an artistic and political vision that reached far beyond the narrow confines within which he felt most at ease.[30]

Falconet's likeness of Peter the Great moved beyond the stereotyped heroic images that Betskoi favored and that earlier artists had imposed upon the equestrian monuments of Rome, Venice, Padua, Paris, and Berlin, for he clothed his hero in neither the garb of a Roman emperor nor the uniform of a commander-in-chief. "I would no more think of clothing my Peter in Roman armor," he wrote to Diderot, "than I would [dare] to dress a statue of Scipio, Caesar, or Pompei in a long Muscovite coat or a French jacket." Dismissing the Roman armor in which modern-

day sculptors had clad France's Louis XIV as being "fit only for a masquerade," he also rejected traditional Muscovite garb as belonging to a
way of life that clashed with Peter's dream of creating a modern nation.
Peter's style of dress had to "be that of all nations, of every man in any
time. In a word," he concluded, "it is [to] be purely heroic."[31] Falconet
therefore chose for his bronze horseman a long sleeved smock that
reached below his knees, a cloak of heavy cloth, and boots such as Russians might have worn when their thirteenth-century prince Aleksandr
Nevskii had led them to victory against the knights of Sweden not far
from the very square on which the statue was to stand. With a bearskin as
his saddle and a circle of laurel crowning his head, Falconet's Peter the
Great thus became everyman's hero, whose garb and bearing blended the
legacies of East and West, lord and peasant, and past and present that had
shaped Russia's historical experience.

Falconet shaped his bronze mount and rider to project the full grandeur
of Peter's achievement. Convinced that the mount upon which his imperial
horseman would be seated had to be more than a passively conceived platform, he shaped it to emphasize the energy with which its rider had worked
to transform Russia. At one with its imperial master in daring to challenge
the unknown, Falconet's horse would never be completely in its master's
grip. Kept in check by reins held only lightly in its rider's left hand, Peter's
bronze steed seemed about to plunge into space, just as its rider had dared
to challenge the past and present in his effort to reshape Russia's future.

The Frenchman's vision of Russia's Emperor was broad enough, as he
later wrote, to become "the symbol of the whole nation he civilized,"[32] but
he nonetheless proved unequal to the task of creating a compelling image
of Peter's features. After Catherine rejected all three of his attempts to
sculpt his horseman's head, Falconet turned to Marie-Anne Collot, whose
genius for capturing human features in bronze and stone had won enthusiastic praise in Paris and St. Petersburg. Working from a mask which
Bartolomeo Rastrelli's father had cast when Peter was still alive, Collot
produced a model that won the Empress's instant approval. Her creation,
Falconet later wrote, was "daring, colossal, expressive, and permeated with
character." In a later letter, he added the word "magnificent."[33]

If the Bronze Horseman symbolized the power, vision, and achievement
that had brought St. Petersburg into being, its huge granite base spoke once
again of the stubborn tenacity of the masses that had made Peter's vision a
reality. Raised from a swamp by the labors of thousands of workers, it stood

as a monument to what the will of Russia's autocrats and the might of its people could accomplish. Here once again was evidence of the raw human power that had always made Russia strong, for the feat that moved this huge boulder from the depths of the Finnish forest to the center of St. Petersburg seems well beyond the limits of eighteenth-century technology. Only the ancient Egyptians had ever moved stones of this magnitude before. Yet the so-called colossus-stone that became the base upon which the Bronze Horseman stands made part of its journey over water.

In the low-lying lands around St. Petersburg, rock in any size and quantity was scarce. Yet some mysterious natural force had placed a huge, towering stone in the midst of a swamp not far from the nearby Finnish village of Lakhta, and rumor had it that Peter himself had watched some of Russia's first naval battles against the Swedes from its highest point. Partly buried beneath a carpet of small birch trees, scrub evergreens, and dirt, this gigantic granite monolith weighed no less than three million pounds and stood nearly thirty feet high.[34] "It seemed well beyond the forces of men and machines to move it," wrote a military engineer who visited the site. "Its huge weight, the marshy land and deep streams around it, and the fact that it lay on the wrong side of [the Finnish Gulf and] the Neva," he added, "all presented obstacles that seemed truly daunting."[35]

To move the colossus-stone across the five miles that separated its swampy resting place from the Finnish Gulf and then transport it over another eight miles of water to the Neva River's southern bank seemed an impossible task. Yet, once Falconet had seen it, he insisted that it must become the base for his bronze horseman. "Without wasting time," Catherine therefore decreed on September 15, 1768, "all assistance [must] be given ... so that [this stone] may be transported [in one piece and] with all dispatch to the Neva embankment" nearest the spot on which Peter's statue was to be set in place. Everyone knew that Falconet would have to cut away huge chunks of the stone to give it the proper form, but no one looked for ways to modify the Empress's order. Giving no thought as to whether its weight might be reduced by removing the useless parts, Catherine's military engineers simply applied that unique blend of brute force and human cunning that has shaped so much of Russia's history. Cost, convenience, human life, and labor—even common sense—all would take second place in carrying out the Empress's command.[36]

Efforts to dislodge the colossus-stone began in the fall of 1768, when a detachment of four hundred soldiers and workers drained all the swamplands between Lakhta and the coast, cleared away the brush, and dug a pit a hundred feet wide and fifteen feet deep to free the stone. As spring approached, Colonel Laskaris-Carburi, a Greek military engineer who had come to Russia in search of the success that had eluded him in the West, had his workers set down the first of the sliding wooden rails between which bronze balls had been set to reduce the friction as the heavy stone slid along them. Then, while scores of men turned six huge windlasses to pull the stone over the rails, hundreds of others cleared the way, moved the rails ahead, and placed the heavy five-inch bronze balls in position between them once again. By November 1769, they had moved the stone 160 feet. Then, as the terrain turned slightly downhill and the freezing ground grew more firm, their pace quickened. By the end of March, the colossus-stone had reached the water's edge.

To move the colossus-stone over water required a vessel such as none of the Imperial Admiralty's experts could envision in the spring of 1770, but during that summer a daring blend of intuition and modern science led them to suspend a huge double-decked barge nearly 150 feet long and 66 feet wide between two three-masted sailing ships. Like the devices used to float cargo ships over sandbars in Amsterdam, the space between its decks could be filled with water and sunk deep enough below the surface for the stone to be slid aboard. Then, when the water was pumped out, the barge floated higher, buoyed by the air between its decks. With its captain ordering repeated soundings to avoid the shoals and shallows at the Neva's mouth, this awkward craft slowly picked its way along the coast and up the Neva's smaller branch to the Peter and Paul Fortress opposite the Winter Palace. Then, it turned west onto the river's main course and floated downstream to its destination. While cheering Petersburgers lined the banks, the unwieldy vessel deposited the colossus-stone in its proper place on September 26, 1770, where Falconet proceeded to reduce its size by nearly half so that his bronze statue of Peter the Great would sit properly upon it.[37]

Catherine planned to present the bronze and stone creation of Falconet, Collot, and Russia's masses to the people of St. Petersburg on the morning of August 7, 1782, in a way that would dramatize the masterpiece they had created. Nowhere that day were there any reminders of the ties between Old Russia and Byzantium that had been so much a part of the pomp with which Russian sovereigns had surrounded themselves in earlier times. Nor were there any symbols to celebrate the new imperial vision with which

Russia's eighteenth-century rulers were beginning to link their realm to modern Europe and the legacy of ancient Rome. That morning, a late summer Sunday, the city was quiet, with hardly a sign that anything out of the ordinary was in the wind, and anyone who passed by the huge square on which the Empress's celebrations were to take place later that day would have found it empty. Empty, that is, except for an awkward structure formed by eight rain-soaked linen-covered plank panels that had been set in the shape of a clumsy rectangle near the Neva River's edge.

Ever since the previous afternoon, a sharp wind had been driving rain in drenching sheets that made it seem more like mid-fall than late summer, and the Neva had started to rise toward the newly built granite embankments that contained it. Then, just after noon, the sodden clouds broke apart, the heavy shadows vanished, and the sun burst through. When the first of the Empress's specially chosen regiments began to assemble just beyond the square around two o'clock, the sky had turned almost entirely blue. Altogether, fifteen thousand elite fighting men waited to enter the square, their damp uniforms drying in the sunshine.

Tall, imposing, and with not one man among them under six feet in height, the Empress's own bottle-green-coated Preobrazhenskii Guards led the way along the Neva Embankment. In their wake came the Izmailovskii and Semenovskii Guards, the Horse Guards, and a contingent of Guards Artillery, all moving in tight formations that walled off the gathering crowd from the awkward form that rose above them. Then, while Russia's foremost field marshal and a suite of adjutants in plumed helmets and sparkling orders of merit rode past the troops in review, dozens of splendidly outfitted yachts swept onto the broad Neva River, their colored sails and gleaming hulls sparkling as they tacked and turned. At five o'clock, Catherine stepped from the imperial yacht and made her way into the building that housed the Ruling Senate, the highest governmental body in Russia.[38]

When their Empress appeared on the Senate balcony half an hour later, the tens of thousands of people in the square burst into cheers and applause. Catherine waved her hand. Then, a rocket exploded high above, and the forty-foot-high wood and linen panels fell away to the thunder of cannon fire to reveal Falconet's gigantic likeness of Peter the Great set high upon a mammoth granite rock. Astride a rearing steed that seemed about to leap from the precipice on which it stood, Russia's "Tsar-Transformer" sat erect, his right arm extended as if to calm the river that flowed from the

*The Bronze Horseman. (Courtesy of the Russian National Library, St. Petersburg)*

heart of his empire to the nearby sea. Like Marcus Aurelius, whose towering bronze likeness had stood as a Roman model for heroes since the days of the Renaissance, Peter had become immortal. Now transformed from flesh and bone into metal, he had become a romantic abstraction and a bridge across which Imperial Russia and its European capital could regain its Muscovite past. Russians now began to reach for that past, even as they drew closer to Europe.

When Peter the Great first had urged the Russians to set their past aside in the name of progress, barely a handful had shared his enthusiasm for the West. As the years passed, the numbers of those who embraced

the ways of Europe increased, and by the middle of the century the culture of the West had become the preferred way of life for the lords and
ladies of Peter's city. Yet Europe offered more than fashions, manners, and
modern technology, for the eighteenth century was a time of intense intellectual ferment in which Europeans challenged the essence of the Old
Regime itself. The Age of Enlightenment raised the individual to the
level of paramount importance in the minds of the continent's leading
thinkers, and individual accomplishment became the standard by which
all people—rich and poor—were measured. By the time Catherine had
reigned for a decade, the thinkers of the West had moved resolutely onto
the path that would bring them to the French Revolution. As the Russians continued to borrow from Europe, it became increasingly difficult
for them to avoid that course as well.

Almost from the beginning of her reign, Catherine had to confront a
disturbing paradox. If she continued urging the Russians to move closer
to the West, as every sovereign since Peter the Great had done, she risked
bringing to Russia ideas that could undermine what Peter and his successors had accomplished. So long as educated men and women saw such
ideas merely as new fashions to be adopted and discarded according to
the whims of their Empress and her court, the immediate danger did not
seem very great. But if the Russians actually embraced liberty, fraternity,
and the rights of man, the danger could quickly become immense. During the 1760s, Petersburgers discussed the ideas of Montesquieu, Diderot,
and Voltaire superficially and as a matter of changing fashion. Then, at
the very end of the decade, their attitudes began to change, and by the
early 1770s there were people in Russia's capital who wanted to embrace
more radical European ideas than Catherine dared to allow.

Intolerant of tyranny in any form, these first critics of Russian autocracy took the teachings of the Enlightenment to heart. They lamented
the ways in which masters abused their serfs, questioned the arrogance of
government officials, and criticized the deep-rooted corruption that
touched every corner of Russian life, all of which their Empress tolerated
in the name of maintaining domestic peace. "You lord tyranny over the
people subjected to your care," one critic wrote of Russia's serf owners.
"These poor creatures seem to you more like horses and dogs than people."[39] To be truly enlightened, such men insisted, a sovereign had to see
life as it really was, not as her counselors wanted her to see it. Because
Catherine had failed to do so, they claimed, she had started down the

path to becoming a tyrant. The Winter Palace, which had shone as a symbol of patronage, culture, and political power for those men and women who shared Catherine's vision, now threatened to cast an ominous shadow across the lives of Russia's first dissidents.

The conflict between Catherine and her critics began in the early 1770s and simmered throughout the 1780s. At the very end of the decade, it burst into a dramatic confrontation over censorship between the Empress and a man in whom she once had placed her deepest trust. Twenty years earlier, Catherine had seen in Aleksandr Radishchev one of the people best able to help her bring enlightened laws to Russia, but in 1790 she condemned him for publishing a book "filled with the most pernicious philosophizing, destructive to civic peace, [and] disparaging of citizens' respect for authority."[40] Fearful that Radishchev's *Journey from St. Petersburg to Moscow* might bring the teachings of the French Revolution to Russia, Catherine ordered all copies, "wheresoever they may be found, to be destroyed."[41] At the same time, she prohibited the sale of Diderot's *Grande Encyclopédie* and even canceled the translation she had commissioned of Voltaire's collected works. Clearly, her enthusiasm for the Enlightenment had waned during the quarter-century that had passed since she had promised France's leading *philosophes* lives of "freedom and tranquility" if they agreed to move to St. Petersburg from Paris.[42] And her certainty that Russia no longer could follow the Western path made her even more resolute in turning toward the model of ancient Rome.

Even in the 1760s, Europe's *philosophes* had sensed that Catherine's efforts to embrace the Enlightenment involved more window dressing than substance, but at the same time Aleksandr Radishchev, a young Russian of great intellectual talent, had taken very much to heart her admonitions to study its ideas. Until his parents enrolled him in the Imperial Corps of Pages at the age of ten, Radishchev had lived in Russia's provinces, and he had come to respect the caring serf nannies and servants with whom his wealthy parents had surrounded him. After he proved himself to be one of the best in the Corps of Pages, Catherine had chosen him to become an apostle of enlightened laws in Russia, and had sent him to study at the University of Leipzig. But the intellectual tumult of Leipzig and Catherine's own wavering enthusiasm for the Enlightenment turned Radishchev's life onto a very different course. Eventually, sovereign and subject became the bitterest of enemies.

Then one of the leading centers of German Enlightenment, Leipzig gave Radishchev a chance to explore the ideas that were shaping the politics of Europe, and his studies provided him with a standard by which to measure the progress of those same views in Russia. Even more than the lectures he heard, his reading at Leipzig convinced him that autocracy, like despotism, violated the most fundamental principles of natural law, and that it represented "the condition most contrary to the nature of men."[43] By the time he left Leipzig in 1771, Radishchev had embraced the ideas of Locke, Helvetius, and Rousseau, each of whom believed that it was the people's duty to judge their sovereign and insisted that an unjust ruler must bear responsibility for every action that violated the law and the social contract. These were the ideas Radishchev carried back to Russia, but he kept them to himself for nearly twenty years.

Upon finding that Catherine had abandoned her earlier plan for a code of enlightened laws in Russia, Radishchev entered the army. Then he became a government official and eventually head of St. Petersburg's Customs House, the busiest in all of Russia. During his leisure time, he wrote, in the style of Laurence Sterne's *Sentimental Journey*, an account of an imaginary trip from St. Petersburg to Moscow, and he used it to comment on the many failings he saw in the enlightened society Catherine had worked to create. Aristocrats, priests, government officials, and even the autocrat herself, Radishchev insisted, all had failed Russia, and he warned that they must mend their ways or face bitter consequences. Infuriated by his criticism, and further angered because he had gotten his book approved by a careless censor, Catherine condemned him to death, though she later relented and sentenced him to exile in Siberia. Her actions defined the point at which the infatuation with Europe that had brought St. Petersburg into being finally diverged from the interests of Russia's established order. Thereafter, autocrats and censors no longer thought that the interests of the Russian Empire and the West were the same. Just as in the eighteenth century St. Petersburg had been the point at which the cultures of Eurasia and the West intersected, so now it marked the place at which the interests of the two diverged. St. Petersburg therefore continued to be Russia's "window on the West," but one that would always be partly closed.

The divergence between Russia and the West that occurred in the nineteenth century was never to be as complete as it had been in Muscovite times—nor would it take place all at once. St. Petersburg would always be Russia's most European city, its aristocrats would continue to take pride in their closeness to the West, and many would see it as a sign of success that aristocratic refugees from the French Revolution found in the city a comforting haven. Still, the waning of Catherine's era marked a turning point for Russia, its nobility, and St. Petersburg, for it was then that Russia began to define itself apart from Europe and to become the Eurasian colossus that history and geography seem to have destined it to be. In no other nation in the world could one encounter such vastness, and nowhere else were the ties with the heritage of ancient Rome stronger or more pronounced. In the nineteenth century, the Imperial Russian giant would embrace a vision larger and more grand than any yet seen in modern times. Like Falconet's Bronze Horseman, it would be larger than life itself and cast on a scale that would always test the limits of human imagination.

PART II

*Imperial
Colossus
(1796–1855)*

FOUR

# THE
# HUB OF EMPIRE

*T*HE PROUD POSSESSOR OF ARMIES that had overwhelmed the most formidable of modern-day conquerors, Russia in 1815 stood triumphant among the nations of the West. Rulers of the nation that had defeated Napoleon, Catherine's grandsons Alexander I and Nicholas I reigned as conquering heroes, the captains of a million men under arms, the greatest military force the modern world had ever seen. Under their command, St. Petersburg became the hub of a colossal Eurasian empire between 1796 and 1855, and the cosmopolitan neoclassicism of Catherine's era gave way to styles that befitted a nation that ruled more than a sixth of the land surface on the globe. Towering buildings modeled on the structures of ancient Rome replaced the more elegant, less pretentious ones from Catherine's time. Built during the first half of the nineteenth century, the Senate, the Synod, the Admiralty, the Ministry of War, the Headquarters of the General Staff, the Foreign Ministry, the Cathedrals of Our Lady of Kazan and St. Isaac, the Imperial Theaters—even the school of the Imperial Ballet—all called to mind the days when Rome had ruled the ancient world.

Identification with the power and glory of Rome thus shaped the transformation of early-nineteenth-century St. Petersburg into the capital of the world's new military giant. Whereas Catherine had been content to see herself as lawgiver, benevolent despot, and patron of the arts, her successors envisioned themselves as military commanders whose authority could best be displayed on the drill field, where the instant response of marching battalions illustrated the immensity of their power. Just as in earlier times the Winter Palace and its court had demonstrated the elegance, sophistication, and worldly authority to which the empresses Elizabeth and Catherine the Great aspired, so massed formations of marching troops symbolized the civilized taste and culture that the force of arms had come to represent.[1] An atmosphere of military command now combined with the transcendental power of classical architecture to set a new tone, as battalions of men in splendid uniforms wheeled against the backdrop of the massive Doric porticoes of the newly built Pavlovskii Guards Barracks at the edge of the Field of Mars. Such martial displays became ever present reminders that discipline and subordination had merged with the Romanovs' earlier aspirations to enlightenment and civility as the values that Russia's sovereigns cherished most of all.

Enthralled by symbols of command, Catherine's grandsons rebuilt the center of their capital into a gigantic parade ground covering more than four million square feet, beginning at the Winter Palace and extending for half a mile along the Admiralty Boulevard to the Senate Square. Here, a hundred thousand men could march in review. Church, state, army, and Romanov dynasty all came together in the grandiose imperial structures that surrounded this drill arena, and for the rest of the century scores of battalions in precise formations would assure the nation's autocrats of the massive power they commanded. Russia's sovereigns hoped that the order of the drill field—the symmetry of formations, the meticulous correctness of uniforms, and the precision of maneuvers—over which the Emperor as God's earthly representative held command would uplift their nation's spiritual life by blending the divine and secular forces of God and Reason. In their eyes, the army offered a way for their dynasty to fulfill its God-given mission in Russia and abroad, and St. Petersburg, as the perfectly designed setting for that instrument, became the city that best represented Russia's present and future.

As the focal point of this military colossus, one observer remarked, "St. Petersburg never looked more like Rome."[2] Triumphal arches and columns, Roman swords and shields, and all the symbols and paraphernalia of Imperial Rome appeared in abundance and on a scale never seen before in Russia. The statue of Peter the Great clad in the armor of a Roman emperor that Carlo Rastrelli had completed in the 1730s was put on public display for the first time at the very beginning of the new century, and not long after that sculptors began to clothe other military commanders in Roman garb to bind the vision of a heroic Russia to the image of Imperial Rome.

That was particularly true of Mikhail Kozlovskii's statue of the great eighteenth-century commander Aleksandr Suvorov, which blended Russian and Roman motifs as a tribute to the first hero of Russia's imperial age.[3] In real life, the thin, wispy-haired Suvorov had been the antithesis of the perfectly proportioned heroic figure that Kozlovskii placed on the edge of the Field of Mars. Nonetheless, his statue projected a "deep inner truth" that radiated the new sense of national pride that had begun to tie St. Petersburg so closely to the heritage of Rome. As in ancient Rome, Russia now paid homage to beautiful men whose perfect bodies expressed great physical power, and relegated the sleek, languid goddesses of earlier times to second place.[4] That was true most of all in St. Petersburg, where people of wealth, power, and position sought to emulate the poses and manners of statues in an effort to project the elegance and eloquence they associated with Ancient Rome.

Even before styles of architecture and sculpture did so, fashions, furniture, and interior design reflected the Russians' new fascination with the Roman Empire. "Alabaster vases carved with mythological images, tripod tables, and incense burners appeared everywhere ... [as did] long sofas where one's arms rested on eagles, griffons, and sphinxes," one Petersburger wrote in his remembrances of the 1810s. "Women's dresses that called to mind statues on the banks of the Aegean and the Tiber," he added, "were imitated on the Neva, and if it were not for the military uniforms and frock coats, the balls would have resembled antique bas-reliefs and ancient Etruscan vases."[5] Life was buoyed by a new feeling of triumph that Petersburgers had not known even in the golden days of Catherine the Great, and this was reflected in the huge buildings that took shape during the age of Napoleon. Many of these were painted a rich yellow color, which called to mind the imperial gold that emblazoned so many military standards and uniforms of the era.[6] Corinthian columns, Doric porticoes, and all the architectural embellishments that evoked the glories of ancient Rome now overshadowed the baroque and neoclassical styles that Elizabeth and Catherine had imposed on the city.

Because St. Petersburg epitomized all of Russia, these themes and motifs spread from it to far corners of the empire. Imperial structures resembling the monumental new buildings of the city's center soon began to tower above wooden cottages and onion-domed churches in towns from Russia's Polish frontier to its Pacific coast. Even in such remote frontier towns as Simbirsk, Perm, Orenburg, and Irkutsk, huge buildings of state offered new reminders of the forces that now bound together the empires of Russia and ancient Rome. Just as edifices glorifying the Caesars had appeared in Roman Britain and Gaul, so huge brick and stucco monuments to Russia's emperors took shape in remote corners of Eurasia.

A rebuilt and redesigned Admiralty became the first of the huge imperial structures that took shape around St. Petersburg's central parade ground at the beginning of the nineteenth century. Dating from an earlier time in which different visions had dominated the city, the Admiralty now stood in painful contrast to the elegant neoclassical style that had shaped so much of Russia's capital during the decades since Ivan Korobov had designed it in the 1730s. In the spring of 1805, Alexander I assigned Andreian Zakharov, a middle-aged professor of architecture at the Imperial Academy of Fine Arts, to redesign the Admiralty to reflect Russia's new imperial vision. Zakharov had learned his trade during the 1780s in Paris, where he had studied with the man who eventually created Napoleon's Arc de Triomphe. Now, after having taught at the Academy for nearly twenty years, he approached the daunting assignment of rebuilding a fifth-of-a-mile-long building with all the naive confidence of a man who did not yet know from experience the limits that practice imposed upon theory.

Zakharov's confidence led him to work on a colossal scale. He extended the Admiralty's facade to just ninety-eight feet short of a quarter of a mile, but he used only the simplest decoration, relying mainly on groupings of towering Greek columns to ornament all but the central pavilion, where a complex blend of sculptures and bas reliefs made it clear that the building served an empire whose lands touched a dozen seas. Four monumental sculptures of Pyrrhus, Achilles, Ajax, and Alexander the Great stood proudly above the corners of its attic, and twenty-eight statues representing the seasons, the winds, and the elements adorned its cornices.[7] Isis, the Egyptian goddess who presided over the waters and the winds was there, and so was Urania, muse of astronomy and patron of navigators in ancient times. Above them all soared the Admiralty's golden spire, which, as a visitor wrote, "resembled the mast of a golden ship planted on the roof of a Greek temple."[8] Beneath it, on granite pedestals outside the entrance, the sculptor Feodosii Shchedrin placed two groups of three caryatids, each supporting a massive globe, just weeks before Napoleon invaded Russia in 1812. As if to show that Russia had the will and the strength to bear the burden of its huge Eurasian empire, none of the figures bent beneath the weight it carried. Shchedrin's caryatids became monuments to Russia's new world mission just when it set out to liberate Europe from the yoke of Napoleon, and the Admiralty they adorned, in defining the northern boundary of St. Petersburg's huge emerging parade ground, became the focal point of the city's center.

Zakharov saw his Admiralty as a "maritime acropolis" that drew attention to St. Petersburg's ties to the sea.⁹ The men who followed him embraced that theme but added others whose monumental scale left no doubt that Catherine's grandsons identified their triumphs with the glories of Imperial Rome. Zakharov had just begun to work when one of the most striking of these efforts took shape on the easternmost tip of Vasilevskii Island, where the Little Neva flowed off from the river's main current. There on a spit of land that had defied the best efforts of Russia's court architects since the days of Peter the Great, Quarenghi had tried to build St. Petersburg's first stock exchange in the 1780s, but his work had been cut short by the costs of Catherine's second war with the Ottoman Empire.

For the next fifteen years, Quarenghi's building had stood half-finished. Then, in the summer of 1805, just a few months after he had assigned Zakharov to work on the Admiralty, Alexander I gave the task of building St. Petersburg's Bourse to Thomas de Thomon, a French-educated architect who had only recently come to Russia to seek his fortune. After razing the remains of Quarenghi's effort, de Thomon set to work in the style of the soaring Greek temples at Paestum, surrounding his Bourse with forty-four towering Doric columns, and framing it with two rostral pillars that spouted flame toward the heavens on holidays. The result was an architectural ensemble that would dominate St. Petersburg's waterfront in much the same manner as the Parthenon ruled the hills of Athens, calling to mind the glories of the fallen empires with which Russia now sought to identify.¹⁰

Just as Imperial Rome had its Pantheon, so St. Petersburg had its Cathedral of Our Lady of Kazan, which celebrated Russia's national saints and heroes in a truly imperial manner. Built at the very beginning of the century by the serf architect Andrei Voronikhin, the Kazan Cathedral became a symbol of the triumphs of the Russian Empire and a monument to its messianic mission. Here the greatest heroes of Imperial Russia lay enshrined among trophies of their finest hours on the battlefield. From the moment of its completion in 1811, the Kazan Cathedral stood for Russian power and Russian glory as no other cathedral in the empire ever could. While Moscow's Cathedral of the Assumption continued to recall Russia's long Orthodox heritage, St. Petersburg's Cathedral of the Madonna of Kazan spoke of its imperial grandeur and its unique Eurasian mission.

By itself, the wonder-working icon from which the Kazan Cathedral took its name reflected triumphs in Muscovite Russia's history of which the Russians were extremely proud. Found in the Volga River trading center of Kazan not long after the armies of Ivan the Terrible had conquered it in the 1550s, it had been brought to Moscow to bless the Russians' victory over the Poles in 1612. Peter the Great then ordered it moved to St. Petersburg when he named the new city Russia's capital, and Voronikhin installed it in his cathedral's two-ton silver iconostasis. From this place of honor, the icon of the Madonna of Kazan would bless Russia's victory over Napoleon in 1812 and the armies that marched against the Austrians, Germans, and Turks in 1914, but it was only the first of many monuments to their empire's triumphs that Russia's sovereigns would set within the cathedral's walls.

In the sanctuary of the Kazan Cathedral, Alexander I enshrined more than a hundred captured French banners and eagles, along with the keys to twenty-five captured cities and fortresses and the baton of Napoleon's great Marshal Louis Nicolas Davout. There, too, beneath the colossal statues of St. John the Baptist, St. Andrew, and the sanctified grand princes Vladimir and Aleksandr Nevskii, the Russians laid to rest in 1813 the body of Mikhail Kutuzov, the Field Marshal who had commanded their armies against Napoleon. Above them all stood the huge stone frieze of Christ carrying his cross to Golgotha, into which Feodosii Shchedrin had cut nearly fifty figures that conveyed the tragedy of Our Lord's final hours and united Russia's triumphs with His resurrection.[11] Here was further proof of the favor the Almighty had bestowed on Russia. The Kazan Cathedral proclaimed that Russia was God's empire, and its triumphs His triumphs. But Imperial St. Petersburg was never to become God's city. Despite its several great cathedrals, it would remain a secular capital, the hub of an empire that prayed to God but drew its imperial vision from the heritage of pagan Rome.

Yet the heritage of Christian Rome was there, too, not only in the Kazan Cathedral but also in the Cathedral of St. Isaac of Dalmatia, which stood on the southwestern corner of St. Petersburg's central parade ground. The largest church in the city and the last classical monument to appear there during the first half of the nineteenth century, St. Isaac's boasted the world's third largest dome and cost more than twenty-five million rubles before it was finished in 1858. Its builder was August Ricard de Montferrand, lately of Napoleon's Imperial Guard, who had come to Russia after his emperor's defeat. In St. Petersburg, he presented as his only credentials an artfully bound volume of miniature paintings to illustrate how such a cathedral might appear if it were designed in the styles typical of China, India, Byzantium, Ancient Greece, Rome, and Renaissance Italy. Montferrand provided no blueprints and had no experience in building large structures or working on the sort of marshy subsoil on which St. Petersburg stood. Yet his paintings won Alexander's confidence and his heart. To an autocrat accustomed to having his way without question, Montferrand's sketchbook was enough to capture the most sought-after commission in all of St. Petersburg at that time.

Appointed court architect in the spring of 1818, Montferrand did not receive full approval of his plans for St. Isaac's Cathedral until 1825. A commission of architects had to correct the structural defects in his initial designs, and their corrections had to be amended as more flaws came to light. As finally approved, the plans featured a ribbed gilded dome that weighed more than twenty-two hundred metric tons and was supported by an intricate network of cast-iron girders. Raised above a huge central drum surrounded by columns of red Finnish granite, Montferrand's dome provided a much-needed focal point for the center of Russia's imperial capital, where, as the builder Carlo Rossi later said, "grandeur of form, nobility of proportion, and indestructibility" had come to take precedence over the elegance and grace that Catherine the Great had demanded.[12]

"Placed upon the skyline of the city like a golden mitre," as one visitor wrote after seeing it from a distance, St. Isaac's Cathedral called to mind "St. Peter's and the Pantheon of Agrippa in Rome, St. Paul's in London, St. Genevieve's in Paris, and the Dome of the Invalides."[13] Unlike any other building in Russia, it was a somber yet sumptuous mass of red granite that turned milky pink in St. Petersburg's winter frosts. Each of the forty-eight columns that supported its four gigantic porticoes weighed over 110 tons, and its interior required 900 pounds of gold, a thousand tons of bronze, and sixteen tons of rare Siberian malachite for its decoration. Not even Rastrelli or Quarenghi had been able to build so lavishly or on such an immense scale. "It is developed like a beautiful phrase of ecclesiastical music that fulfils the promises of its pure, classical theme, and does not offend the eye by any dissonance," a visitor marveled the year after St. Isaac's was completed. "In the evening . . . when the light falls in a particular way [and] the windows are lighted up by rays of the setting sun," he added, "it seems to be illuminated and burning within."[14]

Each of the stunning buildings created by Montferrand, Zakharov, and Voronikhin added a new dimension to nineteenth-century St. Petersburg, yet the city's imperial image was shaped most forcefully by Carlo Rossi, who boldly demolished buildings and redesigned facades to express his larger vision. Of all the architects at work in Russia after Napoleon's defeat, only Rossi dared to ask why Russia should "fear to be compared with [the Romans] in magnificence,"[15] and only he worked on a scale worthy of the Romans, from whom he drew his chief inspiration. No other builder ever linked modern Russia and Ancient Rome more closely, for Rossi saw in the heritage of Rome a means for expressing the full grandeur of Russia's destiny. And in doing so, he transformed St. Petersburg into an imperial metropolis that had no rival in the modern world.

Rossi was the son of an Italian ballerina who had settled in the nearby suburb of Pavlovsk after she had retired from the St. Petersburg ballet. Born in 1775, he studied with the noted architect and decorator Vincenzo Brenna, whose work drew much of its inspiration from Roman interiors, and when Brenna retired to Italy in 1802 the twenty-six-year-old Rossi followed him. In Rome, the opulence and grandeur of what remained of the world of the ancients cast its spell upon the student in search of a style in which to work, and Rossi responded by vowing to build in a manner that would "surpass that which the Romans [had] considered sufficient for their monuments" when he returned to Russia.[16] Yet he had to delay his dreams for nearly a decade. His first assignment in Russia was as a painter in the Imperial Porcelain Works, after which he worked as an architect in Moscow and the provincial town of Tula. Only after Russia had conquered the armies of Napoleon did Rossi have the chance to build in the style that had won his heart and on a scale he thought worthy of Russia. By then he was well into his forties, but his work during the next fifteen years left a mark that would never be erased.[17]

In 1819, Alexander I commissioned the forty-four-year-old Rossi to build a residence for his youngest brother, Grand Duke Mikhail Pavlovich, and the beautiful Württemberg princess he had married. This gave Rossi his first opportunity to blend the Corinthian and Doric styles into a bold and powerful interpretation that was to become the stunning

Mikhailovskii Palace. To create a proper setting, he designed a huge park reaching from the palace to the Field of Mars, into which he carried a variety of Roman themes. Then he redesigned the facades of the buildings that fronted on three sides of the square the palace was to face and did the same to those along the street that led to the Nevskii Prospekt from the square opposite its main entrance. Completed in 1823, the Mikhailovskii Palace surpassed every other residential ensemble in the city in elegance and grandeur. The Grand Duke's wife, Grand Duchess Elena Pavlovna, turned it into one of the most sophisticated salons in St. Petersburg, and after her death the Emperor Alexander III transformed it into what is today the Russian Museum, which still holds the best collection of Russian art to be found anywhere in the city.[18]

Further up the Nevskii Prospekt from the point where the street leading to the Mikhailovskii Palace intersects it, Rossi experimented further with his idea of setting key buildings into larger ensembles. Somewhat more than a long block past the huge Merchants' Arcade on the Nevskii, a large square separates the Public Library from the park surrounding the Anichkov Palace, and it was there that Nicholas I commissioned Rossi in 1828 to build the Alexandrine Theater. Rossi's plan embraced two squares and a street between, beginning with the Public Library and Anichkov Palace, which stand at right angles to the Nevskii Prospekt, and ending with Chernyshev Square bordering on the Fontanka River. The Alexandrine Theater formed the center of this new ensemble, and Rossi altered the facades on all the buildings on the square toward which it faced to emphasize its sumptuous yet sober blend of Doric and Corinthian styles. Behind the theater, he cut a new street called Theater Street leading to Chernyshev Square, and again designed the facades of the buildings along it to highlight his vision.[19] Yet even this did not allow Rossi all the room he needed in which to work. As he began to build the Alexandrine Theater, he was already at work on two even grander ensembles that would complete the vast imperial complex that Zakharov's Admiralty had begun.

Starting in 1819, Rossi rebuilt Russia's Imperial General Staff Headquarters and redesigned the gigantic square that separated it from the Winter Palace. Ever since Rastrelli had finished the Winter Palace in 1762, architects had struggled to define the space that spread out to its south, but all had failed to find a worthy solution. Rossi solved the problem by casting the building that was to house the General Staff, Ministry of Finance, and Ministry of Foreign Affairs in the shape of a huge arc stretching the length of six football fields. In its center, he set three triumphal arches, one behind the other, and topped them with a colossal bronze and iron figure of "Victory" riding in a six-horse chariot. Together, his bow-shaped facade, arches, and heroic figures defined the southern limits of St. Petersburg's Palace Square and created a stunning backdrop against which to silhouette tens of thousands of troops marching in massed formations for the emperor's review. To give the center of the huge square sharper focus, Rossi spoke of installing a great monolith in the manner of Trajan's Column in Rome. Eventually that task fell to Montferrand, who in 1834 carried Rossi's victory theme into the center of the Palace Square in the form of a 600-ton red-granite monolith topped by a bronze angel that was dedicated to Alexander I's triumphs over Napoleon.[20]

Rossi's final achievement stood at the opposite end of St. Petersburg's huge central parade ground from the Winter Palace Square. Beyond the Bronze Horseman and to the north of the Horse Guards Riding School that Quarenghi had built in 1807, he linked the buildings that housed the Senate and the Synod into another gigantic facade that stretched from the Neva Embankment to the edge of the Horse Guards Boulevard. This marked the brilliant culmination of the project to create a vast imperial parade ground that had been begun more than thirty years before with no master plan to shape it. Now, as in the Forum in Rome, the instruments that expressed the secular and religious power of the nation had been gathered around a single central area to signal that St. Petersburg had become a very different city than the one from which Catherine the Great had reigned less than half a century earlier.[21]

The first half of the nineteenth century saw St. Petersburg become the nerve center of a bureaucracy that governed lands stretching from the Vistula River to the Yukon. Yet unlike Rome, which had delegated greater power to its governors and provincial centers as time went on, the Russian Empire between 1800 and 1850 became more and more centralized. Gone were the days when Catherine the Great had allowed her governors to rule Russia's provinces. Her grandsons now insisted that only in St. Petersburg was it possible to find the know-how needed to resolve the many dilemmas the Russians faced. Problems relating to famines, epidemics, serf revolts, building new roads and bridges—even the trivial matter of repairing a flue in a government office stove—all had to be referred to the capital for decisions, and local authorities had to wait while the proper inquiries were sent and the necessary replies received.[22] "The entire life of the people is under governmental tutelage," one nobleman grumbled. "No question

however trifling," he complained, "can be dealt with by the people themselves."[23] St. Petersburg had become the fulcrum on which everything in
Russia was balanced. Now politics, trade, the empire's huge army, and
many of the smaller things that formed the contours of daily life all moved
in response to impulses that came from St. Petersburg.

Because Catherine's grandsons insisted that everything had to be dealt
with from St. Petersburg, the bureaucracy that had been quite small in the
eighteenth century evolved into a veritable army of officials as the nineteenth century moved toward its midpoint. By 1850, Russia's bureaucracy
was nearly five times larger than it had been fifty years before, and it was
growing at an exponential rate.[24] So was the flood of papers, which, an
observer remarked, "seemed to reproduce itself . . . in geometrical proportions."[25] Forms, official procedures, and a mountain of paperwork transformed St. Petersburg's great government buildings into warrens of dark,
crowded offices connected by passageways along which armies of anxious
clerks and copyists scurried with armloads of precious files and official
correspondence. "Every department concentrated upon improvements . . .
in the details of its internal administrative apparatus," a St. Petersburg official wrote, and that all too quickly became an end in itself.[26] A sense of
urgency reigned everywhere, yet often very little beyond creating more
red tape seemed to be accomplished. Each year frantic provincial governors had to sign more than a hundred thousand documents, and ministers
in St. Petersburg had to sign even more. This left Russia's leading statesmen with little time to gain a sense of perspective about the problems
they faced and the people they ruled. "We go one step forward and take
two steps backward," one frustrated official complained. "We shall not get
very far if we keep this up."[27]

No matter what procedures were devised and whatever new forms were
created, St. Petersburg always remained at the center of bureaucrats' visions of what Russia ought to become. Looked at from the provinces,
everything was handed down from the capital, and lesser officials simply
waited for instructions to arrive from on high. In St. Petersburg itself,
most officials saw the process in which they took part as the best way to
lead Russians to a better life, always with the idea of helping them emulate the example being set in the capital. Each instruction and every decree had that purpose and was therefore revered by the men who wrote it
as another step in the long process of making Russia better. "I believed so
absolutely in the usefulness of [our] office work," one official later con-

fessed, "that each new document we produced seemed to me to be a new current of benevolence flowing from [our office near] Chernyshev Bridge into the vastness of Russia."[28]

In this world of official petitions, applications, inquiries, and reports, the production of documents became a yardstick by which St. Petersburg's civil servants measured their importance. The Ministry of Internal Affairs alone generated more than thirty million documents a year in the 1840s, and each one of them had to be signed, registered, and acted upon according to the rules set down in thousands of pages of regulations. Each document had to be prepared according to a specific form, written in precise copperplate script, with copies produced as required by hand. Promotions could depend on the quality of an official's handwriting, the closeness with which he followed the rules, and his loyalty to his superiors and the agency in which he served. And yet all this was done to little real purpose. Far too often, patronage, influence peddling, and corruption remained the true keys to success in St. Petersburg, while talent and merit took a distant second place.[29] "On the surface it all seems splendid," one disgusted official remarked. "But it is rotting away underneath."[30]

As if toward a magnet, everything flowed in the direction of St. Petersburg in those days, for it was the stimulus to which all of Russia and the Russians responded. "We provincials somehow turn our steps toward St. Petersburg," the novelist Mikhail Saltykov-Shchedrin confessed at one point. "It is as if St. Petersburg, all by itself, with its name, its streets, its fog, rain, and snow could resolve something or shed new light on something!"[31] No longer merely Russia's window on the West, St. Petersburg by the 1830s and 1840s had acquired an almost magical aura that drew people to it, and Russians therefore expected something different and somehow better to happen in their lives once they reached Peter's city. This promise of power and success encouraged ambitious young men to abandon the security of friends and home in the provinces in order to try their luck in the capital. "I still do not understand why I came to St. Petersburg," one of them confessed to his diary. "Among the city's half million inhabitants, I had not a single friend or acquaintance."[32]

To govern the empire, St. Petersburg's statesmen and bureaucrats depended upon a flow of information from distant provinces. Poorly educated and sometimes almost illiterate, provincial officials had little inkling about what their superiors in St. Petersburg needed to know, and in turn they did little to help those in St. Petersburg understand what life outside the capital was really like. Yet, if St. Petersburg was to lead Russia into the modern age as the Emperor Nicholas I expected, its statesmen needed to answer questions their predecessors had never had to confront. How many people lived in St. Petersburg? In Moscow? Or in Kiev? What was their standard of living? How rich was the average nobleman? How poor were his serfs? How much did land cost in different parts of the empire? And, how much trade came and went in Russia's towns and cities? What quantities of vital natural resources could Russia claim to have? Where were they located? How could they be used? In the modern age, the reality of what the Russian Empire was like became important. Modern problems required statesmen to have facts before they could govern, and those facts held the key to success in politics and government.

No nation could enter the world that the Industrial Revolution was bringing into being without answering basic social and economic questions, and European statesmen had done so as a matter of course since at least the end of the eighteenth century. But the Russians had kept such poor records that even as late as 1840 high officials could not say for certain how many people lived in any part of the empire including St. Petersburg province itself. If Russia were to follow the example of Europe, then the central offices of St. Petersburg needed to provide all the information that officials in the provinces had failed to supply. Because Russia's central government in the second quarter of the nineteenth century did not have the resources to take on that task, several semi-official organizations dedicated to exploring Russia and learning more about its people came into being in St. Petersburg. Most important was the Imperial Russian Geographical Society, founded in 1845 by scientists from the Academy of Sciences and officials from the Ministry of Internal Affairs and the Admiralty, who dedicated their leisure hours to studying the realities of life in Russia's provinces.

Led by Grand Duke Konstantin Nikolaevich, the Emperor's second son, the Russian Geographical Society explored Russia's Caspian coast, the Altai highlands, and the remote lands that lay beyond the Urals. Some of its members studied the huge fairs that took place every year along the Volga and in the Ukraine and examined the complex patterns of Russia's domestic trade. Then, from its headquarters on Demidov Lane halfway between the Haymarket and the Moika, the Society published all the data its explorers and scholars had compiled, and asked what this new knowledge meant for Russia's future. For the first time, some of Russia's statesmen began to see more clearly what course their nation needed to take if it hoped to remain among the community of Great Powers of which Peter the Great had made it a part. Their ideas would play an important part in shaping the Great Reforms that freed Russia's serfs in 1861.[33]

As the hub of the Russian Empire, St. Petersburg continued to stand at the center of its artistic and literary life, but the relationship between writers and autocrats changed dramatically during the fifty years after Catherine the Great. In the days of Alexander I, a gap began to open between St. Petersburg's writers and its rulers, and by the 1830s and 1840s that rift had become a chasm. Writers now disdained the sorts of favors that Catherine had showered on the literary figures of her day, and while St. Petersburg's poets had sung her praises in the 1780s, their successors preferred to condemn the tyranny of her grandsons.

Among the first of St. Petersburg's poets to turn from praise to criticism was Aleksandr Pushkin, who burst onto the city's literary scene in the early 1820s. As the author of caustic verses that condemned the brutality of serfdom and spoke of killing tyrants, Pushkin had been exiled to Russia's south in 1823, but his praises of liberty continued to stir the hearts of Petersburg's youth in ways that the writings of earlier poets had never done. Pushkin's poems told of "maidens come to flower to satisfy the whims of unfeeling scoundrels," and he cursed savage masters who had no feeling for the serfs they worked to exhaustion. Speaking of the terrible lives that Russia's serfs endured, he looked forward to a time when the emperor would grant them freedom, and he called upon the men and women who oppressed the masses to lighten the load their bondsfolk had to bear. "One could scarcely find a literate ensign in the army who did not know [Pushkin's verses] by heart," a young rebel remembered many years later. "Pushkin was the voice of his generation, a truly national poet the likes of whom Russia had never seen before."[34]

Pushkin's praise of freedom inflamed the hearts of men who had lost faith in their Tsar and run out of patience with oppression. On December 14, 1825, several hundred young officers of the Imperial Guards in St. Petersburg revolted, not to protect or extend their privileges (as those of their fathers and grandfathers who had overthrown several rulers in the eighteenth century had done) but to win human rights for all Russians. Armed and ready to give their lives in the cause of liberty, these noblemen led their men to the Senate Square on the morning of December 14, formed them in ranks around Falconet's Bronze Horseman, and called for a constitution and an end to autocracy. By late afternoon, the field guns that the young Emperor had ordered into action against them had shattered their formations and left the square and the Neva's icy surface wet with blood. Eventually, five were hanged and more than a hundred sent to prison in Siberia, but the sparks of their uprising continued to smolder. On that grim St. Petersburg day, the first shots had been fired in the struggle that would bring down the Romanovs ninety-one years and seventy-eight days later. St. Petersburg had become not only the hub of the Romanovs' empire, but also the seedbed of the new ferment that would lead to the Russian Revolution.[35]

The Decembrist Revolt tarnished the shining facade of Russia's imperial capital forever after. No longer was St. Petersburg a city of untrammeled imperial visions, unstained beauty, and "marvelous buildings gilded by the morning sun [and] reflected . . . in the clean mirror of the Neva," as a young poet had claimed just a decade earlier.[36] Now, amidst the elegance and harmony that radiated from the buildings of Quarenghi, Voronikhin, and Rossi, the men who had seen freedom when they had marched against the armies of Napoleon in Europe sensed a kind of capricious brutality that mirrored the fundamental nature of Russian life and society. For such men, St. Petersburg symbolized the raw power of Russia's autocrats, who wielded the authority to break men's bodies and torment their spirits. In the gleaming gold spire of Trezzini's Cathedral that rose above the Peter and Paul Fortress, they now saw not only the power of the Russians to triumph over Nature, but the awesome authority of the autocrats who ruled the dungeons nearby.

In exile on one of his family's estates some two hundred miles away from the capital in the province of Novgorod, Pushkin had not taken part in the Decembrist Revolt, although he later told the Emperor that he would have done so had he been in the capital. But the revolt darkened his vision of St. Petersburg, and he no longer portrayed the city in the optimistic and praiseworthy terms his predecessors had used. Now Pushkin saw St. Petersburg as a stunning achievement that had been bought at a terrible cost. In just more than five hundred lines of verse, his *Bronze Horseman* told of the rise of modern Russia, the genius of Peter the Great, and the ways in which Russia's imperial "idol astride a steed of bronze" had brought St. Petersburg into being. In a sense, Pushkin spoke no differently than his predecessors, but he also focused on how the masses' pain and suffering had shaped the city's history. It had been the unyielding will of Peter and his successors that had raised St. Petersburg from the swamps, and it was from that darker side of its history that Pushkin extracted his account of how Peter, the "mighty master of destiny," overcame the power of Nature to bring St. Petersburg into being.[37]

St. Petersburg's history showed all too clearly how Nature had rebelled against Peter's demands. As often as every other year, the Neva burst its banks, and its disease-ridden waters infected Petersburgers by the thousands with typhoid and giardiasis. Early in the summer of 1831, a cholera epidemic killed some six hundred people every day, and on June 23 the city's frantic lower classes rioted in the Haymarket until the Emperor Nicholas himself brought them to heel.[38] Then, in 1848, cholera returned with even greater force to strike one out of every twenty Petersburgers and kill one in thirty-six. "It spared no one," an eye-witness wrote of that terrible time. "Terror reigned throughout the entire summer."[39] St. Petersburg became a ghost town in a few short weeks, its streets deserted and its docks unused. "The city is empty," a schoolgirl confided to her diary at the beginning of July. "During the past two weeks about a hundred thousand people have left."[40] By the end of that summer, more than twelve thousand Petersburgers had died. Their deaths became yet another reminder that, although Peter and his successors had brought Nature under control, they had never truly conquered it.[41]

Peter the Great and the people who continued to bear the burdens he had imposed held equal places in Pushkin's *Bronze Horseman,* as the poet balanced the splendor of Russia's beautiful capital against its ongoing human cost. For the first time, a work of art revealed a dark undercurrent flowing beneath Peter's triumphs, and by the poem's end a sense of tragedy had all but blotted out the elation with which its first lines had lyricized the city's past and present. "There was a dreadful time, the memories / of which are still too fresh," Pushkin explained. "And you, my friends, will hear of it / in the tale that follows, and / what a sad tale it will be."[42] Destruction, dismay, and death all but overwhelmed the city's classical elegance in Pushkin's poetic account. Then, when the Neva's flood once again submerged Peter's city, Russia's first Emperor became no longer the far-seeing founder but a fearsome godlike brazen image whose awesome presence called to mind those ancient deities from whose temples St. Petersburg's builders had drawn their inspiration.

The Emperor Nicholas saw enough of an indictment in *The Bronze Horseman* to insist that it not be published in the poet's lifetime, and only after Pushkin was killed in a duel at the beginning of 1837 did he allow a "softened" version to appear. Russians did not see the original text in print until after the Revolution of 1905, but even the toned-down version that appeared in the late 1830s made it clear that the literary and historical image of St. Petersburg had begun to change.[43] For the rest of the century, Russians continued to see St. Petersburg as the capital of their empire, but their emotional ties to Moscow, as a more intimate place that drew them closer to their roots, grew stronger. As Russians became more conscious of their history, especially after Nikolai Karamzin began to publish the first volumes of his monumental *History of the Russian State* in 1818, Moscow became their point of contact with the distant past upon which Peter the Great had turned his back. Aleksandr Radishchev had first pointed the Russians in that direction, when he had cast his criticisms of the empire and its Empress in terms of a journey from St. Petersburg *to* Moscow, not the reverse, and others had followed soon after that. "O, Moscow, darling daughter of Russia, where can your equal be found?" the poet Ivan Dmitriev had asked not long after Alexander I had ascended the throne. "How," his friend Evgenii Baratynskii had added, "can one not love one's own dear Moscow?"[44]

As St. Petersburg became Russia's imperial city, it surrendered any sense of warmth and intimacy to Moscow, to which Russians' hearts were drawn even more strongly after the soldiers of Napoleon's Grande Armée ravaged it in 1812. On an emotional plane, Russians now relished Moscow's charming disorder, while St. Petersburg's regularity seemed somehow to have become too rigid and austere. "Straight, correct, evened out, symmetrical, monotonous, and complete, Petersburg can serve as an emblem of our life," one of Pushkin's friends remarked. "In people, you can't tell Ivan from Peter; in time, today from tomorrow: everything is the same."[45] St. Petersburg thus presented Russians of the 1830s and 1840s with a dilemma. Elegant, harmonious, and splendid in so many ways, a window to the West, and a monument to Russia's modern achievements, the city had become also cold, its beauty as deceptive as the White Nights that turned so quickly into darkness at noon.

In addition to being a capital that represented the breadth and depth of their imperial vision, Russians also saw imperial St. Petersburg as a city of contrasts and contradictions: of unimaginable wealth and wrenching poverty, of elegance and shabbiness, of cold, crystalline harmony and churning, burning disorder, the residence of an autocrat who constantly had to be reassured that his power reached beyond the room in which he was standing and the person to whom he was speaking. Except for the palaces and townhouses of the city's great aristocrats, virtually every residence in St. Petersburg's center embraced those contrasts among the rich and well-born who lived in spacious, high-ceilinged quarters in the front, and the poor and wretched who crowded into the cramped flats in the rear. Every Russian writer who came after Pushkin knew all of these dualities in the city as indisputable facts. But none captured them more brilliantly or with greater urgency than the tormented novelist and playwright Nikolai Gogol.

Born and raised in an out-of-the way village in the southwestern corner of the Russian Empire, Gogol came from a family of doting, overprotective Cossack farmers. "He was a trembling mouse of a boy, with dirty hands and greasy locks, and pus trickling out of his ear," Vladimir Nabokov wrote half a century ago. "He gorged himself with sticky sweets. His schoolmates avoided touching the books he had been using."[46] Shy, sheltered, and shunned at school, Gogol had set off in search of a future that would raise him above the schoolmates who had mocked him, and he gave himself over to dreams of fame and fortune that would never be. "Fate is driving me off to Petersburg," he announced as he set out for the capital at the age of nineteen. As if trying to absorb the city's aura of success, he hurried to gorge himself in its pastry shops, sample its exotic fruits, and explore its many streets, squares, and islands, all the while holding fast to his dreams of finding success in this center of power and possibilities. "It would be terrible to live and leave no mark of my existence behind," he confided in one of his letters. The powerful mystique of St. Petersburg convinced him that a glorious future lay ahead.[47]

Gogol hoped to become a statesman, an artist, a poet, or an actor, but when a few months had passed and he had become none of those things, he settled for a job as a humble clerk in a government office. Trapped in a grimy corner of the bureaucratic underground, he turned angrily against the city he had embraced with such hope. "The idea of the city," he wrote bitterly, "is emptiness taken to the highest degree."[48] But St. Petersburg, which had disappointed him so bitterly, seemed even worse than that. It was, he insisted, demonic and perverse, a place of shifting shadows, "a reflection in a blurred mirror, an eerie medley of objects put to the wrong use," as Nabokov once explained.[49] The St. Petersburg of Peter the Great had become living proof of the autocrat's power to defy Nature, and

Catherine had made it the ultimate expression of rationality and higher harmony. But Gogol's Petersburg now defied rationality on every plane. "The devil himself lights the street lamps only in order to show that everything is not really as it seems," he once wrote.[50] St. Petersburg thus became a place in which "the smug, the vulgar, and the callous are here to stay," as an American critic later explained, while "the pure of heart are crushed by the unbearable discrepancy between their dreams and 'revolting' reality."[51]

And so Gogol created a new image of St. Petersburg that would thrive alongside the imperial vision until the Revolution of 1917. This was to be the St. Petersburg of Dostoevskii and of Andrei Belyi, whose novel *Petersburg* presented, on the eve of World War I, a grim vision of nightmares, distorted perspectives, and shadowy people clustered at the edge of a cataclysm almost too fearsome to describe.[52] Belyi's Petersburg would be Gogol's city of fog and perversity brought to the brink of Apocalypse, a place "of things going backwards the faster they moved forward," as Nabokov said.[53] For Belyi, St. Petersburg would be so far removed from Russian experience as to have become completely "non-Russian."[54] And, as Gogol and Dostoevskii had done before him, Belyi stripped the city of any hint of romance and denied it any place in the larger scheme of Russia's history. Yet to fully understand the nature of Belyi's St. Petersburg, one needs first to see it from Gogol's point of view. For it was Gogol who first presented Russia's capital city in alien, disembodied terms, and it was he who first saw it not as a promise of what Russia could become but as a monument to what Russia ought not to be.

As Pushkin had done when writing from the perspective of his hero in *The Bronze Horseman*, Gogol portrayed St. Petersburg as a fearsome place. As the true enemy of the tens of thousands of men and women who had to struggle to make a living in Russia's capital, it was as hostile as it had been when Peter the Great's adjutants had driven the first hapless workers there to fill its swamps in 1703. Although it might seem warm and inviting to the casual visitor, Gogol's St. Petersburg was a detached place in which a perverse fascination with rank outweighed all human feeling. It was an anonymous city of endless squares from which there seemed to be no escape and where time had little meaning. At the center of it all, forming the greatest of all the city's many contradictions, was the Nevskii Prospekt, at one and the same time enchanting and repulsive. "Oh, do not trust this Nevskii Prospekt," Gogol warned his readers. "I always wrap myself more tightly in my cloak whenever I walk along it, and I try not to take notice of things I encounter. Everything's an illusion. Everything's a dream. Everything's not what it seems!"[55]

The Nevskii Prospekt, Gogol hurriedly explained, made up the very heart and soul of St. Petersburg, for its pavement and sidewalks formed the spinal cord along which flowed all the forces and impulses that shaped life in Russia's capital. In St. Petersburg, Gogol wrote, the Nevskii Prospect was "everything." It was the "universal communication of St. Petersburg," the one place in the city to which people went by choice rather than out of necessity. To see who came and went, what they sought, and how they sought it one needed only to stroll along the sidewalks of the Nevskii Prospekt, sit in its pastry shops, sample its endless offerings, and peruse the wares of its shops. Everything and everyone could be found there or within sight of it. "No directory or inquiry office will provide such reliable information as the Nevskii Prospekt," Gogol insisted. "All powerful Nevskii Prospekt!" he went on. "What a quick phantasmagoria is performed on it in the course of a day! How many changes occur there in the course of a single day and night!"[56] During Gogol's time and afterward, the Nevskii Prospekt held the key to St. Petersburg. To know the Nevskii Prospekt in all its complexity meant to know the city's deepest secrets. That was why Gogol gave its name to one of his best stories. And that is why a detailed tour of the Nevskii Prospekt can provide us now with the story of St. Petersburg life during the reign of Nicholas I, when serfdom was living out its last days and Russia's Old Regime was about to be transformed.

# FIVE

# THE
# NEVSKII PROSPEKT

N O CITY IN THE WESTERN WORLD boasts anything like the Nevskii Prospekt. In the nineteenth century, it was more grand than Oxford Street in London; more so even than the Rue de Rivoli or the Champs Elysées in Paris. Rome had no counterpart, and neither did Madrid, New York, Amsterdam, or Berlin. In imperial St. Petersburg, the Nevskii Prospekt was the place to see and be seen, where the buildings were the cleanest and the shops the best-stocked with the latest fashions. Gogol once wrote that young ladies turned their heads to its glittering shop windows "as sunflowers turn to the sun."[1] Young officers and well-bred dandies followed these elegantly attired creatures in the hopes of winning a favorable nod, while others preened in the reflections of shop windows, perhaps hoping to draw the attention of passersby away from the other sights and sounds that swirled around them. On the ever-changing stage of the Nevskii Prospekt, the drama of St. Petersburg's life played out, hour by hour, and day after day. People brought their hopes and desires there, and from it they drew inspiration that added meaning to their lives. For the Nevskii Prospekt was most of all a state of mind and a way of looking at the world. Somehow, it made people different, more in tune with the world around them.[2]

As if precision could project reality, lithographers seeking to capture the essence of St. Petersburg in the 1830s and 1840s rendered every detail of the buildings on the Nevskii Prospekt and reproduced every sign and advertisement that hung in its shop windows. Such was especially true of Vasilii Sadovnikov, a former serf who produced a *Panorama of the Nevskii Prospekt,* in which a pair of engravings, each measuring forty-seven feet in length and eleven inches in width, portray both sides of the street. Until age thirty-eight the property of Natalia Golitsyna, the willful princess who served as Pushkin's model for the despotic dowager in his *Queen of Spades,* Sadovnikov produced his famed *Panorama* just a few years after his liberation.[3] Here, by looking through the viewing aperture and rolling the huge lithograph from one reel to the other, viewers could pass the Kazan Cathedral, the City Hall, the Merchants' Arcade, and the Public Library all in the space of the thousand meters that separated the palace that Rastrelli had built for the Stroganovs (at the intersection of Nevskii Prospekt and the Moika) and the Anichkov Palace that stood where the avenue crossed the Fontanka. On the opposite side of the Nevskii Prospekt, viewers saw the Dutch Church, the Roman Catholic Church of St. Catherine, the Lutheran Church of Saints Peter and Paul, the Armenian Church of St. Catherine, and scores of shops, including the renowned pastry shop of the confectioner Filippov. Each had a specialty, and each served a particular clientele. All this seemed somehow known to Petersburgers beforehand, as part of the sense of order that pervaded the entire city during the reign of Nicholas I between 1825 and 1855.

This sense of order first blended with modern technology and design in 1848, just a little more than a decade after Sadovnikov had engraved his huge *Panorama,* when St. Petersburg followed the example of several other European cities and opened a glass-covered arcade. Linking the Nevskii Prospekt to Italianskaia Street that paralleled it on the northeast, this "Passazh," or Passage, housed two floors of shops and cafes in which Petersburgers could shop and relax to the music of a small orchestra that played every afternoon. Like the arcades of Milan, London, and especially Paris, St. Petersburg's Passazh drew large numbers of people in bad weather, and it offered a modern alternative to the open-fronted shops of the Merchants' Arcade that Vallin de la Mothe had built on the other side of the Nevskii Prospekt in the reign of Catherine the Great. Yet the Passazh did not fundamentally change the personality of St. Petersburg's main thoroughfare. Especially on its so-called Parade Section that extended from

*An early view of the Nevskii Prospekt. (Courtesy of the Russian National Library, St. Petersburg)*

the Admiralty to the Fontanka, the Nevskii Prospekt continued to reflect the pulse of the city in the same way it had a hundred years before.

The way in which its personality changed with the seasons and the time of day made the Nevskii Prospekt particularly striking. First came the early-morning smells that accompanied its first hints of movement. To Gogol, the entire city smelled like freshly baked bread at that hour, while his friend Apollon Grigorev insisted that "every Petersburg street has its own special smell, peculiar to it alone. Usually early in the morning or late in the evening, in cold weather," Grigorev continued, "these smells become almost palpable, thickening into an ill-smelling fog or warm steam."[4] During the early hours, the city's upper classes remained fast asleep, and even its middle-class shopkeepers and merchants scarcely stirred, especially in the winter, when daylight did not come before ten-thirty in the morning. Peasant workmen, draymen, water carriers, an occasional government clerk, and a flock of beggar women plying their trade on church steps reigned supreme as dawn broke, making the Nevskii Prospekt the unchallenged preserve of the lower classes, whose rough manners and cruder language kept proper ladies from setting foot there anytime before the shops opened at noon. At this time of day,

*Two sections of Vasilii Sadovnikov's* Panorama of Nevskii Prospekt. *The left panel shows the Police Bridge over the Moika River; the right (next page) depicts the State Duma.*

Gogol observed, "no matter how you may be dressed, even if you have on a workman's cap instead of a proper hat, and even if your collar juts too far out over your tie, no one will pay you any mind at all."[5] The Nevskii Prospekt was central to no gentleman's or lady's plan or purpose while the masses reigned. It was simply a thoroughfare used to accomplish particular tasks and errands.

As early morning moved toward noon, the Nevskii Prospekt grew more lively, not all at once but bit by bit. Shopkeepers began sweeping their steps, polishing their counters and windows, and putting out stale pastries and bread for passing beggars. Gradually the people on the sidewalks became more animated. Then as the noontime gun at the Peter and Paul Fortress boomed out over the Neva, tutors and governesses appeared, explaining to the children assigned to their care what each shop sold and what lessons could be learned by observing what each window contained. As they strolled in the orderly manner that proper behavior required, the French governesses and English tutors of St. Petersburg commented on their charges' posture, manners, and deportment, telling them to straighten their backs and lift their shoulders, hold their heads in the proper way and move their arms in a particular manner. Then, just as the workmen and draymen had done earlier, this group also disappeared. At the stroke of two, the crowd on the Nevskii changed once again.

Afternoon on the Nevskii Prospekt belonged to those men and women whose self-esteem allowed them to believe that they served a higher purpose in St. Petersburg's life. "They are people occupied with strolling, and with reading newspapers in corner pastry shops," Gogol explained, and their main concern was to measure themselves against the crowd around them. The people on the Nevskii Prospekt at this time of day, he re-

marked, were the sort who stared at your shoes as you approached and then turned to stare at your coattails after you passed, and they had raised to a fine art the use of shrugs, sideward glances, and signals to indicate where one another stood. "Here you will encounter that special smile— the very perfection of the art—which at times may cause you to dissolve with pleasure," Gogol confided as he took readers into his confidence. "Sometimes, it can make you feel lower than the ground you walk on, and at others it will lift you higher than the Admiralty spire itself."[6]

An army of self-important officials—all clad in the green uniforms of the civil service—soon mingled with this self-indulgent throng. Lean junior clerks trying to look more important than they were, and haughty superiors whom a lifetime in the emperor's service had rewarded with positions as office section chiefs and department heads all joined the Nevskii Prospekt crowd in the afternoons. Like the strollers who had come a little earlier, these self-styled grandees sometimes bore elegantly dressed ladies on their arms, each of whom measured herself against the crowd, as did the man she accompanied. What did it mean to be dressed in beaver instead of marten? Did one dare to appear in the black side-whiskers of a Foreign Ministry official, even if one served only in the Ministry of Justice or the Ministry of Internal Affairs? Were one's lapels too narrow? One's neckline too revealing? One's bonnet too small, or one's shawl too large? Was one's dress the height of this year's fashion in Paris? Or was it the height of fashion in St. Petersburg (and hence at least a year too old for Paris)?

At four o'clock, this self-important crowd drifted away and left the Nevskii Prospekt to an awkward handful of misfits, whose eccentricities entitled them to be there at times when few others were present. These reigned on the avenue while the lamplighters worked, each with his ladder, to light the streetlamps that made the Nevskii Prospekt one of the best-lit avenues in Europe. For an hour or two, there was a sense of anticipation. Then, as daylight gave way to gaslight, another metamorphosis occurred and the Nevskii Prospekt came alive once again. People now moved more quickly, and with a more obvious sense of purpose. It was as if the flickering light of the streetlamps—"that alluring, miraculous light," as Gogol once said—had somehow softened the daytime order and regularity.[7] At a time when uniformity was the order of the day, the men and women on the Nevskii Prospekt seemed to become individuals only at night.

But who were these people individually? What did they hope to accomplish? How did they live? What were their lives like? Nearly twice the size of Moscow by the 1840s, St. Petersburg's population was approaching half a million, of which seven out of every ten were men, and more than two out of every five were serfs. Many of these lower-class people worked on such huge construction projects as the Cathedrals of Kazan and St. Isaac's, the Senate, the Synod, the General Staff Headquarters, and the Admiralty, each of which required thousands of laborers willing to work up to sixteen hours a day. Others worked at shoemaking, tailoring, baking, and scores of other trades, and about one out of ten worked in the new cotton mills that had begun to spring up in the city's Vyborg and Okhta quarters.[8] Such people usually lived from hand to mouth at the bottom of St. Petersburg's economic pyramid. Yet, compared to Russia's villagers who lived in wretched poverty, the men who came to St. Petersburg looking for work found the effort worthwhile, for a man could earn more cash there in a few weeks than an entire serf household could assemble in several months of work in the fields.[9]

Although their wages were paltry, tens of thousands of peasants from villages within a radius of several hundred miles came to try their luck in Russia's capital. This brought into St. Petersburg men who had never before seen a paved street, a proper staircase, or a shop that sold boots or clothing. For such people the prospect of being cast adrift in the city's vastness was so terrifying that most tried to offset it by staying close to others from their home village or county. For that reason, every peasant who came in search of work tried to find someone from home who already worked in the city, and this meant that newcomers usually learned the trades and skills of those who had come before. Waiters therefore tended to come from one province, hackney drivers from another, and carpenters from yet a third. This helped the lower classes to maintain a sense of identity within the emptiness of the city and kept them in touch with family and friends back home. Some of these men and their descen-

dants continued to maintain ties with their villages for several generations. Even at the time of the Revolution of 1917, the practice of going to
St. Petersburg to work for a few months or years and then coming home
continued to be passed down from fathers to sons.

At the other end of the economic spectrum from servants and wage
workers stood St. Petersburg's aristocrats, who numbered around fifty
thousand at the middle of the nineteenth century. Some of these held
important posts in the government, and others served in the military.
Many had already retired from government service, since it was considered perfectly respectable to do so the moment one reached the rank of
major or its equivalent in the civil service. Still others formed a part of the
court and lived on the income their estates produced. The richest of these
men and women enjoyed yearly incomes in the tens of thousands of
rubles, and their townhouses and palaces required the services of scores
(in a few cases, hundreds) of servants who were serfs. Their luxuries came
from abroad or from St. Petersburg's finest shops, but many of their daily
provisions came from estates they owned in other parts of Russia. Every
fall, hundreds of serfs appeared in St. Petersburg bearing their villages'
annual payments of honey, dried mushrooms, grain, meat, and fowl that
they were required to bring to their masters. With such wealth at their
disposal, St. Petersburg's aristocrats lived on only a slightly more modest
scale than their sovereigns, but only a comparative handful belonged to
their ranks.

In fact, barely more than one St. Petersburg aristocrat in twenty actually owned property in the city in those days, but many others rented from
the few who did. The poet Pushkin paid 2,500 rubles a year (the pay for
between 3,000 and 4,000 days' work for a wage laborer) to rent a seven-
room apartment in a fashionable part of town from one of the city's
wealthiest senators in the 1830s, and others paid similar sums to live on
the Millionnaia and in the vicinity of St. Isaac's Square.[10] Other non-pro-
letarians (including many down-at-the-heels aristocrats) paid far less for
more modest quarters, even in the center of town, for nearly every town-
house and apartment building had its rear flats, in which artisans, tradesfolk, and lesser officials crowded into tiny rooms without proper places to
cook or to wash. As in the outlying workers' districts, the poverty that festered in these rear-end flats grew worse with the passing of time. As the
city grew more crowded and the demand for cheap housing increased,
landlords offered less and less space at higher prices. By the 1820s, people

*The Passazh, a shopping arcade at 46 Nevskii Prospekt. (Photo by K. Bulla. Courtesy of the Central State Archive of Kino-Photo-Phono Documents, St. Petersburg)*

were living in rooms rather than flats. Twenty years later, the rooms had become "corners" in which a blanket or bedspread divided one tenement from another.

In the rear of courtyards shielded from those who came and went in the fashionable apartments facing the street, St. Petersburg's lesser folk made their way through unlit passageways clogged with refuse. "It was dark and smelled of putrid water and cabbage," a description of one man's attempt to reach his basement flat in the 1840s began. "He stumbled against a tub and it spilled over," it continued. "He stumbled against a pile of logs and almost fell again."[11] Such obstacles often filled the entryways to those nether regions of which Dostoevskii was soon to write in *Crime and Punishment*. All through the St. Petersburg of Nicholas I, such back-alley entries stood as the antithesis to the order that reigned in the city's squares and streets. What seemed to be neat and polished on the outside too often turned out to be rotten within. In many ways, the city was becoming a pastiche that appeared to be better than it really was, and for that illusion, Petersburgers soon were to pay a heavy price.

*Nikolai Gogol*

*Fedor Dostoevskii*

Many of the lesser officials who made up the majority of those forty thousand impoverished civil servants in St. Petersburg who had not yet reached noble rank lived in straitened circumstances such as these. The costs of food and lodging consumed nearly all of their salaries, and it was not uncommon for two or three of them to share meal tickets in the city's cheapest eating houses because each could not afford an entire ticket for himself. To buy a new overcoat or a second pair of shoes required so many months of careful saving and sacrifice that very few of Gogol's readers must have been surprised to learn that the hero of his short story "The Overcoat" went mad when his new coat was stolen. Dostoevskii and Gogol are to be taken literally when they write of poor clerks coming home to a cot under the stairs at night, for that was a common form of housing for men with education but no wealth in St. Petersburg of the 1840s.[12] As mid-century approached, the gap in means that separated the top of literate Petersburg society from its bottom was nearly as large as that which divided the city's nobles from its lower classes.

Because St. Petersburg formed the political and cultural center of Russia, every educated man who dreamed of making his way in the emperor's service hoped to find a position there. But Russia's central government enjoyed the luxury of having more educated people than its offices could accommodate, and not all those who sought places in St. Petersburg's civil service actually found them. Those who did so had to live on subsistence wages unless their families were well enough off to supplement their meager earnings. By the 1840s, hundreds of men with good educations were working as humble copyists in St. Petersburg's huge office buildings. And, within twenty years, the government's failure to make use of their talents or to pay them a living wage would help to bring a revolutionary movement into being.

The rank and file of the revolutionary movement in St. Petersburg would eventually come from its factory workers, who in the 1840s and 1850s lived in conditions that made even the lives of the city's poorest civil servants seem enviable. Substantial numbers of factory workers did not become a part of the city's life until the 1840s, when their ranks suddenly doubled to almost twelve thousand in a decade. Then, as cotton mills and metalworking plants began to take shape in the Vyborg and Okhta quarters and in some of the districts between the Fontanka River and the outlying Obvodnyi Canal, St. Petersburg began to see the first of those workers' barracks and tenements that had become so common in the West. In 1844, the first government commission to investigate workers' living conditions in the city found as many as fifty men, women, and children, including several with tuberculosis and syphilis, living in a single room that measured no more than twenty feet on a side, and reported that it was not unusual for twenty people to be crowded into a single tenement flat.[13] By the middle of the century it had become common to find workers living in dormitories that allotted them sleeping spaces that were less than two meters wide. Shortages of even this type of accommodation soon meant that sleeping spaces had to be rented in shifts. Such arrangements gave workers spaces on the barracks' plank sleeping platform for twelve hours. Then the next shift arrived, and the first group, whether sick or well, had to relinquish their places.

Even though ugly hovels and filthy tenements became more a part of St. Petersburg life after 1850, the construction of cheap housing and proper sanitation facilities failed to keep pace with the growth of the city's proletariat. By the late 1860s, when public health physicians estimated that more than thirty thousand tons of human feces were lying unattended in the courtyards of buildings in the city's poorer sections, even oozing cellars that filled with excrement-tainted liquid whenever it rained were being rented to workers by greedy landlords. As cholera, typhus, and tuberculosis festered in such slums, St. Petersburg won the distinction of suffering the highest mortality rate of any major city in Europe.[14] Nor were those the only problems. "Drunkenness is unprecedented, even for Russia," one diarist wrote as he lamented the social and moral malaises that ravaged the city's poor. "There have been cases of fatal alcohol poisoning," he added, "even among fourteen- and fifteen-year-olds."[15] Drunkenness had become such an acute social problem by the mid–1860s that one of the city's leading newspapers warned that "it forces us to think about it as a social catastrophe."[16] This was the way of life of which Dostoevskii wrote with such pity and passion as he described how the craving for vodka drove men to sell even their daughters into prostitution. In Dostoevskii's world of destitution, in which fate seemed to have dragged so many into St. Petersburg's lower depths, men of learning committed the basest crimes just to prove that they still had the power to make choices in a world where forces beyond their control seemed to shape human destiny.

If poverty bred drunkenness, it also bred vice. Some two thousand registered prostitutes filled 150 officially licensed brothels in mid-nineteenth-century St. Petersburg, and at least that many more walked the streets without proper official yellow "passports." Many of these crowded the sidewalks in the part of town where the Nevskii Prospekt and Ligovskii Prospekt intersected, but no area of the city lacked its share of streetwalkers. Most had left Russia's villages hoping to find a better life, only to learn they could not survive by any other means. Brothels boasting the youngest and most attractive women catered to the nobility, high officials, and well-heeled army officers. Lesser establishments featured those women who had been treated less kindly by nature or had begun the downward drift that the ravages of age and disease made inevitable. Those whom disease or violence did not claim earlier eventually reached that bottom rung, on which stood those painted and aged unfortunates who sought out customers in back streets and alleys, and accommodated them in courtyards and nearby stairways for a handful of kopeks.[17]

At the epicenter of St. Petersburg's cauldron of poverty and drunkenness stood the Haymarket, to which in the 1760s and 1770s Catherine the Great had encouraged peasants from the nearby countryside to bring their produce for sale.[18] Since then, the huge square had evolved into an arena for pickpockets, hucksters, and petty crooks, who worked the crowds that thronged it from morning to night buying food piled up in vendors' stalls, and pawing through used clothing and various other odds and ends that were offered for sale. Peasants in their greasy sheepskin coats, knee-high boots, and rusty black trousers, working women with their heads wrapped in bright-print kerchiefs, cooks and servants of the well-to-do, and a smattering of aristocrats and various other sorts all made their way through the square and its nearby alleys, where, one observer noted, "the dealers themselves were not much cleaner than their goods."[19] In years to come, the Haymarket would add three huge glass-covered areas, somewhat like Les Halles in Paris, for which vendors would pay more than 200,000 rubles a year in rent. But in the mid-nineteenth century, it remained open to the elements except for the scant shelter that its flimsy slab wood and canvas stalls offered.[20] This was the "belly" of the city in more senses than one, to which all material things at some time flowed.

In winter, St. Petersburg's damp, biting wind cut the Haymarket's vendors to the bone, and the sour smell of cabbage soup oozed through the small window vents of the surrounding tenements to clog the nearby alleys with its putrid odor. In summer a rotten stench rose from the meat and produce that festered in the heat to combine with the sweat of unwashed bodies into a fetid fog. Anything could be had in the Haymarket, and what had been stolen the previous night could often be retrieved for a suitable price the following morning. In the narrow streets that led into the market's central open space, patrons moved between scores of pothouses and cheap brothels as their thirst and inclination dictated. Here men could be drunk for days, and women lost for a lifetime. Yet the irony was that the Haymarket stood less than half a mile from the Nevskii Prospekt. From its center one could walk to St. Isaac's and the Kazan cathedrals in less than fifteen minutes, and the Winter Palace stood no more than a ten-minute walk farther.

Clogged with people from St. Petersburg's lower depths, the Haymarket also marked the starting point from which lower-class tradesmen began their climb into the ranks of the city's respectable merchants. From stalls in the Haymarket, ambitious hucksters moved on to better surroundings, starting with shops in nearby Shchukin Arcade in the vicinity of Chernyshev Bridge where "arcade" denotes not a glass-enclosed shopping street but rather several alleys lined with rough wood shops. Here, a visitor

*The Haymarket, a short walk from the Passazh, drew St. Petersburgers of every description to its wood and canvas stalls. (Courtesy of the Central State Archive of Kino-Photo-Phono Documents, St. Petersburg)*

noted, a shopper could find rare incunabula mixed with "books from every country in the world . . . soiled, stained, and worm-eaten," all sorts of leather goods, furs, lithographs, second-hand furniture, pottery, silver, and, of course, icons of all shapes and sizes. Sellers in the Shchukin Arcade (and the Mariinskii and Apraksin markets nearby) often had already risen into the ranks of the *meshchanstvo*, or petite bourgeoisie, while men and women who worked in various trades in the shops around them were registered as *remeslenniki*, or artisans in the broadest sense of the term. Hence, tailors, seamstresses, carpenters, cobblers, harness-makers, bakers, and workers in some three-score other trades all were among St. Petersburg's artisans, and their combined numbers totaled almost fifteen thousand at mid-century.[21]

At the very top of the pyramid formed by St. Petersburg's non-noble tradesfolk stood the great merchants, with businesses worth tens and hundreds of thousands of rubles. Some owned the city's new cotton mills, while others, like the Putilovs, had built its first metalworking plants. Still others had made fortunes by exchanging for the luxury goods of Europe the furs, dried rhubarb root, and other commodities that poured into St. Petersburg from Siberia and China. Such merchants and their families lived like well-to-do aristocrats, with elegant townhouses, expensive carriages, and armies of servants. But these were few and far between in comparison to the much larger number of petty traders and artisans who lived on a far more modest scale. Even in 1850, St. Petersburg was still mainly a city of nobles, soldiers, civil servants, and serfs. Because foreigners continued to play a large part in trade and manufacture, Russian industrialists would only begin to exert a significant influence on the life of St. Petersburg during the half-century that still lay ahead.

Yet the influence of modern industry and the technology of the Industrial Revolution were beginning to be felt in St. Petersburg, even in the 1830s and 1840s. The first steamboats in Russia appeared on the Neva in 1828, and they made the thirty-five-mile voyage from St. Petersburg to Kronstadt naval base with the "unbelievable speed" of just three hours.[22] Soon after that, the railroad followed, the first being a train that ran from St. Petersburg to Tsarskoe Selo some fifteen miles away. The brainchild of an Austrian engineer, the railroad took nearly eighteen months to build despite the flat terrain and lack of any natural obstacles, but it made possible the trip from St. Petersburg to Tsarskoe Selo in the astounding time (for that day and age) of thirty-five minutes—from "the capital to the cabaret" as one of the Emperor's advisers nastily remarked in referring to the hotel, dance hall, and restaurant that had been built at the station.[23] Then the railroad came to the center of St. Petersburg itself. Horse-drawn trolleys that carried passengers from Znamenskaia Square to the English Embankment had appeared on the Nevskii Prospekt in 1847, and in 1851 a true railroad in the form of a line that connected Moscow and St. Petersburg opened its terminus on Znamenskaia Square in the Nicholas Station designed by the architect Konstantin Thon.[24]

Even though they shared the Nevskii Prospekt as the artery along which the life of their city flowed, St. Petersburgers of the 1830s and 1840s had very little else in common. Serfs, aristocrats, civil servants, and tradesmen all had their own special interests, and no group shared any sense of common purpose with any other. Those who lived in the squalid rear flats of an apartment building were of little consequence to the well-to-do nobles and merchants who lived in the front, nor did the poor clerks, artisans, and

*Horse-drawn trolleys on the Nevskii Prospekt near Anichkov Palace, 1903. (Courtesy of the Central State Archive of Kino-Photo-Phono Documents, St. Petersburg)*

tradesfolk who shared those rear courtyard lodgings have any idea about the lives of those who came and went through the building's front.

What Petersburgers did have in common in those days were the natural disasters they faced. From the moment Peter the Great's soldiers had set the first timbers in place for the Peter and Paul Fortress, the inhabitants of the city had faced the twin scourges of fire and flood. Every Petersburger knew the feeling of helplessness that gripped the hero in Pushkin's *Bronze Horseman* as the waters of the great November 7, 1824, flood swept his fiancée away, for the inundations had come on an average of every second or third year since the city's founding.

During the reign of Catherine the Great, the Catherine Canal had been dug through the city's center to help drain off rising water, and the Obvodnyi Canal had been built for the same purpose in the reign of

Alexander I. Caused in part by contrary winds that forced the waters of the Neva and the nearby Finnish Gulf into its streets with almost no warning, St. Petersburg's three greatest floods came in 1777, 1824, and 1924, in all three cases covering most of the city with more than ten feet of water.[25]

Of the three, the flood of 1824 was the worst, with the water rising higher than thirteen feet in the space of a single night and morning. "The savage waves raged across the Palace Square . . . and poured along the Nevskii Prospekt like a wide river all the way to the Anichkov Bridge [over the Fontanka]," one eyewitness wrote. "Around two o'clock in the afternoon," he continued, "the Military Governor General Count Milo-radovich appeared [on Nevskii Prospekt] in a boat rowed by twelve oars-men to try to give help and comfort to anyone he could. But by three o'clock the water had started to recede, and by seven, people were back driving in their carriages once again."[26] By then, the journalist and profes-sor Ivan Martynov had seen his entire library of rare books float out a broken window and disappear down a water-filled street on Vasilevskii Is-land to join people clinging to doors, beams, and parts of broken roofs. Recently buried caskets unearthed by the flood floated by, along with fur-niture and all sorts of goods from nearby warehouses. All across the city, people struggled to escape the surging waters, while navy cutters follow-ing the lead of Count Miloradovich plied the streets and squares to rescue anyone they could reach.[27]

If floods usually struck late in the fall, fires came at almost any time of the year. Every Petersburger knew the terror of seeing flames soar high into the air and leap from one roof to another, sometimes even shooting across canals and squares. Perhaps for that reason, the men and women of the city had seemed particularly drawn to *The Last Day of Pompeii*, the huge painting that the artist Karl Briullov had created in Rome in the early 1830s. Already acclaimed by Sir Walter Scott as an epic, and deco-rated with the gold medal of the French Academy, Briullov's vision of fire raining from the skies drew Petersburgers by the thousands when it reached the Academy of Fine Arts in the fall of 1834. "Men of power and artists, socialites and scholars, simple folk and craftsmen—all are imbued with the desire to see Briullov's painting," one newspaper supplement re-ported. Everyone seemed drawn to the artist's image of the terror that Nature could inflict upon men and women whose ancestors had dared to defy it. As Aleksandr Herzen, one of Russia's first émigré dissidents wrote a decade before he fled to the West, "the image of a wild, irrational force, destroying people" applied not only to Pompeii. It was also the "inspiration of Petersburg."[28]

Fire that had seemed to rain from the skies had reshaped St. Petersburg in a fundamental way during the summers of 1736 and 1737, when hundreds of wattle and daub shelters in the areas that would eventually become the fashionable Admiralty quarters were burned away during the course of several weeks. Whether the fires were accidental or deliberately set was never determined, but they enabled the Empress Anna's planners to lay out the designs that would determine the city's shape for more than two hundred years. Fire also had been the Empress Elizabeth's greatest fear while she had lived in a temporary wooden palace waiting for Rastrelli to rebuild the Winter Palace in the late 1750s, and in fact a huge fire had consumed part of the city just a few months before she died. Catherine the Great saw enough fires start in the crowded merchant warehouses on Vasilevskii Island during the early years of her reign to encourage St. Petersburg's merchants to spread their storehouses across the city so as to lessen the chances for further damage. Her grandson forbade all open flames in the Shchukin Arcade except in chapels and shops that sold icons for fear that a careless spark would set its tangle of slabwood and rags aflame. And throughout the city it was forbidden to smoke on the street as watchmen anxiously looked for any sign that a flame might be about to break of control.[29]

None of these measures prevented the huge fire of February 2, 1836, that began in a popular burlesque theater on the edge of Admiralty Square and claimed more than 120 lives. Nor did they keep the Winter Palace itself from going up in flames on December 17, 1837. That night, the Emperor Nicholas was at St. Petersburg's Bolshoi Theater to see a ballet in which the great Marie Taglioni was dancing the leading role. On receiving word that a fire had started, he rushed to the burning palace and oversaw much of the Imperial Guards' effort to save its furnishings. When asked by one of his aides what papers needed to be removed from his study, he replied: "None. Just save for me the small case of letters which my wife wrote to me when she was my bethrothed."[30] Driven back by the flames in one part of the palace, he ordered a detachment of Guards to retreat, and when they persisted in trying to remove a huge mirror from the wall, he hurled a pair of binoculars and broke it. "Your lives are worth a lot more to me than a mirror, lads," he roared above the din. "Get out!"[31]

By that time, virtually everything else in the Palace had been saved, including all of the priceless paintings that the empresses Elizabeth,

Catherine, and their successors had bought in the West. But the palace itself burned for three more days, with Nicholas and his wife watching from the private apartments that Rossi had created for Foreign Minister Karl Vasilievich Nesselrode in the Foreign Office just across the Palace Square. "In a year, I will celebrate Easter in the Winter Palace," Nicholas promised as the last embers died.[32] And, thanks in large measure to the efforts of Count Petr Kleinmikhel, who drove his serf workmen so unmercifully that scores died before the rebuilding was finished, he did so on Easter 1839. "He is certainly one of the most, if not the most unpopular of men in Russia," one observer wrote of Kleinmikhel as he tried to explain the confidence that Nicholas placed in his advice, "[but he is] a man of great industry—in availing himself of the labor of others—[and] . . . he has the faculty [to render] order out of disorder."[33]

Done according to the directions of the architect Vasilii Stasov, the reconstruction of the Winter Palace preserved some of its most striking features and added new ones. Stasov rebuilt Rastrelli's famed Jordan Staircase according to its original plans, and he did the same with the Gallery of 1812 that Rossi had designed and completed in 1826. Filled with 332 life-sized head-and-shoulders gilt-framed portraits of the heroes of the War of 1812 against Napoleon, this was restored according to Rossi's original designs, all of the portraits having been rescued from the burning palace by Guardsmen who had braved the flames to save them. Stasov also rebuilt the palace chapel according to Rastrelli's designs but had Montferrand redesign the Small Throne Room. Beyond that, Nicholas added his own touches, especially dozens of monumental ornamental vases carved from the richly colored hardstones of Siberia. Designed by leading architects, these generally were done in the style of the French Empire and still stand as monuments to the Russians' ability to create art on a massive imperial scale. Perhaps most striking of all is the elliptical Kolyvan Vase, which measures fifteen by nine feet and is cut from a single block of jasper found in the Siberian mountains above the town of Kolyvan. Designed on Nicholas's orders, the Kolyvan Vase required more than eleven years to carve and cost more than thirty thousand rubles. Too large to fit into any of the rooms of the rebuilt Winter Palace, the Emperor had a special room built around it in 1850.[34]

Even the burning of the Winter Palace was by no means the most fearsome of St. Petersburg's conflagrations. After several days during

which smaller fires had broken out and were brought under control, the
most terrifying of St. Petersburg's fires destroyed the Shchukin Arcade
and the nearby Apraksin Market at the end of May 1862. Within an
hour some six thousand shops in the very center of the city were ablaze,
and the flames threatened to spread to the nearby central offices of the
Ministry of Internal Affairs and the Nevskii Prospekt itself. "The
Apraksin Market was an immense space, more than half a mile square,
which was entirely covered with small shops—mere shanties of wood—
where all sorts of second and third hand goods were sold," an eyewitness
wrote. "Old furniture and bedding, second-hand dresses and books,
poured in from every quarter of the city, and were stored in the small
shanties, in the passages between them, and even on their roofs," he continued. "This accumulation of inflammable materials had at its back the
Ministry of Internal Affairs . . . and, almost opposite the Ministry, on
the other side of the [Fontanka] Canal, there were extensive timber yards
. . . [which] took fire almost at the same moment." From his vantage
point in the Corps of Pages dormitory just a block away, a young student
watched as the fire spread. "Like an immense snake, rattling and
whistling," he reported, "the fire threw itself in all directions, right and
left, enveloped the shanties, and suddenly rose in a huge column, darting
out its whistling tongues to lick up more shanties with their contents."[35]

As new buildings burst into flame like torches, the fires spread wherever the rising wind took them. There seemed to be stores of rags, oil,
brimstone, and turpentine everywhere, and all of them exploded into
columns of greasy black smoke and flame the instant the sparks touched
them. Hair singed, eyelids swollen, and their faces black with soot, people
struggled to contain the fires, only to have them break out anew whenever
the wind came up. Fearful crowds clogged the streets, seeking ways to escape from what they felt sure was certain destruction. "Wherever you
went," a writer who lived nearby wrote in his memoirs some years later,
"you saw suitcases, baskets, and parcels, in which poor people and those of
modest means had tied up everything that was dearest and most valuable
to them."[36] Everyone was waiting for a chance to flee, convinced that the
coming days would bring something worse. An apocalyptic sense told
these men and women that the fires had not happened by accident.

The crowd's certainty of danger stemmed from rumors that spread even
faster than the flames around them. The fires had broken out at a time

*The Nevskii Prospekt in a growing St. Petersburg. (Courtesy of the Central State Archive of Kino–Photo–Phono Documents, St. Petersburg)*

when St. Petersburg was facing its first wave of student unrest, during which university students defied the authorities and, with the encouragement of some of their professors, demanded a larger voice in university affairs. Some of the most radical students had circulated a manifesto bearing the title *Young Russia*, in which the authors warned that "rivers of blood" would flow and that "a revolution, a bloody and pitiless revolution," was about to strike Russia. They promised that the old order would be swept away, and that all traces of Russia's imperial past would go with it. "We will strike the Imperial party without sparing our blows," they promised. "We will destroy them in their houses, in the narrow streets ... [and] in the broad avenues of the capital."[37] Now, just two weeks after the first copies of *Young Russia* had surfaced, people wondered if these promises lay behind the fires. Had the revolutionaries—now readily called by the fearsome term Nihilists—actually dared to set Apraksin Market ablaze?

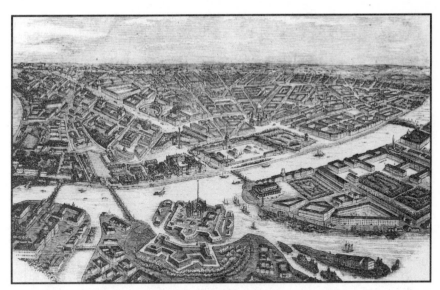

*This late-nineteenth-century view of St. Petersburg scans the city from above the Peter and Paul Fortress on the northern shore of the Neva River southward toward the city's suburbs.*

Many Petersburgers at the time firmly believed that radical students had set the Apraksin Market aflame as a prelude to revolution, but no one has ever proved for certain how the fires really started. Yet the very fact that suspicions of the radicals' guilt was so widely shared marked the beginnings of a split in public opinion that would deepen as time went on. The coming year plunged St. Petersburg into deeper turmoil as its educated and working classes all turned against the radical intelligentsia, and Russia faced a revolt in its Polish lands. What had seemed so certain in 1850, when one writer had triumphantly announced that "in Russia there exists everything necessary for national welfare,"[38] seemed very doubtful twelve years later, when Petersburgers and Russians alike were seeking the path that would lead them most easily into the modern world.

Even more urgently than the rest of Russia after 1860, St. Petersburg faced all the dilemmas of modernization that Europe had confronted two generations earlier, as the Emancipation of 1861 set in motion a migration from village to city that swelled to massive proportions over the next thirty years. By 1880, the city's 12,000 factory workers of 1840 had increased more than twelvefold to over 150,000, with such enterprises as the Putilov metalworking plant growing in size from 650 workers in 1860 to 13,000 in 1900. St. Petersburg had to house, feed, and provide basic public services to a population that grew from half a million in 1860 to nearly one and a quarter million in 1900, of which more than a third were lower class and poor. More than ever before the gap between rich and poor widened, and the dangers of lower-class life increased. That the annual death rate in 1900 ranged from fewer than one in a hundred in the city's upper-class districts to more than three in a hundred in its working-class quarters offered dramatic proof of how poorly public health facilities had met the needs of St. Petersburg's burgeoning poor.[39]

All of these crises in the making were reflected in the fact that as the fires of 1862 died away, St. Petersburg seemed somehow different. No longer simply the majestic imperial capital of Pushkin's poems, the city had become the throbbing, tormented netherworld that Dostoevskii portrayed in *Crime and Punishment.* Of course, elegant, aristocratic St. Petersburg still survived, and its beautiful palaces and imperious vistas continued to cast their spell on the Russians and foreigners who shared them. The White Nights still remained, and the Nevskii Prospekt, as of old, continued to be the place on which people congregated out of choice rather than from necessity. But, by 1860, a new and rapidly changing rival had come to stand beside the crystalline imperial city whose contours had been shaped so precisely by Pushkin, Rossi, and Nicholas I. This was St. Petersburg, the "gloomiest city in the world,"[40] as Dostoevskii once said, which between 1860 and 1917 would be subjected to all of the forces of modernity and transformed to meet its challenges. This St. Petersburg—the city of workers, technology, factories, iron and glass buildings, dark, heavy fog, and poverty—would become Russia's vanguard of modernity at the same time as it remained the bastion of its old order. This St. Petersburg—"the cradle of revolution" and the home of a richer, more sophisticated culture than any that Russia had ever known—would shape the Russians' vision of their future in a different and dramatic way in the years to come.

PART III

*Cradle
of Revolution
(1856–1941)*

# SIX

# MODERNITY'S
# CHALLENGE

ETWEEN THE END OF THE CRIMEAN WAR in 1856 and the Bolsheviks' abandonment of St. Petersburg as Russia's capital in 1918, the city lived through the most massive transformation in its history. During these sixty-two years, the Russian Empire freed nearly fifty million serfs and state peasants, faced the full force of the Industrial Revolution, lived through three foreign wars, and endured three revolutions. The pace of life accelerated from the speed of a team of horses to that of a locomotive, and the telephone and telegraph shrank the empire's huge dimensions to a fraction of their former size. The St. Petersburg of this modern age evolved from a city of symmetry and imperial regularity into a metropolis of striking contrasts in which the beautiful buildings, broad squares, and elegant avenues of its center contrasted with the ugliness of slums that had grown to include more than half a million men, women, and children by the 1880s.

The poverty that had been a blot on St. Petersburg's landscape in earlier times became a festering sore that made it the most unhealthy capital in Europe. By 1870, the number of foundlings had reached seven thousand a year. Daily arrests for drunkenness were approaching a hundred, with another four hundred Petersburgers being taken into custody every day for offenses that ranged from begging to murder. In some parts of the city as many as sixty people out of every thousand died in any given year, and many of their deaths stemmed from diseases connected with bad water, malnutrition, and poor sanitation. More than thirty thousand Petersburg-ers came down with syphilis each year in the 1870s. And between just 1869 and 1872, the number of suicides in the city rose by 270 percent.[1]

St. Petersburg was in the process of becoming the industrial center that produced the field guns, steel-clad warships, high explosives, locomotives, rails, and steam engines that would usher the Russian Empire into the modern age. A black-orange-greenish-yellow pall hung over hundreds of smokestacks, the emblems of progress in a world fascinated by the new-found power of the machine. All across the modern and modernizing world, the dynamo had become the chief inspiration of humankind, and in St. Petersburg this had created a many-chimneyed ring of factories, which squeezed the aristocratic city of Pushkin, Rossi, and Catherine the Great in an ever tightening grip. As the tell-tale smokestacks grew in number along the Schlüsselburg Road and in what had once been outly-ing parts of the city, slums spread around them like mushrooms sprouting from the stumps of rotting trees. With freight wagons clogging the streets and its chimneys belching smoke and ash, by the beginning of the 1880s no part of St. Petersburg was free from the stain of industry. When Em-peror Alexander III ascended the throne in 1881, Russia's capital was suf-fering all of the growing pains associated with the early stages of the industrial revolution. Climate, geography, and the fact of it being the cen-ter of Russia's government combined to make these problems worse.

St. Petersburg's rise as a modern industrial city had begun in the era of Nicholas I, when Russia's sense of being bound to the imperial, militaris-tic heritage of ancient Rome had been the most intense. In those days, Russia's statesmen regarded their empire as the proud inheritor of Rome's glory, and they set preserving the status quo as the main goal of policy and politics. Solid, orderly, and above all imposing, St. Petersburg reflected a sure and certain confidence in the vision of what Russia's future ought to be. All in Russia bowed to its Emperor, and its Emperor bowed only to God. With its newly built cathedrals of St. Isaac and Our Lady of Kazan, and the towering imperial chanceries from which thousands of clerks and statesmen sent their sovereign's orders to every corner of the empire, St. Petersburg had reflected an image of Russia's present and future that had admitted no deviations from the prescribed tenets of orthodoxy, autoc-racy, and nationality. Confident victors over social and political revolutions in 1825, 1830, and 1848, Russia's emperor and the men who served him believed they could tame the industrial revolution as well. Their shared belief in Russia's future and its mission made them confident that stern political and religious principles could shape the very social and economic forces that had brought so much turmoil and hardship to the West.

Yet, it was during this time of great self-confidence that the forces that would change Russia and St. Petersburg in fundamental ways had taken shape. In the 1830s and 1840s, the industrial revolution began to make its way into St. Petersburg in the form of Baron Ludwig Stieglitz's great cotton-spinning mill and the Aleksandro-Nevskii and Rossiiskii mills that soon became its rivals. Then came the Putilov Iron Foundry and Machine Works, soon to be followed by similar ventures bearing the names of Lessner, Siemens, Halske, and Samsonev, all of which became the basis for huge armaments, shipbuilding, and railroad enterprises during and after the Crimean War. The number of Petersburgers who worked in factories increased dramatically in the 1840s, but so long as most Russians remained bound to the land, the labor force for a full-scale industrial revolution remained locked in the countryside. Then the Emancipation of 1861 opened the way. By the 1870s, rural workers began to pour into St. Petersburg in search of jobs and the slim chance at a better future that work in its factories offered.

Many of St. Petersburg's new factories and mills took shape in the lands just to the south of the Aleksandr Nevskii Monastery and in the Vyborg and Petersburg boroughs that lay on the Neva's northern bank beyond the Peter and Paul Fortress. Here, by the late 1860s, abysmal wooden tenements already outnumbered brick buildings by more than four to one, and these became the mainstay for housing the city's working masses. A list of their owners' names reads like a guest list at court or a roster of the city's town council, for some of St. Petersburg's most prominent and prosperous citizens profited from renting substandard housing to the poor. A report prepared by an appalled public health physician in the early 1870s showed that many of St. Petersburg's workers lived in cellars that for periods of time had up to two feet of standing water polluted by human wastes. Running water (usually a spigot in the courtyard, not an indoors faucet) could be found in only one building out of fourteen in the Aleksandro-Nevskaia borough, and in the Vyborg section the ratio was one in fifty-one.[2]

Yet, aside from having water nearer to hand, running water did little to reduce the health hazards that Petersburgers faced in the 1860s and

1870s. The city continued to draw its water directly from the Neva and its tributaries, into which more and more buildings and factories discharged their wastes every year. "The water placed on the table in spring is perfectly pestiferous," a visiting Scotsman wrote in disgust. "Frequently in summer did I meet the nightmen's carts, which discharged their filthy cargo into the Fontanka, so that the very air was poisoned. Then in the morning," he added, "water for breakfast is procured from [the same place]."[3] Public notices in the form of placards with glaring red letters that warned people not to drink unboiled water were posted everywhere. Yet, as an English visitor to Russia reported in 1910, it still was not unusual to see "dirty workmen slake their thirst with water dipped out of their greasy caps from the foulest canals in the city."[4]

Well into the twentieth century, infectious diseases borne by the city's water killed tens of thousands of Petersburgers every year. Nearly half of the fatalities in 1908 stemmed from such diseases, and between 1892 and 1905 the rate of deaths from typhoid fever alone was more than four times higher in St. Petersburg than in Moscow. Another twenty thousand Petersburgers died every year from typhus, a staggering statistic that ranged between eight and thirteen times the rate in Moscow and Warsaw, and amounted to more than in all the cities of the German Empire combined. Britain's Foreign Office continued to receive reports from worried diplomats about St. Petersburg's contaminated water supply, and these were sometimes drawn from official Russian government sources. Yet St. Petersburg's City Council continued to toy with ineffective schemes for filtering and purifying the Neva River water rather than take decisive steps. Not until 1914 did they finally decide that a new source of water had to be found.[5]

All Petersburgers shared the city's foul water, but what they ate varied according to their wealth. Well-to-do aristocrats continued to pride themselves on the rich tables they set, and so did the city's great merchants and industrialists. Wines from France, pâtés from Périgord, the best confections, and whatever else the economies of Russia and Europe had to offer all had places on the tables of St. Petersburg's rich and famous. Restaurants that served the finest in the way of food and wines were well established on the Nevskii Prospekt and in its vicinity, and a meal at Contant's, Donon's, or Cubat's—or in the restaurants at the Astoria, Europe, or Grand hotels—all cost many times what a factory worker earned in a day.

Yet, if the rich lived sumptuously, getting enough food to stay alive posed a growing challenge for people who worked long hours at lathes and looms to keep body and soul together as the nineteenth century neared its end. Rising prices of even the most basic staples meant that some workers had to choose between food and heat in the winter. Others formed cooperatives, which bought and prepared the poorest grades of the cheapest foods to cut the cost of eating. A worker in Moscow once called these communal enterprises "cooperatives for the disposal of spoiled food,"[6] and they were just the same in St. Petersburg, with the only difference being that the quality was even poorer because the cost of staples was higher. A physician who visited one such group at a tanning works on Vasilevskii Island was appalled to learn that the rotten bits of meat and fat its members scraped from hides being prepared for tanning provided the group's main source of dietary protein.[7] At a time when their working day stretched from twelve to fifteen hours, these men and women continued to eat mainly coarse rye bread and sour soup made from water and pickled cabbage.

For St. Petersburg's workers, the consequences of bad water, poor diet, and wretched housing were intensified by an acute lack of medical care. At mid-century, more than thirty charity and government hospitals had offered services to the lower classes in the city itself, but as hundreds of thousands of peasants poured into the city and as its factories spread into the suburbs, St. Petersburg's facilities no longer could meet their needs. Many factories themselves offered no medical services at all, and others provided little beyond a doctor or nurse who was hired to deal with the work-related injuries of thousands of workers. Otherwise, the city's lower classes had no choice but to seek out a physician in private practice. Men and women who saw the prices of housing and food consume most of each week's pay viewed such a visit, which cost almost a whole day's earnings, as something to be resorted to only after every other remedy had failed. Unaccustomed to the hazards of city life and with virtually no health facilities to serve them, St. Petersburg's lower classes fell prey to cholera, typhoid, typhus, diphtheria, measles, and smallpox at a fearsome rate that helped to maintain the city's unsavory reputation as the most unhealthful capital in Europe.[8]

As the Industrial Revolution moved into high gear in the 1890s, St. Petersburg's population exploded, and by 1900 it had tripled compared to what it had been forty years earlier. More than two out of every three Petersburgers in those days had been born somewhere else. Nearly one in three worked in the city's shops, factories, and mills, and more than a sixth of these were women, many of whom gave birth on the floor next to their looms because mill foremen would not allow them to take time off.[9] Everywhere working conditions resembled those commonly encountered during the first decades of the Industrial Revolution. Long hours, low pay, frequent layoffs, heavy fines for carelessness, accidents, or absences all made the workers' lives hard, especially between 1890 and 1900, when the cost of bread, meat, fish, kerosene, and cloth more than doubled while wages rose by barely a fifth.[10]

Apartments in St. Petersburg's crowded tenements in the early twentieth century housed twice as many people as in Vienna, Paris, or Berlin, with an average of nearly sixteen people in each and reports of as many as a hundred being crammed into a single large room.[11] Close to sixty thousand Petersburgers now lived in cellars, and tens of thousands more lived in closets, corners, and the spaces beneath staircases. "The rooms are filthy and the walls and ceilings are thick with soot," a contemporary wrote of a typical Petersburg workers' lodging in the 1880s. "Two rows of cots line each room," the account continued, "and two men are obliged to sleep in each one."[12] Very quickly, such housing rose from being the worst the city had to offer to the level of being well above the bottom. By the eve of World War I, the doss-house had replaced the tenement as the lowest level of working-class life in Russia's capital. Thousands of workers now slept in these night shelters, with no place to spend their leisure time but the street.

By 1910, there were at least thirty-four doss-houses in St. Petersburg being run by the city, a handful of charities, and a number of entrepreneurs anxious to reap a profit from the lower-class housing shortage. Sleeping platforms divided into spaces less than three feet wide stretched along the middle of each room, but once these were full, the overflow slept in hallways, aisles, and under the platforms themselves. The cost of a night's lodging under such conditions ranged from five to thirty-five kopeks, with the charity- and city-run shelters charging the least and providing the most in the way of tea and something to eat. Still, many workers preferred the more wretched but expensive privately run facilities because these allowed alcohol, while those of the city and charities did not. By 1910, more than eight thousand Petersburgers spent their nights in this way, and public health officials estimated that another twelve thousand places could have been easily filled.[13]

As St. Petersburg approached the outbreak of war in 1914, appalling poverty and astounding wealth continued to exist side by side along with the remnants of backwardness and the instruments of progress. A scant twenty minutes' walk from the Haymarket and the rebuilt Shchukin Arcade stood the stunning new red granite shop that the court jeweler Peter Karl Fabergé had just opened at No. 24 Bolshaia Morskaia Street. Workshops of the goldsmiths Ovchinnikov, Bock, Bolin, Tillander, and Denisov all stood within a long stone's throw from Fabergé's door, and the emporium from which the Grachev Brothers sold their famed gold, silver, and enameled masterpieces lay just around the corner on the Nevskii Prospekt. A little further up the avenue on the edge of the Catherine Canal stood the Russian Headquarters of the Singer Sewing Machine Company, with more than two dozen banks within easy reach. France's Crédit Lyonnais had a Russian headquarters on the Nevskii Prospekt in those days, and International Harvester had one not far away.

Electric trams, now used by more than two hundred million passengers every year, ran along the Nevskii Prospekt, and nearly two hundred kilometers of track spread throughout the city.[14] Yet the instruments of backwardness remained, too. Strong holdovers from the village way of life in the form of peasant carters, haulers, and street peddlers continued to play a role in St. Petersburg's commerce, and people still bought more goods in bazaars than in modern retail emporiums. There was still a rural element in St. Petersburg life around 1912 that could not be found in London, Paris, Berlin, or New York, and this helped to preserve traditional— mainly peasant—values in the larger arena of modern city life. On the streets and in factories, trading arcades, and those forms of housing that the rich and poor still shared, the old and new conflicted, blended, and struggled to find new common ground. There was upward mobility in St. Petersburg's modern world as well as downward social movement, and this found its most dramatic expressions in the industrialists and railroad magnates who rose to prominence during the quarter century before World War I began.

Although much of Russia's light industry tended to develop in Moscow under the influence of a colorful, closed circle of Old Believer merchants, St. Petersburg quickly became a major center of heavy industry in the 1860s and 1870s. Thanks to the government's new policy of subsidizing the development of modern industries and to the foreign and domestic capital that poured into the city's banks, iron and steel mills, tool and die plants, cotton mills, and chemical facilities all grew at a steady pace, and the ranks of the city's workers expanded at an even faster rate. These were the years when Ludwig Nobel established his huge Phoenix metalworking plant and steel mill in the city's Vyborg Quarter, and when the Obukhovs, Kudriavtsevs, and Putilovs founded the giant industrial enterprises that dominated the city's factory districts after 1870. The twin forces that drove these new industries were orders for rails and rolling stock, and military hardware for the huge and now rapidly modernizing Russian army and navy. Russia's first ironclad warships were built in St. Petersburg in the 1860s, and, beginning in the 1870s, so was much of the rolling stock that moved along its railroads.[15]

In large measure because managerial talent was in short supply, bigness became a key component in industrial development all across late-nineteenth-century St. Petersburg. By the end of the century, more than two thousand people worked at the Aivaz Machine Construction Plant, the Nevskii Shipbuilding Works employed nearly twice that number, and the Russian-American Treugolnik Rubber Company had more than eleven thousand on its payroll. The Putilov Metalworking Plants employed over twelve thousand, and the huge spinning and weaving mills that silhouetted the skyline of St. Petersburg's suburbs all boasted workforces that numbered thousands more. Even the Laferm Tobacco Company employed over two thousand people by the early twentieth century, as St. Petersburg's labor force tripled between 1890 and 1910.[16]

The handful of families who owned these huge enterprises became wealthy beyond belief to rival the great noble families whose property had been bestowed upon them by Russia's eighteenth-century emperors and empresses. Among them, few equaled in wealth Nikolai Putilov and his son Aleksei. A civilian engineer who had served in the Imperial Russian Admiralty in the 1840s and 1850s, the elder Putilov had made a reputation during the Crimean War as the designer and producer of steam-powered gunboats. Certain that Putilov knew how to harness modern technology in the service of Russia, the government in 1868 sold him a large iron foundry, and he plunged into making rails and rolling stock to supply the railroad boom that had just got under way. Thanks to large government subsidies and contracts, the Putilovs expanded their ironworks into a massive industrial complex that employed some twelve thousand workers. Soon they would branch out into munitions and armaments on such a huge scale that by 1912, war materiel would make up nearly half of their factories' output.[17] Always, the Putilovs lived on a princely scale, with townhouses the size of palaces and staffs of servants that rivaled the households of the great courtiers who had served Catherine the Great. Superb wines, exotic cuisine, ball gowns from Parisian couturiers—the best that money could buy in terms of furniture, comfort, and art—all were a part of daily life of the Putilovs.

Although claiming to believe in "the amazing capacity of the Russian people for mechanical and industrial work,"[18] Nikolai Putilov insisted that paternalism and strict managerial control must shape the relationship between his family's huge enterprises and their workers. By the early 1870s his mills faced some of the first strikes anywhere in Russia, and violent labor protests eventually cost him so many government contracts that the Putilov Works had to be taken over by the stockholders of the Petersburg International Bank. These presided over the firm's successful rebirth in the 1890s as a builder of railroad locomotives, carriages, and armaments, and the early twentieth century saw Putilov's mills again stand unchallenged as St. Petersburg's largest. Yet despite this new success, the unyielding Putilovs continued to face strong worker protest. Their managers had to close the factory doors twice in 1905, and it was not until the powerful Russian-Asian Bank headed by Aleksei Putilov took over a few years later that the factory fully recovered. Then, massive subsidies and huge orders for armaments and munitions helped it to prosper until the Revolution of 1917, when it was nationalized and became the property of the new Soviet state.[19]

The Putilovs' story marks just one of many instances in which St. Petersburg's banks played a major part in modernizing and developing its industries. One of the keys to the city's prominent role in Russia's industrial revolution lay in the founding in 1864 of the St. Petersburg Private Commercial Bank, the first joint-stock commercial bank in Russia, which financed some of the capital's first large-scale industrial establishments. Soon banks from Berlin and Vienna began to invest in St. Petersburg's new industries, and these opened the way for the even larger influx of foreign capital that helped to accelerate the pace of Russia's industrial revolution. Founded in 1870, St. Petersburg's Volga-Kama Bank quickly spread across Russia, with branches in nearly twenty cities before 1880 and two dozen more after that. Soon, it became one of the leading banks in the empire, pouring tens of millions of rubles into the expansion of the capital's industries every year. Thanks to the Volga-Kama Bank, its rivals and its allies, St. Petersburg became the financial nerve center of Imperial Russia well before the end of the century. Its banks (twenty-eight on Nevskii Prospekt alone) held nearly half of all the cash deposits in the entire empire, and its Stock Exchange, which the Alexandrine architect Thomas de Thomon had built at the beginning of the century, dominated the empire's trade in securities and commodities.[20]

The pragmatic new ways of thinking about the everyday world that ruled St. Petersburg's surging economic life in the 1870s, 1880s, and 1890s also shaped its institutions of advanced technical education. Starting in the 1860s, training at the city's Mining Institute, Technological Institute, Institute of Civil Engineering, and Institute for Transportation Engineers began to address broad social and economic questions. Now concerned to harness technology and science in the service of a better life for all Russians, the graduates of these institutes, some of whom founded professional technical and technological societies, helped to bridge the gap between government and St. Petersburg's private sector that had made joint undertakings impossible in earlier times. For the first time in Russia's history, scholars, engineers, technicians, and officials all worked together in St. Petersburg, and their efforts created a whole new technological arsenal that served the city and Russia. The great chemist Dmitrii Mendeleev played a key role in this blending of resources and talents, and so did at least a score of other scientists who had won acclaim for their work in chemistry, physics, hydromechanics, electricity, and the application of steam technology to land and water transport.

Such people now began to ask what impact technology might be expected to have on the city and country in which they lived and if it could play a part in solving larger social and economic problems. Could technology and science, for example, be applied to the problems of public health that had plagued the city since its founding? And could they provide the means for moving people away from the slums in which they lived and worked? Certainly the development of modern public transport networks had become a means for enabling workers to live further from their work in a number European cities, but the process was only beginning in St. Petersburg. By 1900, for example, Berlin's omnibuses and streetcars carried nearly half a billion users every year, but in St. Petersburg they carried fewer than a quarter of that number. Between 1870 and 1914, about a million and a half people moved to St. Petersburg, and most of them continued to crowd into the slums that clustered around the mills

and plants outside the city's center. St. Petersburg's lower classes continued to walk to their looms, lathes, and blast furnaces. Around 1900, only
its upper and middle classes had access to means of transportation that
enabled them to live in one part of the city and to work in another.[21]

The new technology and new ways of creating wealth that the Industrial Revolution brought to St. Petersburg required a host of new buildings, with railroad stations, apartment houses, schools, hospitals, hotels,
banks, offices, and modern mansions all being needed. Architects no
longer came only from the tradition-bound Imperial Academy of Fine
Arts as had been the case during the heyday of neoclassicism, and their
visions were now more far-reaching and diverse. Men trained in building
construction at St. Petersburg's Institute of Civil Engineering had new
ideas about how buildings ought to be built and what purpose they ought
to serve, and they sought to realize their visions of progress by using new
types of materials and designs. "The property of a material and the best
possible means of applying it determine the means of construction,"
wrote Apollinarii Krasovskii, the author of a text on *Civil Architecture* that
would serve as a bible for generations of Russian builders. "Architecture,"
he concluded in the 1880s, "should not tend exclusively toward either the
useful or the beautiful. Its basic rule is the transformation of the one into
the other."[22] Some of these principles were put to work in the huge glass
and cast-iron coverings that were raised over the Haymarket in the early
1880s, but they did not become firmly established until the very end of
the century, when St. Petersburg's builders began to use iron, plate glass,
and reinforced concrete on a larger, more creative scale.

The nouveaux riches of late-nineteenth-century St. Petersburg did not
at first approach the matter of building design with either the pragmatism
or the clear artistic vision that Krasovskii's text suggests. From the mid-
1860s to the late 1870s, a passion for redesigning facades swept the city
and defaced a number of beautiful buildings as men and women with
more money than taste sought to leave a mark. "More and more people
are redoing their facades," Dostoevskii complained in 1873. "You really
don't know how to define our current architecture," he went on. "It's a sort
of disorderly mess, entirely, by the way, appropriate to the disorder to the
present moment."[23] Facades blended neo-Renaissance, neo-baroque, neo-
Greek, Russian Revival, and a jumble of what one expert has called
"mixed or unrecognizable styles,"[24] as the city's new entrepreneurs demanded apartment buildings that resembled the palaces of Venetian

doges and Florentine princes. "If it suits you, here are five yards of Greek 'classicism'; if not, here are three and a quarter of Italian 'Renaissance,'" the critic Vladimir Stasov wrote in lamenting facades "without a single breathing space" that scrambled several styles at once. To satisfy clients with money and no taste, Stasov went on, architects blended bits of anything that came to hand like shopkeepers anxious to please fickle customers. "With us," another critic concluded sadly, "an architect is a hireling, obligated for his remuneration to fulfill someone else's will without thinking."[25]

Yet, by the 1890s St. Petersburg's architects had taken a firmer hold and begun to create a distinctive *style moderne* that matched artistic integrity to modern needs. Commercial buildings, private apartment buildings, two of the city's premier hotels—the Hotel Astoria and the Hotel Europe—and a number of private townhouses built at the turn of the century all displayed significant elements of this new style, and these remain today as monuments to the mark that the modernist vision left behind. Brick, stone, concrete, cast iron, steel, and glass all took on new forms in this work, as building styles moved quickly toward stripped and modernized forms of classicism in the early twentieth century.

Foremost among the creators of this new style in St. Petersburg was Fedor Lidval, who studied at the Academy of Arts during the first half of the 1890s and built his first important building—an apartment complex registered in the name of his wife—in 1899 at the age of twenty-nine. Unlike so many of St. Petersburg's earlier builders, Lidval at first chose to work in the Petersburg Quarter, not far from the place where Peter the Great had built his first log house in 1703. There in the midst of what was soon to become a comfortable center of middle-class life, he used cast and wrought iron, stained glass, brick, and stucco in ways that enabled him to replace the cramped inner courtyard that had characterized St. Petersburg apartment buildings of the Rossi era with a landscaped area that gave a sense of openness and depth. Lidval then moved on to build several more apartment buildings on Bolshaia and Malaia Koniushennaia streets in the city's center before he returned to the vicinity of his earlier work in the Petersburg Quarter.[26]

Other architects followed the course Lidval had set, especially along the Petersburg Quarter's Kamennoostrovskii Prospekt, which by 1910 boasted more than a dozen modern apartment buildings designed by such builders as Nikolai Vasilev, Ippolit Pretro, and Sergei Korvin-Kriukovskii in addition to Lidval. All of these took advantage of the greater space available away from the city's center, and each found new ways to blend modern materials with innovative visions. Rough-cast and reinforced concrete, textured stucco, heavy stonework—even glass and steel, which made walls into membranes that transmitted light—all were featured in these new designs that took shape during the twentieth century's first decade.[27] Together they transformed the vision that had defined St. Petersburg since the days of Elizabeth and Catherine the Great.

In commercial buildings, the modern style that distinguished the apartment houses on Kamennoostrovskii Prospekt evolved quickly into what has been called "stripped, modern classicism."[28] Among the first of these new buildings was the headquarters that the goldsmith Peter Karl Fabergé engaged the architect Karl Shmidt to build for his family's workshops in 1899. Known around the world for the superb workmanship and true originality of his art, Fabergé had become famous as a creator of the objects of pure fantasy and decadence that illuminated Imperial Russia's twilight. His masters shaped lilies of the valley from pearls, diamonds, and nephrite, created exquisitely enameled miniature sedan chairs with rock-crystal windows, produced miniature grand pianos of enamel and gold, and, of course, crafted the fabulous Easter eggs that knew no equals anywhere.[29] As demand grew faster than he could engage artists to fulfill new commissions, Fabergé decided to move from the cramped quarters he had inherited from his father to 24 Bolshaia Morskaia Street, just a few minutes walk from the Nevskii Prospekt and the Winter Palace. There Shmidt blended polished red granite columns, plate glass, and various combinations of rough-cut and smooth gray granite into a "Gothicized premoderne" style that opened the way for several other modern buildings on the nearby Nevskii Prospekt.[30]

The most flamboyant of these new structures was designed by Gavriil Baranovskii for the food emporium that G. G. Eliseev maintained at No. 56 Nevskii Prospekt. An 1885 graduate from the Institute of Civil Engineering, Baranovskii had worked in Moscow, Nizhnii-Novgorod, and Estonia and had played a leading part in shaping Russian architectural taste in his role as editor of the influential journal *Stroitel* (*The Builder*). For Eliseev, Baranovskii drew upon new architectural trends from Vienna, Brussels, and Paris that relied heavily on curved iron beams and huge expanses of plate glass, and he sought to place these into a setting that would highlight their contrast with the classical style that dominated that part of St. Petersburg's central avenue. When completed in 1904, the Eliseev building added character and interest to the north side of the Nevskii Prospekt, which had been perpetually overshadowed by the grandiose Stroganov Palace, Kazan Cathedral, Aleksandrinskii Theater, Public Library, and Anichkov Palace, all of which stood on the opposite side of the street.[31] A striking contrast to the designs of Vallin de la Mothe, Rossi, and Rastrelli that had shaped the character of the buildings nearby, the Eliseev emporium continued even in Soviet times to stand as a beacon to the best that the city had to offer in the way of food and wine.

The trend started by Shmidt and Baranovskii seemed even more striking in the block across from the Kazan Cathedral, where the architect Pavel Siuzor built the St. Petersburg headquarters for the Singer Sewing Machine Company at No. 28 Nevskii Prospekt. As the dean of St. Petersburg's architects at the opening of the new century (he had graduated from the Academy of Fine Arts in 1866 and was fifty-six in 1900), Siuzor had worked through the eclecticism of the 1860s and 1870s to play a major part in the neoclassical revival that followed, and he already had built nearly a hundred projects when Singer's representatives approached him in 1901. For his American clients, Siuzor used bronze, iron, and plate glass, including a metal ribbed cupola, a large stone stairway, and three Otis elevators to connect the building's seven floors, and he decorated the three main window shafts with helmeted nude females and a large American eagle of bronze. All of this gave the Singer Company a forceful architectural presence in St. Petersburg that no other European or American enterprise could match, even as a number of banks and commercial establishments struggled to do so.[32]

Architects who designed buildings in early-twentieth-century St. Petersburg worked easily within an eclectic framework that embraced "Gothicized premoderne," *style moderne,* and stripped-down neoclassicism. But, by the end of the new century's first decade, a certain reverence for reviving the grandeur of neoclassicism began to take shape within this blend of sometimes conflicting influences. Condemning "pathetic parodies in the deutsche Renaissance, in French Rococo, [and] in the Gothic,"[33] the advocates of this reform style argued for a restoration of those influences that had shaped St. Petersburg in the days of Catherine the Great, Alexander I, and Nicholas I. Here Lidval led the way by blending neoclassicism and modern bourgeois architecture in the Azov-Don Bank and the luxury Astoria Hotel on St. Isaac's Square. Others turned instead to Renaissance Italy for inspiration. Still others drew upon Muscovite designs of the sixteenth century, while those who opposed their efforts to look back in time continued to forge ahead with such strikingly modern works as Marian Lialevich's and Marian Peretiatkovich's plans for an indoor market and the Jewish Synagogue that Iakov Gevirts built on the edge of the city's Jewish cemetery.[34]

As the clouds of World War I began to gather, the eclecticism that had characterized much of the new architecture in turn-of-the-century St. Petersburg began to refocus on the neoclassicism that had been so closely associated with Russia's imperial brilliance a hundred years before. "After an epoch of agitated searching for a new form, new beauty and ornamentation," a leading architect told the Fourth Congress of Russian Architects in 1911, "architecture . . . is again joyously . . . taking as its base the old national forms." This came at a time when Ivan Fomin, a brilliant young modernist architect, had already proclaimed that the "amazing structures" of neoclassicism were the "poetry of the past," and worthy of serious attention as models for the future. Soon, some of St. Petersburg's leading critics embraced Fomin's designs as the antidote to "the contemporary economic spirit of calculation and triviality, of contemporary cheapness and bad workmanship." Fomin's work, the influential Georgii Lukomskii insisted, stood "close to the very basis of Old Petersburg" and was "wholly based on splendid traditions."[35]

To evoke the drama and brilliance of Russia's heroic past, Fomin and several other neoclassical revivalists designed private mansions, both in central St. Petersburg and on Stone Island, which lay across the Malaia Nevka from the northern shore of the Petersburg Quarter. Here the great late-eighteenth-century architect Vasilii Bazhenov had built a three-story palace for the future emperor Paul I, and the imperial family had continued to maintain extensive parks around it. Otherwise the island had remained relatively undeveloped until well past the middle of the nineteenth century. Then a group of aristocrats and wealthy businessmen began to build summer mansions that signaled the last wave of great private construction the city would see before the end of the twentieth century.

Directly across the Malaia Nevka from the magnificent Elagin Palace that Karl Rossi had designed for the mother of Alexander I, Fomin built a summer house for the heirs of Senator and State Counselor Aleksandr Polovtsev. Done on a scale unrivaled in the early twentieth century, the villa's Gobelin Hall housed five magnificent Gobelin tapestries. Paintings of classical ruins adorned other rooms, and the Italian ceiling of its White Columned Hall rivaled that of Rossi's Mikhailovskii Palace. Nearby, other builders soon created mansions on a more modest scale for the Chaevs, the Mertens, the Bekhterevs, and the Krilichevskiis. In other parts of the city neoclassical revivalists who shared Fomin's views designed apartment houses and several more private mansions, the best known of which was the Abamalek-Lazarev house that Fomin himself built in the year before World War I broke out. Some of these radiated a museum-like quality that tended to set them apart from the mainstream of modern life, but they all marked an effort to make contact with the past and recall those glories that, in the days when the armies of Alexander I defeated Napoleon, had made Russia great.[36]

The new tastes and values that altered the face of turn-of-the-century St. Petersburg also transformed its cultural and intellectual life. By 1910 nearly eight out of every ten of the nearly two million people living in the city could read and write, and this brought them into contact with a larger and more complex world than their parents and grandparents had ever imagined.[37] In 1810, the number of magazines and newspapers being published in St. Petersburg had not yet reached half a dozen, and the figure for all of Russia had totaled fewer than twelve. A century later, those numbers stood in the hundreds for St. Petersburg alone, while for all of Russia the output of the periodical press counted far into the thousands.[38] Best sellers, which had been defined in terms of a thousand copies in the days of Alexander I, now enjoyed printings in the tens of thousands. Thanks to modern science and communications, a vast amount of information that had been unknown a hundred years before was now readily at hand, and modern education made that knowledge available to hundreds of thousands of Petersburgers who could never have dreamed of having access to it in earlier times.

More people were being educated in early-twentieth-century St. Petersburg than had been able to attend school in all of Russia a century before, and this completely changed the content and focus of the dialogue between society and the government. In earlier times, only a very small number of educated men and women had debated the issues of progress, modernization, and social change, and then only within the narrowest of frameworks allowed by the government. Now Petersburgers had to take responsibility for their lives, and that meant they had to confront real and practical questions about the future and what direction it ought to take.

True, the autocracy until 1906 continued to deny its subjects any part in the national legislative processes that had become so much a part of life in the West. But on a less exalted plane, Russians had to begin to take responsibility for their communities and themselves. Public services, public health, and the protection of property all became questions that elected officials suddenly had to confront in St. Petersburg and elsewhere as the nineteenth century turned toward its end. No longer did tsar, lords, and ladies take responsibility for the welfare of those men and women over whom fate had given them command. How the Russians proceeded in this entirely new milieu would determine a great deal about their lives as they entered the twentieth century.

On the national level, the Great Reforms of the 1860s and the debates they stirred transformed Russians from subjects into citizens. In the space of barely more than a decade between 1861 and 1874, Russia's government freed nearly fifty million serfs and state peasants, introduced trial by jury, established local self-government, and made its people responsible for censoring their press and defending their homeland. Certainly this did not mean that Russia's political climate remained stable, or that the emperor and his closest advisers had a clear vision of what part Russians ought to play in shaping their nation's future. But it did mean that government and governed began to share common goals and could join forces from time to time, especially in the realm of technology and science, where learned men and state officials could work together most easily.

Especially in St. Petersburg, the growing contact between Russians and their government that developed between the end of the Crimean War and outbreak of World War I meant that the city's social and civic dialogue reached further and spread to a larger audience. Not just a handful of intellectuals, but scientists, businessmen, bankers, professional people, and in fact anyone who could read and write had some concern about issues that had been regarded as strictly government business in earlier times. Perhaps most striking of all, the men and women who had debated the dilemmas of progress in the 1840s had defined them in terms of abstract theories that had no practical application, but those who sought to establish Russia's course half a century later thought in much more realistic terms. A few revolutionaries continued to think of utopia, but by the turn of the century the experience of life in the modernizing world had taught most Russians to think more pragmatically. The "superfluous man" who had ruled St. Petersburg's literary world in the 1840s had no place in the great novels of Dostoevskii or among the men who embraced the era of "small deeds" in the decade after his death in 1881. How people confronted the social questions of the time, how willingly they shouldered their new civic responsibilities, and how they proposed to deal with the dilemmas of poverty and disease in Russia's cities became far more important.

Depending on their material and intellectual circumstances, Petersburgers viewed the dilemmas of modern life in different ways. Some segments of the old aristocracy continued to live as before, assuming that life would continue in the pattern to which they and their ancestors had long since become accustomed. Others faced the challenges of change and progress more squarely and sought to understand how the problems of modernity affected their city. As daily life became more complex and the new problems posed by machines and modern ways of creating wealth grew more troublesome, people had to ask how their city's intellectual and economic resources could be used best. As in the West, Russians tried to study their society "scientifically" in the belief that the laws determining human behavior could be discovered in the same manner as had the laws governing physical phenomena. This gave them greater faith in science and a new hope that its laws and methods could help to eradicate age-old problems from modern life. Science could be used to fight disease and make life more comfortable and rewarding in material terms, while the methods of science could be applied to solving those social and economic problems of poverty and unequal opportunity that had plagued humankind since the dawn of history.

But how did the laws that governed the workings of society function, and how might they best be understood? In 1863, a daring young radical literary critic and publicist by the name of Nikolai Chernyshevskii described his vision of a new socialist society in the progressive St. Petersburg monthly *Sovremennik (The Contemporary)*, but unlike those utopians who had come before him he drew up a practical blueprint for how his brave new world could be created. Like many of the men and women who would shape St. Petersburg's history during the second half of the nineteenth century, Chernyshevskii had grown up in the provinces and had come to the capital in search of education and a better future. A true pragmatist in the style of the hero in Turgenev's famous novel *Fathers and Sons*, he insisted that the key to understanding life lay in embracing the world as it really was, its flaws and failings not withstanding. "Life is beauty," he exclaimed at one point. "Reality is not only more animated, but also more perfect than imagination."[39]

The reality that overrode all others, Chernyshevskii insisted in 1862, was the poverty of Russia's masses and the need to bring the tens of millions of men and women who had been freed from serfdom the year before into the modern world. The task of providing these superstitious, uneducated people with the benefits that all citizens deserved must take precedence, he warned, or the masses would eventually rise up and destroy everything St. Petersburg and modern Russia stood for. "The people are . . . dominated by primitive prejudices and by blind hatred for anything different from their own barbaric customs," he wrote that spring in an essay called "Letters Without an Address." "Without exception," he went on, "they will spare neither our science, our poetry, nor our arts, [and] will destroy our civilization." For the time being, the masses seemed calm, obedient, and willing to bow to the forces of authority, but Chernyshevskii believed that their apathy only made the danger worse. The longer the day of reckoning was postponed, the more terrible its violence would be when the smoldering fires of popular anger finally burst into flame.[40] Statesmen, bureaucrats, aristocrats, and thoughtful citizens all knew the danger, he insisted. Still no one had yet found the means to create a society that would give the masses their due.

Because censorship obliged many thoughtful Russians to speak through the mouths of fictional characters in those days, Chernyshevskii chose to set down his vision for the future in a novel he entitled *What Is To Be Done?* Determined not only to confront the burning questions of his time but to seek answers, he asked how the talents of all men and women could be used to benefit the society in which they lived. How could people of limited means gain access to the education? How could they have a fair chance of living better lives? And, how could the constraints which excluded women from professional careers (and therefore cut Russia's reservoir of talent in half) be cast aside? To ask such questions about the masses was particularly dangerous in St. Petersburg of 1862, for government and people both were on edge after the fires that had swept through the Shchukin Arcade and Apraksin Market that spring. Many feared that the uprising "Letters Without an Address" had predicted was about to burst forth, and the authorities worried that, as the moral leader of the government's opponents, Chernyshevskii himself might play a role. By midsummer, the authorities decided that they had tolerated his radicalism long enough and issued an order for his arrest. Some eight months before *What Is To Be Done?* appeared in the March, April, and May 1863 issues of *Sovremennik*, its author was already a political prisoner in St. Petersburg's Peter and Paul Fortress.[41]

*What Is to Be Done?* became a bible for Russia's revolutionaries. Some paid as much as twenty-five rubles (more than a month's wages for a factory worker) for a single copy. The mere fact that its heroine was a woman encouraged young Russians who dreamed of building a new society to follow the path of female liberation. Yet for others, the pace of Chernyshevskii's plan for improving life in all of Russia seemed too slow. While Chernyshevskii languished in Siberia, where he remained for all but the last four months of his life, other more bitter, radical, and alienated young men and women sought to move history at a quicker pace. Rather than wait for society to transform itself into Chernyshevskii's hoped-for utopia, these people vowed to sweep aside the authorities who stood in their way.

Such feelings set the stage for the nefarious plans of Dmitrii Karakozov, a tormented young man who came to St. Petersburg at the beginning of 1866 after promising his friends that he would kill Alexander II. Pale, worn, and careless about how he looked, Karakozov had twice been expelled from the university, and he suffered from psychological disturbances that made him think often of suicide. Tormented in mind and body, he decided to combine suicide with regicide, and at the age of twenty-six set out to fulfill that mission. At the end of February 1866, he bought an old double-barreled pistol, powder, and ball in one of St. Petersburg's back-alley shops, and by the beginning of April he was ready to carry out his mission.[42]

Still spread out along the Neva's southern bank and now more than a hundred and fifty years old, the tree-shaded walks of the Summer Gardens had been one of Petersburgers' favorite promenades ever since the Empress Elizabeth had dedicated so much money and effort to making them beautiful. This was the place to see and be seen, and Alexander II liked to go there on pleasant afternoons to enjoy the shade and to chat in an off-handed way with whomever he found. Here was a chance for sovereign and people to meet informally, for the Emperor to feel the city's pulse and gain a sense of where its people were moving and how. Peter the Great had done so in the 1710s, and so had the empresses Elizabeth and Catherine the Great later in the eighteenth century. No sovereign had ever faced danger in the Summer Gardens, and the need for security in this favorite strolling place was not a thought that entered the minds of courtiers or the police.

And so it was that Alexander II strolled in the Summer Gardens on the afternoon of April 4, 1866, chatted with the Duke of Leuchtenberg and several other people who crossed his path, and returned to the carriage that waited just outside the main gate. Suddenly, Karakozov stepped from the crowd, pointed his pistol at the Emperor, and fired. Official reports later insisted that a peasant—one of the traditional saviors of Russia's rulers since before the Romanovs had mounted the throne—had struck Karakozov's arm and spoiled his aim. Then the police seized the assassin, took away his weapon, and dragged him to the Emperor, who questioned him about what he had hoped to accomplish and why. Five months later, Karakozov was hanged, but the shock waves of the shot he had fired continued to reverberate through Russia.[43] Henceforth St. Petersburg would become a battleground on which a handful of daring revolutionaries pitted their meager resources against the massive power of the Russian state. Pistols, hand grenades, dynamite, double agents, and a tenacity that few could match all would be a part of their arsenal in a struggle that would continue until they had driven the Romanovs from their capital and Russia's throne.

Karakozov's shot signaled the beginnings of a life-and-death struggle between Russia's revolutionaries and the forces of law and order. Inevitably centered in St. Petersburg, this new movement changed the course of the city's history, for it added an element of terror and instability that had not been a part of its story before. As Russia's most European city and greatest industrial center, St. Petersburg had stood for more than a hundred and fifty years as a symbol of imperial power, modernity, and progress to which all the rest of Russia had paid homage. Then, by proclaiming that the very progress of which its people had been proud for so long was in fact a sign that their nation had gone wrong, Karakozov and the revolutionaries who followed him saw in St. Petersburg proof of Russia's failure. In the city's soaring population they saw not progress but slums filled with hundreds of thousands of proletarians living from hand to mouth. In the great mills whose smokestacks darkened the skies they saw not harbingers of modernity but instruments for denying the masses what was theirs by right. And in the regularity and grandeur of the city itself, they saw proof that their nation's rulers had betrayed the essence of

Russia. All of this seemed sure and certain proof that Russia needed different values and a new sense of direction. It then became the revolutionaries' task to chart the untried course they believed Russia ought to take.

As the center of Russia's revolutionary movement, St. Petersburg now embraced the empire's champions and its enemies, with each being consigned symbolically, at least, to opposite banks of the Neva River. On the south bank stood the Winter Palace, home of Imperial Russia's sovereigns and symbol of the new power that Peter the Great had brought into being. Nearby stood the Admiralty, the Senate, the Holy Synod, the General Staff Headquarters, and the Ministries of War and Foreign Affairs—all of which expressed the awesome power of the Russian state and the autocrat who reigned over it. Across the river lay the Fortress of Peter and Paul, originally built to protect the city from the gunfire of enemy ships, but in the nineteenth century the place of imprisonment for those men and women who challenged the course that Peter the Great had set. Idealistic young nobles who had tried to overthrow the autocracy in the name of a republic in December 1825, utopian socialists who had dreamed of building communes in Russia, the novelist Fedor Dostoevskii, Chernyshevskii, terrorists, populists, and socialists all languished in the dungeons of the Peter and Paul Fortress before they were made into monuments to the heroes of the Revolution after 1917.

From its place in St. Petersburg's very heart, the Peter and Paul Fortress promised protection against the specter of revolution for some at the same time as it loomed darkly as a repressive instrument that denied others the just fruits of their labor. In both cases, its gray granite walls stood as solid as the empire itself, a symbol that Russia's rulers could sweep their enemies from the face of the realm they ruled. Depending on whether the observer's vision of the future included the Romanovs and the Russian Empire or a society and government that belonged to the masses, the fortress offered comfort or intimidation, for its massive dimensions left no doubt of the immense power of the state. Liberation, oppression, truth, falsehood, good, and evil—the Peter and Paul Fortress embraced all these and more. And in the stories of the men and women who suffered in its dungeons lie important insights about how the people of St. Petersburg and their rulers tried to confront the problems created by modernity's many challenges.

# SEVEN

# THE PETER AND PAUL
# FORTRESS

ONE OF THE FIRST TASKS THAT PETER THE GREAT had assigned to the Russian troops who occupied Hare Island in May 1703 was to build a fort to guard the Neva River's mouth. Some twenty thousand men worked throughout that summer and fall, and by November a log and earth fort to defend Sankt Piter Burkh was finished. Three years later, Peter ordered the architect Domenico Trezzini to transform its crude defenses into the Peter and Paul Fortress, and in May 1706 the Tsar himself laid the cornerstone for its first bastion. Over the next twenty-eight years, Trezzini built six bastions in all, and named them for Peter and his five closest advisers. During the architect's last years, two of the bastions were renamed for the Empress Anna and the teenaged Emperor Peter II, and by the time Trezzini died in 1734 his great stone fortress had spread across virtually all of Hare Island. In the 1770s, Catherine the Great ordered its rough walls to be faced with gray granite to give it the appearance it has today. During the half century after that, more barracks were built to house a larger garrison. The arsenal was enlarged, and so were the Alekseev and St. Ioann ravelins at the eastern and western ends of the island.[1]

Deep within the bastions of his fortress, Trezzini built cells that served the Russian Empire as prisons for nearly two hundred years.

More were added in the 1730s, the 1750s, the early 1800s, and again in the 1830s.[2] The first prisoner of note to be confined there was Peter the Great's son Aleksei Petrovich, who after having been accused of treason against his father was brought to the Trubetskoi Bastion in the middle of June 1718 and died there after two weeks of torture.[3] Peter the Great's long-time comrade-in-arms Menshikov spent time in the fortress before the Emperor Peter II exiled him to Siberia in 1728, and a number of statesmen who had chosen the wrong side in the various "palace revolutions" that spanned the 1730s to early 1760s were confined there, too. Aleksandr Radishchev, whose *Journey from St. Petersburg to Moscow* enraged Catherine the Great in 1790, spent more than two months in the fortress prison before the Empress commuted his death sentence to Siberian banishment.[4] Then in the nineteenth century, as thoughtful men and women began to dispute the course their rulers had chosen, the numbers of political prisoners in the fortress increased.

The arrests that followed the Decembrist Revolt of 1825 filled the cells of the Peter and Paul Fortress to overflowing. On December 14 of that year, the flower of Russia's nobility rose up, hoping to replace their Emperor with a constitutional government, and they led more than three thousand Imperial Guards in revolt on the Senate Square. The young Emperor Nicholas I shattered their ranks with cannon fire, and in the aftermath sent several hundred officers to the fortress bastions, where all windows were painted over and neither light nor fresh air could enter. Mold and slime—the aftereffects of the huge flood of November 1824—still covered the floors and walls, and the interrogators allowed more filth to build up in order to make the place even more terrifying as the prisoners were shunted from one bastion to another to confront their accusers. On some occasions, high police officials and senior officers took turns questioning the accused; other times, the Emperor himself took the lead in trying to discover how far the conspiracy had spread.[5]

No interrogations had taken place in Russia on such a large scale since the revolt of the *streltsy* musketeers early in the reign of Peter the Great, and none had ever been conducted in St. Petersburg. Young men from some of Russia's noble families were starved, deprived of sleep, kept in solitary confinement, and terrorized into confessing their part in a revolt whose reasons their Emperor could never comprehend. But

*The Peter and Paul Fortress, originally built to guard the Neva River's mouth, was later used to imprison some of Russia's most infamous revolutionaries. (Courtesy of the Central State Archive of Kino–Photo–Phono Documents, St. Petersburg)*

apart from their interrogations, silence reigned. "The remotest place of exile, or life in the Aleutian Islands, or even penal servitude would have seemed to me an act of great mercy in comparison with the close confinement I experienced," one of them later wrote. "The solitary, grave-like confinement was terrible," another added many years later. "Anyone who has not spent time in solitary confinement simply cannot imagine how bad it is."[6]

When Nicholas and his adjutants sent more than a hundred of the Decembrists to Siberia and hanged five others, the Peter and Paul Fortress became Russia's main symbol of repression. A cell in its bastions awaited every man and woman who raised a hand against the government, and although other Petersburg prisons eventually shared its notoriety, the Peter and Paul Fortress continued to symbolize coercion and torment. Once inside its gates, prisoners entered a capricious world of fear in which their lives were never their own. This was a world of night-time interrogations and frequently uttered threats. The rest of the time, they were alone. "My vocal chords became weakened and atrophied from disuse," a woman prisoner remembered. "From a deep contralto [my voice] became thin, strident, and quavering. . . . Together with this physical breakdown of my organ of speech came a psychic change [and] the desire arose in me *to be silent*."[7] Yet despite fear and overpowering loneliness, life in the cells of the Peter and Paul Fortress remained more humane than its Soviet counterpart would prove to be. Books, newspapers, and writing paper were a part of virtually every prisoner's daily life in the fortress, which was a far cry indeed from the ravages of life in the Soviet Gulag during the 1930s, where men and women fought for crusts of bread and rotten bits of fish to stay alive.

The severity of the Decembrists' punishments caused many of St. Petersburg's intellectuals to turn inward, and for somewhat more than twenty years they sought freedom in the realm of the mind and spirit rather than in the world around them. Then in the late 1840s, a group of young Petersburgers began to gather in the rooms of Mikhail Butashevich-Petrashevskii, a strangely complex young man who served as a minor clerk in the Imperial Ministry of Foreign Affairs. These petty clerks and junior officers drank too much, complained too often, and criticized their superiors too loudly. From time to time they spoke of socialism as an antidote to the economic traumas that were transforming the cities of Europe into breeding grounds for revolution, and a few asked if such a system might work in Russia. In the West and in America, where dozens of high-minded people crafted utopian visions of a better world, such talk was of little consequence. But in Russia, where the authorities made no distinction between thought and deed, it became an act of rebellion that led agents of the imperial gendarmerie to Petrashevskii's lodgings in April 1849 and send everyone they found there to the Peter and Paul Fortress. Among them was Fedor Dostoevskii, an army engineer-turned-novelist, whose *Poor Folk* had won him accolades from the city's leading literary critics.[8]

As in the days of the Decembrists, the arrests of Petrashevskii, his friends, and acquaintances filled the cells of the Peter and Paul Fortress. For the better part of a week, the authorities searched the city for nearly three hundred men whose names had been turned in by double agents, only to release some quickly and let a few more go free after questioning them briefly in their rooms. Arrested at four o'clock in the morning in his small apartment at the corner of Malaia Morskaia and Voznesenskii Prospekt not far from St. Isaac's Cathedral, Dostoevskii was locked in cell No. 9 in the Alekseev Ravelin, where he spent the next eight months being interrogated and awaiting news of his fate. As spring turned into summer, fall, and winter, he drafted plans for new novels, wrote, and worried about the future. "If it isn't possible to write, I'll die," he confessed. "Better fifteen years of confinement if only one can keep a pen in one's hand."[9]

When it was announced, the punishment was death by firing squad. Just three days before Christmas 1849, Dostoevskii and twenty others were marched from the fortress in the predawn darkness to Semenovskii Square, where three black execution stakes loomed starkly against the snow as it began to grow light. "We all were made to kiss the cross, a sword was broken over our heads, and we were told to don our white execution shirts," Dostoevskii wrote to his brother a few days later.[10] "My entire life . . . passed before me with lightning speed," he added in a letter to another friend, "its scenes shifting and merging into each other as they do in a kaleidoscope."[11] The first three men were bound to the stakes and the firing squad marched onto the square. Then the drums beat retreat, and an imperial aide-de-camp galloped up to announce that the Emperor had decided to grant them their lives. Sentenced to four years of penal servitude in Siberia's Omsk Prison, Dostoevskii left the Peter and Paul Fortress for the last time on Christmas Eve. "Life is a gift," he wrote to his brother then. "Each moment of life can be a century of happiness."[12]

A decade of penal servitude and frontier military service as a private soldier transformed Dostoevskii into a devout Christian dedicated to defending Russia's autocratic government. But, as the ideas of other Russians moved in the opposite direction, the numbers of those ready to declare war against the government grew larger. At the beginning of the 1860s, the students at St. Petersburg University marched through the streets proclaiming that "public opinion, literature, our professors, countless circles of freethinking people, Western Europe, and everything that is good and progressive are with us," and more than a hundred ended up in the Peter and Paul Fortress.[13] All but three were set free by the end of the year, but their protests, followed by Karakozov's assassination attempt, made it clear that once people began to see the Tsar as their enemy, he would never again be safe in his city. In the 1870s and 1880s others would follow in Karakozov's footsteps. More than half a dozen attempts would be made to kill Alexander II between 1876 and 1881. In 1887, a band of revolutionaries including Lenin's older brother would try to assassinate Alexander III.

Opposition to Russia's government blossomed into a true revolutionary movement during the spring and summer of 1874, when several thousand young men and women "went to the people" to spread the gospel of socialism among them. Many who were arrested and brought to St. Petersburg for trial were later released, but some found themselves in the Peter and Paul Fortress, "the terrible fortress," one of them later wrote, "where so much of the true strength of Russia had perished during the last two centuries, and the very name of which is uttered in St. Petersburg in a hushed voice."[14] Prince Petr Kropotkin, educated in the Imperial Corps of Pages and already famous for his geographical explorations in Siberia was among the revolutionaries brought to the fortress that fall, and his memoirs reveal what life was like within its walls. "We entered a small room where darkness and dampness prevailed," he began to describe his arrival. "I was required to take off all my clothes, and to put on the prison dress— a green flannel dressing gown, immense woolen stockings of an incredible thickness, and boat-shaped yellow slippers, so big that I could hardly keep them on my feet when I tried to walk. . . . Then I was taken through a dark passage, where I saw armed sentries walking about, and was put into a cell. . . . A heavy oak door was shut behind me, a key turned in the lock, and I was alone in a half-dark room."[15]

Trying to get his bearings, Kropotkin surveyed his surroundings. A small opening cut in the outer wall showed a tiny slit of sky and revealed that the masonry was at least five feet thick. Canvas and heavy felt covered the walls and floor to absorb every sound. "Silence, as of the grave, reigned around me," Kropotkin wrote. "In vain I knocked on the walls and struck the floor with my foot, listening for the faintest sound in reply. None was to be heard. One month passed, then two, three, fifteen months, but there was no reply to my knocks. . . . I tried to catch any sound from the Neva or from the town on the opposite side of the river, but I could not," he explained at another point. "This dead silence began to oppress me," he added, "and I tried to sing." But after a few days that feeling passed. Like so many others who entered the fortress, Kropotkin let the silence of the prison envelop him.[16] Hour after hour, day after day, the only sounds were the bells of the fortress cathedral, which rang the Orthodox chant "Lord Have Mercy" every fifteen minutes. Then at midnight, they chimed the anthem "God Save the Tsar," which lasted a full fifteen minutes. Sudden changes in temperature sometimes made the chimes ring off key. Then, Kropotkin remembered, they became "a horrible cacophony which sounded like the ringing of bells at a burial."[17]

The torment of Kropotkin's isolation was relieved by the freedom to read and write. He was allowed to order scientific books and journals from the library of the Academy of Sciences, and to write every day until sunset. When his pencils and pens were taken away, he read the ancient Russian chronicles, books on history, lives of saints, and novels. "My relatives managed to send me the Christmas stories of Dickens," he remembered many years later. "I spent the festival [of Christmas Eve] laughing and crying over those beautiful creations of the great novelist."[18] Eighteen months after that, Kropotkin escaped and—irony of ironies—celebrated by having dinner with a friend at Donon's on the Moika Canal before fleeing to the West. As the two young men had guessed, the authorities never thought to look for him in one of the city's most elegant restaurants.

Throughout the 1870s, the Peter and Paul Fortress continued to receive new prisoners as the secret police brought group after group of revolutionaries to trial. Depending on the whim of the authorities, some stayed for brief interludes while others remained for years. Some went mad from the psychological strain and others committed suicide, despite the best efforts of their guards. A few found that incarceration made them stronger, but these were a handful among the much larger numbers of people to whom months and years in the Peter and Paul Fortress brought sickness, premature aging, and death. In the 1870s, one of the most feared parts of the fortress was the Trubetskoi Bastion, a diamond-shaped structure that projected from its southwest corner. Here prisoners like Kropotkin were kept in solitary confinement for years at a time.

Still dedicated to the belief that the revolution's greatest chance for success lay in stirring up Russia's peasants, the populist Sergei Kravchinskii found the prison regime much worse when he arrived at the Trubetskoi Bastion in 1879, several years after Kropotkin had escaped. "For a minute or two you see nothing, so deep is the gloom," he remembered of the moment when his jailers brought him to his cell. "The coldness of the place chills you to the bone," he went on. "There is a damp moldy smell like that of a charnel house or an ill-ventilated cellar. . . . Then, when your eyes have become accustomed to the obscurity, you perceive that you are the tenant of a cell a few paces wide and long. In one corner is a bed of straw, with a woolen counterpane—as thin as paper—nothing else. At the foot of the bed stands a high wooden pail with a cover. This is the *parashka* [which will serve as a toilet and] which later on will poison you with foul stenches." None of the "luxuries" such as books, paper, pens, or soap that Kropotkin had enjoyed were available in Kravchinskii's time, when the vermin that infested the subterranean cells of the Trubetskoi

Bastion spilled into other parts of the prison. "Rats enter by scores, try to climb upon the beds, and bite the prisoners," Kravchinskii wrote. "It is in these hideous dungeons," he added, "that those condemned to death spend their last hours."[19]

Kravchinskii soon was taken from the Trubetskoi Bastion to serve a long sentence of penal servitude in a remote corner of Siberia, but others filled his place. Foremost among the prisoners sent to the Peter and Paul Fortress in the early 1880s were terrorists from the Party of the People's Will, who had passed a sentence of death against Alexander II on August 26, 1879. Hoping that the murder of Alexander II would ignite a revolutionary conflagration in Russia, these young men and women turned to assassination to avenge the suffering their comrades had endured at the hands of the Emperor's police. Earlier that year, a twenty-three-year-old schoolteacher by the name of Aleksandr Soloviev had fired five shots at the Emperor as he had strolled through the Winter Palace Gardens that spring. Now Soloviev's comrades vowed to "substitute the will of the people for the will of one individual" and to "free the nation from the yoke of the existing government."[20] They insisted that the first requirement for doing that had to be the death of Alexander II.

Although no attempts had been made against Alexander's life between 1866 and April 1879, when Soloviev fired his shots, assassination continued to serve the revolutionaries as a weapon. On January 28, 1878, a young woman by the name of Vera Zasulich shot the Governor General of St. Petersburg to avenge the flogging of one of her revolutionary comrades in prison, and the authorities chose to have her tried by a jury in the hope that her conviction would lead public opinion to condemn the revolutionary movement. Moved by Zasulich's plea that she had shot the general because all other avenues for seeking justice were closed in Russia, a Petersburg jury acquitted her of the crime to which she had already confessed. Public opinion cheered the verdict, and only a very few understood that her acquittal had glamorized assassination as a political weapon. The great novelist Lev Tolstoi had been one of the handful to sense that dark days lay ahead. "The Zasulich verdict is no joke," he had written when he heard the news. "This is like a prophecy of revolution."[21] The very next year, the young men and women of the Party of the People's Will proudly embraced assassination as their weapon of choice. Early in September 1879 they began their campaign to kill the Tsar.

For eighteen months after they made their decision, the terrorists pursued their prey back and forth across European Russia. Bound by an oath that forbade them to abandon their cause on pain of death, they never numbered more than a handful. On several occasions, they attempted to blow up the Emperor's train as he traveled from one part of Russia to another, but each time chance or some careless mishap intervened. In the fall of 1879, the terrorists decided to confine their hunt for the Tsar to St. Petersburg and to concentrate on killing him in the Winter Palace. The first step in their plan was to gain entrance to the palace itself, and with that in mind one of their number got a job there as a carpenter. The man's passport stated that he was a peasant by the name of Batyshkov from the North Russian province of Olonets. Pleasant, honest, but apparently not overly intelligent, "Batyshkov" seemed the sort of fellow who made friends easily with superiors and comrades alike. Unknown to the authorities who employed him, he was in fact Stepan Khalturin, a key figure in the Party of the People's Will, and he had come to the Palace to kill the Tsar.

Over the next several months, Khalturin smuggled bits of dynamite into the cellar quarters where the Palace workmen lived and hid them in his mattress. Toward the end of January 1880, the conspirators decided that he had enough explosives to do the job. Although Khalturin argued that more was needed, his comrades overruled him. Told to go ahead, he planted his bomb two floors below the Emperor's private dining room, and on February 5, he lit the fuse and walked out by the workers' entrance. Half an hour later, the dynamite shattered the guardroom on the floor above, killing eleven and injuring fifty-six, but the force did not reach the dining room, and Alexander escaped unharmed. Although the Emperor remained alive, the psychological impact of Khalturin's bomb was immense, for it proclaimed that Russia's Emperor could never feel safe even in his own home. To protect himself and Russia, he turned to a committee of generals, which immediately put extraordinary measures into effect. These men used all the resources of the imperial government to guard Alexander II against any further danger.[22]

With arrests thinning their ranks over the next several months, the twenty-seven radical activists of the People's Will watched and waited. Seven were women and all but six were younger than thirty. Seven would be dead in six months, and another eleven would die before the decade reached its end. Only six would survive to see revolution sweep the Romanovs away in 1917. Most had never used a firearm before, and only three had any experience with explosives. Between them, they had fewer than two hundred rubles, a sum so small that it could not even feed them all if it had been needed for that purpose. Nonetheless, they turned to face

Alexander's army and secret police convinced that the "honor of the Party demands that the Emperor be killed,"[23] and that the salvation of Russia required them to make one more attack. Led by Andrei Zheliabov, they vowed again to assassinate the Emperor or die in the attempt.[24]

A former serf who had studied law at one of Russia's provincial universities, Zheliabov had not become a revolutionary leader until well into the 1870s. "Tall, magnificently built, broad and with strongly marked features," according to a friend, "he was a man who compelled attention at first glance" and believed that terrorism could move the revolution at a quicker pace.[25] During the last year of his life, he fell in love with Sofiia Perovskaia, the daughter of a one-time governor-general of St. Petersburg and great-granddaughter of the Empress Elizabeth's lover Kyril Razumovskii. Small, blond, almost childlike in appearance, she was as dedicated to the terrorists' cause as he. Perovskaia returned Zheliabov's love, but both put the revolution first and ended their lives on the hangman's scaffold.

Led by Perovskaia, five terrorists set out at the beginning of 1881 to discover what routes Alexander II preferred to use when he traveled from one part of St. Petersburg to another. This time, they planned to set a charge of dynamite under a street over which he passed, but they also agreed to hold in reserve a new and untried weapon in case he changed his route or their dynamite failed to explode. Invented by Nikolai Kibalchich, a brilliant scientist who had joined them at the very beginning, the terrorists now had the world's first fuseless hand grenade. Filled with bits of jagged metal shards and almost suicidally volatile, its center contained two crossed glass vials of nitroglycerine that would explode on impact.[26]

Zheliabov and his comrades used a small inheritance to rent a basement shop at No. 56 Malaia Sadovaia, a street that ran along the Catherine Canal and intersected Nevskii Prospekt across from the Kazan Cathedral. They chose two of their number to act as shopkeepers to prevent the neighbors from becoming suspicious, and dug a tunnel under one of the Emperor's oft-traveled routes from one of the shop's unused rooms. The police had at long last begun to penetrate the curtain of secrecy with which they had surrounded themselves, and in mid-January, 1881, three of their number were arrested. A few weeks later, another fell into the clutches of the authorities, and at the end of February Zheliabov and another comrade walked into a police trap. Zheliabov's quick thinking concealed his identity and bought his comrades a few more days, but time was running out.

The remaining terrorists planned their attack for the morning of March 1, 1881, with a sleepless Kibalchich having spent the previous seventeen hours putting together four nitroglycerine hand grenades. When Alexander changed his usual route at the last minute, these became their only weapon of attack, and they used them against his carriage as it sped along the Inzhenernaia and turned onto the Catherine Embankment. A gift from Napoleon III, Alexander's bombproof carriage suffered little damage when the first grenade thrown by Nikolai Rysakov exploded. But when the Emperor got out to inspect the damage, a second terrorist hurled a device directly between his feet. When the heavy smoke cleared, Russia's sovereign lay mortally wounded, his legs torn away by the blast. An hour later he died, and within a week most of the terrorists had been incarcerated in the Peter and Paul Fortress. Kibalchich and another conspirator were turned in by their landlady. Perovskaia was identified by a woman from whom she had sometimes bought milk, and Gesia Helfmann was captured by the police in a raid on another suspect's apartment. Nikolai Rysakov, of course, was caught after he had thrown the first hand grenade, while Ignacy Hryniewicki, a Pole who had joined the Russians' cause and thrown the fatal grenade, died several hours after his victim from wounds the explosion had inflicted. Several others, most notably Vera Figner, escaped to continue the struggle for another year or two before the police caught them, too.[27]

Deep in the Trubetskoi Bastion of the Peter and Paul Fortress, the six terrorists thought to be the most guilty—Zheliabov, Perovskaia, Timofei Mikhailov, Kibalchich, Rysakov, and Helfmann—faced days and nights of questioning as the police tried to learn how they had laid their plans and who had helped them. Always Zheliabov and Perovskaia remained aloof and arrogant, refusing to yield anything the authorities demanded. Rysakov and another of the grenadiers by the name of Mikhailov proved less strong. Kibalchich spent most of his time in the bastion drafting plans for a rocket-powered flying machine, which proved to be so impressive that Count Totleben, a high police official, urged the Emperor to lock him up and make him work for the government rather than to hang him.

The terrorists' trial began on March 26 and lasted three days, during which the court sat from eleven in the morning until two-thirty in the afternoon and again from eight in the evening until midnight. Nineteen witnesses were called to describe their attack, but none were summoned in their defense. At three o'clock in the morning of March 31, the judges pronounced all six guilty. Then, just as the cold gray morning light was beginning to show in the courtroom windows three and a half hours later, they announced that they all were to be hanged. "It was not expected even by the public present," *The Times* correspondent telegraphed to London, "that all the accused would be indiscriminately condemned to be hanged." Later that day, Helfmann revealed that she was pregnant, and her sentence was suspended because imperial law forbade the killing of her unborn child. The others were informed that they had the right to appeal, but none did. When Mikhailov and Rysakov begged the new Emperor to spare them, their petitions were summarily denied.[28]

At eight o'clock on the evening of April 2, 1881, five Orthodox priests entered the Peter and Paul Fortress to be taken to the cells of the five condemned prisoners. Rysakov made his confession and took Holy Communion, while Mikhailov confessed but refused the Sacrament. Kibalchich spoke at length with his priest but did not make confession nor take Communion. Zheliabov and Perovskaia refused to see any priest at all. Then at six o'clock the next morning, they were all taken from their cells and ordered to change into the prescribed black garments. After that they were taken into the prison yard, chained to seats on heavy springless carts on which twelve-foot-high platforms had been erected, and paraded through the city to the same Semenovskii Square where Dostoevskii had been taken for his mock execution almost thirty-two years before. In addition to detectives and police, some twelve thousand troops lined the streets to make certain that no attempt was made to free the condemned. By that time, so few of the terrorists remained at large that no such effort would have been possible.

At the square, the prisoners were brought to the gallows and allowed to kiss the cross before the executions began. Because it was not the Russian way to construct drop platforms in scaffold floors, death usually came by slow strangulation, and that grim fact alone made the hangman's trade so unpopular that there was only one practitioner in all the empire. This man, Frolov, invariably steeled himself for his gruesome task with large tumblers of vodka, and the morning of April 3 found him more intoxicated than usual. He therefore managed to dispatch only three of his victims without incident and bungled the hangings of Mikhailov and Zheliabov. After Mikhailov's noose had slipped twice and Frolov had hauled him up to be hanged a third time, the enraged crowd surged toward the scaffold in a vain attempt to spare him. Angry, drunk, and cursing, Frolov tied Zheliabov's noose in a double knot to prevent a similar incident, but by doing so he slowed his death even more. Eventually the prison doctor pronounced all five victims dead, but it had taken Zheliabov and Mikhailov each several minutes to die.[29]

What Vera Figner called a reign of "White Terror" waged against all opposition in Russia began the moment Alexander III took his father's place. As one of the few terrorists to escape from St. Petersburg, Figner fled to the south, where she remained at large until she was betrayed by a double agent early in 1883. When her police escorts brought her to St. Petersburg in the middle of February, she was kept in the Alekseev Ravelin of the Fortress, and like so many before her, she too faded into silence. "A gray, monotonous life began," she remembered many years later. "For whole days and weeks . . . I lost the inner impulse for speaking [and] when it was necessary to move my lips to speak, I had to summon all my strength of will."[30] For a full twenty months, Figner remained in the Fortress awaiting trial, alone with her thoughts and her silence. "We had been deprived of everything: of our native land and humanity, of our friends, our comrades and families," she wrote. "We were cut off from every living person and thing. . . . Of all the world they left us but a prison courtyard. . . . And of all people, only gendarmes remained . . . as deaf as statues and their faces as immobile as masks."[31]

After the commutation of Figner's death sentence to life in prison in 1885, the authorities moved her to the old Schlüsselburg Fortress, some forty miles upstream at the point where the Neva River flows out of Lake Ladoga. Her transfer marked an important moment in the history of the Peter and Paul Fortress, for the government had now decided to keep its most dangerous prisoners outside the capital. Yet, the old fortress on Hare Island remained a symbol of oppression even though Schlüsselburg and several of Siberia's prisons replaced it as centers of penal servitude. Just two decades after Figner's transfer to Schlüsselburg, St. Petersburg's workers would take to the streets in what became known as the Revolution of 1905 to win a constitution and National Assembly for all Russians. Twelve years after that, the masses to whom Figner, Zheliabov, Perovskaia, and their comrades had dedicated their lives would drive the Romanovs from Russia's throne.

What connected the terrorists of the early 1880s with the triumphant revolutionaries of 1917 was a handful of men and women who survived the White Terror by fleeing to the West. Throughout the 1870s, Russia's revolutionaries had put action ahead of contemplation and preferred head-on confrontation to debate. Their vision of revolution centered upon millions of peasants marching in support of a just cause, but the men and women who escaped the White Terror soon began to see things in a different way. Georgii Plekhanov, Pavel Akselrod, and Vera Zasulich all turned to Marxism, whose founder claimed to have discovered those "scientific" laws about the workings of society that Russia's intellectuals had been seeking for the better part of a generation.

Although the first volume of Marx's *Das Kapital* had been translated into Russian in 1872, its Russian readers had not seen its revolutionary implications until the end of the decade, when Plekhanov first dared to ask who The People really were and if they would really fight in a socialist revolution. Until then, Russia's revolutionaries had believed that the communes in which so many of their nation's peasants lived and worked were a form of primitive socialism, but no one knew for a fact if that was really true. The first hard answers to these questions began to emerge in 1879, when a young sociologist and ethnographer by the name of Maksim Kovalevskii showed that conflicts between rich and poor peasants had caused communes to disintegrate in countries more advanced than Russia. But Kovalevskii's data could not predict if Russia would follow the path of other nations or if, as so many of its revolutionaries wanted to believe, its communes were in some way different. The answer to that question came just a few months after Kovalevskii's work appeared in print, when a thirty-one-year-old statistician by the name of Vasilii Orlov showed that Russia's peasant communes had already begun to disintegrate under the forces of modernization. "It was impossible to disagree with [Orlov's] figures," Plekhanov's wife wrote as she recalled how her husband had struggled to save his populist faith.[32] Orlov's data were simply too overwhelming and his conclusions too clear to be disputed.

Vowing to build a new faith on firmer foundations, Plekhanov searched the realm of economic and political theory throughout the early 1880s. With skepticism and caution he finally turned to Marx, whose writings led him to conclude that *"the very development of Russian capitalism"* was a vital "new guarantee of the revolutionary movement's success. . . . Like Ariadne's thread," he later confessed, "the theory of Marx led us out of the labyrinth of contradictions in which our ideas had struggled."[33] Convinced that he had replaced his blind faith with the last word in the scientific study of society, Plekhanov insisted that Russia's revolutionaries must concentrate on making the industrial proletariat into a revolutionary force. Because he no longer believed that its communes had a part to play in bringing socialism to Russia, he saw no point in making any further attempt to build a revolutionary movement among the peasants.

Now living in Switzerland, Plekhanov, Zasulich, and Akselrod formed the Emancipation of Labor Group, the first Russian Marxist organization. As they worked to apply Marxism to Russia's backward economic life, they had no vision about how Russia's revolutionary experience would unfold, how the proletariat would seize power, or how long it would take them to do it. When Alexander III died and the weak-willed Nicholas II took his place in 1894, Russia's Marxists still had no practical plan of action. "[We thought that] gradually the number of workers studying Marxism would increase, and that they would bring into their circles still more new members," one of them wrote some years later. "In time . . . we [expected to] form a socialist workers' party," he added. "[But] what it would do and how it would struggle [for the workers' cause] still remained unclear."[34] In the meantime, the first step had to be to convince Russia's workers to follow their lead. In St. Petersburg, the city with the largest concentration of factory workers in the empire, a handful of study circles had taken shape in the late 1880s. But no one had yet bound them together or convinced them to follow a Marxist program.

In 1893, the first of two young men who would galvanize the city's workers arrived in St. Petersburg. Already balding at the age of twenty-three and barely five feet five inches tall, Vladimir Ilych Ulianov was known to his friends as "Ilych" or "the Old Man," and he brought with him a stern sense of discipline that tempered his passion for action. He had once practiced law in the provinces, and he used the incisive ways of thought he had learned as an attorney to plan new tactics for bringing Russia's workers into the political arena. During his first years in St. Petersburg, Ulianov concentrated on turning revolutionary theory into action, and he urged the city's scattered study groups to unite in demanding shorter hours, better pay, and safer working conditions. Eventually, he adopted the revolutionary name of Lenin. Twenty-four years after he first set foot in St. Petersburg, he would take command of Russia from the steps of Rastrelli's famed Smolnyi Convent.

As Lenin urged Russia's workers to stand firm against St. Petersburg's factory owners and managers, he found an ardent supporter in Iulii Tsederbaum, the son of well-to-do Jews from Odessa. Later to become better known by the pseudonym of Martov, Tsederbaum had sought shelter in the revolutionary movement from the violent pogroms that had shattered thousands of Jewish lives and fortunes in Southern Russia in the 1880s. "Would I have become what I am," he asked many years later, "had not Russian reality . . . impressed its coarse fingers upon my pliable young soul?"[35] Certainly Martov's hatred for a society that allowed innocent men and women to be treated so brutally drove him to war against the authorities who represented it. Sent into exile for the first time when he was still in his teens, he was just twenty-two in 1895 when he and Lenin first met in St. Petersburg. Starting in that year, Martov led the *molodye*—the "youngsters"—of St. Petersburg's Social Democratic movement, while Lenin commanded its *stariki*, or "old men."[36] Together they formed men and women who knew well the misery of life in St. Petersburg's lower depths into the Union of Struggle for the Liberation of the Working Class. Many of these new recruits had spent their lives in the city's huge textile mills, where for fourteen hours every day, they had walked more than eight miles back and forth in front of clanging looms and jennies. Because the threads they wove and spun were more pliable when warm and damp, they worked in high temperatures and stifling humidity. A government report described them as "emaciated, haggard, worn out [and] with sunken chests [which] gave the impression of sick people just released from the hospital."[37] Too tired to eat at the end of the day, St. Petersburg's textile workers dragged themselves home to live in the worst poverty imaginable.[38] They lived from day to day, for even a day out of work meant hunger. A fortnight's unemployment could bring them to the brink of starvation.

Lenin's and Martov's efforts to organize St. Petersburg's workers bore fruit in the spring of 1896, when some of the weavers and spinners who had joined their Union of Struggle went on strike. Promising to confront the city's factory owners with "unified, unanimous, and unyielding resistance,"[39] these men and women demanded shorter hours and better pay, and after three weeks they won their first concessions. Yet, when the strike ended in the middle of June, neither Martov nor Lenin could share the workers' triumph. Early in December 1895, the security police—now called the Okhrana—had put Lenin and most of the *stariki* in prison, and a month later they had arrested Martov and most of the *molodye* who supported him. The rank-and-file Marxists who faced the factory owners that spring thus did so without the men who had formed their ranks and shaped their tactics. What carried them through those hard, dangerous days was the firm belief that they had the power to shape their destinies.[40]

"When you get hungry enough, you'll come back to work," an arrogant plant manager told a group of strikers at one point. "We'll die right here," they replied. "But we won't come back to work under the conditions we had before!"[41] In the Union of Struggle for the Liberation of the Working Class, St. Petersburg's striking workers had discovered self-respect and a sense of power. In the years ahead they would press their demands with greater force as their numbers increased.

Textile workers had dominated the Petersburg strikes of 1896, but that changed when dissatisfaction among the city's steelworkers deepened toward the end of the decade. When a new wave of strikes swept the capital in 1901, the more skilled, literate, and politically assertive men who worked in the Obukhov Steel Mill insisted that the time had come to "fight for freedom against the tyranny of Tsar and capital."[42] At the beginning of May, the Obukhov men fought the police with cobblestones thrown from upper windows and doorways, forcing the government to call in armed sailors and infantry. By May 8, a week after the strike had begun, seven workers had been shot and a thousand arrested, but fifteen thousand from other steel mills and foundries had joined in the strike. Hoping to avoid further confrontations, the government agreed to some of the strikers' demands. Clearly, labor protest was growing in Russia's capital, but the mass movement that might one day overwhelm Nicholas II and his government had not yet begun. That was about to change as the tensions of the Russo-Japanese War weakened the forces that had previously suppressed the men and women who confronted the government and factory owners in 1896 and 1901.[43]

The morning of January 30, 1904, found St. Petersburg in turmoil. Less than four days before, ships from the Japanese fleet had attacked Russia's Far Eastern naval bastion at Port Arthur, and Russia and Japan were now at war. Whipped by a raw wind that made the freezing temperatures seem even colder, thousands of people began to gather on the Palace Square while it was still dark. Students from the university surged across the Nikolaevskii Bridge, while crowds from the Nevskii Prospekt thronged through the great arches with which Rossi had joined the General Staff Headquarters with the Ministry of Finance and the Foreign Ministry. Massed in front of the Winter Palace, they sang "God Save the Tsar," prayed, and cheered for Tsar, Army, Fleet, and Country. In contrast to the strikes of a few years before, the people of St. Petersburg now seemed united.

Surrounded by their children, Nicholas and Alexandra appeared on the palace balcony to acknowledge the crowd's cheers and hymns. In the

square below and on the Nevskii Prospekt, "everyone was mixed together," a correspondent reported the next day. "Generals and tramps
marched side-by-side, students with banners and ladies, their arms filled
with shopping. Everyone was united in one general feeling," he added.
"Everyone sang."[44] To this enthusiastic throng, Nicholas II was still
*Batiushka*—the "Little Father"—who answered to God for their well-
being. These lower classes blamed the pain and suffering they had borne
for so long on men who had failed to serve the Tsar as they should, and
they felt certain that their *Batiushka* would right the wrongs they suffered
if only they could tell him the truth. The masses had believed this for
hundreds of years, but that, too, was about to change. The place where it
would change was St. Petersburg. And the man who made that happen
was Father Georgii Gapon.

A slender man with fiery black eyes, "thick, wavy hair, and a beard the
hue of a raven's wing,"[45] Georgii Gapon had grown up in the heart of the
Ukrainian steppe, where the Cossacks had fought Poles, Turks, and Russians since the seventeenth century. His peasant mother's religious fervor
made him become a priest, but his Cossack father's hatred for social injus-
tice convinced him to use his place in the Church to help Russia's masses.
By the time he graduated from the Theological Academy at St. Petersburg's Aleksandr Nevskii Monastery in 1898, Gapon had learned to
charm the masses with his words, and he vowed to use that gift to serve
the city's proletarians. He took to spending long hours in the harbor district, where, he later explained, "the poorest people lived in the greatest
poverty." Urging his listeners to avoid violence, he preached that "some
sort of workingmen's organization" would better serve their cause than
did "clashes with the authorities."[46]

With the support of high officials who hoped government-supported
unions could control the city's proletarians, Father Gapon founded the Assembly of Factory and Mill Workers late in the summer of 1903. "The basic
idea is to build a nest among the factory and mill workers where . . . a truly
Russian spirit would prevail," the people's priest explained. "From there," he
predicted, "healthy and self-sacrificing fledglings can fly forth to defend
their Tsar and country and aid their fellow workers."[47] Gapon wanted his
Assembly to become the center of a larger movement. "In two or three
years, all two hundred thousand Petersburg workers will be members of our
union," he vowed.[48] "[Then] we shall unite the workers in all of Russia."[49]
He wanted his union also to become "a place where factory workers can

truly undertake earnest, practical efforts to refine and educate themselves ... [in] an environment for the sensible awakening and strengthening of Russian national consciousness among the workers."[50] By the outbreak of the Russo-Japanese War, the Assembly had become "the largest concentrated organization" anywhere in Russia, and it seemed ready to follow his program. St. Petersburg's workers had not joined the labor unrest that flared in other parts of the empire that year, and for the moment it seemed that Gapon had found a way to bind government and workers together.[51]

At the beginning of 1905, workers at St. Petersburg's Putilov Plant vowed "without shouts and noise, and without violence" to protest the firings of several men who had played a key role in their Assembly.[52] Their peaceful protest burgeoned into a strike, and by the end of the first week more than a hundred thousand workers had walked away from their benches. Still, Gapon's organization urged passive resistance, not violence. "A kind of mystical, religious ecstasy reigned for the whole time," an observer wrote in recalling one of the Assembly's mass meetings. "The content of the speeches was meager," he went on, "but they were all pronounced with such ... touching sincerity ... [that one was] compelled to feel ... that it was really necessary ... to do something [and] give vent to this worker bitterness and dissatisfaction."[53] The best course, they decided, was a mass appeal to the Tsar. "Go to the Tsar, as children to their father," the bishop of St. Petersburg urged them. "Tell him of your woes, asking for help and justice," he added. "What Russian heart would not respond to this call?"[54]

During the first days of 1905, Gapon turned up everywhere, urging workers to join the peaceful march he had planned for Sunday, January 9. His plan was to lead the workers to the Winter Palace and deliver a petition to the Tsar that described their plight and asked for his help. "We are regarded not as human beings but as slaves who must endure their bitter fate in silence," the petition stated. "Neither we nor the rest of the Russian people enjoy a single human right—not even the right to speak, think, assemble, discuss our needs, or take steps to improve our condition. ... If Thou ... dost not respond to our pleas," their petition concluded, "we will die here in this square before Thy palace.... We have nowhere else to go."[55]

But how many workers would follow Gapon? And what if the Tsar did not respond? In St. Petersburg's streets where men and women huddled in groups against the biting wind, in smoke-filled cafes and taverns where workers guzzled watery beer and rotgut vodka, and in workers' clubs of the Narva, Petersburg, and Vyborg districts, Gapon asked his audiences: "What if the Tsar will not receive us and won't read our petition?" And from them all he heard the same answer—again and again, fearsome in its monotony: "Then we have no Tsar!"[56] "Like an echo," an eyewitness remembered, "the phrase repeated itself from all sides: 'No Tsar! No Tsar!'"[57] Hoping that the Tsar would hear their pleas, the workers of St. Petersburg prepared to march. At the same time, Governor-General Ivan Fullon brought twelve thousand infantry and cavalry into the city. "Petersburg resembled a city that had been seized by enemy soldiers," one commentator wrote. "Campfires burned brightly. Ambulances stood ready to take on wounded, and great kettles of soup steamed in company mess kitchens that had been set up in the open."[58] Workers and soldiers all waited for the morning. "Many turned their attention that evening to the huge blood-red moon that rose above the horizon," one worker remembered. "On this night, St. Petersburg was the very heart of Russia."[59]

With the temperature standing at five degrees below freezing, January 9, 1905, dawned bright and clear, one of those rare Petersburg winter days with no wind. Gapon had spent the previous evening speaking to crowds of workers, comparing the coming day to the Resurrection when, like Christ, they all would walk with the Lord. When word spread that the police were seeking his arrest, Gapon took shelter in a worker's apartment, where no one dared to touch him. Plans already had been made for the marchers to assemble at several points and follow the great avenues that converged on the Winter Palace Square. Everyone came dressed in his or her Sunday best without any weapons or revolutionary symbols. "We must save Russia from the bureaucrats under whose weight we suffer," some of them said as they crossed themselves and repeated the Lord's Prayer. "We are going to the Tsar for truth."[60] As their columns advanced, the workers in the lead hoisted huge portraits of Nicholas and Aleksandra. Then came people carrying icons, religious banners, and large crosses, who sang "save us, O Lord. How glorious is our Lord in Zion!"[61] "The crowd reminded one of the ocean's dark billows," the Bolshevik writer Maksim Gorkii remembered. "The gray faces of the people were like the turbid, foamy crests of the waves."[62]

When a squadron of Horse Guards failed to drive back workers from the Putilov Plant at the Narva Gates on the southeast side of the city, two companies of the Ninety-Third Irkutsk Infantry replied with aimed volleys that cut down dozens of marchers. An hour or so later, more shooting took place on the Troitskaia Square, not far from the Peter and Paul Fortress, where the Pavlovskii Guards shot more than a hundred marchers after saber-swinging Cossacks had failed to disperse them. Yet all this was a prelude to the confrontation on the Winter Palace Square itself, where tens of thousands of marchers faced two thousand infantry and cavalry supported by artillery. Again the workers refused to disperse, and once again officers ordered their men to fire, leaving the square littered with torn bodies from which blood poured onto the new-fallen snow.

Troops swept through the nearby streets, firing from time to time into crowds that contained onlookers as well as marchers. The English satirist H. H. Munro, who wrote under the pen name of Saki, narrowly missed being shot that day, and so did the writer Dmitrii Merezhkovskii, who had been walking in the Summer Gardens. Gorkii had been among the marchers at Troitskaia Square, as had Lenin's sister Anna. All four escaped, but others were not so lucky. Old men carrying portraits of Nicholas and Alexandra, children who had climbed trees to get a better view, mothers walking hand in hand with toddlers all had been cut down, nearly a thousand in all.[63] "There is no Tsar!" Gapon proclaimed in a letter that Gorkii read to a huge crowd the next day. "Long live the beginning of the popular struggle for freedom!"[64] The myth of the Tsar as the "Little Father" of all the Russians was dead. For centuries it had stood between the autocracy and its enemies. Now it was gone, swept away by the gunfire of a single day.

Bloody Sunday, as the events of January 9 in St. Petersburg became known, ushered in what the Dowager Empress Mariia Fedorovna called a "year of nightmares,"[65] in which crisis piled upon crisis, and tragedy followed tragedy. Just a few weeks after Bloody Sunday, the Grand Duke Sergei Aleksandrovich was blown to bits by a nitroglycerine grenade of the type that had killed Alexander II. Then, news of huge Russian defeats at Mukden and the Tsushima Straits flowed in from the Far East. Soldiers and sailors mutinied, and so many strikes and peasant riots broke out that Nicholas and his generals had to assign thousands of infantry companies and cavalry squadrons with 224 cannons and 124 machine guns to suppress them.

All through the spring and summer, the Russian Empire continued on its collision course with revolution. Yet, when the real revolution came that fall no one recognized it at first. It began in Moscow on October 7 as a railroad workers' strike that spread across the entire empire. When it became a general strike in St. Petersburg a few days later, factory workers, telephone and telegraph operators, servants, and janitors all walked off their jobs, and so did physicians, lawyers, teachers, clerks, and even the entire corps de ballet of the Imperial Mariinskii Theater. For the better part of a week, St. Petersburg had no streetlights, no newspapers, no streetcars. Food and fuel grew scarce. No one knew what the morrow would bring, but everyone was on edge.⁶⁶ On October 14, St. Petersburg's Governor-General Dmitrii Trepov issued his famous order to "use no blanks and don't skimp on bullets!"⁶⁷ By that time, the city's workers had begun to arm themselves.

A novelist and rare book dealer by the name of Sergei Mintslov lived through the Petersburg strike, and his diary entries between October 12 and October 17 tell how a patriotic Russian, who believed in his Tsar, Church, and country, saw the events that began the Revolution of 1905 in St. Petersburg.

> *October 12th.* Piter is now cut off from the rest of Russia. . . . Panic is beginning to spread through the city. People are certain that by evening all shops will shut their doors and go on strike. . . . Sausage shops, bakeries, and grocers' shops are all besieged by customers as everyone tries to lay in a stock of provisions. [Today] the price of meat soared from 16 to 22 kopeks a pound.

> *October 14th.* Shop windows are all boarded up for protection. There is no electricity today. Shop interiors are dully lit by a few candles or by some sort of cheap oil lamps. Everything looks as if it has been fixed so that, with the very first tremors, the proprietors need only shut their doors and douse the lights in order to turn their shops into little strongholds.

> *October 15th.* Reinforcements have arrived in Piter. They say that infantry have been brought from Pskov and the Guards' Cavalry from Tsarskoe Selo. . . . There are no newspapers today. . . . The Tsar is at Peterhof where the Imperial yacht, *Polar Star*, remains under full steam and ready to take him aboard and flee to Denmark.

> *October 16th.* Evening. The electricity has been playing tricks. One minute the streets are pitch dark. Suddenly, there is a crackling sound and all the street lamps flame with light only to go out again

in a few minutes. A huge searchlight [atop the Admiralty] illumi-
nates the Nevskii Prospekt. . . . Rumors are flying that the "revolution" will break out on the 20th, and now all workers and
revolutionaries are laying in weapons.

> *October 17th.* The mood of alarm continues. . . . Institutions of
> higher education are occupied by soldiers and machineguns.
> . . . Everyone is convinced that the Tsar does not want to hear of any
> concessions, and that, in the highest circles of government, they are
> firmly resolved to "spill the blood of the revolution."[68]

"The ominous signs of a terrible and stormy explosion," one statesman
wrote, "make themselves felt more strongly each day,"[69] and the sense of
crisis that Mintslov perceived seemed to be everywhere. For a brief moment, everything seemed to turn on the actions of Trepov and the Petersburg Soviet of Workers' Deputies, which had first convened on October
13 with a membership of about thirty. Soon its numbers grew to 562,
with Lev Davidovich Bronshtein playing a leading part in directing its
struggle against the government. Better known by the revolutionary nom
de guerre of Trotskii, Bronshtein had just turned twenty-six when the
October days began, and he had raced to St. Petersburg from Finland
hoping to change the course of history. In the meantime, Governor-
General Trepov, a cavalryman who gave no thought to politics and was
ready to crush any who stood in his way, continued to bring more troops
into the city. Trepov had no doubt that he could put down St. Petersburg's
strikers and demonstrators. But, as Nicholas later explained to his mother,
he warned that it would "cost rivers of blood" to do so.[70]

Trotskii later remembered that in St. Petersburg "the Soviet united the
revolution around itself."[71] Convinced that "decisive events in Russia will
be accomplished in the coming days," it urged the workers of St. Petersburg to continue their general strike, and warned that a premature return
to work could prevent a "decisive blow [from being delivered] to the tottering autocracy."[72] At the Nevskii and Obukhov plants, seventeen thousand workers gathered on October 17 to support the Soviet, and a few
thousand made ready for an armed uprising against Trepov's forces. The
majority feared that Trepov's units were too strong and urged caution, but
it was the government that backed down first. Confronted by the stark
choice between granting concessions to his subjects and giving Trepov the

order to slaughter them, Nicholas II chose the first course—although not before giving very serious consideration to the second. Indeed, he preferred bullets to ballots, but the urgings of his advisers forced him not to use them.

And so on October 17, the day of the mass meetings at the Obukhov and Nevskii plants, Nicholas II signed the October Manifesto, granting civil rights to all Russians and summoning a National Assembly, or a Duma, as it was called in Russian. Mintslov, who saw it as a chance for Russians to shape their destiny, exclaimed, "Hurrah! We are now free people," when he read the Tsar's proclamation.[73] But other Petersburgers saw things differently. To conservatives, the October Manifesto signaled disaster, for it threatened the principles of autocracy, orthodoxy, and nationality on which they based their view of Russia's past, present, and future. To Trotskii and the Petersburg Soviet it seemed only to offer minor concessions that would keep the old order intact. "The proletariat . . . does not want a *nagaika,* a Cossack whip, wrapped up in a constitution," Trotskii announced after he read the Tsar's manifesto.[74] The proletariat, he insisted, must continue to fight for freedom. But when the government arrested three hundred members of the Soviet of Workers' Deputies at the beginning of December, the Revolution of 1905 in St. Petersburg passed into history. When Trotskii proclaimed that "the Revolution is dead. Long live the Revolution!"[75] not even he dared to imagine that the fall of the Romanovs was just twelve short years away.

For half a decade after the Revolution of 1905, labor protest in St. Petersburg fell on hard times. New waves of arrests sent the city's leading revolutionaries to prison or drove them into exile and left its proletarians without leaders. Men and women who had never taken part in strikes were pouring into St. Petersburg in search of work. Between 1908 and 1913, the number of metalworkers in the capital increased by two-thirds and the number of textile mill workers by a quarter.[76] Only when factory owners tried to tighten their grip on these new arrivals did the city's workers become more willing to take to the streets once again. One hundred thousand Petersburg workers went on strike at the end of September 1913. A hundred and forty thousand more stopped work to commemorate the ninth anniversary of Bloody Sunday on January 9, 1914, and the number of strikes continued to rise throughout the first half of that year.[77] By the time war came in July 1914, every second worker in Russia had joined in some form of labor protest within the past twelve months, and the ratio was even higher in St. Petersburg, where the average worker had taken part in twelve work stoppages between 1912 and 1914. Some had been on strike for as much as four months during that time. Many more had been on strike for two or three months.[78]

The outbreak of World War I brought labor peace to St. Petersburg, but only briefly. During the first fortnight of the war, the city was renamed Petrograd because that was thought to be more Slavonic and less Germanic. Petrograders gathered on the Palace Square to sing the national anthem and to pray for their Tsar and Russia, and for a few brief days people and sovereign seemed united as they had not been since the tragedy of Bloody Sunday. But by the spring of 1915, the strikes began again, and when the government tried to crush them, more workers joined in protest. Anger seethed in Petrograd's streets, and by early 1917, a flash point had been reached. The crowds that appeared to celebrate International Women's Day on February 23 grew larger each day, and on March 2 Petrograd's workers drove Nicholas II from his throne.

During the spring, summer, and early fall of 1917, Petrograders struggled to come to terms with several Provisional Governments, the continuing war, and the growing wave of revolutionary sentiment that crested late in October, when Lenin and the Bolsheviks seized power. Just before two A.M. on October 26, a detachment of revolutionary guards burst into the room in the Winter Palace where the ministers of the Provisional Government were meeting, demanded their surrender, and placed them under arrest. When the men who had sought to steer Russia away from a workers' revolution found themselves in prison a few hours later, their destination marked one final ironic moment in the history of St. Petersburg and Imperial Russia. "5:05 A.M.," one of them wrote in his diary. "I am [in the Peter and Paul Fortress] in cell No. 54."[79]

EIGHT

# ON THE EVE

WHILE THE CITY OF PETER and Catherine the Great, the poet Pushkin, and Emperor Nicholas I had radiated visions of imperial power and a glorious future, the capital of Silver Age Russia blended brilliance with decadence, and combined a taste for debauchery with the hope of salvation. Between 1898 and 1918, St. Petersburg's writers, painters, and composers searched for new ways to give life meaning in a world from which science and technology had erased many of the mysteries that had once drawn people to God. Not knowing what tomorrow might bring made life for many of them uncertain, and a deepening sense of doom began to darken their vision of St. Petersburg's present and future. Gripped by a sense of impending Apocalypse, they awaited a final clash between Good and Evil in the belief that its cleansing fires would give birth to a new order in which their city's fate would determine whether Russia would be European or Asiatic.

In 1917, the future turned out to be even more revolutionary than they had dared to imagine, when the events of a single year transformed St. Petersburg, the "granite diadem of Great Russia," into "Red Piter," the second city of a shrunken territory ruled by the Bolsheviks.[1] When Lenin moved Russia's capital back to Moscow in the spring of 1918, Petersburg's intellectuals then had to confront the most apocalyptic prediction of all. For "if Petersburg is not the capital," the Symbolist Andrei Belyi had written on the eve of World War I, "then there is no Petersburg. It only seems that it exists."[2] Of all the apocalyptic visions that swept the city be-fore the carnage of war and revolution transformed it, Belyi's had been the most daring. Yet it reflected a broader sense of doom that gripped Russia's capital at a time when a feeling of being "on the eve" of a brave new world held writers and artists in its grip.

Perhaps the first to express the sense of foreboding that gripped Peters-burgers on the eve of World War I was Petr Ilych Chaikovskii (Tchaikovsky). A man whose homosexuality tormented him to the end of his life (and played a part in his suicide), Chaikovskii composed music that swept audiences off their feet only to be scorned a few years later as frivolous and trite. "It is customary not to criticize Chaikovskii's music but to sniff at it," a prominent commentator wrote on the eve of World War II.[3] Only in the 1960s did critics again celebrate the brilliance that contemporaries had perceived when Chaikovskii composed his greatest works. The finale of his *Sixth*—and last—*Symphony*, his biographers wrote then, "was so original that musicians were to ponder it for years to come. It cannot be improved upon," they insisted. "It is unique."[4]

Although he lived most of his adult life in Moscow, Chaikovskii re-mained closely tied to St. Petersburg, for he had gone to school there, served there as a government official, and had been among the first stu-dents to study in its newly opened Conservatory at the beginning of the 1860s. He loved the city's vibrancy, the excitement of the Nevskii Prospekt, and the theater and balls that were open to him as an up-and-coming man-about-town, and those feelings stayed with him throughout his life. "Everything that is dear to my heart is in Petersburg," he once confided. "Life without it is positively impossible for me."[5] In St. Peters-burg Chaikovskii touched a world that stretched beyond Russia's borders, for although he always claimed to be "a Russian in the fullest sense of the word,"[6] he needed the audiences and milieux of the West to which St. Pe-tersburg still served as Russia's gateway. In that, his life personified the contradictions that were to rule the Silver Age, for the more he turned to Russia the more he was drawn to Europe. Russia and Europe both played a part in his life, and he brought them together in his music.

The St. Petersburg that Chaikovskii knew as a young man was a musi-cal melting pot of aristocratic themes, lower-class melodies, and folk mo-tifs from East and West. "Italian tunes were whistled on Nevskii Prospekt, and a few steps away one could hear an organ grinder playing Viennese ländler," a commentator once explained. Everywhere, soldiers marched to the music of military bands. Italian operas still dominated the stage of the Imperial Theater, while French ditties reigned in the city's dance halls, and the songs of peasants and gypsies filled its taverns. The waltz—regarded as sufficiently dangerous for society to require a young woman to ask special permission from a chaperone before dancing it in public—brought a sense of sexual daring to aristocratic ballrooms. And *romansy*, those "beautiful, darkly erotic flowers that grew in fashionable salons after a complex cross-fertilization of Russian folk tunes and Italian arias," found particular favor among the upper classes for the way in which they blended tenderness, anguish, and passion. Chaikovskii listened and absorbed them all. "The whole variety of musical sounds from . . . [Chaikovskii's] St. Petersburg," a critic wrote not long ago, "lives on in . . . [his] first three symphonies: the sorrowful marches, the aristocratic, sultry waltzes, the *romansy* of its salons and suburbs, the ballet scenes and arias from its imperial stages, [and] music from its folk festivities, fairs, and holidays."[7]

More than any other artist of the 1880s and 1890s, Chaikovskii used music to reflect his vision of Russia and St. Petersburg. He prominently featured the national anthem, "God Save the Tsar," in his *Slavonic March* and *1812 Overture,* and he used both works to highlight the themes of Pan-Slavism and national triumph. His *1812 Overture* glorified the greatest of all Russian victories, the expulsion of Napoleon from Russia, which had signaled the fullest flowering of the imperial age. Yet toward the end of his life Chaikovskii replaced his hopeful paeans to Russia's greatness with a sense of melancholy and foreboding that shaded quickly into presentiments of doom. Nowhere did that apply more to St. Petersburg than in *The Queen of Spades,* the opera based on a poem by Pushkin, which he completed in 1890. There, as in the *Sixth Symphony* he would complete three years later, Chaikovskii sensed the impending doom of Peter's city. In this single extraordinary work, a critic once explained, Pushkin's vision of the city as "a place with a glorious past and future" was "almost completely dissolved in the waves of Chaikovskii's music in order to take part in the fading away of the old mystique of Petersburg and the creation of a new one."[8]

Elegant, tattered, rock solid, yet built on shifting sands, St. Petersburg seemed to hold equal measures of exaltation and despair as the twentieth century began. The city was growing faster than any other capital in Europe, spreading further into what had once been an empty and desolate countryside. Rails, freight cars, locomotives, heavy guns for the army, battleships for the navy, machines of all sorts, hundreds and hundreds of miles of cotton cloth—everything that Russia needed—poured from factories and mills that worked day and night. The wealth produced was astounding, and its possessors would spend it lavishly to pursue fame as patrons of the arts. But the poverty was appalling, too, as the number of people living from hand to mouth grew larger. "Why do we feel more and more frequently two emotions: the oblivion of rapture and the oblivion of depression?" one poet asked. To some the city had never seemed more beautiful; to others it seemed on the verge of catastrophe. Looking out the window one evening at the factories that spread across the suburbs, one Petersburger felt as if he were "a guard looking down from the city tower at the Huns at the city gates."[9] As with the Huns, no one knew how to estimate the danger. Some feared it, others felt drawn to it, and still others thought it of little consequence. All the writers, artists, and composers of Silver Age St. Petersburg struggled to understand it, and their efforts brought into being a flood of painting, poetry, fiction, and music more diverse and vibrant than any the city had ever known.

Among the first of the avant garde who felt drawn to Chaikovskii's vision were a small group of aesthetes who gathered at the apartment of Aleksandr Benois, a young artist with a passion for music and theater whose family had come to Russia from Italy, France, and Germany in the late eighteenth century. As Europeans who brought their talents to Russia, members of the Benois family had stood near the center of St. Petersburg's artistic life for the better part of a century, and they felt so much a part of it that young Aleksandr adopted the slogan "Petersburg über Alles" as a rule to live by. Most of all, the Benois family saw the city as a means to bind Russia closer to the West. "I knew very little about Russia," Aleksandr confessed when he recalled those days in his memoirs, "but I loved St. Petersburg."[10] Chosen from among the young men he had met at Karl May's exclusive boarding school, Benois's circle of friends in the late 1880s included the writer Dmitrii Filosofov and the artist Konstantin Somov, both of them, like him, under the age of twenty. Soon they invited the painters Lev Bakst and Nikolai Rerikh to join their afternoon discussions, and in 1890 they added Filosofov's "country cousin" Sergei Diagilev. Art, they insisted, was "a form of mystical experience, a means through which eternal beauty could be expressed."[11] Daring, arrogant, and uninhibited, they vowed "to establish the first principles for Russian art, Russian architecture, Russian philosophy, Russian music, and Russian poetry."[12]

After becoming infatuated with Chaikovskii's *Sleeping Beauty* at one of its first performances at the beginning of 1890, the young men anxiously awaited the opening of *The Queen of Spades* at the Imperial Mariinskii Theater that fall. *"The Queen of Spades* literally *drove me mad,"* Benois recalled many years later, "for through it I could enter the world of shadows that had been beckoning me for a long time."[13] He and his friends had first embraced this "kingdom of shadows" when they had discovered in *Sleeping Beauty* an affirmation that "life continues beyond the grave." That, in turn, had convinced them that "not only separate personalities but entire epochs continue to live on."[14] Applied to St. Petersburg, they called their veneration of the past "passeism," which, Benois insisted, involved not only the city's history but "a countless number of the most beautiful creations of art and literature."[15] Nothing was more worthy of an artist's attention, they thought, than the glorious architecture of Peter's city. Like Chaikovskii, Benois and his friends insisted that Russia's writers, composers, and artists needed to show the European side of their national life. The time had come to turn away from the dark criticisms that Dostoevskii and Gogol had leveled against St. Petersburg and return to the "unique romance" of the city that represented Russia's greatness and ties with the West.

Having changed their name from the Society for Self-Education to the Nevskii Pickwickians, Benois and his friends moved their meeting place in the late 1890s to Diagilev's apartment on the corner of Liteinyi Prospekt and Simeonovskaia Street. There among the collection of Renaissance bronzes, antique Italian furniture, and neo-Impressionist landscapes that their host had gathered during his early foreign travels, they vowed to reject "everything which reflected a literary, political, or social tendency."[16] Determined to chart a new course, they insisted that no artist should "serve any idea or any society,"[17] and they embraced art for the sake of art alone. While they sat around Diagilev's huge sixteenth-century Italian table, argued, and drank tea served by the old nanny whom Bakst would later capture in the background of his 1906 portrait of Diagilev, they worked out the ideas that brought a stunning new monthly periodical into being.[18] As one of the first journals in Russia to concentrate exclusively on the arts when it appeared in 1898, *Mir Iskusstva (The World of Art)*, became the mouthpiece for what Diagilev once described as "a generation thirsting for beauty."[19]

Although the ideas that shaped it came mainly from Benois, Filosofov, and Bakst, the moving force behind *The World of Art* was Diagilev. When he had first appeared in St. Petersburg as a raw provincial from the Siberian borderlands of Perm, Diagilev had stunned his new acquaintances with his childish naivete. "We were shocked by his indifference to our purely aesthetic and philosophical debates," Benois confessed. "He would openly doze off during our discussions . . . [and] he particularly irritated us by the way he acted at the theater."[20] Yet Diagilev surpassed them all in charm, stubbornness, and raw strength of will. "By leaps and bounds he would go from utter ignorance and indifference to demanding and even passionate study . . . [so that] he suddenly would acquire competence in areas that demanded a notable amount of specialization," Benois remembered.[21] But most of all, Diagilev had seething energy and a truly rare ability to draw attention to artists and their work. "I think that I have no real gifts," he once confessed to the stepmother with whom he shared his most intimate feelings, "[but] I think I have found my true vocation [in] being a Maecenas."[22]

Benois once wrote that Diagilev had "painted no pictures, and with the exception of a few (very talented) articles did not write either. He had not the slightest interest in architecture or sculpture," he added, and "he very quickly became thoroughly disillusioned with his efforts to compose music, and he even gave up singing. . . . He was," Benois concluded, "rather unimaginative . . . but he would greedily seize upon anything that developed in the minds of his friends in which he sensed a spark of life. And he would passionately set out to bring to life those ideas, even though they were not his own."[23] As the Nevskii Pickwickians searched for new ways to understand the arts, Diagilev exploded in a frenzy of enthusiasm. "I am looking at the future through a magnifying glass," he exclaimed. "I mean to bring together the whole of our artistic life."[24] Financed by two wealthy patrons whom Diagilev charmed into supporting it, *The World of Art* set out "to recognize individuality under every guise and at every epoch."[25] "*The World of Art* is above all earthly things," Bakst announced just before the first issue appeared. "It stands among the stars, where it reigns arrogantly, enigmatically, and alone, like an eagle on a snowy crag."[26]

Among other things, *The World of Art* supported the passeism of the Nevskii Pickwickians. Embracing Benois's belief in "Petersburg über Alles," they applauded the city's beauty and proclaimed it a monument to Russian and European culture. To recapture the feelings that had once bound Russians to its past, Benois devoted a whole series of watercolors to St. Petersburg life in the eighteenth century, and then went on to create thirty-three illustrations for Pushkin's *Bronze Horseman* to celebrate the two hundredth anniversary of the city's founding. "At last we have drawings worthy of the great poet," the Symbolist Valerii Briusov exclaimed when Benois's illustrations appeared in *The World of Art.* "In them Old Petersburg is as alive as it is alive in the poem." It was "as if the artist had just been there, in the streets of Petersburg in centuries past," another declared. A third critic thought the illustrations "profound . . . [and] with all the naivete and simplicity of a dream."[27]

Not all of St. Petersburg's artists and critics shared those views. In 1863, thirteen young artists had revolted against the rigid conservatism of St. Petersburg's Imperial Academy of Fine Arts and had struck out on their own. Vowing to lay the foundations for Russia's first national school of modern painting, they had called themselves the *Peredvizhniki,* the Wanderers, and they had made it their aim to portray Russian life as it really was. Throughout the 1870s and 1880s, viewers had been astonished by their raw realism, and the greatest among them, the one-time peasant icon painter Ilia Repin, had shaken Russians to the very depths of their souls by the pain he expressed in his art. Petersburgers had waited in line for hours to see Repin's *Ivan the Terrible and His Son Ivan* when it was featured at an exhibition at the Iusupovs' Petersburg palace at the beginning of 1885, for they never had seen the tragedy and torment of their nation's history so forcefully compressed into a single moment. "Women fainted when they saw it," one visitor reported as he recalled Repin's portrayal of the bleeding mortal wound Tsar Ivan had inflicted on his son. "High-strung people," he added, "even threw up."[28] Before and after, Repin had enjoyed similar triumphs, and the portrait he had painted of the booze-sodden composer Modest Musorgskii as he lay dying in a St. Petersburg hospital still stands as a monument to the self-destructive power of genius.[29] Realistic portrayals of the past and present thus stood at the center of the Wanderers' creed. The idealized remembrances and distorted visions of the Nevskii Pickwickians stirred their anger.

Especially Vladimir Stasov, St. Petersburg's reigning critic from the 1860s to the turn of the century and a staunch defender of the Wanderers' realism, found *The World of Art* offensive. When he dismissed Diagilev as a "decadent cheerleader" and branded his journal "a courtyard of lepers,"[30] the Petersburg art world exploded. In the 1860s and 1870s, a similar conflict had won new enthusiasts for the paintings of such Wanderers as Ivan Kramskoi, Vasilii Surikov, and, of course, Repin himself. Now the result was to draw more attention to such artists as Somov, Bakst, and Rerikh, and to encourage the avant-garde theater that the Nevskii Pickwickians and *The World of Art* supported. In Moscow, the railroad magnate and art patron Savva Mamontov had already established the revolutionary practice of commissioning theater sets from leading artists instead of hack set painters. Soon Diagilev would bring that practice to Paris by having Bakst, Rerikh, and Benois paint sets for the dazzling Ballets Russes.

Just as Stasov had used his pen and powerful personality in the 1870s and 1880s to win support among Petersburg's audiences for the Wanderers and such composers as Musorgskii, so Diagilev used *The World of Art* to bring many of Russia's most contentious writers and painters together, if only for a moment at the beginning of the new century. The painters Valentin Serov and Isak Levitan, Bakst and Rerikh, Konstantin Somov and Mikhail Vrubel all found common ground in the pages of Diagilev's journal. So did the writers Filosofov, Dmitrii Merezhkovskii, and Vasilii Rozanov, and the poets Zinaida Gippius, Andrei Belyi, and Konstantin Balmont, who were changing the course of Russian poetry with their daring images and bold metaphors. Convinced that every artist's reactions to what was seen and felt held the key to a mystical experience that expressed eternal beauty, they all now insisted that the sole purpose of art must be pleasure. Believing that no single art form could ever express all the dimensions of beauty by itself, Diagilev sought to bring philosophy, architecture, music, poetry, and painting together in ways that would enable them to combine and come closer to that goal.[31]

In days to come, music would hold a key to Diagilev's vision of blending the arts, as the painters, poets, and novelists of the avant garde looked forward to a time when a "symphonic society" would resolve all social conflicts and reconcile all economic differences. Painters called their studios "nests of music," described their works as "sonatas," and introduced their exhibitions as "auditions." One of Russia's greatest Symbolists, Andrei Belyi, called his new works "symphonies," while others spoke of escaping from calendar time to "musical time" and sought to play upon words in "the alphabet's strings." Belyi's friend Aleksandr Blok called one of his collections of poems "harps and violins," and as World War I drew Russia closer to its rendezvous with revolution, the tango became the musical theme for a society that stood on the brink. Gypsy violins, Spanish guitars, domras, and balalaikas blended into a plaintive symphony of longing and doom that provided the background music for a world in which St. Petersburg and Russia were about to be turned upside down.[32]

Among those who sought new harmonies in realms that lay above and beyond the real world, the beautiful Zinaida Gippius and her husband, the introspective and eccentric Dmitrii Merezhkovskii, followed *The World of Art* in believing that the everyday world was only a symbolic reflection of a higher, more vital realm. Merezhkovskii saw it as the tragedy of modern life that men and women had been condemned to live between the death of the ancient gods, who had bound human creation and nature together so perfectly, and the birth of new ones that might do so once again. He explored the conflict between these "two equally powerful but irreconcilable forces"[33] in *Christ and Antichrist*, a trilogy of novels that presented history as a struggle between the world of the flesh and the realm of the spirit, and he concluded that "a new earth and a new sky" could be found only in the Apocalypse that would signal the collapse of modern civilization and the emergence of a harmonious new world that would reconcile art, man, and God.[34] Some saw Merezhkovskii as a prophet. Others saw him as a man of mediocre intellect. Andrei Belyi, who knew him well, remembered him as a small, thin, brown man who "bleated" like a sheep and seemed most like "a cross between a sexton and a minor civil servant."[35]

Once described as standing "a full twenty-five heads higher than Merezhkovskii in the subtlety of her thoughts and feelings," the poet Zinaida Gippius altered many of her husband's convictions in subtle but meaningful ways.[36] Notorious for her flamboyant beauty and scandalous public behavior, Gippius is remembered as a Petersburg Hedda Gabler and a Russian Messalina[37] who struggled to create the Kingdom of God on earth by fusing life and religion into a higher form of freedom. "We are seeking new forms, a new death, and a new resurrection," she proclaimed in *The World of Art*.[38] Unable to integrate the opposites she encountered in life and art, she tried to blend the trinity of love, life, and death into a new religion, but in the end found the pull of its opposites too strong. "God is close to me, yet I cannot pray," she once wrote. "I yearn for affection, yet I cannot love."[39]

At least once a week (usually on Sundays) the avant garde of turn-of-the-century Petersburg gathered at the apartment of Gippius and Merezhkovskii on the fourth floor of the Dom Muruzi, the building that Prince Aleksandr Muruza had engaged the architect Aleksei Serebriakov to

*The Gippius Salon in the Dom Muruzi: Zinaida Gippius, Dmitrii Filosofov, and Dmitrii Merezhkovskii, 1914. (Courtesy of the Central State Archive of Kino-Photo-Phono Documents, St. Petersburg)*

build at No. 24 Liteinyi Prospekt in the 1870s. Here Gippius presided imperiously, tossing forth judgements about young artists and their work that shaped the city's artistic scene for the better part of a decade. She dismissed the young poet Nikolai Gumilev as being of no consequence ("His sententious ideas are as old as the hat of a widow visiting the cemetery"),[40] and she whispered to several friends that the leader of Moscow's Decadents Valerii Briusov reminded her of a chimpanzee.[41] But she was entranced by the young Symbolist Andrei Belyi, and even more infatuated with his friend Aleksandr Blok. "His face was straight and motionless, as calm as if it were made or wood or stone," she remembered after their first meeting, when Blok had "pronounced every word slowly, and with effort, precisely as if he were tearing himself away from some meditation." She found "something endearing" in him, yet she could never completely penetrate the wall of reserve with which he surrounded himself.[42] "Even when he was right there with you," she once confessed, "he always was somewhere else too."[43]

In those days Gippius dyed her long blond hair a flaming red and favored white or black dresses that fitted her like a second skin and sometimes featured pink-lined pleats that gave the impression that she wore nothing underneath.[44] Her Tuberose-Lubain perfume hung heavily on the drawing room's thick rugs and dark brick walls, and she waved the long holder through which she smoked scented cigarettes as if it were a wand for working her charms. Her green eyes and sensuous mouth drew men to her, and so did her slenderness and her unusual height. Arising late in the afternoon, she went to bed at dawn after spending hours stretched on a settee, as one visitor remembered, with "her luxuriant red-gold tresses illuminated by the red flames of the fireplace."[45] Her cruel tongue, capricious moods, and propensity for spreading vicious gossip endowed her with great power. Many felt drawn to her, others feared her, and some truly hated her. The great Petersburg poet Anna Akhmatova remembered her as "nasty and mean,"[46] and the thinker Nikolai Berdiaev, who was in the process of exchanging the gospel of Marx for the Gospels of Christ, remembered her salon as "a place where you would not meet a real person."[47] At first infatuated with her, Belyi later called her "a wasp in human attire."[48] But Gippius was a brilliant poet, had a sixth sense that allowed her to perceive the weaknesses of humankind, and never ceased to be the axis on which the world she ruled turned.[49]

While Gippius held court, Merezhkovskii shuffled back and forth in his gown and slippers. Surrounded by a haze of cigar smoke, he spent much of the time closeted in his study, from which he emerged to issue pronouncements that Gippius would often dismiss with the exclamation: "Dmitrii, you are out of order!"[50] Yet Gippius and her husband continued to share the hope that God and humankind could be united in a new religion that would lead to a higher form of freedom. She spoke of a Third Testament that would proclaim the Kingdom of the Third Humanity in which people would be free and strong. Especially with Belyi, she would speak about religion, the Trinity, and the flesh throughout the night. "For God's sake!" Merezhkovskii would call out from the other room. "It's four o'clock in the morning! You're not letting me sleep!"[51]

Although an ardent Muscovite who did not actually visit St. Petersburg until 1905, Andrei Belyi was an important part of the Gippius-Merezhkovskii circle. Gippius insisted that he "never walked . . . but danced," and other friends remembered him as being "thin, slight, with a high forehead and a chin that jutted forward [so that] with his head always slightly tilted back he seemed not to walk, but to fly."[52] He was a passionate disciple of the philosopher Vladimir Soloviev, whose belief in the redeeming power of a Beautiful Lady "clothed in the sun" he shared. Belyi believed that music held the key to understanding the universe because it alone could transcend those limits of time, space, and place that separated people from God. In the first issue of *Novyi put* (*The New Way*), which Merezhkovskii and Gippius began to publish in 1903, he announced that the final struggle between Good and Evil had begun. And, while Merezhkovskii insisted that Christ and Antichrist had been at war throughout modern history, Belyi saw their clash as the more immediate product of the twentieth century. Now, he argued, Soloviev's Beautiful Lady, the symbol of divine wisdom, would confront the "Great Whore" in a final struggle for the soul of humankind.

In his vision of the Apocalypse Belyi found common ground not only with Merezhkovskii and Gippius but also with Aleksandr Blok, the Petersburg poet whose readings, one literary critic confessed, affected his audiences "as the moon affects lunatics."[53] Blok was the son of a man who had been driven from his home for beating his wife, and he had grown up in the home of his grandfather, the rector of St. Petersburg University. At the age of eighteen he had fallen in love with the writings of Soloviev and the person of Liubov Mendeeleva, the beautiful daughter of the great chemist who had just created his periodic table of elements in St. Petersburg. Like Belyi, Blok was drawn to the salon at Dom Muruzi, but only briefly, and by the beginning of 1905 he had begun to explore the raw, real world that he found in St. Petersburg's back streets and taverns.[54]

As a friend remembered, Blok was "unbearably, unbelievably" good looking, and the solemn manner in which he declaimed his carefully crafted lyrics made him irresistible to audiences wherever he read his poetry.[55] Listeners captivated by his hypnotic monotone bought tens of thousands of postcards with his photograph from street kiosks all over Russia, and even the cheap yellow press printed his poems. "In those days, there wasn't a single 'thinking' young woman in Russia who wasn't in love with Blok," one of his admirers remembered, and they showered him with tokens of their passion.[56] Young women would go to the door of his apartment to kiss the handle he touched whenever he entered, while others who were more daring sent him invitations and propositions for intimate meetings.[57] Yet, as he struggled to reconcile his belief in Soloviev's Beautiful Lady with the rawness of life as he was coming to know it, Blok remained aloof. "Cries, madness, and—often—painful dissonances" filled his work.[58] By the end of 1905, "with everything whirling . . . into darkness,"[59] the Beautiful Lady to whom he had written his first book of poetry had become a "Woman Arrayed in Purple and Scarlet." Blok now wrote of "The Unknown Woman" of the streets who lived in a Dostoevskian realm of pain and poverty and cries for help that went unheard. Women, "their breasts adorned with a crumpled rose . . . with their heads tilted back, their lips half-parted" entered his poems.[60] "Christ was never there," he wrote in describing to Belyi the realm in which these fallen women lived. "He is walking somewhere very far away."[61]

In St. Petersburg, the defeats of the Russo-Japanese War, the tragedy of Bloody Sunday, and the turmoil of the Revolution of 1905 obliged the habitués of the salon at the Dom Muruzi to admit that the line between East and West was more stark than they had wanted to imagine. "You are sober, we are drunk; you are rational, we are frenzied; you are just, we are lawless," Merezhkovskii exclaimed in contrasting Europe and Russia in those days. "For you, politics is knowledge," he added. "For us it is religion."[62] Blok's aunt remembered that some of the Symbolists "urged people to renounce happiness"[63] as they abandoned the joyous expectations that had filled their poetry just two or three years before. Like Blok they had began to notice the masses, and to those who did not share his sympathy for the lower classes, the discovery brought fear and dread. "Who are these strange people . . . who have so unexpectedly revealed themselves?" one of them asked. "They're not even savages. . . . Savages are visionaries, dreamers, with shamans, festishes, and incantations, while here [among the Petersburg masses] all we have is some sort of hole of nonexistence."[64]

Even people like Blok and Belyi began to carry guns. Many of their friends spoke of suicide, and some succeeded in joining the ranks of the fifteen hundred Petersburgers who killed themselves in 1908.[65] For them all, the Apocalypse was no longer a mere figure of speech to be contemplated with delicious dread from afar. Now it seemed near at hand and somehow connected to the scent of rot that was starting to seep into the city. No amount of perfume could cover it up. Whiffs of decay even reached the salon in the Dom Muruzi, where Gippius still lay bathed in the heavy scent of her Tuberose-Lubain. Everything that had seemed so clear such a short time ago now seemed clouded and uncertain.

*The Admiralty, designed by Andreian Zakharov. Nearly a quarter of a mile long, its square marked the center of an immense parade ground that stretched from Winter Palace Square to Senate Square. (Courtesy of the Russian National Library, St. Petersburg)*

*The Stock Exchange and Rostral Columns on the eastern tip of Vasilevskii Island. (Courtesy of the Russian National Library, St. Petersburg)*

*Kazan Cathedral, a monument to Imperial Russia designed by Andrei Voronikhin in the early nineteenth century, dominates the Nevskii Prospekt. (Courtesy of the Russian National Library, St. Petersburg)*

*Cathedral of St. Isaac of Dalmatia. An equestrian statue of Nicholas I adorns the square that faces the mammoth structure. (Courtesy of the Russian National Library, St. Petersburg)*

*Interior view of St. Isaac's Cathedral. (Courtesy of the Russian National Library, St. Petersburg)*

*The Catherine Garden, which Rossi designed to fill the space between the Public Library and Anichkov Palace, leads to his Aleksandrinskii Theater. (Courtesy of the Central State Archive of Kino–Photo–Phono Documents, St. Petersburg)*

*Carlo Rossi*

*The Mikhailovskii Palace, designed by Carlo Rossi for Grand Duke Mikhail Pavlovich.
(Courtesy of the Russian National Library, St. Petersburg)*

*Arch of the General Staff Headquarters connecting the Nevskii Prospekt with Palace
Square. (Courtesy of the Russian National Library, St. Petersburg)*

*The Senate, one of Rossi's final creations, housed Russia's highest judicial and administrative offices. (Courtesy of the Russian National Library, St. Petersburg)*

*The Senate, the Bronze Horseman on Senate Square, and St. Isaac's Cathedral as seen from the bridge connecting Vasilevskii Island with the Admiralty Quarter. From a drawing by Vasilii Sadovnikov. (Courtesy of the Russian National Library, St. Petersburg)*

*Aleksandr Pushkin*

St. Petersburg's avant garde tried to escape the uncertainty that descended after 1905 by living outside of time and space in the famous "Tower" of Viacheslav Ivanov. A brilliant student of classical antiquities who was once described as "quite possibly the most urbane, cultured, and esoteric man in Europe and certainly in Russia,"[66] Ivanov did not publish his first book of verse until after he had turned forty. When it appeared, he had lived for many years in the West, and he came to Russia only briefly to bask in the critics' acclaim before fleeing to Switzerland once again. Then in 1906 he moved to St. Petersburg with Lidia Zinovieva-Annibal, a writer of modest talent and a distant relative of the great poet Pushkin. They made their home in a penthouse atop a stylish new building on No. 25 Tavricheskaia Street, not far from the famous Tauride Gardens and Palace, which just a few weeks before had become the home of the first Russian Duma or National Assembly. Every Wednesday, St. Petersburg's avant garde flocked to their salon, where Ivanov, always wearing black gloves to cover his chronic eczema, welcomed them to the temple of a new faith that sought to erase the lines between past, present, and future.

Ivanov and his wife demolished the walls of three apartments to create what Belyi once described as "capriciously interlaced corridors, rooms, and doorless anterooms: square rooms, rhomboids, and sectors, where thick carpets swallowed up the sound of footsteps."[67] Their antique furniture was of heavy, carved, highly polished dark wood, and upholstered in rich fabrics that complemented the red-orange tapestries covering the walls. Clocks were banished and calendars were banned, for their idea was to create a sense of timelessness. "Day became night and night became day," Belyi explained. "You'd forget what country you were in and what time it was. . . . You'd blink, and a month would have passed."[68] The air in this esoteric realm was always heavy with the scent of lilies mixed with fumes from the burning wax of many candles. There was plenty of wine and an enormous quantity of the black tea that the host himself liked to drink. Time, like life, slipped away unnoticed. "One time I planned to stay at the Tower for three days, and ended up living there for five weeks," Belyi wrote some years later.[69] Mikhail Kuzmin, whose novel *Wings* outraged conservative critics for its defense of pederasty, once dropped in for a visit and stayed for more than a year.[70]

At the Tower of "Viacheslav the Magnificent," as Ivanov was known in those days, the poets, philosophers, and artists of St. Petersburg challenged every belief that had shaped Russia's past and present. For hours and days on end, they debated the existence of God, the meaning of Symbolism, and the future of the Romanovs in a headily apocalyptic blend of Nietzsche, Dostoevskii, Ibsen, and Maeterlinck tinged with lesser amounts of Baudelaire, the ancient Greeks, and Schopenhauer. There was talk of orgiastic rites, Dionysian mysteries, and human sacrifice, and during one of Petersburg's magical White Nights, Blok climbed onto the Tower's sloping roof and declaimed "The Unknown Woman," which revealed the identity of his fallen Beautiful Lady, to the stars. Just as there were no walls in the Tower, so there were no barriers to ideas. "We were citizens of the universe, the custodians of the great cultural museum of humanity," one woman remembered. "In a certain sense," she added, "we were the revolution before the revolution—so profoundly, mercilessly, and fatally did we destroy the old tradition and build bridges to the future. But our depth and daring were combined with an unescapable sense of decay," she concluded sadly. "We were the last act of a tragedy."[71]

As a way of heightening their awareness of the "real" world of the spirit, the avant garde saw love as the key to life. Belyi at that time was in love with Blok's wife and insisted that an "artist-phoenix" could overcome death with love.[72] At the same time, Blok had fallen into a morass of seething tensions that separated him from the woman he loved. He wanted other women, but he also wanted to be alone. "Mysticism requires ecstasy," he wrote in one of his notebooks then. "Ecstasy is solitude."[73] Then, insisting that "anyone who does not love is dead," Ivanov married Zinovieva-Annibal's daughter after her mother succumbed to scarlet fever. "One only needed to fall in love," a young poet concluded, "to have all the necessary elements for one's first lyrics: Passion, Despair, Exaltation, Madness, Vice, Sin, and Hatred."[74]

The lack of barriers in Ivanov's Tower mirrored the way in which the various artistic media flowed together in St. Petersburg on the eve of World War I. Of that, Diagilev and his friends provided the most stunning example by using the ballet to blend sight, sound, and motion into intense musical pictures. Expanding dramatically on the beginnings Savva Mamontov had made in the 1880s, Diagilev combined the painting of Rerikh, Benois, and Lev Bakst, the choreography of Mikhail Fokin, and the music of virtually every major Russian composer with the dancing of Vatslav Nizhinskii and the three prima ballerinas Anna Pavlova, Tamara Karsavina, and Ida Rubinstein into stunning kaleidoscopic productions. Even the drawings the young Parisian poet Jean Cocteau used to decorate the programs for Diagilev's Ballets Russes showed that the lines between the arts were dissolving. But Diagilev failed to heed the axiom once expressed by the director of Imperial Theaters that "we must first of all please the royal family."[75] When his art and personal life both proved too daring for the taste of Russia's sovereigns, Diagilev found Petersburg's Imperial Theaters closed to him. Paris, not Petersburg, thus became the scene of the brilliant Ballets Russes productions that astounded European audiences before and after World War I.

In one of the Ballets Russes's most stunning productions, Diagilev used art, ballet, and the music of Igor Stravinskii to recall old St. Petersburg. Born, raised, and educated in Russia's capital, Stravinskii was destined to win fame in the West for the brilliance with which he blended and interpreted the heritages of Russia and Europe. At Diagilev's urging, he wrote the music for the ballet *Petrushka* between mid-1910 and early 1911. By then, the twenty-eight-year-old Stravinskii—"a young savage who wears loud ties and kisses women's hands while stepping on their feet," according to Claude Debussy[76]—had already been hailed as a genius for *The Firebird,* which Diagilev had staged in Paris in the summer of 1910. He now set out to bring to life St. Petersburg's carnival with its organ grinders, singing beggars, and lusty coachmen all celebrating *maslenitsa,* Butter Week, the last seven days before Lent. Stravinskii scored his ballet, one critic wrote, so that "flutes bubbled like the reeds in a fun-fair organ; trombones and tubas, released from their Wagnerian servitude, filled exciting new roles as circus clowns; [and] hurdy-gurdy tunes, churned out to the tinkling rhythm of triangles, infused a delicate flavor of irony into the music."[77]

Asked by Diagilev to create a plot and to design sets and costumes for *Petrushka,* Benois saw a chance to bring his passe-ist dreams to life by reviving all the drama and old-time folk color of Butter Week. Set in the reign of Nicholas I, a time thought by the Nevskii Pickwickians to have been a lost golden age of autocratic Russian values, the entire plot revolved around the escapades of the ill-starred puppet Petrushka, whom fate had swept up in a wave of human passions. Emotionally, Benois's interpretation drew heavily upon his long-standing fascination with the ideas of E. T. A. Hoffmann, but in flavor and substance his *Petruskha* was purely Petersburgian. Harking back to a time when St. Petersburg had been the envy of all Russia and when its people had been certain of where they were going and how they would get there, the creation that Benois shared with Stravinskii and Fokin won acclaim in the West as "refreshingly new and refreshingly Russian," "supremely clever, supremely modern, and supremely baroque."[78] No one in the West noted the profound nostalgia that had moved Benois to re-create the favorite carnival character of his childhood. Nor did they sense the pure fun that had inspired Stravinskii to envision in musical terms a puppet "suddenly endowed with life," whose escapades so "exasperate[d] the patience of the orchestra with diabolical arpeggios" that they were obliged to "retaliate with menacing trumpet blasts."[79]

Because of Diagilev's troubles with the authorities, Petersburg audiences were never permitted to enjoy the gay nostalgia of *Petrushka*. Nor could the ballet have diverted the political and artistic forces that seemed about to overwhelm the city. "It was as if something was in the air hovering over each and every one of us," Gippius remembered. "People . . . rushed about, never understanding why they did so, nor knowing what to do with themselves."[80] Blok lamented that "the literary circles in Petersburg have reached the last stages of putrefaction . . . and have begun to stink,"[81] while one of his friends bemoaned the "sickness of the soul" that had descended upon them all.[82] "One could already begin to sense the smell of burning, blood, and iron in the air," Blok remembered.[83] "Come back to Russia," he wrote at the beginning of the year to Belyi who was traveling through Europe and North Africa. "It may turn out that there is not much time left to know her as she is now!"[84]

By 1911, a sense of impending Apocalypse had begun to overwhelm the avant garde in St. Petersburg. The philosopher Vladimir Soloviev had first raised the alarm in 1900, when he warned of a new Mongol horde rising in Asia. Then, the first decade of the new century had brought Russians' vision of the Apocalypse to St. Petersburg itself. The shattering and completely unforeseen defeat by Japan in the Russo-Japanese War, the Revolution of 1905 and the weakening of autocracy, and a whole series of events ranging from the death of Tolstoi to the reappearance of Halley's Comet convinced Russians that life as they knew it was coming to an end. For many, the modern city—of which St. Petersburg was the empire's most striking example—had become the personification of evil, and they believed that it would be there that the final struggle between Good and Evil would be played out. Here was "the curse of the beast," the "final curse of man,"[85] in which factories replaced cathedrals as the great monuments of a new society in which the instruments of technology had come between humankind and God. "We live *daily* in horror, stink, and despair, in factory smoke, in the rouge of lascivious smiles, in the roar of disgusting automobiles," Blok wrote. "Petersburg is a gigantic whore-house, I feel it."[86]

Belyi brought all these feelings together in *Petersburg,* a novel of star-tling apocalyptic imagery that portrayed Russia's capital in grimmer terms than any writer had yet dared to imagine. Vladimir Nabokov ranked *Petersburg* with Joyce's *Ulysses,* Kafka's *Metamorphosis,* and Proust's *In Search of Lost Time* as one of the "greatest masterpieces of twentieth century prose,"[87] and others have seen it as the quintessential work of Russian Symbolism.[88] *Petersburg* is a social, philosophical, political, psychological, historical work cast in the form of a novel of suspense. And, as its transla-tors explained some years ago, it is so richly textured and endlessly subtle that "it is all but immune to paraphrase."[89] Here Belyi pursued the dark vision of Dostoevskii to the terrifying conclusion that St. Petersburg must "go to pieces" and "sink" before the sun could "rise in radiance" over Rus-sia.[90] Here was the Apocalypse in its most terrifying form, set in the very center of Russia's greatest urban monument to modern civilization and progress.

In Belyi's vision, St. Petersburg became a nightmarish industrial city peopled by men and women with "small, compressed, cubic souls." Here amidst "blackish-grayish cubes" of buildings that could barely be per-ceived through the "greenish-yellow fog" that hung over them, Belyi found a "human swarm of many thousands that dragged itself to many-chimneyed factories every morning." There was none of Catherine the Great's classical elegance in Belyi's vision. Nor was there any hint of the glorious olden days that Benois had recalled so fondly in *Petrushka.* Be-lyi's St. Petersburg was damp, cold, and full of germs that made people sick, a realm of "bodies, bodies, and more bodies, bent, partially bent, just slightly bent, and not bent at all." It stood between the earthly and the cosmic, and divided Europe from Asia. "I was shaken by the strength of its inner meaning and the depth of its abundant insights," Viacheslav Ivanov confessed after Belyi had taken the better part of a week to read *Petersburg* aloud at his Tower. Esoteric, mysterious, and infinitely complex in its vision, the novel brought Russian letters to the edge of a new liter-ary universe. It obliged Petersburgers to confront both the meaning and fate of their city just as it was approaching its rendezvous with the forces that would change its place in history.[91]

When *Petersburg* first appeared in serialized form in 1913, less than a year remained before the outbreak of the Great War that would become

Russia's—and Europe's—Armageddon. That year the Romanovs celebrated their three-hundredth anniversary on Russia's throne, and St. Petersburg commemorated the 210th year of its founding. By that time St.
Petersburg had grown to over two million, just more than half again as
large as it had been in 1900. More than seven out of every ten Petersburgers were peasants, while one in 39 was a soldier, one out of 173 was a government official, one in 150 was a policeman, one out of 75 was a
tradesman, and somewhere between one in 30 to 50 was a prostitute.[92] All
their lives were changing. For one thing, eight out of every ten Petersburgers could read and write by 1913, and the number of dime novels and
"penny dreadfuls" published and sold in the city stood at well over seven
million a year.[93] There were 555 newspapers and magazines published in
St. Petersburg then, nearly twice as many as in Moscow and a full quarter
of the number published in the entire empire.[94] For the first time in St.
Petersburg's (and Russia's) history, large numbers of women had become
readers. After Anastasia Verbitskaia's *Keys to Happiness* sold over thirty
thousand copies in four months in 1909, women's magazines and novels
won prominent places in the city's bookstores. All of these broadened the
horizons of the lower classes, and while Russian translations of Nat
Pinkerton's adventures may hardly strike us as uplifting now, they were a
far cry from the primitive homilies that Petersburg's lower classes had
read thirty or forty years before.

Most of all, the horizons of lower-class Petersburgers were broadened
by movies, the new form of mass entertainment that was enthralling audiences all across the industrialized world. By the end of 1913, there were
twenty-three movie houses on the Nevskii Prospekt alone, and the entire
city boasted nearly a hundred and fifty. At first, these showed only foreign
films, which gave the city's lower classes—including illiterates—a broader
sense of what life was like beyond the narrow confines of the corners in
which they lived and the factories in which they worked. Above all, they
showed a way of life that was more daring and more liberating, and this
was reinforced by the rhythms of the ragtime and jazz music with which
Petersburg piano players sometimes accompanied the films on screen. As
in America and Western Europe, this raucous, exuberant music brought
to Russia's capital a message of social and sexual liberation,[95] which
helped to broaden and deepen the urgings to nonconformity that the
Symbolists and Decadents had already brought to the city's avant-garde
salons. The advent of off-the-rack, up-to-date clothing added a further

dimension at about the same time. During the first decade of the twentieth century, it became possible for the young swells of Petersburg's lower
classes to aspire to being modern by dressing in new fashions and imitat-
ing the ways of life they had seen at the movies.

In 1907, Russia's first film studio was established in St. Petersburg, and
the next year its founders brought to the screen *Stenka Razin,* the story of
the legendary seventeenth-century rebel, robber, and folk hero. Within
less than a decade the city had nine studios that were turning out hundreds of films a year. Stories by Dostoevskii, Chekhov, Pushkin, Tolstoi,
Lermontov, and Turgenev all were made into films, thus making it possible for the city's masses, even the illiterate, to discover their nation's literary treasures.[96] Movies brought together, for the first time in history, all
classes and all occupations. Students, policemen, workers, aristocrats,
shopkeepers, priests, intellectuals, and beggars all found themselves on
common ground in St. Petersburg's movie theaters, if only for a moment.
But worlds of difference still stood between them once they left the magic
world of the silver screen, for nowhere was the gulf that separated the upper classes from the working masses greater than in St. Petersburg.

For comfortably well-off and truly well-to-do Petersburgers, the last
year before World War I seemed more promising and gayer than ever.
Few of these men and women paid attention to the apocalyptic preach-
ings of the avant garde, and many saw the Romanovs' three hundredth
anniversary as a promise of better things to come. They had everything at
their fingertips: oysters, champagne, and fine clarets from Paris, Pears
soap, fruitcakes, and smelling salts from London, and striped blazers and
football jerseys from Oxford and Cambridge. They took their vacations
on the Italian and French Rivieras, where hotel and restaurant proprietors
laid in special stocks of the cloying champagnes that they preferred to the
drier styles favored in the West, and they moved more easily between East
and West than ever before. Many—including Gippius, Merezhkovskii,
Benois, and Diagilev—now took to spending part of each year in Paris,
and a number of the revolutionaries who still plotted the overthrow of the
Romanovs also spent their days and nights in the cafes there. Among the
well-to-do Russians who stayed in St. Petersburg, names and origins continued to count. Except for treasures made by Fabergé, what was made in
France, England, or Germany invariably outclassed anything Russian.

As aristocrats vied with each other in the size of the orchestras they
employed, the menus they served, the fashions they wore, and the favors

they presented to their guests during the winters of 1912–1913 and 1913–1914, there was an endless succession of balls and dinners, each more memorable than the last. The ballerina Matilda Kshesinskaia gave a Christmas party for her son, complete with the famous clown Durov and an elephant that reclined on a bed and used a chamberpot on cue.[97] In townhouses and apartments along the city's fashionable embankments, Petersburgers celebrated Shrovetide in the usual manner—with paper-thin pancakes heaped with beluga caviar and eaten with toasts of vodka—while lesser folk gathered around snow slides in the parks and enjoyed the offerings of vendors who sold spicy meat- and cabbage-filled pies and apple tarts on the city's streets and squares. Nicholas II celebrated the last Shrovetide before the war—in early February 1914—with a formal regimental dinner for the Hussar Life Guards, where everything was served on silver and regimental songs were sung until four in the morning. The Empress Aleksandra remained in seclusion. By that time, her dislike of St. Petersburg high society had become the talk of the city.

And so St. Petersburg's upper classes lost themselves in festivities as the winter of 1913–1914 moved toward Lent. Then began six weeks of fasting and self-denial followed by a joyous celebration of Christ's resurrection that coincided with the first signs of spring. As always, spring spurred the well-to-do to make plans for spending the summer months away, and by May the packing had begun in earnest. Some looked forward to the cool breezes of the Finnish and Estonian coasts, others to weeks spent on rural estates, and a few to visits to Paris or London. But when the too-dry spring moved toward summer, Petersburgers' sense of well-being changed. The first two weeks of June were unseasonably hot, and forest fires started easily. A pall of smoke hung over the city, its source never really known. Some thought it came from nearby peat bogs having been set afire by lightning. Others thought it came from Siberia, or maybe from the mead-owlands between St. Petersburg and Moscow. Apprehensions deepened. Gippius and Merezhkovskii actually came back from Paris to spend the summer in St. Petersburg, and others began to have second thoughts about going away.[98] Nicholas, Aleksandra, their friends, and their children stayed at the Alexander Palace at Tsarskoe Selo and then went to the palace at Peterhof, both an easy hour's ride from the capital. Although very few spoke of it out loud, all of them seemed to be waiting for something.

The murder in Sarajevo of Archduke Franz Ferdinand, heir to the Austrian throne, on June 15, 1914, set off a crisis among the monarchs, states-

*A demonstration in support of Serbia after its rejection of the Austro-Hungarian ultimatum proceeds along the Nevskii Prospekt, July 1914. (Courtesy of the Central State Archive of Kino-Photo-Phono Documents, St. Petersburg)*

men, and parliaments of Europe that would lead to war. At six o'clock on the evening of July 19, Nicholas II ordered Russia's general mobilization, and six hours later, Count Friedrich Pourtales, Germany's ambassador to Russia, demanded that the order be canceled. When Russia refused, Pourtales made his last visit to the Russian Foreign Ministry the next evening to deliver Germany's declaration of war, and by July 23 (August 5, according to Europe's Gregorian calendar) the nations of the Western world were at war. "The part played by reason in the government of peoples is so small that it has taken merely a week to let loose universal madness," France's ambassador to St. Petersburg had confided to his diary that day.[99] "We could foresee the course of events," Russia's foreign minister commented, "[but] we were powerless to change them."[100]

Petersburgers greeted Germany's declaration of war against Russia with outpourings of patriotism and outraged national feeling. "Faces were strained and grave," a young grand duchess remembered, when courtiers, ladies-in-waiting, senior army officers, and high officials gathered in the Nicholas Hall of the Winter Palace on July 20 to hear the Emperor tell them that Russia was at war. "Men frowned thoughtfully, shifting from foot to foot, readjusting their swords, or moving their fingers over the

*A gathering on Palace Square in front of the General Staff Headquarters to hear Nicholas II read the Declaration of War signaling Russia's entry into World War I, July 20, 1914. (Photo by K. Bulla. Courtesy of the Central State Archive of Kino-Photo-Phono Documents, St. Petersburg)*

brilliant decorations pinned on their chests," she wrote.[101] Women wept. When they heard Nicholas II vow "never to make peace so long as a single enemy soldier remains on our soil," everyone cheered.[102] The crowd outside on the Palace Square took up the cry for Russia and the Emperor, and when Nicholas and Aleksandra went to the balcony, a quarter of a million men, women, and children knelt and sang the Russian national anthem. Petersburgers and their Emperor seemed to be at one again. The feeling on the Winter Palace Square and in the streets around it, one visitor remarked, was such as "may be felt in a great cathedral or at any moment when the community is everything and the individual only has significance as a member of it."[103]

Two days later, the Petersburg crowd stormed the German Embassy, which had been completed only two years before. A monument to all that was tasteless in Wilhelmian Germany, its "vulgar and gaudy eloquence"

*Mobilization of reservists, shown here making their way to barracks accompanied by friends and family, July 1914. (Photo by K. Bulla. Courtesy of the Central State Archive of Kino-Photo-Phono Documents, St. Petersburg)*

was criticized by France's ambassador as being "abominable as a work of art,"[104] and the building certainly fit poorly with the others that stood near it on St. Isaac's Square. Seeing it as a symbol of their national enemy, Petersburgers destroyed the embassy's furniture and paintings, smashed its windows, and hurled Ambassador Pourtales's collection of rare Renaissance bronzes onto the square below, while the police looked benignly on. Nor did the authorities intervene when the mob attacked the bronze horses and naked giants that adorned the embassy's roof. Through it all, St. Petersburg's mayor and the Imperial Minister of Internal Affairs stood just a few feet away. Then, four days later the Duma met in a special one-day session at the Tauride Palace and voted the credits needed to finance the war. A month after that, Nicholas and his ministers changed St. Petersburg's name to the more Slavic-sounding Petrograd, which diplomats greeted as "a protest of Slavic nationalism against Germanic intrusion."[105] Briefly, that gesture appealed to some of the city's intelligentsia, too. But for the masses, the city remained "Piter," just as it had been since the days of Peter the Great.[106]

The war changed more in Russia's capital than its name. As the empire's greatest producers of armaments, Petrograd's mills and plants worked day and night to turn out field guns, shells, and all the other armaments that could be crafted from iron and steel. Jobs were plentiful, and workers' pay went up. Then prices started to inch upward, too. At first, they moved more slowly than wages, but when they overtook them, strikes increased. In August 1914, labor protest had all but died out, but the crises of the war's first year brought it back. By August 1915, casualties at the front had passed four million with no end in sight.[107] The infantry was running out of rifles and cartridges, and the artillery had run out of shells. By late summer 1915, three out of every four of Russia's cities were reporting food shortages, and the number seemed to be growing despite that fall's bumper harvest. Too quickly, the patriotism of 1914 gave way to cynicism and self-interest. War profiteers had become a common sight in Petrograd by the summer of 1915. So had able-bodied men whose social and political connections helped them to avoid duty at the front.

For Petrograd's avant garde the war changed everything. Set against the slaughter of 1914 and 1915, the raging declarations of disenchantment with which these "children of Russia's terrible years" had greeted the last days of peace now rang off key.[108] For the fact was that life on the eve of the Great War had been the best that St. Petersburg's artists and writers had ever known, nor would any of them live to see such a time again. Not only had it been possible for the first time in Russia's history to earn a good living from the arts, but censorship had been all but nonexistent. For a brief moment, the future had been theirs to claim, but now, as their friends died in the marshes of West Poland and East Prussia, Petrograd's writers and artists realized that they had missed their chance and that war could never be invigorating or uplifting. The Apocalypse, they now knew, could never bring rebirth, for the fires of Armageddon to which they had looked so hopefully to cleanse the world had proved to be destructive beyond all imagining.

Knowing that the world could never be the same again, these men and women finally realized that "in war there is no room for dreams" and began to see the present and future in different terms. Many thought that escape from the "well-equipped factory for the annihilation of mankind" into which fate had cast them could come only through a revolution that would obliterate the old world and replace it with a new society.[109] But, as with the visions of Apocalypse and Armageddon that had dominated their writings before the war, any sense of when the revolution would come and what it would leave in its wake remained unclear. To Petrograd's avant garde at the end of 1914, Revolution still seemed little more than a substitute for the visions of Apocalypse and Armageddon that had proved to be so terrifying in reality.

Petrograd's poets no longer proclaimed their verses to the stars from the rooftop of Ivanov's Tower. Now the city's bohemians gathered at the Stray Dog, a cellar cabaret on the corner of Mikhailovskaia Square and Italianskaia Street that stank of overflowed toilets and cheap tobacco smoke. There, beneath vaults on which the artist Sergei Sudeikin had painted flowers and birds, "where all the 'stray dogs' on the different roads of contemporary art could come together,"[110] the avant garde of the city gathered after midnight to read their poetry and debate its meaning. Unlike "Viacheslav the Magnificent," who had presided over the Tower's discussions a few years earlier, the Stray Dog's proprietor, Boris Pronin, followed the example of Aristide Bruant in Paris and let artists and writers in free of charge, but extracted outrageous admission fees from a crowd of well-heeled politicians, war profiteers, and other sorts of philistines who were willing to pay generously to sit near the city's leading painters and poets. Invariably these onlookers greeted readings and performances with shouts of *"Homage! Homage!"* all the while (as one memoirist remembered) "squeezing each other's lustful knees under the tables."[111]

The Stray Dog was "the only islet . . . where the literary and artistic youth, without a cent to their name as a rule, felt at home" in wartime Petrograd.[112] Pronin would sometimes organize "special Mondays" and "extraordinary" Wednesdays and Saturdays, or arrange evenings around special themes that featured, for example, the founder of Italian Futurism, Filippo Marinetti, or the ballerina Tamara Karsavina, just returned from a triumphant tour of London. On other evenings the attraction might be Arthur Lourie or Ilia Sats, the latter renowned for the music he had written for plays performed at Stanislavskii's Moscow Art Theater, the former to win fame for his music only when he fled to America after the Revolution. Futurists, Acmeists, Cubists, and Constructivists—the Stray Dog was home to them all as they debated what art is, what it ought to be, and where Russia seemed to be headed. Supported by the philologists Viktor

Shklovskii and Boris Eikhenbaum, the Futurist poet Vladimir Maiakovskii in those days demanded a new kind of poetry written in "language beyond the mind." His rivals the Acmeists insisted that the time
had come to stop seeing objects as symbols of a higher, mystical world
and allow a rose once again to "become beautiful in and of itself."[113]

On winter evenings, the Stray Dog was visited frequently by a young
novelist, Aleksei Nikolaevich Tolstoi, who, in his Stalin Prize–winning
*Road to Cavalry*, would later describe Petrograd as "coldly seething and
satiated," a city that "lived as if awaiting the fateful day of judgement." As
he stormed through its streets in his mammoth raccoon fur coat and huge
beaver hat, Tolstoi found Petrograd "tormented by sleepless nights, deadening its misery with wine, gold, and love without love."[114] Called by some
"the king of aesthetes" and the "Russian Beau Brummel," Mikhail
Kuzmin often visited the Stray Dog in those days, too.[115] Like so many of
the avant garde, Kuzmin had dreamed of a career in music, but had become a poet instead. At the Stray Dog he sometimes sang and accompanied himself on the piano while the "pharmacists" (the disdainful name
Pronin gave to his paying customers) clapped and cheered.

Tolstoi, Kuzmin, the poets Benedikt Livshits and Nikolai Gumilev, and
scores of other Petrograd bohemians frequented the Stray Dog during its
short lifetime between New Year's Eve 1912 and the late spring of 1915.
But the two around whom life in the cabaret turned most persistently
were the poets Anna Akhmatova and Vladimir Maiakovskii. Of the two,
Akhmatova was at first better known, having been a frequent visitor at
Ivanov's Tower in addition to being the wife of Gumilev and the friend of
the poet Osip Mandelshtam. "I have never seen a woman whose face and
entire appearance . . . set her apart anywhere and among beautiful women
everywhere," one of her friends once wrote. People thought her "more
than beautiful," and her poems about love and passion drew listeners even
more powerfully than her beauty.[116] Love to Akhmatova seemed at the
same time beautiful and terrible, and she wrote of all its phases with a
sense of intimacy that compelled her readers to ask what lover or lovers
she had in mind.

Especially after she returned to St. Petersburg from Paris in 1912,
Akhmatova began to highlight the opposites that she found in life and
love. "We are all revelers, we are all whores. How unhappy we are together!" she intoned when the Stray Dog's patrons celebrated New Year's
Eve, 1913.[117] Yet those were the happiest times in Akhmatova's life. "Yes, I

loved those noisy, crowded nights," she confessed many years later as she looked back on the months just before the war when the greatest challenge confronting Petersburg's bohemians was to discover the real meaning of life. "We did not know [then]," she added, "that we lived on the eve of the first European war and the October Revolution."[118] Nor, she might have added, did her friends at the Stray Dog have any sense of the horrors that awaited those who would live into the era of Stalin and World War II.

In 1915, the Jewish Petrograd artist Natan Altman painted a portrait of Akhmatova that became the icon of the modernist movement her poetry represented. Allowed to live in the city only because he had been certified as a sign painter (Jews who did not have wealth, higher education, or certification as craftsmen were forbidden to live in the capital), Altman was influenced by Cubism and Acmeism, and his depiction of Akhmatova in her blue-black dress, bright yellow shawl, and with an oval cameo at her waist won instant acclaim as his greatest work. Altman had met Akhmatova by chance in Paris in 1911, when, as she later wrote, "the spirit of art had not yet transformed [us and] . . . everything that had happened to us up until that point was the prehistory of our lives."[119] Now, he made her "the embodiment of the general spiritual unease"[120] that enveloped Petrograd as the end of the war's first year approached. Patriotic passions had long since waned, and everyone was growing tired of the bad news that still poured in from the front. Even the government's supporters felt they were "dancing a 'last tango' on the rim of trenches filled with broken corpses" in those days.[121] For the moment, they held their tongues. But the bohemians at the Stray Dog did not.

From the Stray Dog's small inner room, the twenty-one-year-old Futurist poet Vladimir Maiakovskii spoke as the voice of rebellion and outrage. Tall, dark, and strongly built, he formed part of the avant-garde generation that stood between those who, like Merezhkovskii and Gippius, had practiced art for the sake of art, and those early Soviet Constructivists who wanted to enlist art in the service of politics.[122] Before the war, he had embraced the city, the factory, and the machine as symbols of the world he wanted to create, and had claimed to look down on the "insignificance" of Tolstoi, Dostoevskii, and Pushkin "from the height of skyscrapers."[123] In August 1914, he had tried to enlist in the army but had been rejected because of his close connections with Lenin's Bolsheviks. He had moved to Petrograd, drawn a few posters to support the invasion of East Prussia, and then had turned against the war. At the Stray Dog, one of his friends remembered, Maiakovskii took to looking on in stormy silence, "half lying in the position of a wounded gladiator, on a Turkish drum" that he beat whenever one of his fellow Futurists walked in.[124] In that pose, he had watched the "pharmacists" come and go, had watched them flaunt the wealth they had made from war profits, but continued to hold his peace.

Then in February 1915, Maiakovskii spoke out, rising from his position by the door to speak in the velvety voice that always seemed incongruous when compared to the harsh words he loved to use. *"Vam!"*—"To You!"— he began as his unsuspecting audience looked on expectantly. *"Vam!* Who live only from orgy to orgy." Laying down what he called a barrage of "words like gunshots," he continued his attack: "Aren't you ashamed to read in the newspapers / About the presentations of the Crosses of St. George [for valor]?" He spoke just a few more lines more and then concluded as he turned away in disgust: "Why should I give my life for you? / I'd rather serve pineapple water drinks / To the whores at the bar!"[125] It had taken Maiakovskii a mere seventy-seven words compressed into sixteen lines to shatter the veneer of self-righteous patriotism with which the men who served Tsar and country in the name of profit had summoned themselves. Soon afterwards, when the authorities who had rejected his patriotism in 1914 tried to draft him into the army, his friends saved him only by a series of bureaucratic subterfuges.

By the time Maiakovskii spoke his piece, Petrograd had become swollen with refugees. The war continued to hang over the city like a black cloud, "brutifying," as Merezhkovskii said, people and everyday life. In August 1915, Nicholas II took command of Russia's armies and went to the front. Neurotic and neurasthenic, the Empress Aleksandra remained in what they now both called "rotten Petrograd" to rule Russia. During the next year, life in the city turned increasingly sour, and its people grew correspondingly impatient. "We're heading for revolution," Russia's former prime minister, Kokovtsev, told France's ambassador as they dined at Donon's one evening in the fall of 1916. The third man at the table, Aleksei Putilov, thought differently. "We're heading for anarchy," he told them. "There's a vast difference. The revolutionary has the intention to reconstruct; the anarchist thinks of nothing but destruction."[126]

Well-to-do men like Putilov and Kokovtsev could debate such distinctions, but to most Petrograders the real problems were food shortages and soaring prices. Boots cost five times as much at the end of 1916 as they had at the beginning of the war. Coal prices had quadrupled, and the cost of a meal in a cheap workers' café had risen by a factor of seven.[127] At the beginning of 1917, blizzards and plummeting temperatures cut supplies and drove prices higher still, until the cost of a loaf of bread was rising at the rate of two percent a week. The price of potatoes and cabbage rose at a weekly rate of three percent, sausage at seven percent, and sugar at more than ten.[128] When the bitter cold of February descended on Petrograd, firewood became so expensive that workers had to choose between heat and food, and many people lived in buildings in which the temperature never rose above twelve degrees centigrade, even at midday.[129] That the city's masses were angry and restless was an open secret, and the reasons were painfully obvious. "Children are starving," a secret police agent reported. "A revolution, if it takes place . . . will be spontaneous, quite likely a hunger riot."[130] "Every day," another added, "the masses are becoming more and more embittered. An abyss is opening between them and the government."[131]

By early February 1917, politicians, high officials, diplomats—virtually everyone in Petrograd except Nicholas and Aleksandra—had become seriously alarmed. Again the suicide rate soared.[132] "Everyone has lost heart," one of the leading progressives in the Duma confessed. "They all realize how powerless they really are."[133] To France's ambassador, it seemed that "the forces of disintegration [were] silently at work in the very heart of Russian society."[134] That seemed especially true in Petrograd's weapons factories, where on February 14, demonstrations by nearly ninety thousand workers who had gone on strike to celebrate the end of the Shrovetide holidays had to be broken up by mounted police and Cossacks. Despite the wave of bitter cold that settled on the city during the next week, another two hundred thousand workers joined more than one hundred and fifty new strikes in different parts of the city. All of them marched against the war and the shortage of bread.[135]

Then, the weather cleared, the sun turned warm, and the snow began to drip away from balconies and windows. On February 21, seven hundred men at the huge Putilov armaments works went on strike, and two days later, on Thursday, February 23, thirty thousand workers from other factories in the city joined fifty thousand women from the textile mills who were celebrating International Women's Day and demanding higher wages. Still hardly anyone seemed concerned. Zinaida Gippius dismissed that day's demonstrations as an "ordinary sort of hunger riot like those that have been happening in Germany," the French ambassador had twenty-six guests in for dinner that evening, and the Princess

*Soldiers' wives demand increased rations in a demonstration along the Nevskii Prospekt following the celebration of International Women's Day, February 23, 1917. (Photo by K. Bulla. Courtesy of the Central State Archive of Kino-Photo-Phono Documents, St. Petersburg)*

Radziwill went ahead with plans for a large party she was planning for Sunday.[136]

To everyone's surprise, the numbers of strikers in the streets doubled the following day, and on Saturday, the day after that, the Putilov men joined their ranks. By then, the numbers of demonstrators had passed two hundred thousand, and in mid-afternoon, when it had already begun to grow dark, they marched up the Nevskii Prospekt to Znamenskaia Square in front of the Nicholas Railroad Station. There angry men and women called for the city to open its flour warehouses and give them more bread. When the police tried to disperse them, they turned sullen and started to build barricades in some of the side streets within sight of the Nevskii Prospekt. Because the authorities continued to avoid any major confrontation that would draw firm lines of conflict, an uneasy peace still reigned. As night closed in on the city everyone wondered what Sunday would bring.[137]

Several hundred miles away at Stavka, the headquarters of Russia's High Command, Nicholas II had spent Saturday in a very different way.

That morning he had gotten up late, enjoyed a leisurely breakfast, and spent an hour or so listening to reports. After a leisurely lunch, he had jotted a note to the Empress, prayed at a nearby monastery, and then taken the afternoon walk he never missed unless he was ill. Later in the afternoon, a letter from Aleksandra had mentioned the demonstrations in passing, but seemed to attach not much importance to them. At the same time, Nicholas's chief of staff received more detailed reports from Petrograd, and he passed some of them (though by no means all) to the Emperor at dinner.[138] When Nicholas settled down to a quiet evening of staff work, the situation in Petrograd was on his mind, but he dealt with it quickly and moved on to other things. "I order you to bring all of these disorders in the capital to a halt as of tomorrow," he wrote in a telegram to the commander of the city's garrison. "These cannot be permitted in this difficult time of war with Germany and Austria."[139]

Almost without thinking about it, Nicholas had put his government and Petrograd's masses on a collision course. For, if the workers refused to disperse, the only way to bring the disorders to a halt was with gunfire. Yet, what if Petrograd's peasant soldiers refused to fire upon their peasant brethren who had taken jobs in the factories? There is no evidence that Nicholas ever considered that possibility, but Petrograd's commander understood it full well. If the soldiers did not shoot down the demonstrators in Petrograd's streets, the workers' protests would become a revolution. "Even the tiniest spark could start a conflagration," the wife of the Duma's president told a friend just a few days before.[140] Now it seemed as if the spark had been struck by a sixteen-word telegram penned by the Emperor himself.

NINE

# COMRADES

*W*HILE NICHOLAS WAS WRITING his fateful telegram on the night of February 25, some thirteen thousand Petrograders sat in the plush seats of the Aleksandrinskii Theater, just off the Nevskii Prospekt. That evening, the theater was presenting what one viewer called a "gorgeous revival" of Mikhail Lermontov's *Masquerade,* the product of the author's own revolutionary yearnings in the 1830s, when he had struggled to prevent the censors of Nicholas's great grandfather, Nicholas I, from defacing his poems and novels. "Stupidity and perfidy," Lermontov had written then, "are what make the world turn," and for many years *Masquerade* had been banned "because of the violence of [its] passions and characters."[1] Now directed by Petrograd's daring Vsevolod Meyerhold, whose avant-garde techniques were destined soon to fuse the diverse artistic currents of Symbolism, Futurism, and Expressionism into revolutionary new theatrical perspectives, *Masquerade* had been five years in the making. In terms of actors, sets, costumes, and theatrical effects the play commanded the best that Imperial Russia had to offer, yet an aura of fatalism had surrounded it from the very beginning. By 1917, actors, musicians, and stage hands had nicknamed it "Sunset of the Empire."[2]

Despite shortages of everything from munitions to bread brought on by the war, the Imperial Treasury had paid thirty thousand gold rubles for *Masquerade*'s sets. Aleksandr Golovin designed them, and he had made four thousand drawings before he was entirely satisfied. Meyerhold matched Golovin's passion for detail at every step, seeking to coordinate every word the actors spoke with a corresponding choreographed gesture. Some in the audience called his effort "an opera without music," and everyone was stunned by the overpowering artistic tapestry that actors, director, and designer created that night. The play's message that Russia's court, high society, and government were all a false masquerade must have struck the audience as especially appropriate to the situation in which they found themselves, for the contrast between the lavish setting and the sullen anger of Petrograd's hungry masses could not have been more stark. "What were we going to do afterward?" one critic remembered asking himself as the audience heaped laurel wreaths and bouquets on the stage. "Go to Lucullus to eat nightingales' tongues, and let the hungry bastards howl, seeking bread and freedom?"[3] At that very moment, more than two hundred thousand workers were preparing to return to Petrograd's streets. Having just received Nicholas's telegraphed order "to bring all of these disorders in the capital to a halt as of tomorrow," General Sergei Khabalov, commander of the city's garrison, had begun to move more than fifteen thousand soldiers, Cossacks, and police into position.

It was nearly midnight when *Masquerade*'s audience left the theater. As they made their way to townhouses on the Moika and the Fontanka, and apartments across the river on Vasilevskii Island and in the Petrograd District, they had an eerie sense of being part of history in the making. The night was dark. Squads of infantry and small groups of cavalry moved past silently, sometimes staying in the shadows, at others moving into the open. From time to time, stray gunshots broke the silence. Streetcars had stopped running, and the poet Anna Akhmatova had to search for some time before she could find a hackney driver who dared to take her to her apartment in the workers' Vyborg District, where gunfire continued to be heard. Zinaida Gippius had no such difficulty in getting to her apartment in the more fashionable Dom Muruzi, but she felt no less apprehensive. "It's like some sort of gigantic corpse is suffocating," she confided to her diary that night. "A strange sensation."[4] The city was being turned into an armed camp. Before dawn, machinegunners had taken up positions on rooftops and in attic windows, from which they could command strategic avenues and intersections. Infantry platoons guarded key buildings, and Cossack squadrons patrolled the streets. Held by its own army against its own people, Petrograd had become an occupied city for the only time in its history.[5]

In the course of the next four days, Petrograd's garrison joined forces with its workers. Early on Sunday morning, General Khabalov had ordered his men to "give three warnings and then—open fire" if they confronted crowds that were "in any way threatening."[6] A few had done so, and by mid-afternoon, one soldier-memoirist wrote, "the blood of workers had stained the snow."[7] That evening several military units had turned against the police. On Monday—always an unlucky day according to Russian superstition—soldiers and workers had broken into the Liteinyi Arsenal and seized more than seventy thousand rifles and pistols along with at least four hundred machine guns.[8] Well before the watery winter sun had set that day, Sunday's general strike had become Monday's armed insurrection against Nicholas and his government. All day Sunday and Monday, telegrams from Petrograd's high officials and concerned citizens poured into the Emperor's headquarters, but he ignored them all. Then came Khabalov's admission of defeat. "I beg you to inform His Imperial Highness that I am not able to carry out his instructions about the restoration of order in the capital," he telegraphed the duty officer late on Monday evening. "The majority of army units . . . have refused to fire on the rebels," his report continued. "Other units have joined with the insurgents and have turned their weapons against the troops still remaining loyal to His Highness."[9]

By the time Khabalov's telegram arrived at Nicholas's *Stavka* just after midnight, the Tsar had decided to grant no concessions and to bring Petrograd's crowds to their knees by force. On the morning of February 28, he sent General Nikolai Ivanov to the capital with the St. George Battalion of battle-hardened heroes who had won the coveted Cross of St. George for valor in combat and could be counted on to follow orders. When he learned the full extent of the garrison's defection, Nicholas's more level-headed chief of staff General Mikhail Alekseev ordered Ivanov to return, lest a pitched battle in Petrograd drive more army units into the arms of the revolution. That same day, Petrograd's workers and soldiers organized a Soviet of Workers and Soldiers' Deputies in hopes of seizing control of the revolution, and by that time soldiers, sailors, and workers in several nearby towns and cities had come over to their side.

To prevent armed proletarians from overwhelming Petrograd, moderate and conservative members of the Duma demanded Nicholas's abdication and struggled to form a Provisional Government. At first, the Emperor would hear none of their pleadings, and when asked about several telegrams that had been sent by the Duma's President Mikhail Rodzianko, he remarked that he would "not even deign to reply."[10] Two days later, on March 2, Nicholas bowed to the inevitable and signed a manifesto of abdication. At one o'clock the next morning, March 3, 1917, he set out for Tsarskoe Selo, where Aleksandra waited with their children in the Aleksandr Palace. "[My] heart is heavy over what has just happened," he confided to his diary as he set out. "All around me there is nothing but treason, cowardice, and deceit!"[11]

Petrograd's workers cheered Nicholas's abdication. Speeches and mass meetings became a way of life, for everyone had something to say, and there was always someone ready to listen. For a few days, the palaces and townhouses of the well-to-do became fair game, as "searches" inevitably ended in pillaging and looting. A huge red flag replaced the imperial banner above the Winter Palace, and cheering crowds stripped two-headed imperial eagles from government buildings and threw them onto bonfires. Now truly in his element, the poet Maiakovskii, who had joined Lenin's Bolsheviks at the age of fifteen and celebrated his sixteenth birthday in solitary confinement, cheered them on. "We have triumphed! / Glory to us all! / Glo-o-o-r-y to us all!" he wrote in his "poetry chronicle" of the revolution. "Death to the two-headed eagle! / Sever its long-necked head / With a single stroke!"[12]

For the next eight months, the Revolution of February 1917 held Petrograd in its grip. Command of democratic Russia passed formally to the Provisional Government on the day after Nicholas's abdication, but the Soviet of Workers' and Soldiers' Deputies controlled the munitions plants, railroads, army, postal service, and telegraph, so that it alone commanded the masses and had real power. During the spring, summer, and early fall, several Provisional Governments rose and fell, each being succeeded by one that had moved further to the left. Everyone sensed the power of the masses, but no one yet could tell if it would be used for good or ill. The poet Aleksandr Blok hoped that "blood, violence, and bestiality" would soon give way to "pink clover," and he urged his friends to remember that "the heavy hammer breaketh glass but forgeth steel."[13] Having himself risen from the lower depths and knowing the masses'

*Funeral procession along the Nevskii Prospekt to honor the victims of the Febru-*
*ary Revolution, March 1917. (Photo by K. Bulla. Courtesy of the Central State Archive*
*of Kino–Photo–Phono Documents, St. Petersburg)*

pent-up brutality at first hand, the hugely popular novelist Maksim Gorkii knew better. "All the dark instincts of the crowd, irritated by the disintegration of life and by the lies and filth of politics will flare up and fume, poisoning us with anger, hate and revenge," he predicted as Petrograd's summer nights began to cool and the fall days shortened. "People," he concluded grimly, "will kill one another, unable to suppress their own animal stupidity."[14]

As Russia continued to stumble, Lenin laid his plans for seizing power. "The present task must be an *armed uprising* in Petrograd and Moscow, the seizure of power, and the overthrow of the government," he wrote from the refuge to which he had fled in Finland.[15] "The whole future of the Russian revolution is now at stake."[16] On the night of October 10, he slipped into Petrograd under the cover of an icy drizzle to meet with the

*Burial of the victims of the February Revolution in the Field of Mars (formerly Tsaritsyn Meadow), March 1917. (Courtesy of the Central State Archive of Kino-Photo-Phono Documents, St. Petersburg)*

eleven members of the Central Committee who opposed his call for an armed uprising, and after several hours of argument he won over a majority of nine. Now committed to action, most of these men still had doubts. "We really seem to be pygmies thinking of moving a mountain," one of them told a friend.[17] Hunted by the Provisional Government police, Lenin slipped back into hiding, and the task of leading the Bolshevik Revolution in Petrograd fell to Trotskii, the brilliant, dynamic son of a South Russian Jewish farmer. "He was the central figure," one observer wrote not long afterward. "[He was] the real hero of this remarkable page in history."[18]

Petrograd in October 1917 was a city filled with desperate people facing desperate futures. After the Russians' last great offensive had crumbled that summer, the war effort had all but collapsed, and a sense of hopelessness about a conflict that could not be won and would not end pervaded everything. Everyone feared that winter would bring even greater shortages of food and fuel than those of the previous year. Prices soared, money lost its value, and once-rich men and women began to trade jewelry and antique treasures for food. People stood for hours in lines to buy tobacco, chocolate, sugar, and milk, and rumors spread that the bread ration might be cut at any moment to half a pound a day. Only recently arrived in the city, Jack Reed, an American socialist who had come to see the revolution with his own eyes, found "a great throbbing city under grey skies rushing faster and faster toward—what?"[19] Lenin knew, and so did Trotskii. A revolution of a very new kind was in the making, and Petrograd was to be its center. All that was needed, Trotskii explained, was for Russia's "revolutionary leaders" to determine the proper moment to strike. "They must feel out the growing insurrection in good season and supplement it with conspiracy," he wrote. "Intuition and experience" were needed. So were energy, dedication, and daring.[20] No task seemed beyond Trotskii's strength in those days, when not even the huge amphitheater of the Petrograd District's Cirque Moderne could accommodate the crowds that came to hear him speak. A sense of mission drove him on, and in Lenin's absence he took firm command.

All through that summer and early fall, the headquarters that the Bolsheviks had established at the Smolnyi Institute had been the place to feel the Revolution's pulse, for there one could mix freely with revolutionary leaders and followers at one of the rare sources of plentiful food in Petrograd. Reed often went to the Smolnyi's cellar dining room, "where twenty

*Red Guards and revolutionary soldiers guard Bolshevik headquarters (formerly the Smolnyi Institute for Young Noblewomen), October 1917. (Photo by P. Otsup. Courtesy of the Central State Archive of Kino-Photo-Phono Documents, St. Petersburg)*

men and women ladled from immense cauldrons cabbage soup, hunks of meat and piles of kasha, and slabs of black bread" onto plates held by a thousand revolutionary workers who sat at trestle tables.[21] And then, at a single command from Trotskii in late October, the open camaraderie vanished. While Trotskii's newly organized Military Revolutionary Committee laid its final plans for an armed insurrection in Petrograd, a tight curtain of military security cut Smolnyi off from the rest of the city. Only a few days more were needed. Then the Bolsheviks would be ready to strike.

On Sunday October 22, the Bolsheviks celebrated Petrograd Soviet Day by holding mass meetings all across the city. Since the Provisional Government's order for his arrest was still in force, Lenin remained in hiding, but Trotskii seemed to be everywhere. "Soviet power," he told a huge gathering at the People's Palace not far from the city's zoo, "will give everything in our country to the poor and the men in the trenches. You have two sheepskin coats, bourgeois—give one to a soldier who is freezing in the trenches," he went on with a dramatic flourish calculated to win

Petrograd's lower classes to his side. "Do you have warm boots, too?" he asked his hypothetical middle-class subject. "Stay at home. A worker needs your boots!" With thousands of workers and soldiers hanging on his words, Trotskii extracted from them an oath "to support with all our strength and at any cost the Soviet, which has taken upon itself the great burden of leading the revolution to victory."[22]

The following day, one eyewitness wrote, Trotskii won the cheering garrison at the Peter and Paul Fortress along with the weapons they commanded at the nearby Kronverk Arsenal over to the Bolsheviks' cause by delivering "not so much a speech as an inspirational song."[23] Along with Red Guards drawn from Petrograd's factories, Trotskii was counting on these men to overwhelm the Women's Shock Battalions, military cadet units, senior officers, and scattered Cossack detachments that had not yet sworn to support the Bolsheviks. For more than a week, Petrograd's Red Guards had been prepared. Ready to move into the street at a moment's notice, men at the huge Putilov works kept their rifles near to hand. At another factory, a Red Guard remembered some years later, "turners were at their workbenches with cartridge pouches over their shoulders," rifles within easy reach.[24] By October 22, many of the Red Guards had taken to sleeping in their factories, just to be ready when the time came. The point from which there could be no looking back was very near, a Bolshevik friend told Jack Reed. "The other side," he said, "knows it must finish us, or be finished."[25]

Through it all—the mass meetings, the speeches, the recruitment of Red Guards—Lenin stayed in hiding at the apartment of Margarita Fofanova, a dedicated Bolshevik who lived on the outskirts of the Vyborg District. From Fofanova's corner bedroom, surrounded by chintz curtains and flowered wallpaper, Lenin unleashed a flood of letters urging his comrades at Smolnyi not to waste a single precious moment. "We must not wait [or] we may lose everything!" he wrote in a note that Fofanova delivered on the afternoon of Tuesday, October 24. "The government is tottering. It must be *given a death blow* at all costs!"[26] Unsure if the thirty-eight-year-old Trotskii had firm control of events and still fearful that his Bolsheviks might falter, Lenin struggled to gain a clearer picture of events that were moving more rapidly than any hand-delivered notes could indicate. "Everything now hangs by a thread," he fumed a few hours later as he continued to pace Fofanova's small apartment. "The matter must be decided without fail this very evening, or this very night."[27]

Had Lenin known the details, he might have been less worried, for the fall of the Provisional Government seemed more like a comedy of errors than a revolution. Outside the government itself, no one resisted and no one complained. Not long after Fofanova delivered Lenin's first note of the day to the Central Committee at Smolnyi, two of Trotskii's agents, both of whom had forgotten to bring their weapons, took command of Petrograd's Central Telegraph Office in the name of the Bolsheviks' Military Revolutionary Committee. By four o'clock on the morning of October 25, Bolshevik commissars from the Military Revolutionary Committee had added the Electric Power Station, the Main Post Office, and the Nikolaevskii Railroad Station to their list of conquests, as well as all the bridges across the Neva. "The moonlight created a fantastic scene," one of the Bolsheviks wrote later. "The hulks of the houses looked like medieval castles."[28] Petrograd's State Bank fell at six A.M., the Central Telephone Exchange at seven, and the Warsaw Railroad Station at eight. Unable to find loyal troops anywhere in the city, Russia's Prime Minister Aleksandr Kerenskii fled the capital at nine, huddled in the back seat of a huge Pierce Arrow touring car that had been commandeered from the U.S. ambassador. Not until early Wednesday afternoon, when they gathered at the Winter Palace for a meeting did the ministers of Kerenskii's fallen Provisional Government discover that he was gone. Soon after that, the Bolsheviks' Red Guards closed their ring around the palace. The last act of the Great October Revolution was about to begin.[29]

"In general," an eyewitness reported, "military operations seemed more like a changing of the guard" than a revolution.[30] While the Bolsheviks were seizing key posts throughout the city on Wednesday, Count Louis de Robien, a French diplomat, had lunch at Donon's, dined at Contant's, and noted nothing unusual. That evening, Fedor Chaliapin gave a concert to a packed house at the People's Palace where Trotskii had spoken a few days earlier, and the Aleksandrinskii Theater featured a revival of Aleksei Konstantinovich Tolstoi's half-century-old *Death of Ivan the Terrible*. No one paid much attention to what the Bolsheviks had in mind, nor did many seem to care. "The indifference of the crowds in the streets and on the streetcars is astounding," a General Staff officer remarked as he watched Petrograders making their way home that night.[31] Gippius felt the same way. "The darkest, most idiotic, dirtiest 'social revolution' that history has ever seen is upon us," she wrote in her diary when she got home. "To hell with them all," she added. "It's boring and disgusting. . . . The element of struggle is completely lacking everywhere."[32]

"Boring and disgusting" to Gippius, perhaps, but not to the Bolsheviks, who sensed a chance to change the course of history. Unable to contain his impatience, Lenin had slipped away from Fofanova's apartment just before midnight on October 24 and had made his way to Smolnyi, his bald head covered by a curly wig and his face wrapped in a dirty bandage. By that time, Jack Reed remembered, "Smolnyi, bright with lights, hummed like a gigantic hive," its gate bristling with machine guns and cannon and its courtyard filled with armored cars ready to go on the attack.[33] By the next night, the Bolsheviks held all of Petrograd except for the Winter Palace, in which the Ministers of the Provisional Government continued to meet without Kerenskii. They were defended only by a group of four hundred military cadets who passed the time by chasing each other up and down the sidewalk, a handful of Cossacks, and one of the Women's Shock Battalions that Kerenskii had organized that summer. "It all had an operatic air, and a comic one at that," Jack Reed's wife Louise Bryant told her friend Bessie Beatty, the redoubtable American war correspondent of the *San Francisco Bulletin* who had come with them to Petrograd.[34] Inside the palace, the ministers of the Provisional Government felt differently, more like "doomed rats, abandoned by everyone, roaming around inside a gigantic mousetrap," one of them later said.[35]

Then the defections began. At six o'clock on the evening of October 25, some of the cadets slipped away, soon to be followed by the Cossacks and part of the Women's Shock Battalion. Outside, the Bolsheviks drew their ring tighter, but not without some difficulties. When told that the guns of the Peter and Paul Fortress could not be fired, a group of Red Guards struggled for several hours to move artillery into position to shell the palace before they discovered that a quick cleaning would put the fortress guns back into service. After the cruiser *Aurora* had steamed into position near the Nikolaevskii Bridge and fired one blank round, the newly cleaned fortress guns fired some three dozen live shells, only two of which actually hit the palace. Then Red Guards began to work their way into the palace through doors and windows that the defenders had forgotten to lock. When their numbers grew large enough, they disarmed the last of the Provisional Government's forces. The set-piece assault that was later to be dramatized in Soviet film and song never took place, even

*Military cadets defend the Provisional Government in the White Hall of the Winter Palace during the Bolshevik coup, October 1917. (Photo by K. Bulla. Courtesy of the Central State Archive of Kino–Photo–Phono Documents, St. Petersburg)*

though several machine guns continued to fire at the palace's walls and windows from time to time.[36]

In the Tsar's private dining room on the palace's second floor, members of the Provisional Government waited, the tension among them deepening as midnight passed into the early morning hours of Thursday, October 26. Then, a few minutes before two o'clock, the door to the dining room burst open. "Like a chip washed up by a wave, a little man flew into the room under the pressure of the crowd [of Red Guards] that poured in behind him," one of the ministers later wrote. "He had long rust-colored hair and glasses, a short trimmed reddish mustache, a small beard . . . colorless eyes and a weary face," he continued. "His collar, shirt, cuffs, and hands were those of a very dirty man."[37] As one of the commanders of the Red Guards, this seedy-looking tactician of the streets who sometimes went by the code name of "Bayonet" placed the Provisional Government under arrest. For the moment, at least, the Bolsheviks had command of Petrograd. Only time would tell if they could hold it.

Like an army of besieging invaders, Petrograd's soldiers, sailors, and workers had their way with the city in whose slums they had worked, starved, and suffered for so many years. Palaces and townhouses were looted, furnishings defaced, and treasures stolen. But what received their fondest attention were the city's wine cellars, beginning with those in the Winter Palace, which were legendary for the rarity of the wines they held. None of the Bolsheviks' efforts to guard them worked. "The Preobrazhenskii [Guards] Regiment assigned to guard these cellars got totally drunk," a Red Guards commander later wrote. "The Pavlovskii [Guards], our revolutionary buttress, also couldn't resist. Then we sent guards from various other picked units—all got utterly drunk. We posted guards specially chosen from Regimental Committees—and they succumbed as well. We dispatched armored cars to drive away the crowd. After patrolling up and down a few times they also began to weave suspiciously. . . . We tried sealing up the entrances with brick," he continued, "but the crowd came back through the windows, smashing in the gratings and seizing whatever remained. We tried flooding the cellars with water—the firemen sent to do the job got drunk instead."[38]

For days, the masses' orgy continued as the looting spread to the cellars of Grand Dukes, rich aristocrats, and such legendary restaurants as Donon's. "It's sickening to see such good stuff thrown away," the Comte de Robien lamented in his diary. "There were bottles of Tokay [in the Winter Palace] from the time of Catherine the Great, and it all has been guzzled down by these vodka swiggers. . . . [It was] as if guerrilla warfare was being waged for the right of entrance to the kingdom of Bacchus," he added after hearing that bottles containing some of Chateau Mouton-Rothschild's greatest vintages had perished in the mob's attack on the palace of Grand Duke Pavel Aleksandrovich at Tsarskoe Selo. At the last minute, Contant's restaurant managed to save its cellars by hiring special detachments of guards and arming them with machine guns.[39] Not even Lenin knew what to expect in a world in which such "vodka swiggers" guzzled the Tsar's best wines. "You know," he mused to Trotskii soon after word reached Smolnyi that the Winter Palace fallen, "to pass so quickly from persecutions and living in hiding to power—it makes one's head spin!"[40]

Other problems soon made the Bolsheviks' heads spin even faster. Within the next few months no fewer than twenty-eight governments would take shape on the lands of the fallen Russian Empire, twenty-seven of which were anti-Bolshevik. More immediately, three years of war and eight months of revolution had unleashed the brutality of Russia's masses, and this ran rampant once the Bolsheviks' victory wiped away the last vestiges of order in Petrograd. The Comte de Robien saw two soldiers shoot an old peasant street vendor rather than pay for two of the stunted green apples she had for sale,[41] and similar incidents quickly showed that no one in the city was safe. As soldiers and armed workers killed for money, clothing, food, and for no reason at all, violence became a way of life, and the number of robberies soared to eight hundred a day. One night, robbers even dragged the chief of the Bolsheviks' newly established security police in Petrograd from his sleigh, stole his clothes, and sent him home naked.[42]

In vain did Lenin urge his followers to "learn discipline from the Germans," while Trotskii called for "work, order, persistence, [and] self-sacrifice." Soon they all realized that force must be used to impose from above the kinds of restraint to which Russia's masses were accustomed. "The only way to save ourselves is by dogged labor and revolutionary discipline," Trotskii insisted.[43] That had always distinguished the Bolsheviks' revolutionary organization from its rivals. And that, combined with terror applied unforgivingly, eventually enabled them to hold Petrograd and Russia. Until the Civil War ended in 1921, terror remained a hallmark of Russian life, as Reds and Whites applied it with a degree of brutality that appalled Western onlookers. But while the Whites used terror in anger and with passion, the Bolsheviks applied it more coldly and with vengeance. Superbly efficient and unremittingly cruel, the All-Russian Extraordinary Commission to Combat Counter-Revolution and Sabotage—the Cheka—which the Council of People's Commissars created at the end of 1917 "to wipe out all acts of counterrevolution and sabotage anywhere in Russia," became the instrument with which the Bolsheviks destroyed any who would not embrace their vision of Russia's future.[44]

Beginning with a single assistant, a small office just a few minutes' walk from the Admiralty and the Winter Palace at No. 3 Gorokhovaia Street, and only a thousand rubles in cash, the Cheka quickly grew into the "avenging sword" of the Revolution and one of the most feared security police forces in the history of the modern world. That it did so was the work of Feliks Dzerzhinskii, one of the most self-denying, austere men ever to enter the ranks of Russia's revolutionaries. Tall and slender, with a sharply sculpted Vandyke beard that called to mind one of the fanatic Spanish grandees who had directed the Inquisition, Dzerzhinskii had a flint-hard revolutionary spirit that never broke in the face of adversity.

"The most remarkable thing about him was his eyes," one of the men who knew him wrote. "They blazed with a steady fire of fanaticism. They never twitched. His eyelids seemed paralyzed."[45]

A third of his adult life spent in Tsarist prisons had given Dzerzhinskii a prisoner's unruffled patience, which he combined with a monk's austerity and a legendary capacity for work. He put the Revolution ahead of family, friendship, and personal comfort, slept in the Cheka offices, and dealt ruthlessly with any who did not share the Bolsheviks' beliefs. "I am in the front line of battle," he wrote in 1918 to the wife and son he had not seen in six years. "My thought induces me to be without pity, and there is in me an iron determination to follow my thought to the end."[46] Cold, ruthless, and unyielding, "Iron Feliks" would defend the Revolution at any cost. He saw himself as a moral guardian of those values around which the Bolsheviks wanted to shape Russia's future, and he truly believed he was building a better world.

As the Bolsheviks struggled to take control, the lives of Petrograd's once well-to-do fell apart. "Everything was being canceled," Aleksei Tolstoi remembered at the beginning of *Nineteen-Eighteen*, the second part of his Stalin Prize–winning trilogy about Russia's Revolution and Civil War. "Ranks, honors, pensions, officers' epaulettes, the thirtieth letter of the alphabet, God, private property, and even the right to live as one wished," he went on, "all were being canceled."[47] As the Bolsheviks limited withdrawals from personal bank accounts to a few hundred rubles a month, all citizens were expected to put their wealth and labor at the service of the state. Promising that "gold will cease to have power," special agents confiscated whatever gold, platinum, silver, and precious gems they found in private hands, thus driving their prices to unheard-of levels on the black market. By the spring of 1922, a ten-ruble tsarist gold coin cost twenty-four million paper rubles![48]

Everywhere people who had lived at the apex of life in Petrograd fell to its lowest depths. "Officers, barristers, schoolmasters, and engineers got employment as house-porters [and] messengers . . . [while others] were breaking [up] ice, selling newspapers, cigarettes, and chocolate," one observer reported.[49] Oblivious to the priceless paintings by Rubens, Van Dyck, and Claude Lorrain that hung above them while they smoked their coarse cigarettes, leaned against Donatello's bust of Ludovico Gonzaga, and spit sunflower seed hulls on the parquet floors, sailors from the Baltic Fleet turned Rastrelli's baroque Stroganov Palace into an off-duty club.

Princess Obolenskaia was seen clearing snow nearby, and a former colonel of the once proud Imperial Guards was said to have been seen begging a bowl of soup from the headwaiter at the Hotel Europe.[50] Everywhere, life in Petrograd seemed to reflect the promise Trotskii had made when he had exclaimed: "Our grandfathers, great-grandfathers, and fathers all had to clean up the shit and filth of your grandfathers and fathers. Now you are going to do the same thing for us!"[51]

Yet, for the masses life was only a little better. Shortages of fuel, food, goods, and public services threatened to overwhelm Petrograd, especially when four blizzards struck the city during the last ten days of December. As each day saw the cold deepen, the lines of people waiting to buy food grew longer. In November, the average adult Petrograder's daily calorie intake fell to 1,395, then to 1,039, and in January 1918 to 698. By February, the bread ration was only a quarter of a pound a day, with so many ingredients substituted for grain flour that it produced a pitiful 306 calories.[52] According to a survey done at the beginning of 1918, nearly half of all the railroad locomotives in Russia had broken down, and Russia's railroads were in disrepair. Without the fuel and raw materials for which they depended on the railroads, so many factories shut down that more than two-thirds of Petrograd's mill hands were out of work before the Bolsheviks' revolution celebrated its first anniversary.[53] "Starving Petrograd ... [was a] city without coal or bread, with its factory chimneys gone cold," Aleksei Tolstoi wrote. It was, he remembered "a terrible place."[54] Once darkened by the smoke from hundreds of smokestacks, the sky over Petrograd turned a brilliant blue in the winter of 1918. Now the darkness lay in its squares and streets and in the hundreds of thousands of corners where people huddled without electricity, with only a few ounces of kerosene or a handful of candles.

After the Bolsheviks moved Russia's capital to Moscow in the spring of 1918, life in Petrograd got even worse. With the simplest kinds of food commanding astronomical prices on the black market, people struggled to stay alive on the watery soup and thin gruel they were served in communal dining rooms in exchange for the official meal tickets that men and women who were thought to be necessary to the Bolsheviks' new order received. Pitirim Sorokin, a sociologist who lived through the Civil War years in Petrograd, thought that his colleagues, "standing in line [at the university dining room] with dishes and spoons which everyone had to bring from home, were like the beggars' line at church doors in former times." Even after one of Sorokin's cynical colleagues calculated that it took more energy to walk to the dining room than they received from the food they were served, the professors continued to appear. "I hope you will be alive tomorrow," they used to say as they left the dining hall in those days. "As the days went by," Sorokin remembered sadly, "fewer and fewer of us were left to say it."[55]

Every winter, Petrograd's bone-chilling dampness produces a peculiar kind of frost that coats cold stone and turns the granite pillars of St. Isaac's Cathedral into pink-silver shafts. In the winter of 1919–1920, this same kind of frost covered the outer walls of the city's townhouses, palaces, and apartment buildings with a silvery film that was broken only by an occasional heated room. During the days when everything in Petrograd was divided into "combustible and noncombustible," the literary critic and philologist Viktor Shklovskii remembered, these rare havens of warmth "showed up from the street as occasional dark patches on the silver." Shklovskii knew an author who wrote in a tiny shelter he had made in the middle of his apartment out of four chairs, a tarpaulin, and some rugs that he warmed with his breath and an electric light that came on whenever there was electricity. Other friends often came to Shklovskii's apartment to warm up because the temperature in one of its rooms sometimes got as high as forty-five degrees Fahrenheit.[56]

The avant-garde artist Iurii Annenkov remembered the winters of 1918 through 1920 in Petrograd as "an epic era of rotten, frozen carrion, of moldy bread crusts, and inedible substitutes." Starving people ate dogs, cats, and rats, and tore apart any dead animal carcass they came upon in the street. Men became impotent, and women stopped menstruating. Everyone seemed to be burning anything and everything, and Annenkov burned his furniture, his bookcases, and his books. "If I'd had wooden hands and feet," he confessed, "I'd have burned them too." People started tearing the doors off abandoned apartments to burn in their stoves. Then they tore down abandoned buildings. "It was a regular holocaust festival," Annenkov wrote. "The larger buildings consumed the smaller ones."[57] Under such conditions people's ways of looking at things changed. Those were the days, Sorokin remembered, when "the most valuable present one could give or receive was a piece of firewood."[58]

Along with hunger and cold came typhus, its spread facilitated by the chronic lack of toilet facilities caused by wastewater pipes that had frozen and burst. Carried by lice that flourished in the filth that festered in every courtyard and corner, typhus rivaled hunger as a killer, for the bite of even a single infected louse could kill people who had grown too weak to live through the disease's fever. Not counting Red Army soldiers, whom the disease infected at four times the rate of civilians, six thousand Petrograders came down with typhus in January 1920, with the number rising to eight thousand in February and nine thousand in March.[59] Hungry, cold, and afraid of getting sick, more than two-thirds of city's population fled. Life in Petrograd fell apart so completely that wildflowers began to bloom in what once had been busy city streets.[60] Yet something—perhaps the caustic sense of humor with which Russians so often face adversity—kept Petrograders from total despair. One morning in 1919, Iurii Annenkov and the poet Andrei Belyi came upon a bored policeman, rifle slung across his back, standing feet wide apart while he wrote his name in the snow with his urine. Overcome by the absurdity of it all, Belyi shouted. "Ink! Just give me a small bottle of ink and a scrap of paper! I don't know how to write in snow!" The embarrassed policeman buttoned his fly. "Move along, citizen," he muttered. "Move along."[61]

While Petrograd's people starved in the fall of 1919, General Nikolai Iudenich led a small anti-Bolshevik army of tsarist fighting men, Estonian allies, and British advisers on a dash toward its gates that stunned everyone by its swiftness. Fearful that the city's exposed position near Russia's frontiers might lead to just such an attack, Lenin had ordered Stalin to bolster its defenses that spring, and Stalin had launched a wave of terror that had lasted through midsummer. Yet Petrograd remained weak, and despite Stalin's claim that the city was safe, its defenses were still in disarray when Iudenich launched his offensive from Estonia at the beginning of October. When the White armies reached the Pulkovo Heights overlooking the city in less than three weeks, Lenin sent Bolshevik Commissar of War Trotskii to take Stalin's place. Proclaiming that "the enemy is at the very gates" but that "Red Petrograd must remain . . . the torch of the Revolution [and] the iron rock on which we will build the church of the future," Trotskii called for "a few thousand people who have firmly resolved not to surrender."[62] When these forces drove Iudenich from Pulkovo four days later, Trotskii hurried to Moscow to report that, on the second anniversary of the Bolshevik Revolution, "Soviet power . . . stands on its feet firmly and indestructibly."[63] Petrograd still starved, and another year of misery had to pass before the shortages began to ease. But the city that Trotskii once called the "revolutionary barometer of the Red Soviet Republic" remained firmly in Bolshevik hands.[64]

Intoxicated by visions of freedom but fearful that its dangers would make life short, Petrograd's avant garde indulged in a frenzy of experimentation with every form of art while the Civil War raged around them. Perhaps no one dreamed brighter dreams or suffered darker disappointments in those days than Aleksandr Blok, who saw in the events of 1917 an "absorbing novel with a thousand characters and the most fantastic combinations." Certain that the "swelling music" of the Revolution would make it possible to "organize things so that . . . our false, filthy, boring, hideous life should become just, pure, merry, and beautiful," he concluded that "the music of . . . [Russia's] intelligentsia is the same as the music of the Bolsheviks."[65] When the Revolution in Petrograd produced a hundred kinds of suffering in its aftermath, Blok struggled to discern the meaning of its opposites. Could good come from evil? Peace from violence? Happiness from misery? As the New Year dawned in 1918, he thought he had found an answer. "Trembling inside" he began to write *The Twelve*, the most brilliant poetic icon ever created for any revolution. Here one felt the power of revolution and the raw strength of the masses. As the workingmen and women of Petrograd marched in step with the Revolution, a sense that the future would be better shone forth.[66]

A brave new world was in the making, but how could it attract the masses and control them at the same time? Even more than in fiction and poetry, the Bolsheviks saw in the theater a means to reveal the future to the masses and draw them into the world they planned to create. "A theater of rapid action, major passions, rare contrasts, whole characters, powerful sufferings, and lofty ecstasy" was needed, Commissar of Enlightenment Anatolii Lunacharskii explained. To "create lofty Socialist art," he went on, it was necessary to "resurrect Shakespeare, Schiller, and many of the other past titans in order to link great art with the great lords of the future—the people."[67] Until Stalin harnessed the theater as another of the Soviet state's many instruments, the question of how Lunacharskii's goal could be accomplished remained open to debate. Playwrights and directors sought ways to reach across the footlights to make the masses active participants in the sort of "people's theater" with which Meyerhold and his friends had experimented in his studio on Borodinskaia Street before the Revolution. The decade after 1917 therefore saw some of the most amazing theatrical experiments ever to be staged in Russia.

In search of new visions that could free them from the misery of daily life, people poured into theaters all across Russia during the Civil War years. "In this terrifying world made of frost, stale herrings, rags, typhoid fever, arrests, bread lines, and armed soldiers," Shklovskii wrote from Petrograd, "one first night followed the other and the theaters were jammed every evening." In theaters without heat during the winters of 1918 and 1919, makeup froze on actors' faces, and musicians played in fur coats and hats with earflaps. "Isadora Duncan danced by the light of torches brought on the stage," Shklovskii remembered, "while thousands of voices, hoarse from the cold, sang 'Bravely forward, Comrades. Keep in step.'"[68] In those days, Duncan, who had moved from America to Petrograd to show her support for the Bolsheviks, loved to dance in a red tunic while she waved a red banner. Some Russian balletomanes criticized her dancing, one calling it "a curious combination of morality and gymnastics" that never allowed her to have "free mastery of her 'liberated' body." Bolshevik loyalists cheered the way her dancing showed the "thorny path of the Russian working class, oppressed by the tsarist boot, and eventually tearing off its chains," while Georgii Balanchivadze, later to win fame in the West as George Balanchine, thought her clumsy and fat. "She dances," he once told a friend, "like a pig."[69]

To celebrate the first anniversary of the Bolsheviks' Great October Revolution, Meyerhold staged Maiakovskii's *Mystery-Bouffe*, one of Red Russia's first revolutionary plays, at Petrograd's Communal Theater of Musical Drama. Drawing on earlier efforts to stage mass spectacles, and with sets painted by the brilliant Cubo-Futurist Kazimir Malevich, the play blended modernism, folk theater, and visions of Apocalypse to glorify revolution as the gateway to the future. *Mystery-Bouffe* retold the Biblical story of the Flood as a parable of revolution in which, as Lunacharskii once explained, the working class "gradually rids itself of parasites on its way through hell and heaven to the Promised Land—which turns out to be our own sinful earth."[70] Moving rapidly from revolutionary Apocalypse to Utopia, the play brought Maiakovskii's image of the new socialist city to Petrograd's masses, and the Promised Land became the final sum of his apocalyptic equation. Here was the Bolsheviks' world of the future, in which the "halls are packed with furniture, / The rooms fashionable with electrical services," all presented in a form that illustrated the sort of daily life that all Russians were supposed soon to enjoy.[71]

Almost immediately, *Mystery-Bouffe* became a model for massive attempts to re-create Russia's revolutionary history. The grandest of these was *The Storming of the Winter Palace*, a mass spectacle involving eight thousand performers and five hundred musicians with which Petrograd's Bolsheviks celebrated the Third Anniversary of the Great October Revolution on November 7, 1920. (Lenin's government had adopted the Western Gregorian calendar, thirteen days ahead of the tsarist Julian one in the twentieth century, on February 1, 1918, thus moving the anniversary of the October Revolution to November.) Iurii Annenkov, the Cubo-Futurist who had illustrated Blok's *The Twelve*, was named the spectacle's artistic designer, while the task of directing it was assigned to Nikolai Evreinov, Meyerhold's rival in Petersburg's cabarets before World War I. Called the "Russian Oscar Wilde" by some,[72] Evreinov saw the theater as a means to create new identities and to transform events. In *The Storming of the Winter Palace* he did not try to record history or explain it. Instead, he wanted to extract dramatic material from the past's events so as to give them focus and meaning.

While a hundred thousand Petrograders looked on, searchlights shifted their attention from one part of Petrograd's Palace Square to another. Trucks bristling with soldiers carrying rifles and fixed bayonets roared back and forth, machine guns coughed and chattered, and the *Aurora* fired once again the blank shot that had made it famous. A mass of Red Guards surged through the huge arch with which Carlo Rossi had divided the General Staff Headquarters from Russia's Ministry of Finance and Foreign Office to storm the Winter Palace, while grappling silhouettes in the palace windows portrayed their struggle against its defenders. More dramatic by far than the Bolsheviks' seizure of power had ever been, *The Storming of the Winter Palace* also involved several times more people than the events of October 1917. In Evreinov's version, Kerenskii fled dressed as a woman, while a huge red banner unfurled over the Winter Palace. As a finale, the actors and audience sang the "Internationale" to signal the beginning of a new age.[73]

After nearly three long years, the Civil War seemed to be dying down. Far to the south, the last of the White armies was driven out of Russia at the end of November 1920, and the Bolsheviks turned their attention to rebuilding the shattered land they now ruled. Yet there was not enough time to save Petrograd from another miserable winter, during which shortages of fuel and food would bring it to the brink of disaster once again. Freight trains limping over Russia's war-torn railroads could not bring coal to Petrograd through the blizzards that struck in January. Nor

*Celebration of the first anniversary of the Great October Revolution on Sen-
ate Square, November 7, 1918. (Courtesy of the Central State Archive of Kino-Photo-
Phono Documents, St. Petersburg)*

could they deliver even a sixth of the eighteen thousand freight cars of
wood the city needed for heat every month. Between the Revolution's
third anniversary and the end of January 1921, Petrograd's City Council
gave permission for 175 buildings to be razed for fuel, and in February
they agreed to the destruction of fifty more.[74] Ninety-three of the city's
largest factories had to be closed that winter and the workers' recently increased rations cut by a third. Real wages stood at less than a tenth of
what they had been in 1913, and the price of bread had risen by a thousand percent in the last year alone. In the first thirty days of 1921, the
prices of bread and potatoes tripled again. The value of a gold ruble,
which had cost just a bit less than eight paper ones in 1917, soared by a
factor of 1,250. Then it kept climbing until a single gold ruble was worth
nearly a quarter million paper ones in the spring of 1922.[75]

Their growing numbers ominously reminiscent of the events that had
preceded the February Revolution in 1917, Petrograd's workers moved

into the streets early in February 1921 to protest the hard times they faced. But four years of hunger, shortages, and terror by the Cheka had taken a terrible toll, and the men and women of the city's slums had no taste for confronting the heavily armed special forces the Bolsheviks sent into the streets. "The handling of the strikers was by no means very comradely," the deported American anarchist Emma Goldman later wrote in a masterpiece of understatement.[76] A group of sailors from the nearby Kronstadt naval base had even harder things to say. "These were not factories," they reported after a visit to some of Petrograd's mills. "[They were more like] forced labor prisons of Tsarist times."[77] Since the first protests of 1917, the Kronstadt sailors had always supported the Bolsheviks, but the more they saw of Lenin's tyrannical methods, the more they changed their minds. Opposed to all forms of coercion and political restraint, they began to mutter that the Bolsheviks were "thieves" and "plunderers of the peasants."[78] Even before the first fragile signs of spring touched Petrograd's frost and snow, the atmosphere at Kronstadt had turned truly poisonous.

Set almost exactly midway between the northern and southern coasts of the Gulf of Finland just twenty miles west of Petrograd, the Kronstadt naval base forms a seven-and-a-quarter-mile triangle that measures just more than a mile at its widest point. Supplemented by seven low-lying forts and thirteen stone and concrete batteries housing heavily armored Krupp guns, Kronstadt barred the Neva's entrance with such an array of fortifications that the editors of the 1914 edition of Baedeker's *Russia* called them "impregnable." Free-spirited and restless as sailors often are, the Kronstadt men had risen in rebellion in 1905 and 1906. When they had done so again in 1910, the government had shot more than a hundred and drowned hundreds more. After killing nearly forty of their senior officers in a single night in February 1917, they had supported the Bolsheviks in pushing the Revolution further left. Lenin became so certain of their loyalty that he used them as a praetorian guard in the weeks after the October Revolution.[79]

The Civil War had seen black-jacketed men from Kronstadt fight for the Reds on scores of battlefields. Yet as they fought they had begun to ask if the Bolsheviks weren't leading Russia in the wrong direction. "When we returned home [to our villages on leave]," one of them wrote, "our parents asked why we fought for the oppressors. That," he added, "set us to thinking."[80] Bolshevik Party membership in the Kronstadt garrison plummeted by half during the last six months of 1920, and more than five hundred sailors deserted in January 1921 alone. Then, on March 2, 1921, Kronstadt exploded in revolt. "The Communist Party has cut itself off from the masses and does not have the strength to pull Russia out of her complete economic collapse," the angry sailors announced.[81] Russia now needed a "true government of toilers," not the "commissarocracy" that Lenin had imposed from above, for only a government that enjoyed the people's confidence could save the nation now.[82] For almost a week the Bolsheviks negotiated, issued ultimatums, and waited for replies. Then on the evening of March 7, they opened an artillery barrage that lasted for ten days. Listening to the gunfire from her room in Petrograd's Astoria Hotel, Emma Goldman jotted notes about "the fearful suspense" that festered while Red fought against Red.[83] "Something has died within me," her friend Alexander Berkman wrote in his diary that night. "The people on the street look bowed with grief, bewildered."[84]

While the Kronstadt men drove back attack after attack, the Bolsheviks railed against the "petty bourgeois counterrevolutionaries" who dared to oppose the forces that had been sent to destroy them.[85] Lenin and his lieutenants knew all too well that the spirit of rebellion sustaining Kronstadt's defenders had its roots in hundreds of years of anarchic tradition that lay buried in every peasant village. And they knew that if the fires of rebellion burned their way back to these sources from Kronstadt, Bolshevik Russia would collapse into thousands of shattered pieces. For that reason alone, every spark from the uprising had to be stamped out. Then Nature added to the urgency of their concerns. As March neared its midpoint, the ice around Kronstadt began to thaw. Once it started to break up, the Bolsheviks would no longer be able to reach the fortress and battleships that its rebels commanded. These could then be resupplied by the Bolsheviks' enemies by sea.

Commanded by the not yet thirty-year-old military genius Mikhail Tukhachevskii, architect of some of the Reds' most brilliant Civil War victories, the Bolshevik forces launched their final assault against Kronstadt early on March 17. For the entire day they stormed the island's defenses, attacking again and again, and each time they were driven back. Just before midnight, they destroyed the last strongholds on the island and Kronstadt's guns fell silent. "The stillness that fell over Petrograd was more fearful than the ceaseless firing," Goldman wrote. Then, when word of Tukhachevskii's triumph reached the city, she continued her account.

"Petrograd was hung in a black pall, a ghastly corpse," she added. When she heard some of Tukhachevskii's victorious fighters singing the "Internationale" the next morning, she took up that theme again. "Its strains," she concluded sadly, "now sounded like a funeral dirge for humanity's flaming hope."[86] Goldman did not know then that the Kronstadt sailors had already written the epitaph for the revolutionary dreams that she and Russia had cherished. "It has become impossible to breathe," the last issue of the sailors' revolutionary newspaper announced on the morning of Tukhachevskii's assault. "All of Soviet Russia," it concluded, "has been turned into a penal colony."[87]

When the Bolsheviks had moved their government to Moscow in the spring of 1918, Petrograd's transformation from an imperial capital into the second city of the Soviet Union increased its people's suffering. For if life in Moscow was hard during those years, in Petrograd it was harder still, because the Bolsheviks' new capital had first claim on every necessity that the lands they ruled could produce. Men and women hoping to win favors from the new regime all turned toward Moscow. At the same time, as food and fuel shortages brought them to the verge of death, Petrograders abandoned their city by the hundreds of thousands, hoping to find ways to stay alive in the villages whence they or their parents had come. From 2,300,000 at the beginning of 1917, Petrograd's population had fallen to 720,000 by the end of 1920, and its industrial production stood at a mere eighth of what it had been eight years earlier.[88] There were no raw materials with which to repair the damage the city had suffered, for Russia's railways were in shambles, and Petrograd's port, for all practical purposes, had been closed since the middle of 1914. Food, supplies, fuel, public services, and most of all people—the city needed them all when Tukhachevskii's victorious Red forces returned from crushing the Kronstadt uprising. No one yet seemed to know where they would come from, but as the spring thaws began, the city started to come to life once again.

Throughout the Civil War, Petrograd's cultural life had stayed alive, as its poets, painters, and composers struggled to confront the devastation around them. Blok wrote his greatest poem then, and Anna Akhmatova, whose poetry would capture the soul of the city for half a century, joined a dozen others in suffering along with the place they still called "Piter." Like the poets, Petrograd's artists recorded its misery. Iurii Annenkov illustrated Blok's *The Twelve* in 1919, and Mstislav Dobuzhinskii, a member of the World of Art circle, created his remarkable lithographic record of *Petersburg in 1921*. "Before my very eyes, the city died a death of extraordinary beauty," Dobuzhinskii wrote in recalling those days many years later. "I tried to capture its terrible, empty, wounded look. This was the epilog of its entire life," he concluded. "It was turning into another city—Leningrad, with completely different people and an entirely different life."[89]

In 1924, the Bolsheviks changed Petrograd's name to Leningrad. A few months later, the city suffered its greatest flood in a hundred years, which swept away much of the flotsam that remained from the days of the old regime. For two centuries Russia's center of power and privilege, Leningrad now was to become a city of the people, a Communist metropolis in which all things connected with daily life were to be for the masses. One of the first efforts in this direction had taken place on May Day 1918, when Mozart's *Requiem* was performed for an audience of seven thousand at the Winter Palace. Many in the audience had never heard classical music before, and at the *Requiem*'s first strains one small boy sank to his knees and stayed on them for the entire concert.[90] Hoping to lift the lives of the masses to a higher level, some of the city's avant garde embraced these efforts for a time, but as bureaucratic and ideological interference lowered the level of city life, many of them turned away. Like Dobuzhinskii, some slipped away to the West, never to return. Others made their peace with forces they thought too powerful to resist, and a few struggled to defend the vision they thought the Bolsheviks had betrayed. Doing so brought Akhmatova's former husband, the poet Nikolai Gumilev, to his death in a Cheka execution cellar in 1921. For Akhmatova and most of her friends, resistance to the proletarianization and politicization of art meant long years of persecution and suffering as the Bolsheviks began to bring culture down to the masses.

After embracing the Bolsheviks' dream during the Revolution, Blok was among the first to declare it had failed. "I'm suffocating!" he complained to a friend early in 1921. "We're all suffocating. World revolution is turning into world angina pectoris!"[91] Blok died later that year after Russia's new masters refused to let him seek treatment for a heart ailment abroad. Then the poet Sergei Esenin killed himself in a Leningrad hotel room in 1925, and Maiakovskii followed his example five years later. After writing *The Bathhouse*, in which he condemned Russia's new bureaucrats for having grown fat by betraying the Revolution, the Bolsheviks' greatest poet shot himself through the heart rather than live with a dream that had turned so sour. Had less than two decades passed since the days of Ivanov's Tower and Pronin's Stray Dog? To the men and women who still remembered those days, the brief span of time that separated Leningrad in 1930 from St. Petersburg in 1910 seemed like an age.

All things in Soviet Leningrad now belonged to the people, but the people's leaders used them as they saw fit. Almost immediately the Bolsheviks seized the art collections of the city's great aristocrats, bringing paintings by Rubens, Van Dyck, Claude Lorrain, Rembrandt, and a score of other masters who had dominated European art over the previous half millennium into government hands. Many of these were transferred to the Hermitage, the art gallery of Catherine the Great now expanded to include most of the Winter Palace, and to the Russian Museum, the palace that Rossi had built on Mikhailovskaia Square for the Grand Duke Mikhail Pavlovich and the Grand Duchess Elena Pavlovna early in the previous century. Over the years, these two museums would come to hold paintings from the collections of the aristocratic Panins, Stroganovs, Vorontsovs, Sheremetievs, and Iusupovs, not to mention the Moscow merchant princes Sergei Shchukin and Ivan Morozov. Other paintings of Europe's great artists were sent from Leningrad to other museums in the Soviet Union, with the Pushkin Museum in Moscow ending up with more than four hundred Petersburg paintings. But many of the treasures of Imperial Petersburg were sold abroad during the 1920s and 1930s, as Russia's Bolshevik masters struggled to buy the technological know-how their nation had not yet learned to produce. Objects of lesser import went first, but by 1928 the great masterpieces of Rembrandt, Raphael, Botticelli, and Titian were beginning to be sold for the wherewithal to buy from such industrial giants as Siemens, General Electric, and Ford the equipment to build modern steel mills, drill oilfields, and manufacture trucks, trains, and automobiles.

The sales of art treasures began at the very end of 1918, and were carried on in utmost secrecy. At first they concentrated on items made from precious stones, silver, and gold, much of which was melted down and sold by weight. Silver and gold crosses, silver icon coverings, silver church book bindings—even the stunning solid silver iconostasis that Andrei Voronikhin had designed for the Kazan Cathedral—all were thrown into the smelters' furnaces. The Sarcophagus of Saint Aleksandr Nevskii, designed by Rastrelli and made by Russian masters in the middle of the eighteenth century, barely escaped the fate of Voronikhin's iconostasis, and only after the Hermitage's director sent personal pleas to the Chairman of the All Russian Central Executive Committee and to Trotskii's wife. There were reports of warehouses crammed with antique religious art treasures, rare porcelains, Gobelin tapestries, bronzes, and paintings whose value had been estimated in the tens of millions of rubles before the Revolution—all awaiting sale to buyers in the West. During the early days of the Civil War some of these were bartered across Russia's northern frontiers for weapons, trucks, and tractors. Later, the Soviet state set up a special office for selling its treasures, but with only a few exceptions none of these sales—whether of objects from Leningrad or elsewhere—included the greatest masterworks. Those went on the market in 1928 to help pay the costs of Stalin's First Five-Year Plan, and they continued to be sold until 1932, when the impact of the Great Depression shrunk the Western art market to a small fraction of its former size.[92]

Working through several prominent European and American art dealers, several renowned collectors and museums acquired a dazzling array of treasures from the Hermitage between 1928 and 1932. The first to buy from the Soviets was Calouste Gulbenkian, an Armenian who headed the Iraq Petroleum Company and was a naturalized citizen of Britain. Gulbenkian began by acquiring some of the finest silver and gold objects ever to be produced in the ateliers of eighteenth-century Paris and then moved quickly on to buy a portrait by Rubens, three paintings by Rembrandt, and Jean-Antoine Houdon's marble statue of the goddess Diana.[93]

Two years later, in 1930, the U.S. Secretary of the Treasury Andrew Mellon replaced Gulbenkian as the Bolsheviks' leading customer for the Hermitage's art. Working through agents in New York, London, and Berlin, Mellon paid just over a million dollars for two of Rembrandt's portraits, Franz Hals's *Portrait of a Young Man*, and Van Eyck's *Annunciation*. Then he purchased nearly a score more, including Botticelli's *Adoration of the Magi* and Raphael's *Alba Madonna*. In less than a year, he spent $6,654,053 for twenty-one stunning masterpieces, including two more by Hals, five Rembrandts, a Rubens, two Raphaels, a Titian, a Perugino, another Botticelli, four Van Dycks, a Van Eyck, a portrait by Velázquez, a painting by Chardin, and another by Veronese. After that, Soviet sales of Leningrad's treasures dwindled, in part because the curators of the Hermitage finally found some friends in high places to argue against them, but also because the Great Depression had driven prices down and émigrés seeking to reclaim family paintings had started to file legal challenges against their new owners. In May 1931, Stalin's government made one final effort and auctioned paintings and other art objects from Leningrad's Stroganov Palace through a Berlin dealer. But the sale netted only a paltry $613,326 for 256 pieces, including Rembrandt's *Christ and the Samaritan at the Well*, which fetched less than $50,000.[94]

With lines of proletarians threading their way through palaces that had been transformed into museums, Leningrad became the people's city. But, if the art of the past belonged to the people, what of the present? By the time the city's name was changed to Leningrad in 1924, its avant garde had scattered. Of the men and women who had shaped St. Petersburg's artistic life on the eve of World War I, Gippius and Merezhkovskii now lived permanently in Paris, and Benois was about to slip away to join them. Maiakovskii and Aleksei Tolstoi had moved to Moscow. Blok and Gumilev both were dead, and Anna Akhmatova, the poet Osip Mandelshtam, and many of their friends had been driven into a corner where they were out of the mainstream and increasingly ignored. No longer the preserve of Russia's elite, Leningrad's cultural life was focused on the masses. Yet for the time being it still remained tied to the West, as Leningraders aimed lower and reached further—to America, where jazz played a key part in shaping the culture of the masses.

The year 1922 marked the first anniversary of the New Economic Policy, which Lenin had decreed in 1921 in a desperate attempt to bring the Soviet economy back to life. In small enterprises all across Russia, millions of private entrepreneurs began to produce and sell consumer goods, provide services, and grow extra food. In the theater, literature, the cinema, and music, everything had to pay its way, and that meant catering to tastes that both Party and avant garde disdained. Passionately wanting to be "modern," the youth of Leningrad entered the Roaring Twenties intent upon embracing those Western ways of life they considered "up-to-date." These included such dances as the fox-trot and shimmy—and for those they needed jazz. Throughout the decade, Soviet authorities vacillated about whether jazz was the voice of the oppressed masses or the vice of the upper classes. And while they hesitated, jazz made its way far enough into Russia so that by 1922 many of the men and women who had sung the "Marseillaise" in 1917 were now humming the pop hit "The Sound of Nocturnal Marseilles."

Jazz, the shimmy, and the fox-trot all came officially to Petrograd in the summer of 1924, when Meyerhold used the jazz band that Valentin Parnakh had organized two years earlier in Moscow as part of his production of *The Trust D. E.*, a play based on a novel by Ilia Ehrenburg. Thanks to the New Economic Policy, night clubs boomed and small shops poured forth the flapper fashions in which Leningraders danced their way into the Jazz Age. The first ensemble of American dancers, singers, and jazz musicians—called the Chocolate Kiddies and led by the bandleader Sam Wooding—reached the city two years after Parnakh, and within a year Leningrad had its own Concert Jazz Band, complete with American instruments that its founder Leopold Teplitskii had brought with him from a recent tour of Philadelphia and New York. After that, jazz bands sprang up everywhere, and Leningraders danced to "Yes, Sir, That's My Baby," "Sweet Sue," "My Blue Heaven," and "The Charleston," even though the controversy over whether jazz was properly proletarian or improperly decadent continued to rage.[95] That debate would continue well into the Stalin era, long after the market forces of the New Economic Policy had made other imprints on the popular culture of Leningrad. Whether or not jazz was decadent continued to be an issue in Soviet life into the 1970s. During the Stalin era alone, the official position changed several times.

Most Leningraders became acquainted with jazz and learned the steps to the dances that went with it at the movies, the form of mass entertainment that the Bolsheviks embraced as a means of communicating with Russia's illiterate and barely literate masses. During the Jazz Age—and before the advent of "talkies"—movies from abroad were overwhelming favorites in Russia, and particularly in Leningrad, where three hundred titles from the West arrived in late 1922 alone.[96] Usually accompanied by a piano or an orchestra that played the latest American music, these reaped huge profits, which helped to finance the production of films in Soviet studios that were more serious or more ideological. The suffering of the masses under the Romanovs, the torments endured by imprisoned revolutionaries, and high moments in the Revolution of 1917 all were favorites of early Soviet film makers, and none more so than the moment when the Bolsheviks seized power. These once again put Leningrad at center stage as the cradle of the Russian Revolution. To celebrate the tenth anniversary of the Great October Revolution, Sergei Eisenstein produced *October*, a film in which Leningrad stood at its very heart.

"A typical boy from Riga," as he once called himself, Eisenstein had joined the Red Army in 1918 and used his training as a military engineer to help strengthen Petrograd's defenses. After the Civil War, he studied for a career in the theater with Meyerhold, but quickly decided that his teacher's ideas worked better in cinema than on the stage. Between 1924 and 1926, his first two films, *Strike* and *The Battleship Potemkin* made him famous, and *October*, frequently shown in the West under the title *Ten Days that Shook the World*, raised him to the ranks of cinema's immortals. Here Eisenstein's portrayal of the events of 1917 seemed so real that they acquired the legitimacy of documentary footage over the years. The cinematic rival to Blok's *The Twelve* as the icon of the Russian Revolution, *October*, was greeted by Lenin's wife Nadezhda Krupskaia as "a fragment of the art of the future," for it gave the impression of depicting life as it really was even though its most dramatic moments never happened.[97]

If movies reshaped Leningraders' views of the past and present during the 1920s and 1930s, novels blended their vision of the present and future. Following a 1923 *Pravda* article that called upon them to write novels on the lines of American detective stories and adventure novels to celebrate the triumph of Soviet Communism, Russian authors brought out a flood of stories in which a handful of dedicated Communists foiled plot after plot by greedy capitalists. The most famous of these pulp novels was *Mess-Mend, or A Yankee in Petrograd*, which Marietta Shaginian published under the pseudonym Jim Dollar in 1924. Shaginian's novel took place in a futuristic Petrograd called Radio City, an industrial complex where products were grown, processed, and turned into manufactured goods to be sent to all corners of the Soviet Union and the world. Shaginian's Radio City was in every sense a revolutionary utopia, in which everything moved at superhuman speed. People did not age, were always safe from enemy attack, and lived in a homogeneous, standardized world. "Here there is everything," the author promised. But "everything" in fact existed only in Petrograd, the center of Shaginian's new society. This utopia of the near future was threatened by a series of capitalist plots, all of which were thwarted by a secret society of workers who called themselves "Mess-Mend" and were led by a single awe-inspiring hero.[98] Here, as one commentator recently explained, "the Jazz Age met revolutionary utopia," and life flowed like a symphony in which "each performs his partiture but hears only the symphony."[99]

But how far was Shaginian's utopia from reality as the 1920s passed their midpoint? And what progress did the people of Leningrad make toward realizing the Communist vision in the two decades that separated the end of the Civil War from the Nazi invasion that began their city's nine-hundred-day siege? Virtually from the moment they seized power, there was a strong sense among the Bolsheviks that Leningrad's center represented an unneeded monument to the fallen ruling classes, and that the city's industrial slums needed to be rehabilitated. Solidly built workers' housing, with modern conveniences, schools, clinics, and facilities for leisure time enjoyment, all linked by cheap public transportation, could make the city's once fetid slums into beacons to the future. That became one of the goals of each of Stalin's first three Five-Year Plans, which demanded Russia's modernization at any cost.

Leningrad's intelligentsia opposed any plan to abandon the city's center, for they believed that its palaces, monuments, cathedrals, and gardens needed to be protected at any cost. Nikolai Antsiferov defended that view in *The Soul of Petersburg*, a book published in 1922 by a publishing house that still identified its location as "Petersburg" on the title page. Russia's fallen capital, Antsiferov wrote, had become "a city of tragic imperialism" that had "ceased to crown 'Great Russia' with its granite diadem."[100] Here in the Neva and its granite embankments, the buildings of Rastrelli, Quarenghi, and Rossi, the shadowy light of the street lamps on the Nevskii Prospekt, and Falconet's Bronze Horseman most of all, this sensitive and grieving man found parts of the city's soul. "Here everything that I consider best in life is concentrated," he wrote, quoting the nineteenth-century writer Vladimir Korolenko. Making no effort to restrain his passion, he insisted that "Petersburg life is full of mirage-like originality."[101]

Antsiferov pleaded for Leningrad's workers to respect their city's past. That, a critic responded, represented "an incorrect, anti-proletarian perspective," for the key to understanding Petersburg must by definition be found in "the large area where there . . . [had been] factories, poverty, and slavery" before the Revolution.[102] Antsiferov had worried that in becoming "Red Piter,"[103] the world's revolutionary beacon, Leningrad risked losing the historical treasures that made it unique. That was precisely what the Bolsheviks had in mind. The time had come, they insisted, to wipe away the aristocratic character that Antsiferov and his friends so loved in old Petersburg and to concentrate on providing the conveniences of modern life for the proletarian men and women who were starting to pour into the city once again.

The dream of transforming "Red Piter" into a workers' metropolis underlay the officially approved 1936 plan to abandon its historic center and reshape the city around a new and grander avenue to be named International Prospekt. Beginning at the slum that had festered around the Hay-

*A parade in celebration of Constitution Day, 1933, pauses at a reviewing stand in front of the Winter Palace. (Courtesy of the Central State Archive of Kino-Photo-Phono Documents, St. Petersburg)*

market since tsarist times, this new avenue was to reach southward for nearly ten kilometers and to become the main focus of Communist city life with apartment houses, department stores, movie theaters, clubs, medical facilities, and schools for the masses all within easy reach. In this way, Leningrad, the crucible of the Bolshevik Revolution, would become a model for the future. Together with Moscow, which was undergoing similar transformations, it would become a place in which the workers at last could receive a fair return from their labor.

Like so many grandiose Soviet plans, the International Prospekt project was realized only in part. Noting that "serious inconveniences" would result if the original city center was abandoned, a new team of architects in 1938 reduced the amount of land involved in the plan from ninety-nine acres to twenty-eight. International Prospekt made its way through empty land in the midst of which arose the city's ponderously neoclassical new House of Soviets that embraced a gargantuan nine acres of office space. Eventually, the avenue would be flanked by some of the facilities that its planners had originally proposed, especially apartment buildings and schools. In 1910, it had been rare for working families to have their own apartments, and fewer than half of their children had been in school. But because education could be easily measured for propaganda purposes and also made it easier for the government to reach the people it ruled, the Bolsheviks paid serious attention to it as well as to housing. Of the city's children, 99.6 percent were in school by 1931. Between 1936 and mid-1941 alone, the Leningrad authorities built more than 400 new schools and nearly 2.75 million square feet of new housing for the city's proletarians, mostly in new areas such as those along International Prospekt.[104]

Soviet efforts to transform Leningrad into a workers' metropolis also meant rebuilding its industries. At the end of the Civil War, the city had little food, less fuel, and almost no raw materials. Then the New Economic Policy brought more than eight thousand small workshops into being during the next half decade. When these restored Leningrad's flow of consumer goods and food products, the Bolsheviks were left free to concentrate on reviving the city's heavy industry by restoring the supplies of electric power, fuel, and raw materials on which its large mills and factories depended. By the end of the First Five-Year Plan in 1932, the number of workers had grown to eight times what it had been a decade earlier, and they were producing five times as many iron and steel products as they had in 1913. Tens of thousands of tractors for Stalin's newly created collective farms were pouring from assembly lines at the "Red Putilov" and Obukhov plants by the early 1930s, along with nine out of every ten of the Soviet Union's hydrogenerators and eight out of every ten of its telephones. By 1932, Leningrad's factories were producing a quarter of the Soviet Union's iron and steel goods and nearly a third of its chemicals. During the next two Five-Year Plans, that output would rise even higher so that by 1940 it would be more than twelve times what it had been in 1913.[105]

Leading the workers of Leningrad in those days was Sergei Mironovich Kirov, first secretary of the city's Party organization from 1926 until 1934. Born in the far northern province of Viatka, Kirov had been a Communist since the age of eighteen and one of Stalin's allies since at least the mid-1920s. More honest than most Bolshevik bureaucrats, he was neither servile nor vicious, as so many of the men in Stalin's inner circle turned out to be. The system within which he worked made him ruthless, but he had a huge following among the city's masses and in the high ranks of the Party. By the early 1930s, many thought of him as one of Stalin's closest associates, but as the Soviet Union embarked upon the Second Five-Year Plan, he and Stalin began to differ, especially on the matter of food supplies for Leningrad's workers. Publicly, Stalin continued to bestow marks of favor on Kirov and talked of moving him to Moscow. But in his heart he had another scheme for dealing with the man he thought too independent and popular. His plan, a number of experts have shown, involved murder. One pistol bullet fired by a single assassin could free Stalin from Kirov's shadow forever. More than that, it could be used as a pretext for unleashing a reign of terror that would sweep away all other enemies, both real and imagined.

Carefully and with great malice aforethought, Stalin laid his plans in the fall of 1934. Working through NKVD chief Genrikh Iagoda, he recruited an assassin by the name of Leonid Nikolaev, had him provided with a Nagant service revolver, and arranged for Kirov's guards to be diverted at the proper moment. Just after 4:30 P.M. on the afternoon of December 1, 1934, Nikolaev shot Kirov in the back just outside his office at Smolnyi. Immediately Stalin used the assassination to unleash a tidal wave of terror that would submerge the entire Soviet Union until the outbreak of World War II. Grigorii Zinoviev, Leningrad's first Party chief and one of Lenin's oldest allies, was purged for having plotted Kirov's murder. For that and for other reasons, so were virtually all the Old Bolsheviks who had once held high office.[106]

Then, a wave of arrests surged across the Soviet Union. By 1936 there were five million Soviet citizens in slave labor camps spread across Russia's Far North and Siberia. Seven million more were arrested in 1937 and 1938, of which a million were shot and another two million died of malnutrition, disease, and abuse. The purges claimed virtually all of the Red Army's senior officers, including all but two of its fifteen army commanders and fifty of its fifty-seven corps commanders. Only thirty-two (of 186) divisional commanders survived, and only nine of the 108 high ranking military commissars serving in 1935 were still at their posts when the Russo-Finnish War broke out five years later.[107] Stalin's reign of terror eradicated most of the delegates to the Party Congress of 1934, Communist Party members from the 1920s and early 1930s, and many senior officers of the NKVD.

In Leningrad, where Stalin's henchman Andrei Zhdanov replaced Kirov, there were "particularly large losses," many of whom "were annihilated without a trial," a speaker informed the delegates of the XXII Party Congress in 1961.[108] The Leningrad purge began right after Kirov's murder, with the deportation of more than thirty thousand Leningraders to labor camps in Siberia and the Arctic. Then Akhmatova's son Lev Gumilev and her friend the poet Osip Mandelshtam were swept up by the secret police, and so were hundreds of other scholars, scientists, poets, painters, novelists, and composers throughout the city. Meyerhold was arrested and shot. So was the Futurist poet Benedikt Livshits, whose memoirs, *The One-and-a-Half-Eyed Archer*, told so brilliantly the tale of life among the avant garde around the time of World War I. Aleksei Tolstoi, having long since moved to Moscow, survived by writing nonsense that claimed (among other things) that one of Dostoevskii's main characters "was a typical potential Trotskyite."[109] "It was an apocalyptic time," Akhmatova remembered of the days when she wrote the poems "Crucifixion" and "To Death."[110] There seemed to be no escape for anyone. "It was impossible to tell who would be killed by the next bolt of lightning," one of the survivors remembered. "People died in delirium confessing to such outrageous crimes as spying, sabotage, terrorism, and wrecking. They vanished without a trace, and then their wives and children, entire families, were sent after them."[111]

"Plots" were being uncovered everywhere. Among the Egyptologists, numismatists, archaeologists, epigraphers, and the like at the Hermitage, the NKVD discovered "German spies" (in the museum's Coins and Antiquities Department), "Japanese spies" (in its Oriental Department), and "class enemies" everywhere. One curator, a long-time collector of antique arms and armor, was found guilty of "storing weapons with the aim of using them in the organization of an armed uprising," and others were accused of having ties to "Armenian terrorists" and "Ukrainian nationalists."[112] Fifty curators at the Hermitage were arrested and sentenced to terms in prison or forced labor camps, and a dozen more were shot as spies.[113] People received ten- and fifteen-year sentences just because they received letters from the West, attended social events where Westerners were present, or knew someone who had. Ballerinas and actresses who danced too long with Western diplomats at official receptions found themselves arrested. So did veterinarians who treated the pets of foreign diplomats.

Even writers and illustrators of children's books suffered. Under the direction of the poet Samuil Marshak and the artist Vladimir Lebedev,

Leningrad had become the Soviet Union's leader in producing books for children in the 1920s and 1930s. In the mid-1930s, the press began to refer to them and the group of writers they directed as "a counterrevolutionary, sabotaging gang of enemies." Like Akhmatova, Marshak and Lebedev were allowed to remain free, but their associates suffered cruelly. Perhaps most tragic of all, Zhdanov and his henchmen sent Vera Ermolaeva, one of Leningrad's most talented illustrators of children's books, to a forced labor camp in Kazakhstan, where the guards tormented her so brutally that her paralyzed legs (she had fallen from a horse as a child) had to be amputated. After that, Ermolaeva was sent to a desert island in the Aral Sea and abandoned. No one ever heard of her after that.[114]

Everyone lived in fear, and no one knew how to act or react. "How can you run when you know you're not guilty?" one victim asked. "How do you act during interrogations?"[115] Month after month the terror continued, with tens of thousands of Leningraders being interrogated, starved, beaten, and deprived of sleep. When Akhmatova protested, her complaints were dismissed as "the whining of a woman who either was born too late or did not die in time."[116] Then in 1937, after hundreds of thousands had been punished, the terror got worse. During that year and the next, the numbers of victims soared into the millions. This time, they included Marshal Mikhail Tukhachevskii, Aleksei Rykov (one-time chairman of the Council of People's Commissars), Nikolai Bukharin (former head of the Comintern), and NKVD chief Iagoda himself.

"*Zachem?*" "*Dlia chego?*" "*K chemu?*" "*Otchego?*" "*Pochemu?*" Everyone kept asking "why?" and "for what?" People asked these questions when they were taken to the NKVD's execution cellars, as cell doors clanged shut, as they were crammed into cattle cars for the long journey to Siberia, and as friends and relatives were dragged away in the middle of the night. People asked them of the men who starved and tortured them, and of those who carted off armloads of precious letters, diaries, and never-published manuscripts that would disappear forever. They wrote them on prison walls, and scratched them on freight car doors. They asked them millions of times, but never got an answer. "What do you mean *what for?*" Akhmatova used to ask indignantly. "It's time you understood that people are arrested for nothing!"[117] By that time, her son had been rearrested and sent to a forced labor camp. "Husband in the grave, son in prison," she wrote. "Say a prayer for me."[118]

Leningraders were disappearing by the tens of thousands and Russians by the millions. At first the Great Purge swept away the city's intelligentsia and anyone else who seemed capable of independent creative thought. But then its scope broadened to people who, as Akhmatova rightly said, had been "arrested for nothing." Death seemed to be everywhere, and it became difficult to find a family in Leningrad who had not lost someone. Yet through it all, a semblance of normality remained. People went to work, shopped for food, dined in restaurants, and went on holidays. They went to the theater and the ballet, and bought rare books from the collections that appeared in used book shops out of nowhere. They fell in love. They got married and had children. And, as the supply of consumer goods increased, the material level of their daily lives improved. Most of all, the authorities tried to keep alive the sense that life was normal. Except for the show trials, little was said about the purges in the press. The Black Marias that carted people off to torture and prison were disguised as delivery trucks with signs that read "meat" or "milk" or "bread."

Stalin assured everyone that "life has become better, gayer." And, to Leningrad's young people—the students, the new technicians, and the recent school graduates who moved ahead quickly to fill the empty places the purges had created—that seemed especially true. Was the terror coming to an end as 1939 turned toward 1940 and 1941? In fact, it was, but not because Stalin and his henchmen had slaked their thirst for the people's blood. In 1941, the purges were submerged in an even larger wave of tragedy, the horror of which swept aside everything else. That summer, the armies of Nazi Germany blockaded Leningrad, and its terrible siege began. It would last for nine hundred days, during which Leningraders would freeze, starve, and die by the millions as shells and bombs rained upon them. At times, the life of their city hung by the slenderest of threads. But as the writer Ilia Ehrenburg once said, this, too, was an eternal city and it survived. Like the firebird of Russian folklore, Leningrad was destined to rise again from the ashes. Its near destruction and painful rebirth still stand as the most heroic moment in its long history.

PART IV

*"Hero City"*
*(1941–1991)*

# TEN

# NINE HUNDRED DAYS

*I*F ANYTHING SEEMED OUT OF THE ORDINARY in Leningrad on the morning of Sunday, June 22, 1941, it was the weather. It had rained for most of the previous week, an unwanted continuation of a damp, cold spring. Then, just the day before—on the shortest of the White Nights, the longest day of the year—a breeze from the south had blown away the clouds, and the weather had turned warm. That evening, crowds celebrating the summer solstice and the end of classes at the university had flowed across the Neva's bridges and filled Nevskii Prospekt. Many Leningraders never went to bed that night, preferring the midnight sunlight to the crowded rooms and apartments they called home. Those who caught a few winks got up to find the Sunday sun already high in the sky, an irresistible invitation to spend the day in the country, where the smell of lilacs and wild cherry blossoms blended so magically with the pungent tartness of the still damp pine woods.

With picnic baskets and rucksacks full, young couples hurried toward the Vitebsk Station to catch trains for Tsarskoe Selo and Pavlovsk, where the huge parks of the imperial palaces had long since been made into picnic sites for Leningrad's masses. Others headed in the opposite direction—to the Baltic Station for trains that would take them to the seaside palace grounds at Peterhof and Oranienbaum on the Finnish Gulf. Some carried accordions or seven-stringed Russian guitars. Many licked at ice cream cones or nibbled eskimo pies as they pushed their way onto the crowded trains that left the stations every thirty minutes. On such a Sunday, few thought about the week ahead. For now, it was enough to know that the day was theirs to enjoy until the factory whistles called them back the next morning.

Elena Iosifovna Kochina, a chemist at one of Leningrad's research institutes was well ahead of the crowds that Sunday. She and her husband Dima had gone to the country a few days earlier and had rented rooms in a dacha, a summer cottage, where they planned to spend their vacation. After a late breakfast, Elena had just taken their infant daughter into the garden, when the woman who owned the cottage came running to say that they had just announced on the radio that the Germans had invaded Russia. There had been fighting in the outskirts of Petrograd in the fall of 1917, and again two years later. Then there had been the war with Finland, finished just less than a year ago. And so Elena knew what war meant. "I am thirty-four years old," she told herself grimly, "[and] this is the fourth war of my life."

In addition to putting loved ones in harm's way, war to Leningraders meant too little food, too little heat, and too many difficulties in meeting the needs of everyday life. That very afternoon, housewives started to buy up sugar, lard, butter, sausage, kasha, matches, and anything else that could be stored. "I bought four and one-half pounds of millet," Kochina wrote, "[and] I hate porridge made from millet."[1] Those who didn't think of food first went to the banks, withdrew their savings, and headed for the commission shops that sold pre-Soviet jewelry and antiques. Diamonds and emeralds from Siberia, oil paintings from everywhere, gold coins from the reign of Nicholas II, gold watches—anything that had real value—was what they wanted. Who knew what paper rubles would be worth in a week? A month? Or a year?

Connected to radio stations all across the Soviet Union, loudspeakers mounted high on building cornices and telephone poles broadcast a speech by Commissar of Foreign Affairs Viacheslav Molotov right after noon that day. In the flat, expressionless tone that had made him one of Stalin's favorite bureaucrats, Molotov announced that the armies of Nazi

Germany had attacked the Soviet Union without provocation. He promised that Russia would be victorious, but people wondered. Could Soviet Russia overcome Hitler's huge fighting machine? What did Stalin think? Midnight came and went and still no word from Stalin. Some people wondered about that, too.

In June 1941, the population of Leningrad numbered 3,544,000, with another 3,200,000 living in the region around it. Machine tools, locomotives, generators, turbines, chemicals, field artillery, light T-28 tanks, workhorse T-34 tanks, the Red Army's new sixty-ton monster KV tanks, radio transmitters, shoes, and textiles—the list of vital goods that Leningrad produced went on and on, for the city accounted for more than an eighth of all the Soviet Union's industrial output. It boasted the largest machinery plant in the country—the Red Putilov, now renamed the Kirov Works—and the largest number of skilled machinists and tool-and-die makers. The Red Army depended on Leningrad. So did the Red Fleet.

In peace or war, Soviet Russia needed Leningrad. But the city was even more precariously situated than it had been in imperial times. In 1939, the Finnish frontier had stood a scant fifteen miles to the northeast, with the Estonian border barely a hundred miles to the west. Neither country was particularly fond of the Soviet Union. Territory won that year and the next in the Russo-Finnish War had enlarged Leningrad's cushion of territory to the north, but only at the cost of making the Finns bitter enemies. When war began in 1941, the Finns joined the Germans. Nearby Estonia, Latvia, and Lithuania were sympathetic, too. Forcibly annexed to the Soviet Union in 1940, all three offered the Germans good staging areas from which to attack Leningrad. In these countries, a holiday atmosphere prevailed while the people awaited the arrival of Hitler's armies. In Tallinn, the capital of Estonia, almost no one paid any attention to the freshly printed Soviet posters that urged them all "to stand as one in defense of freedom." Instead Tallinners sipped cocktails and coffee in the city's outdoor cafés and waited for the Germans. "They looked like angels when they came," one woman remembered of the first SS units to arrive. "Later on they acted like devils."[2]

Some people in Leningrad felt the same way. Who could forget the tens of thousands of men and women who had been dragged from their beds and workbenches never to return? What of the Putilov and Obukhov men who had been lost in the purges? What of the professors? The poets? The people from the ballet and the opera? What of the men and women who had devoted their lives to the Party and the Communist cause and been declared "enemies of the people" anyway? Even once-staunch Communists remembered these losses as the Germans advanced, and some asked themselves if the Nazis offered a chance to be freed of Stalin's yoke. Would Hitler be a greater tragedy for Russia than Stalin? Or might it be the other way around?

Only too happy to look forward to Stalin's fall, many of Leningrad's intellectuals thought about these questions seriously. But they also had to ask if Stalin's overthrow was worth the death of the city they loved. Well before summer's end they knew what Germany's High Command had been told at the beginning of July. "It is the Führer's firm decision to level . . . Leningrad and make . . . [it] uninhabitable, so as to relieve us of the necessity of feeding the population during the winter," Hitler's Chief of Staff had written in a secret memorandum. "The city will be razed by the Air Force," he went on. "Tanks must not be used for that purpose."[3] Thinking that their city's obliteration was too high a price to pay for getting rid of Stalin, Leningraders embraced the words of the poet Olga Berggolts. "No, I have forgotten nothing," this woman who hated Stalin wrote that first Sunday of the war. "My Motherland with the crown of thorns. With the dark rainbow above your head. . . . I love you—I cannot do otherwise."[4]

Even knowing that Estonia, Latvia, Lithuania, and Finland all might help the Germans, the men in Moscow had done little to prepare for Leningrad's defense. There were not enough weapons, not enough ammunition, and military units defending the city were under strength. The High Command had not yet recovered from the shattering purges of 1938 and 1939. Nor had Leningrad's officials and factory managers done so. Worst of all, the purges had made everyone afraid of telling the truth. As in the fairy tale, no one dared to say that the emperor had no clothes when it came to defending and supplying the city.

The truth was that civil defense training in Leningrad had been slipshod and superficial. Firefighting units had not been trained to deal with the massive fires incendiary bombs would ignite, tank traps and trenches had not yet been dug, and the supply system was totally unready to face the strains of a siege. Leningrad had little more than a thirty-day reserve of food when the war began, and its stockpiles of fuel were designed only for peacetime needs. But its people and factories needed 13,000 tons of kerosene every month, 60,000 tons of fuel oil, and 2,240 tons of gasoline.

For heat and cooking, Leningraders consumed nearly two million cubic feet of firewood every year, and millions of tons of food. Even after rationing began on September 2, Leningrad's bakeries and shops required 2,000 tons of flour a day, the equivalent of almost three-quarters of a million tons a year.[5] By no stretch of the imagination was Leningrad ready for a siege when the fighting began. Nor was it ready when the Nazi ring closed around it two and a half months later. Even when the German bombardment began, people in charge of the city's defense believed that the blockade, somehow and in some way, would be broken before winter set in.[6] Only gradually did they come to realize that it would not.

As the Germans advanced in July and August, the people of Leningrad tried to slow them down by digging row upon row of ditches and tank traps, some as far away as the Luga line, more than seventy miles to the south. Many of the men had already joined the army—over 200,000 in just the first week of fighting—so most of the workers were older people, young teenagers, and women, especially women, their kerchiefs flashing like so many bright flowers in the fields.[7] Factory workers dug ditches after their regular shifts were over. Students went to dig after classes. Curators at the Hermitage, librarians from Leningrad's many libraries, professors from the university and technological institutes all went to help with the digging.

Tens of thousands who could be spared from their regular duties worked with picks and shovels all day, every day. "We have worked for 18 days without a break, 12 hours a day," one 57-year-old woman wrote to a newspaper. "One had to work a lot with a pick," she went on. "The dry clay was hard as rock."[8] Leningraders worked in the summer heat, and in the rain when it came. Sometimes they had to go without food, for no one had told them how much to bring with them or how long they'd need to be away. German planes attacked every day, diving, bombing, strafing. Elena Kochina was nearly hit. Later, she remembered the bullets from the Nazi fighter's machine guns "rustling like small metallic lizards" as they struck the ground nearby.[9]

Before the first of September, Leningraders had dug nearly 16,000 miles of open trenches, 340 miles of anti-tank ditches, and laid 400 miles of barbed wire entanglements. They had felled tens of thousands of trees and piled them up as barriers stretching 190 miles, and they had built 5,000 wooden or concrete firing points.[10] In the meantime, Russia's fighting men fell back. "We're digging well enough," one old woman told a

Red Army general that summer, "but you guys are fighting badly."[11] That wasn't quite fair. On the Russian side, tanks and artillery were in short supply. So was air cover. "We start our attack," a soldier told his commander, "and the Germans start to run. Then out of nowhere their tanks and planes hit us. . . . We have no planes, no tanks, just infantry. How can we stand up against that kind of force?"[12] By late August, the Germans were at the edge of Leningrad's suburbs. At the same time, the Finns had retaken most of the Karelian peninsula and regained the frontiers of 1939.

As the Germans advanced, Leningraders tore apart the plants that produced optical instruments, aircraft, and tanks, crated up the machines, and loaded them onto trains that carried them to safer places in Siberia. Before the end of August, 164,320 workers were sent along with them.[13] Still others packed up the city's treasures. They piled sandbags high and thick around Falconet's Bronze Horseman and took down smaller statues and buried them in the Summer Gardens. Windows had to be covered with plywood or crisscrossed with tape. From the Public Library, 7,000 incunabulae, the second oldest surviving Greek text of the New Testament, Voltaire's personal library, a prayer book belonging to Mary Queen of Scots, a Gutenberg Bible, and 360,000 other precious items out of a collection of 9,000,000 volumes all were crated up and sent away, along with precious historical archives containing two hundred years of Leningrad's history, the letters of Pushkin, manuscripts of Dostoevskii, secrets of the ancient East, and information about tens of thousands of other topics.[14] Then came the most stupendous task of all: the evacuation of a million and a half priceless treasures from the Hermitage.

When rumors of a German attack had begun to circulate early that spring, the museum's director, Iosif Orbeli, had begun to stockpile packing materials including fifty tons of wood shavings, three tons of cotton wadding, and sixteen kilometers of oilcloth in the Hermitage's basement and a couple of key warehouses.[15] The moment Molotov made his announcement on Sunday, Orbeli ordered forty of the museum's most valuable paintings to be taken to the steel-lined vaults that housed the famous Scythian gold collection. Then on Monday, the Hermitage staff started to pack, working for six days and nights and sleeping only when exhaustion drove them to it. They placed smaller paintings in large wooden crates, separating one from the other with cloth-padded dividers, while many of the larger paintings had to be taken from their stretchers and rolled up. Rembrandt's huge *Descent from the Cross* had to be packed in that way, despite the danger of cracking its surface. His somewhat smaller *Prodigal Son*, still eight and a half by nearly seven feet, was crated by itself. Some worried that it might be too large to fit into a railroad car.

All the Scythian gold and the imperial jewels were packed. So were the madonnas of Raphael and Leonardo da Vinci. Huge crates held the *Holy Family* by Andrea del Sarto, the Titians, the Giorgiones, the Tintorettos, the Van Eycks, the Van Dycks, and the works of Velázquez, Murillo, and El Greco that made the Hermitage the rival of the Prado in its collection of Spanish paintings. The one-and-a-half-ton sarcophagus of Prince Aleksandr Nevskii, made by Petersburg silversmiths in the middle of the eighteenth century from some of the first silver to be taken from newly discovered mines in Siberia's Altai, had to be taken apart and packed, and Michelangelo's *Crouching Boy* was fitted into a specially made double-walled crate. Fragile Oriental and European porcelain, porcelain from factories founded by the empresses Elizabeth and Catherine the Great, Roman and Greek intaglios, some three hundred thousand rare coins from all historical periods and places, and Carlo Rastrelli's wax figure of Peter the Great, dressed in the Tsar's own clothes, all had to be dismantled and packed away along with Houdon's marble statue of Voltaire and the fabulous Chertomlyk silver vase dating from the fourth century B.C. Museum workers who helped with the packing bent over so many times that their noses bled. "You'd lie down and rock your head until the bleeding stopped," one woman remembered, "and then [you'd] rush back to the boxes."[16]

On the ninth day of the war, trucks carrying the packed treasures left the Hermitage for the railyard behind the Moscow Railway Station, two miles up the Nevskii Prospekt. Gradually a special train was loaded, the workers watching anxiously as the huge crate holding *The Prodigal Son* finally squeezed through the doorway. Then the rest of the treasures—more than a thousand boxes containing half a million items—were carried aboard, and by the early hours of July 1 the train was ready to leave. Preceded by a pilot engine to check the tracks, it was pulled by two locomotives. Then came an armored car with the rarest works of art, followed by a flat car with a battery of anti-aircraft guns pointed skyward to drive away any German planes that might attack. After that came four Pullman cars with other valuable paintings and artifacts, twenty-two freight cars, two passenger cars, and another flat car with more anti-aircraft guns. Three weeks later, a second train left with another three-quarters of a million artworks to join the first at Sverdlovsk, formerly called Ekaterinburg, where Nicholas, Aleksandra, and their children had been killed during that same month in 1918. A third train, packed and ready, could not get away in time. When the Germans cut the last railway connection between Leningrad and the rest of the Soviet Union on August 30, these final 351 crates stayed behind in the city along with the treasures that could not be packed. These included the fresco Fra Angelico had painted for the San Domenico monastery in the 1440s. Because it was too fragile to be moved, Hermitage curators built a breastwork of sandbags thirteen feet high and almost ten feet wide to protect it in case bombs fell nearby.[17]

While director Orbeli and his staff worried about moving the Hermitage treasures, the Leningrad City Council searched for ways to get 392,000 children out of the city. From the first, the evacuation mixed terror with desperation, as parents tried to balance the need for safety against their children's fears of loneliness. Elena Kochina thought the children looked "like frightened little animals" as they moved toward the railroad station—the "demarcation line of their childhood," she called it—because "on the other side life without parents would begin." The little travelers carried small khaki knapsacks with a few clothes, some food, and some money. A few lucky ones carried notes to friends or acquaintances their parents hoped they might stay with when they reached their destinations. Kochina remembered how trucks took the youngest ones to the station, "their little heads stuck out of the body of the vehicles like layers of golden brown mushrooms."[18] The image couldn't have been more unfortunate. Babushkas—those "grannies" of indeterminate age (one hardly knew if a babushka was forty-five or sixty)—muttered that fall that the many mushrooms growing in the parks of Leningrad meant many deaths. In the coming weeks, this would prove to be tragically true. Some parents like Kochina couldn't let their children go, intending to keep them just a few days more. Then it was too late. When the Germans cut the last rail line between Leningrad and the rest of Russia, only a few more than half of the city's children had been sent away.[19]

After Nazi forces took the Imperial palaces at Oranienbaum, Peterhof, Gatchina, Pavlovsk, and Tsarskoe Selo (renamed Pushkin by the Soviets), their offensive ground to a halt. Uncertain about storming Leningrad's defenses, Hitler's generals decided to destroy the city by aerial bombardment and artillery, beginning on September 1 with a handful of long-range 240mm guns that killed 53 people and wounded another 101 in the first barrage. Then they closed their ring around the city, not as tightly as they had first hoped, but tight enough for regular heavy artillery to fire with telling effect. The German vise had caught nearly three million people in its jaws, and the men who manipulated it intended to let none escape. "I wrote a deposition . . . [saying that] it was essential not to let a single person through the front line," one of Germany's leading experts on nutrition told a Russian officer after the war. "The more of them that stayed there [in Leningrad]," he went on to explain, "the sooner [I thought] they'd die, and we'd enter the city without . . . losing a single German soldier!"[20]

Despite such recommendations, the Germans pounded Leningrad with bombs and artillery while they waited for its people to starve. Using the biggest guns in Europe they fired 5,364 shells into the city in September, 7,590 in October, 11,230 in November, and 5,970 in December. Fired from a distance of nearly seventeen miles, some of their high-explosive projectiles weighed close to a ton. Others were smaller and were fired from positions nearer the city against which the Red Army's artillery could retaliate. But the firing continued for a long time, inflicting tremendous damage. Even worse, the Luftwaffe dropped more than a hundred thousand bombs on Leningrad during the fall and early winter of 1941. Sometimes as many as six hundred planes took part in a single raid, and to see two or three hundred at a time was commonplace. These were the days, Akhmatova wrote, when the "dragon's shriek" of falling bombs was everywhere.[21] People were also killed by mines, rifle bullets, and bullets fired from airplane machine guns. Bombs with delayed fuses killed them, too, although these were sometimes disarmed in time. One such bomb—weighing over a ton and painted blue with yellow spots—landed near the big Erisman Hospital. With hundreds of anxious wounded soldiers looking on, it took three days to defuse it and a week more to haul it away.[22]

Leningrad in late August and early September 1941 saw none of the unsettled gray turbulence that so often precedes the coming of what the Russians call *bab'e leto*, or Indian summer. The grass in the parks stayed green until well into September, while the lindens turned brilliant shades of purple and gold, the birches a vivid yellow, and the maples a shining scarlet to mark the onset of autumn. With the Germans continuing their artillery barrages and bomber attacks, key buildings in the city—the Winter Palace, the General Staff, Smolnyi, even the needle spire of the

Peter and Paul Fortress Cathedral—had to be covered with camouflage nets that mimicked these colors. In winter the nets would have to be changed, and changed again in the spring if the city stood that long. Unable to be rigged for camouflage, the huge Admiralty spire had to be painted dirty gray by amateur Alpinists. The idea was to give German pilots the fewest possible reference points as they flew their bombing runs over the city.

From the beginning, Leningraders worried about enemy agents. "Spy mania," Kochina wrote, was "like an infectious disease"[23] in that it touched everyone and left a mark that lasted for decades. Even in the 1970s, it was still forbidden in Leningrad to take photographs from the dome of St. Isaac's Cathedral or take pictures of ships anchored in the Neva River. During the first days of the siege everyone was on the lookout for spies who might be collecting information for the Germans, charting map coordinates, or plotting sabotage. People wearing foreign clothes, beards, or strange hats got arrested by security patrols. So did men and women who limped, carried cameras, or asked directions to military headquarters or police stations. On August 27, the authorities forbade anyone from being on the city streets between 10 P.M. and 5 A.M. without a special pass. Everyone was on edge, and no one knew what to expect, for no city of this size had ever before been placed under siege. Leningrad covered sixty-five thousand acres, had over five hundred miles of tram and bus lines, and held three million people. What it faced at the beginning of September 1941, one of the best observers of wartime Russia wrote, was "the greatest and longest siege ever endured by a modern city."[24]

That fall, no one knew if Leningrad could hold out. With the German armies crowding up against their suburbs, Leningraders threw themselves into the task of building more defenses, on which nearly 100,000 men, women, and teenagers worked every day in September, with the number rising to an average of 113,000 each day in October. They built 17,000 embrasures in buildings, through which snipers could fire at the enemy, and 4,126 pillboxes.[25] The Egorov factory turned out hundreds of steel "hedgehogs" weighing one and a half tons each, and these were put in the city streets to slow down enemy tanks. When Iudenich's White Army had approached in 1919, Trotskii had called for the workers of Petrograd to make their city a fortress in which "every house will become an enigma, a threat, or a mortal danger."[26] That had not been needed after Iudenich's advance had collapsed unexpectedly, and it had been more than a year since an assassin acting on Stalin's orders had killed Trotskii in Mexico. But what Trotskii had called for in 1919 happened in 1941.

Every section of Leningrad had its workers' squads, companies, and battalions. Every open area into which German airborne troops might drop—the Haymarket, Theater Square, Mars Field, and a score of other locations—had machine gun emplacements set up and ready. Anti-aircraft guns, artillery, and antitank guns were everywhere, all camouflaged so as not to be seen from the air. No one knew how long the city could hold out, but Leningraders were ready to make the Germans fight for every building and street. Hoping to lose any attackers in the maze of city streets, they painted out all the street signs and house numbers. "In the southern part of Leningrad, every house had, in effect, been turned into a fortress, with the principal machine-gun nests and anti-tank strongholds set up in the basements and ground floors of large buildings dominating crossroads and main thoroughfares," one war correspondent wrote. "This network of little fortresses—cemented, sandbagged, and propped up with masses of steel girders and wooden walls nine, ten, twelve logs thick," he continued, "extended with varying degrees of density across the whole of Leningrad."[27]

Along with German bomber raids and artillery barrages, Leningraders faced the problem of food. Rationing had been imposed only eight days after the war began, but food consumption remained near normal until early September. Restaurants and cafés stayed open. Meat and fish continued to be sold, and so did sweets and other products that were more luxuries than necessities. Then, Nazi victories started to take a toll, and not just because their armies were closer to Leningrad. The West Russian and Ukrainian lands seized by the Germans during the first four months of fighting had produced nearly two-fifths of the Soviet Union's grain in 1940, more than four-fifths of its sugar, two-thirds of the coal, cast iron, and aluminum, almost two-fifths of the cattle and two-thirds of the hogs, so the quantity of food available for the entire country was cut dramatically before winter set in. Then, when the Germans closed their siege, the authorities in Leningrad discovered that they had just more than a month's reserves in their warehouses. On September 2, they cut workers' rations to a little more than a pound of bread a day, gave office workers a little less, and children only half. Still it was enough to survive, but only barely. Any further cuts, if continued for any length of time, would start to claim lives.[28]

In Moscow at the beginning of September, the State Defense Committee decided to appoint Dmitrii Pavlov as Leningrad's Chief of Food Supply, effective immediately. Honest, straightforward, hard-headed, and fair, Pavlov at age thirty-six was one of the best supply experts in the Soviet Union. The moment his Douglas DC-3 touched down at Leningrad airport on September 9, he began demanding hard facts—no propaganda, no lies, and no excuses—and he found that the situation was worse than the Leningrad authorities had reported. Too many loopholes in the distribution system had cut the city's reserves by half in a week. Knowing that shortages of boats and dock facilities would make the water route across Lake Ladoga on which Moscow's planners had counted impractical until the lake froze hard enough to bear the weight of trucks, Pavlov set out to do the best he could with the little he had.

The day before Pavlov landed in Leningrad, the Germans dropped phosphorus and napalm bombs on the Badaev Warehouses, which lay in the city's main freight yards just south of Vitebsk Station and the Obvodnyi Canal. The fires went on for several days over an area of more than four acres, the huge flames lighting the sky at night in a way that had not been seen since the Shchukin Arcade and Apraksin Market had burned almost eighty years before. Built of wood at the beginning of the century and set too close together, the warehouse buildings were firetraps, but several of them were empty and others only partly full. Before the flames were put out, they consumed some three thousand tons of flour and another twenty-five hundred of sugar, and people began to talk about how "the streets had run with melted chocolate" the first night they burned.[29] In the larger scheme of things, these were minor losses (three thousand tons of flour amounted to a day and a half's consumption based on the September 2 ration), but the psychological impact of the days and nights filled with flames and the smell of burning meat, sugar, and flour was immense. Almost everyone thought that the Badaev losses had brought the city to the brink of disaster. "It's the end—famine," the babushkas muttered.[30] This time, many people believed them. The story spread that the city had lost enough food to last for several years. That was not true, but the belief persisted long after the war had ended.[31]

Fears of food shortages became self-fulfilling prophecies long before supplies ran out. People bought canned vegetables and, whenever possible, canned crabmeat and canned caviar. Generals, high-ranking Party people, and even correspondents had access to special stores where the pickings continued to be good for several weeks more. The wife of the head of the Leningrad Writers' Union bought an enormous can of caviar "just in case," but her husband made her take it back because he thought it set a bad example. "Oh, Lord! Didn't we regret it afterwards," he told a British correspondent who visited the city in the fall of 1943. "Throughout the months of the famine we were haunted by the memory of that eight-kilo tin of caviar. It was like Paradise lost!"[32]

Pavlov needed to get Leningrad's food supplies and rationing system under control quickly. Knowing that potatoes were waiting to be harvested in the fields that lay between the city's suburbs and the German outposts, he sent factory workers and office clerks to help bring them in. "They gathered the potatoes mostly at night, creeping over the fields on hands and knees, hiding in shell holes, lying prone to dig the potatoes up and pile them in heaps," he remembered.[33] Apples were picked and cabbages cut, but there were only enough for something less than nine pounds a person to last the entire winter. Bread, the staff of life for all Russians, concerned Pavlov most of all. He sent agents to comb every warehouse in the city and had them check freight cars on railroad sidings and the holds of barges that had been caught in the harbor. In the middle of September he began to dilute the flour with oats, barley, soy, and malt. Later, he would order the addition of flax cake, cottonseed-oil cake, bran chaff, hemp, and hydrolyzed cellulose, all the while cutting the daily bread ration until it slipped below half a pound per person.[34]

By November, Pavlov was using anything that had any possible food value, and some things that didn't. Floors at breweries and flour warehouses were torn up, and the residue that lay beneath them collected. That winter, scientists at the Academy of Sciences discovered how to extract yeast and yeast milk from cellulose to make soup, and it was served in many of the factory and office cafeterias in which most Leningraders received part of their daily rations. By boiling two thousand tons of sheep guts that had been found in the hold of a ship in the harbor, a meat jelly was made, but oil of cloves had to be added to disguise its stench. Pavlov's scientists also saved two tons of oil each day by substituting a mixture of soap stock, water, and oil for the vegetable oil that was used to grease bread-baking pans at the city's bakeries. Some of these products, in Pavlov's own words, were "revolting."[35] But anything that could be eaten was preferable to things that could not. By the end of 1941, most of the pets, rats, birds, and mice in the city had long since disappeared, and Leningraders were scraping the flour paste from wallpaper and the glue from book bindings to make soup. Soon they grew more desperate. "I remember coming home and so wanting to eat!" one woman wrote many years later. "I took a [pine] log [that lay by the stove] . . . and began to gnaw. . . . Resin oozed out," she went on. "The fragrance of resin gave me a sense of enjoyment."[36]

Everyone thought of food and hatched schemes to get it. Ration cards—one for bread, one for meat, and one for fats—held the key to life in Leningrad, even though "meat" often meant meat jelly, vegetable-and-blood sausage, or powdered eggs, and "fats" might mean candy or even sugar-soaked earth from beneath the Badaev warehouses. Pavlov's agents issued new cards every month, and demanded that each holder present clear proof of his or her identity. Since extra ration cards were worth many times their weight in gold, forgers did a flourishing trade in counterfeit cards, and there was fear that the Germans might drop counterfeit ration cards into Leningrad to disrupt its food supply even more. Pavlov used the sternest measures to halt forgeries and card theft. For counterfeiting a card, the penalty was death by shooting, and for selling blank cards it was the same. When people started filing claims for new cards because their old ones had been lost in bombardments or stolen, Pavlov instituted an iron-clad policy that allowed almost no replacements, even though that condemned hundreds of unfortunates whose cards had been legitimately lost to starvation.[37]

To stay alive, Leningraders melted lipsticks to fry bread, tried to use face powder for flour, and boiled down the rawhide belts that ran machines in factories to make something resembling "meat" aspic. They used linseed oil for frying pancakes, and toothpowder added to a little potato flour or starch to make "pudding." One woman knowingly consumed seventy laxative tablets in an afternoon because the saccharin they contained gave her the impression she was eating something good. Many Leningraders ate peat from nearby bogs since it was thought to have food value, but nearly everyone at one time or another had to buy food on the black market, which survived throughout the siege in the narrow streets around the Haymarket, for more than 150 years the center of Leningrad's underworld. Even in the darkest days of December 1941, bread could still be bought at astronomical prices—a gold coin, a rare antique vase, a snuffbox given to someone by the emperor might net a pound. A diamond ring might bring a little more.

In those days, Leningrad was rife with tales of cannibalism, and few dared to inquire too closely into the origins of the meat patties that hard-eyed, well-fed men and women began to sell soon after the winter frost set in. No one ever admitted to actually seeing human flesh being consumed, but many claimed to have come upon corpses with thighs and arms cut away and other evidence that the scant remains of famine victims were being eaten by the living. "God alone knows what terrible scenes went on behind the walls of apartments," one survivor later remarked. Had husbands eaten dead wives? Wives their dead husbands? Had parents consumed their dead children? No one ever said so for certain. But many people thought that had happened during the terrible days of December 1941 and January 1942.[38]

Death came to Leningraders at work, at home, and in the street, mostly from hunger and cold. After the warm, sunny fall, the first snow came on October 14, and it continued after that with little respite. Heat came from whatever one's own ingenuity could supply, usually a tiny sheet metal stove called a *burzhuika*, into which tiny slivers of wood were fed to create a small, hot flame for short periods of time. Bit by bit, sliver by sliver, rolled-up page by rolled-up page, Leningraders fed their furniture, books, and whatever scraps they could find into these stoves, but they never generated enough heat to lift the temperature above freezing. Even in the city's hospitals, the temperature in the wards hovered between thirty and thirty-five degrees Fahrenheit, with patients being covered by coats, blankets, and extra pallets. Excrement froze in bed pans, and doctors and nurses worked in gloves, fur hats, and overcoats. "The cold never let up," the writer Lidia Ginzburg remembered, "not during sleep, not at mealtimes, not at work."[39] People began to crowd together, several families to a room to share the warmth their bodies produced. Some people moved into the hallways of their buildings, where there were no windows. That way, less heat could escape and there was less danger of being hit by flying shrapnel.

By November, Leningraders' appearance began to change. Friends and neighbors spoke about it, and people noticed it themselves whenever they looked in a mirror. Shoulder blades began to protrude, arms and legs turned to toothpicks, cheekbones stood out. Then people began to swell, first in the feet and hands, then in the face and neck. "People are all bloated, frightful-looking, black, dirty, and emaciated," one diarist wrote. "We've all aged," she added. "Young people have become so ghastly-looking, like old people, that it's simply awful to look at them."[40] Starved for fat, people even ate the grease used to lubricate tanks and trucks. "How we enjoyed it!" one man remembered. "What a miraculous thing!"[41] Thanks to the indigestible things they ate to make their stomachs feel full, most Leningraders had diarrhea. When the water towers were destroyed and the water pipes froze, people began to take their water from holes cut in the ice on the Neva, and that made the diarrhea worse. People were dying in very large numbers—fifty-three thousand in December 1941 alone—which was as many as had died in the city during all of the previous year.[42] But those numbers were guesses at best, and many thought they were much too low. "Ten days ago," the young writer Pavel Luknitskii recorded in his diary on December 29, "I heard that six thousand people a day were dying of hunger. Now, of course," he added, "it's more."[43]

For many, death came easily. "It is so simple to die," one woman wrote. "You just begin to lose interest, you lie on the bed, and you never again get up."[44] Men died before women, teenagers before invalids. People got so weak that any disease could finish them off—flu, grippe, an ulcer—almost anything was enough to kill a person in Leningrad during the winter of 1941–1942. People sometimes just sat down and died, or never got up in the morning. Sometimes they died while they were walking to work, while dragging the body of a loved one to the cemetery, or while standing in line to get their ration of bread. "There are a lot of corpses," Kochina noted at the end of December. "Death is . . . constantly hanging around among the living. People die easily, simply, without tears. The dead," she went on, "are wrapped up in sheets, tied up with a rope, and carried off to the cemetery, where they are stacked up in piles . . . [and] buried in common graves."[45] Wrapped and tied, the corpses looked like Egyptian mummies being dragged across the snow and ice on sleds.

Everything moved on sleds that winter. Their tracks buried under snow and ice, all the trams had stopped running by the end of 1941, and buses had stopped long before that. "The only transportation now is children's sleds," Kochina wrote. "They move along the streets in an endless stream."[46] Sleds—not the large kind on which dogs pulled heavy loads in the Arctic, but small children's sleds, the type on which millions of children have zipped down icy hills in northern countries all over the globe—filled the streets of the city, each moving slowly toward a destination known only to the exhausted human who dragged it. Some carried a relative or friend too weak to walk, others held precariously balanced loads of wood or pails of water. Many bore a mummy-like corpse, wrapped and tied in whatever scraps could be spared, making a final journey to the cemetery. All the while it was quiet, the sleds and the people pulling them being the only source of movement. Beautiful Leningrad, the imperial city of Elizabeth and Catherine the Great, of the emperors Alexander I and Nicholas I—Leningrad of the magical White Nights and gay winter days—had become a ghastly tomb of cold, gray granite, ruled by the wind, the weather, and people's desperate desire to eat. Even the Nevskii Prospekt, the nerve center of the city for more than two hundred years, had now fallen into ruin. "It was almost deserted and lay under a thick blanket of snow," a woman wrote just after the New Year. "Many houses were half ruins," she went on. "Most windows were boarded up . . . [and] the Merchants' Arcade department store was charred and black."[47] A huge bomb had fallen there on the nineteenth of September and the arcade had burned for days. Nothing had been done to fix it. For the time being, there seemed to be no reason to.

People retreated into themselves. "We've never been as remote from one another as now," Kochina wrote of herself and her husband not long after the first week of the New Year had passed. "There's no way we can help one another," she continued. "After all, it's my heart (only I hear its irregular beat), my stomach (only I feel its aching emptiness), and my brain (only I feel the whole weight of unexpressed thoughts). . . . We realize now that a person must be able to struggle alone with life and death."[48] Everything seemed tainted with death, as if the cold had frozen it into everything one touched, drank, or ate. Frozen corpses lay stacked up like cordwood in front of almost every building. After the temperature reached forty below zero on January 24, the plumbing broke down everywhere. Then people simply threw their sewage out the window or dumped it in the courtyard of the building in which they "lived."[49]

One of Leningrad's writers decided to celebrate the New Year by visiting his old apartment in the hope of salvaging some unpublished manuscripts he had left behind when a German bomb had landed early in the siege, but he didn't get around to doing it until January 17th. Pulling a small sled behind him, he plodded through the frozen city, its streets and sidewalks clogged with ice and frozen human waste. Everywhere he saw dead bodies, sprawled on the snow, partly buried with arms and legs sticking out of drifts, or stacked up on sledges and sleds. All seemed the same—pitifully thin, the red and purple marks of death spotting whatever skin was exposed. From time to time he had to turn aside to avoid getting tangled in the long hair that dragged from a corpse on a passing sled, or to avoid behind run into by someone too weak to turn aside. What separated the dead from the living? Was it pure chance or a different kind of will? Only one man he met seemed different—well-fed looking, with greedy eyes. Was he a speculator, the writer wondered? An apartment house manager who collected the rations of his dead and dying tenants and traded them for treasures in the Haymarket? People like that, he thought, "they all need to be shot!"[50]

Like Dostoevskii's long-suffering heroines, women held Leningrad together at the end of 1941. At the beginning of the fighting, it had become their duty to replace the city's men in its factories and to carry on the heavy digging involved in strengthening its fortifications once the men had gone to the Front. Women did the housework, brought in the wood, carried the water, took care of the children, washed and ironed clothes, tried to prepare meals from bits of bread, wallpaper paste, and all the inedible things people ate in those terrible times. And they stood in lines, the endless lines that ruled life in besieged Leningrad. Men avoided standing in lines and expected women to do it. "Men cope particularly badly with queues," Lidia Ginzburg once pointed out, "since they are used to the idea that their time is valuable." Patience was not a part of their character, nor was the ability to consign themselves to the compulsory idleness that the city's lines demanded. "A man considers that after work he is entitled to rest or amuse himself," Ginzburg explained, "[but] when a working woman comes home, she works at home."[51]

"Hunger," Chief of Food Supply Pavlov remembered in looking back on the terrible months of 1941–1942, "revealed character [and] it laid bare hitherto undiscovered feelings and traits."[52] That was especially true of the city's women, for it was they who maintained the will to survive, and supplied the inner strength that kept not only them but their children, fathers, and husbands alive as well.[53] But could even the stout-hearted women of Leningrad go on if there was no hope at all? When the Germans seized the key rail junction at Mga Station at the end of August they had severed Leningrad's rail connection to the rest of Russia. Then on November 8, their advance on the Tikhvin railhead cut off the flow of supplies by rail and road from the Russian interior to Novaia Ladoga on Lake Ladoga's southeastern shore. Desperate to restore the flow of goods, the Russians built 215 miles of road through the wilderness in barely a month to take advantage of the small break that Lake Ladoga's shoreline created by projecting into the Nazi's line of siege. On December 6, a trickle of supplies began to flow along the Novaia Ladoga road, but it was not until the middle of the month that the ice became hard and thick enough to support trucks with a full two-and-a-quarter-ton load. By that time, the Russians had driven the Germans out of Tikhvin, and that cut the length of the land route from the railhead to Novaia Ladoga down to 128 miles. At that moment, Leningrad had only enough grain left for nine or ten days. Oilcake, bran, mill dust, and all other "reserves" had been completely used up.[54]

By the middle of December, Pavlov later said, Tikhvin became a "gigantic ant hill," with workers and soldiers working around the clock to unload trains that arrived from the interior and load a never-ending line of trucks ready to carry supplies through the wilderness and across the lake. Once on the lake, their route was carefully plotted to avoid soft spots in the ice, but constant attacks by German planes and long-range artillery forced the drivers to do much of their traveling at night. It required twenty thousand men and women to keep the line going, but by late December the shipments to Leningrad had risen to more than six hundred tons a day, not even a third of what was needed to supply the city but more than enough to make the difference between gnawing hunger and certain starvation. On Christmas Day, Pavlov increased Leningraders' bread ration for the first time since the war began. Workers had their ration raised by a half. For the rest it was nearly two-thirds.[55]

Thanks to more Russian victories at the end of December, the men in charge of the winter road celebrated New Year's Day, 1942, by opening through-train service from Tikhvin to Voibokalo Station, a scant thirty-seven miles by road from Lednevo and Kabanova, which stood much closer to Leningrad than to Novaia Ladoga. Then the lifeline began to grow stronger and its flow of supplies increased to nearly two thousand tons a day. By February, the daily shipments had risen to over three thousand tons, and in March and April they exceeded thirty-six hundred. Pavlov now raised Leningraders' rations again on January 24, and yet again on February 11. The problem now was to move the supplies from Lake Ladoga's western bank into Leningrad itself. That continued to pose difficulties into the spring, when the melting ice temporarily brought all shipments across the lake to a halt.[56]

No one was willing to let the trucks that delivered food and fuel across Lake Ladoga return to the "mainland" empty. On January 22, 1942, the same State Defense Committee that had appointed Pavlov decided to evacuate half a million Leningraders, starting with children, old people, and women. Just more than half a million left the city between January and April, and another 448,010 between late May and November. By then, deaths and evacuations had cut Leningrad's population to about a million, less than a third of what it had been in the summer of 1941.[57]

Tens of thousands more left Leningrad who were not a part of the official count. Pavel Luknitskii, who had spent the winter of 1941–1942 trying to save his fellow writers and was finally sent out of the city early in February, remembered that every vehicle he saw along the way was crammed with passengers, many of whom had bribed the drivers with cigarettes, vodka, bread, or gold. Luknitskii noted that no one did anything for nothing. Even starving people near death had to pay their fare in bread. To describe the rigors of the journey from Leningrad to the eastern side of the lake demanded all of Luknitskii's talents as a writer. Trucks, buses, and cars crawled, halted, broke down, and were abandoned, leaving the route littered with disabled machines around which vehicles further back in line had to pick their way. There was no food, no shelter, no provisions for dealing with the thousands who made the journey on their own each day, and even after they had crossed the lake many of the evacuees could not find food or a place to get warm. With temperatures at thirty and forty below zero centigrade, people died at every step of the way, their bodies being pushed to the side of the road to be dealt with when the spring thaw came. Desperation drove them on. No one knew where their journey would end.[58]

The winter road brought Leningrad's black market back to life. Many of the drivers, dispatchers, and people who loaded and unloaded trucks found the chance to buy and sell food at a profit too tempting to pass up. The official who accompanied Luknitskii across the lake took all of his relatives, too, and he had every intention of returning to the city with goods for the black market. On such journeys, starving refugees met the people who had flourished at their expense during the siege—a hospital manager and his family all dressed in their expensive best, who stuffed themselves with fried chicken, chocolate, and powdered milk along the way, for example, and the son of a high-ranking supply official, who traveled in the same car as Elena Kochina and her family. "During the blockade we ate better than before the war," he bragged to Kochina's husband. "We ate whole boxes of butter and chocolate," his girlfriend added. "I didn't see that before." Many of these people had connections with Leningrad's Haymarket, where they could sell flour, for which they had paid 25,000 rubles a case, and other goods at a huge profit.[59] The fact that the punishment continued to be death by shooting deterred them not at all. Most people assumed that they paid "protection" to the very officials who were supposed to punish them.

By the time the thawing ice interrupted the flow of goods along the winter road in April 1942, everyone knew that Leningrad had survived the worst torments the Germans could inflict. With the Russians firmly in control of a rail link from Tikhvin to the eastern shore of Lake Ladoga, the shipments across the lake were resumed by boat as soon as the ice cleared away. The railroad line was improved, and so were the warehouses and dock facilities. That summer, the Russians laid an oil pipeline beneath the lake, despite repeated air attacks by the Germans. That way the city would not have to live through a second winter without fuel if the siege continued.[60]

While they waited for food and fuel during the winter of 1941–1942, Leningraders read. Many read Dostoevskii, Turgenev, and Chekhov, and thousands more read Tolstoi. "Whoever had energy enough to read," Lidia Ginzburg remembered, used to read *War and Peace* in besieged Leningrad. "Tolstoi had said the last word as regards courage, about people doing their bit in a people's war," she went on. "No one doubted the adequacy of Tolstoi's response to life. The reader would say to himself: Right, I've got the proper feeling about this. So then, this is how it should be."[61] People without the strength to read listened to the radio, on which some of Leningrad's writers and poets read their works to break the monotony of the siege. Many of their writings gave people heart, for they told of the resilience of the human spirit, the power of memory, and the duty they had never to forget. That winter, people planned books about the siege, kept diaries, and wrote poems and novels about it. They needed to be needed—and to have a point in the future toward which they could direct their lives. When there was no one to read on the radio, the sound of a metronome could be heard, always ticking, never stopping, the ceaseless heartbeat of a city that was too strong to die. Never once in the entire course of the siege did it stop. It was always there, the sound of life even when it seemed that life could not go on.

Hungry, weak, sometimes on the verge of death, Leningrad's musicians did their part that winter by giving concerts that were broadcast throughout the city. The most magical moment of all came in the spring, when Leningraders heard Dmitrii Shostakovich's Seventh Symphony, dedicated to their city. Shostakovich had begun his Seventh Symphony just before the war. On the night of September 19, when a German bomb destroyed the Merchants' Arcade, he invited some of his closest friends to his apartment, where they found him surrounded by sheets on which he had scored the symphony's first three movements. As they heard him play it they were stunned. When the air-raid sirens sounded, Shostakovich sent his wife and children to the bomb shelter and continued to play. Amidst the thunder of bombs, the screech of sirens, and the thump-thump of anti-aircraft guns, his music reached what one critic later called "a powerful, screaming climax with a level of sound that is unbearable physically and mentally."[62] His friends knew they had witnessed a rare moment in the culture of Russia and the world. Shostakovich and some higher force seemed joined, able to reach above and beyond the time and place in which they lived.

Soon afterward, Shostakovich was evacuated by plane to Kuibyshev, a city on the Volga River to which a number of artists, writers, and composers were evacuated that fall. There, he finished the symphony and wrote on the title page "dedicated to Leningrad." In later years he would insist, quietly and only to his closest friends, that the agony and anger of his symphony's music were directed as much against Stalin as Hitler. "This is music about terror, slavery, and oppression of the spirit," one friend remembered him saying. "[It is] not only about fascism but about our country and generally about all tyranny and totalitarianism."[63]

In the middle of March 1942, the Leningrad poet Olga Berggolts was flown out of the city to Moscow, and she was in the Soviet capital for the premiere of Shostakovich's new symphony. Afterward, she saw the composer rise to take a bow. "I looked at him," she remembered, "a small, frail man with big glasses, and I thought: 'This man is more powerful than Hitler'."[64] And so it seemed to other Leningraders, when they heard the *Leningrad* Symphony broadcast on the radio for the first time. "The very performance of the Seventh Symphony in besieged Leningrad," the radio announcer stated before the music was broadcast, "is evidence of the inextinguishable patriotic spirit of the Leningraders, their stalwartness, faith in victory, [and] readiness to fight to the last drop of blood."[65] From Shostakovich's music, Leningraders took heart, for like Akhmatova's poetry, it spoke for them and to them of the terrible burdens they had been called upon to bear. Even by the middle of April 1942, when the siege was already 248 days old, the dimensions of that burden remained still unknown and not fully measured.

Although no one knows for certain even now, those first 248 days of siege probably had claimed the lives of more than a million Leningraders, at least twelve times as many people as would perish at Hiroshima in 1945. There simply was no way of comparing the siege of Leningrad with those endured by any other modern cities. The siege of Vicksburg in the American Civil War had lasted only forty-eight days, from May 18 to July 4, 1863. No one had starved to death, and barely more than a hundred women and children had died. Vicksburgers had eaten mules, horses, dogs, and cats during those days, but even though Confederate soldiers outnumbered civilians by more than seven to one, fewer than one person in fourteen had perished. On a single day during January, February, March, or April 1942, more people died in Leningrad than in the entire siege of Vicksburg. Even the siege of Paris from September 19, 1870 until January 27, 1871 paled in comparison. By the middle of April 1942, the siege of Leningrad had lasted more than twice as long as that of Paris. Like Vicksburgers, Parisians had eaten domestic animals, and they had even killed and eaten a rhinoceros at the Paris zoo. But they had eaten the kinds of things on which Leningraders had survived that first terrible winter. Too, they had plenty of wine, and the weather was far less cold.[66]

Melting snow in the spring of 1942 revealed the full extent of Leningrad's devastation. Aside from thousands of shattered buildings, and thousands more craters in streets and sidewalks, the city's water and sewage systems had been severely damaged. Mountains of snow, debris, and human filth lay piled in some twelve thousand city courtyards. More than two hundred million square feet of street surface lay buried under waste, snow, and dead bodies, and the frozen crust of snow and ice that overlay every street was close to three feet deep. Leningrad needed to be cleaned up, and soon, before the human wastes and refuse exploded into an epidemic of unimaginable proportions. But to do so, the poet Vera Inber wrote, was going to be like "trying to clean up the North Pole if it were covered with refuse."[67]

Leningraders—sometimes as many as 300,000 at one time—dedicated themselves to cleaning up the city during the last week of March and the first two weeks of April. "Everybody turned out, just like a single person," a visiting journalist from Moscow reported. "There were housewives and school children and educated folk—professors, doctors, musicians, old men and old women. One turned out with a crowbar, another with a shovel, another with a pick-axe. Someone had a broom, somebody else had a wheelbarrow, some other person came with a child's sled. Some of them hardly had the strength to drag their legs. Five people would harness themselves to a child's sledge and pull and pull until they had no strength left."[68] By the middle of the month, Leningraders had cleaned a million tons of debris and human refuse from streets and courtyards of their city.[69] "The Augean Stables were child's play compared with this stupendous feat done by people worn down by a terrible winter," the elderly poet Nikolai Tikhonov wrote in May. "Anyone who had seen Leningrad in January or February," he added, "would fail to recognize the city today."

Spring came, the street cars started to run, the White Nights returned, and the siege continued. During the long summer days, the Germans intensified their aerial and artillery bombardments, bringing as many as eight hundred heavy guns to bear on the city. By now people had gotten used to them. "People heard the whistle of shells over their heads with indifference," Lidia Ginzburg remembered. "Waiting for a shell you know is coming is considerably harder," she went on, "but everyone knew that if you heard it, it wasn't going to land on you this time." Only a few let their fear show. A certain artist, Ginzburg recalled, "differed from the majority of Leningraders in his fear of the bombing." This artist would move in with friends who lived on lower floors than he, and during bombardments he could never keep still. "Come and have some tea," his friends would say. "They'll soon be finished." To that he would invariably reply: "You have no imagination, that's why you're not afraid. You have to be really clever, you know, to be afraid properly."[70]

On the Field of Mars and in the Summer Garden, people planted cabbages and potatoes, already planning for the winter ahead. There were "gardens" everywhere, wherever there had once been lawns or parks. While they waited for the vegetables to grow, people ate weeds and wild grasses to satisfy their hunger for something green. "When grasses and herbs appeared, people seemed to be transformed into animals," one survivor remembered. "They tore up any kind of grass and ate it. Not a blade of grass remained to be seen anywhere." Weeds of all sorts made their way onto people's tables and into the canteens of factories and office buildings, too. "Plantain soup, nettle and sorrel puree, beet-top rissoles, goosefoot rissoles, and cabbage-leaf schnitzel," all appeared that spring to supplement "liver made from oilcake, oilcake pastries, fishmeal sauce, casein pancakes, and yeast soup." One woman remembered visiting the Botanical Gardens with a colleague after being assigned to test various local grasses and herbs to determine if any were poisonous. While they waited to see the person in charge, they began to eat the chervil that grew nearby. "May we pick some chervil?" they asked. "It's a weed," the researcher assigned to work with them replied. "I said that it was all the same to us," she recalled. "So we stuffed two bags with it, and brought it back to the laboratory. We ate it all up, and were content. What enjoyment it gave us to eat that weed. We'd eaten our fill of chervil!"[71]

That summer, Leningraders picked daisies, chamomile, mignonettes, and field roses, and brought them home, trying in every way they could to make life seem "normal" again. In some ways, life *was* becoming normal. Civility was returning, and kindness, too. People were still weak, but they helped each other over the rough spots. Aleksandr Fadeev saw a Red Army soldier, a peasant lad from the country, lift an old woman into a streetcar when she couldn't climb the steps herself. "Thank you, little son," the old lady replied. "Because of that, you'll come through alive. Mark my words—a bullet won't get you!"[72] But "normality" was only a veneer, as on the Nevskii Prospekt, where false fronts were set up to conceal the bomb damage from the street. Everyone knew that hardly a building remained unscathed after almost a year of German bombing and shelling.[73] It was that way with people, too.

People recovered slowly, for the strains of hunger and months of seeing loved ones killed had taken a heavy toll. Unlike people who had known no such disasters, Leningraders now understood what really counted and what did not, but the marks of the siege remained—in their strangely dark skin, their gaunt looks, and most of all their eyes. "Those faces and eyes told me more than could be gathered from all the stories of the horrors of famine," Fadeev wrote after seeing Leningrad's children for the first time. The children he saw had forgotten how to play and kept to themselves. Often they were silent for hours on end. "I'm thinking all the time about mama," one small orphan said. "I remember how mama died at home," another added. "When she came in [from standing in line for bread] she fell down on the floor. . . . I put her on the bed, she was very heavy, and then the neighbors said she was dead."[74]

At lunch one little girl Fadeev visited at an orphans' kindergarten kept putting bits of her bread aside. "I wanted to remember mummy," she explained when questioned. "We always used to eat bread together late at night in bed . . . and I wanted to do the same as mummy. I love my mummy," she concluded, "and I want to remember her." Adults masked their feelings more easily, but the strain of life still showed. "I had known her as a handsome woman," Fadeev wrote in April of a cousin he had not seen since the beginning of the siege. "[Now she] was almost an old woman, withered, with puffy eyelids, darkened face, and swollen legs. Her dark, smoothly combed hair was heavily streaked with gray. Her delicate hands had coarsened and had become the rough, knotted hands of a manual laborer."[75]

People whose thoughts had been turned inward for so long began to reach outward through books. "I see people reading books everywhere," Pavel Luknitskii wrote in his diary on July 15. "They sit on benches in the squares, in gardens, in parks, and on the boulevards. [Others sit] on chairs and even in armchairs they've brought out on the pavement near the shell-shattered buildings in which they still live." That summer Leningrad's book trade really came to life. The city had been a haven for bibliophiles since at least the middle of the eighteenth century, and the treasures that had been handed down from great-grandparents, grandparents, and parents simply could not be imagined. During the winter, starving people had sold their books to buy bread, people who had been evacuated had sold their books, and so had the heirs of those who had died or been killed. Thieves had looted thousands of apartments from which people had fled to escape the bombing and shelling, often taking any valuable books. Now these reappeared for sale in used bookstores, in kiosks, and in the Haymarket. Rare first editions that had not been seen in Leningrad's bookstores for decades, books with precious original illustrations tipped in by hand by prerevolutionary printers, books in fine leather bindings, some of them true monuments to the bookbinder's art—these and tens of thousands more all appeared for sale that summer.[76]

On August 9, 1942, the Philharmonic played Shostakovich's Seventh Symphony in war-torn Leningrad. The score had been flown in by special military plane from Kuibyshev in June, and rehearsals had gone on for more than a month. The performance took place in the Philharmonic Hall, its great auditorium still a brilliant blend of white, gilt, and raspberry velvet. "No one will ever forget this concert," one observer wrote. "The motley orchestra, dressed in sweaters and vests, jackets and collarless shirts, played with inspiration and agitation. . . . When they played the finale, everyone in the audience stood up. It was impossible to listen to it sitting down. Impossible."[77] Throughout the concert, heavy artillery fire punctuated Shostakovich's music, but this time the guns were Russian. Lieutenant General Leonid Govorov, an artillery specialist who had commanded the Leningrad Front since April, had brought up three thousand heavy guns to prevent the Nazi artillery from attacking the Philharmonic Hall during the performance.[78] As the gunfire and the power of Shostakovich's music blended with the strength of Leningrad's spirit, people wept, remembering those who had died. Others remembered those far away, who they hoped still lived.

The guns of the Red Artillery signaled the beginning of another attempt to break the Germans' grip. On September 8, General Govorov's commanders hurled three rifle divisions across the Neva near Schlüsselberg, only to have them driven back. A few weeks later, he tried a second time and failed again. The Red Army did not yet have the strength to break the Germans' siege, but the sixty thousand losses it inflicted on the units that occupied the Nazis' forward positions freed Leningrad from the danger of another direct assault. A second siege winter was approaching, and Leningraders knew it would bring more hardships. But they also knew that the worst was past. The city had laid in large reserves of food, and the evacuations and deaths of the previous eight months meant that many fewer needed to be fed. With the Germans pushed back from Tikhvin, the winter road could be opened as soon as the ice froze on the lake. Starvation rations now were a thing of the past.

Repairs had been made all through the summer and fall. Roofs had been fixed, water and sewer lines reconnected, electric wires restrung. Windows had been replaced or covered with plywood. Stoves had been installed in some apartments and fixed in others. Tramlines had been repaired and shell holes in the pavement filled.[79] Much damage still remained, but Leningraders' mood had changed. Now they spoke of when the blockade would be broken, not if it would be. To many it seemed only a matter of time, and they had learned how to wait.

Whatever Leningraders' hopes may have been in the late fall of 1942, their liberation still lay more than a year away. After his two attempts to break the German siege in September and October failed, Govorov waited to gather more strength. The fall came and went, and still he waited. Leningraders were not starving now, and their munitions factories were producing many of the shells, bullets, and hand grenades that Govorov's front-line troops needed. Hatred for the Germans drove the city workers on. The first time prisoners of war were paraded on the Nevskii Prospekt, soldiers and police had to hold the enraged women of the city back. Some of the prisoners, it was said, burst into tears when the Russians told them that they would have to rebuild everything they had destroyed before they would ever be allowed to return to Germany.[80]

The poet Olga Berggolts celebrated New Year 1943 with a poem, looking back on the terrors of the year before. For much of that year, she had lived in the building that had housed the Leningrad Radio Committee. Along with other artists, poets, and composers, she had read poetry, and when all else had failed she had kept the metronome that signaled the city's life. Her husband had died, and she had begun to suffer from dystrophy. She had grown terribly weak, but still she had continued to talk, read, and write. The previous winter, Leningraders had listened breathlessly to the lines of her *February Diary*, in which she had told of their struggles. "We do not weep: they speak the truth, that tears froze within the people of Leningrad," she read. "We'll die, but Red Piter we'll never surrender!"[81] Now Berggolts spoke again. "Again it's winter. The snow is swirling. The enemy is still at the city gates," she began. "But we'll greet the New Year with a party. . . . And we'll breathe warmth into the building, in which death held sway and darkness reigned [a year ago]. Here there'll be life!"[82] Life for Leningrad, perhaps, but death for Germans. That was Leningraders' fondest hope—and they soon were to have their wish.

Now serving as a war correspondent with General Mikhail Dukhanov's Sixty-seventh Army across the Neva from Schlüsselberg, Pavel Luknitskii found himself ordered back to Leningrad on the evening of January 11, 1943. Fifteen hours later, at 9:30 the next morning, forty-five hundred Russian guns opened up on the Germans' positions. Heavy artillery, mortars, Katiushas—those multibarreled rocket launchers whose piercing screams one could never forget—all fired at once and continued for more than two hours, concentrating tens of thousands of shells on the Germans' lines. When Luknitskii was allowed to return to the front on the afternoon of the following day, he found that Dukhanov's divisions had already forced the Neva crossing. Five days later, Schlüsselberg fell, and the German lines retreated ten to fifteen miles from the south shore of Lake Ladoga. Direct rail connections between Leningrad and the rest of Russia could be reopened. Although not to be entirely lifted for another year, the ring around Leningrad had been split apart. "The blockade is broken. We shall triumph," Olga Berggolts rejoiced on Radio Leningrad. "We know that we still have much to live through and much to bear," she added. "But we'll endure everything."[83] Leningraders poured into the streets. "This snow-strewn moonlit night of January 18–19 will never vanish from the memory of those who experienced it," Vera Inber told the city's radio audience right after Berggolts finished. "This happiness, this happiness of liberated Leningrad, we will never forget."[84]

But the siege went on. Nazi guns remained trained on Leningrad, and the trains that reached the city from the "mainland" did so only by running a deadly gauntlet of artillery fire. More than four million tons of freight came through, but the cost in lives was high. The Germans hoped to close the gap, the Russians to widen it, and both relied heavily on artillery. On May Day 1943, the Germans intensified their barrages against Leningrad with heavy railroad guns that hit the Public Library and destroyed trams on the Nevskii Prospekt. Sometimes Olga Berggolts found it hard to write even two paragraphs without being interrupted by the scream of shells and the sound of explosions. The authorities put up thousands of blue and white signs that read: "Citizens! During an artillery bombardment, this side of the street is more dangerous." "As if we didn't already know," Berggolts muttered to herself. "We've lived under continuous shelling for so long."[85] Nonetheless, life got better, slowly but surely. Theaters and cinemas reopened. There was even a summer soccer season. People started telling jokes again.[86]

As Leningraders prepared to welcome the New Year 1944, Olga Berggolts made the listeners of Radio Leningrad a promise. "This is the third New Year we've celebrated under siege," she reminded them. "We won't have a fourth one like this. Enough. That's it!"[87] That thought was in Govorov's mind, too, and also in the minds of Leningrad's Party boss Andrei Zhdanov and Stalin. All fall, the buildup had gone on until the Russian assault force of a million and a quarter men outnumbered the Germans by more than two to one. So many heavy guns and Katiusha rocket launchers had been brought in that they averaged two hundred guns for each kilometer of front, one every seventeen and a half feet. That did not take into account the guns of the Soviet Baltic fleet or the batteries at Kronstadt and the smaller fortresses that supported it. More than a thousand freight cars loaded with shells had been brought up, not counting those produced inside Leningrad itself. The Leningrad shells could be identified by their inscriptions, painted in carefully stenciled letters on their projectiles: "[As payment] for the blood of Leningrad's workers," "For our children's anguish," "For our murdered friends."[88] Now promoted to Colonel-General, Govorov continued to press Stalin and the Soviet Union's Chief of Artillery Marshal Nikolai Voronov for still more guns, more shells, and more men, for he wanted to overwhelm the Germans with his first assault. "The fate of Leningrad hangs on the speed of our advance," he warned his commanders. "If we are held up, Leningrad will be subjected to such a terrible shelling that it will be impossible to stand it—so many people will be killed, so many buildings demolished."[89]

On the morning of January 14, 1944, the 867th day since the Germans had closed their ring around Leningrad, Govorov ordered a murderous artillery barrage that rained more than a hundred thousand shells on the fog-drenched enemy positions in just sixty-five minutes. That first day the Second Soviet Shock Army pushed forward for about two miles along a six-to-seven-mile front, not enough to be decisive, but enough to keep the Germans from regrouping. That night snow fell, and the next morning Govorov opened the heaviest barrage of the war. Between 9:20 and 11:50 that morning, Soviet artillery poured half a million shells and Katiusha rockets onto the Germans' front, more than at Stalingrad, more, even, than the Germans had used in the "Von Mackensen Wedge" maneuver with which they had pulverized Russian positions in World War I. "This morning, I got up long before dawn as usual," Pavel Luknitskii wrote in his diary. By the light of a kerosene lamp, he began to read a French novel until the windows in his apartment on Leningrad's Griboedov Canal suddenly began to rattle violently. When the whole building started to shake, Luknitskii jumped out of bed, hurried to the window, and opened it to find that the windows of the buildings across the canal were full of people, too. What could it mean? The sound of artillery seemed to fill the entire city, but no one heard any shell explosions.[90]

Suddenly, it dawned on people what was happening. "This isn't a bombardment!" they shouted. "Those are our guns!" "It's begun!" someone exclaimed. "It's begun!" Luknitskii grabbed his felt boots and fur hat, threw on a short sheepskin coat, and bolted out the door. By the time he got to the correspondents' briefing room, the Second Shock Army had already advanced six miles.[91] This time the attack did not peter out. During the next few days, the Soviet advance picked up speed, but it still could not keep pace with the retreating Germans. In just a few days, Govorov's armies took back Pulkovo, Pushkin, Pavlovsk, Ropsha, Krasnoe Selo, and Peterhof, and they captured the heavy guns that had bombarded Leningrad for so many months. Everything they took back was in ruins. The golden Samson Fountain and Grand Cascade at Peterhof, and the Catherine Palace and its beautiful Cameron Gallery at Pushkin were shattered. The Amber Room into which Rastrelli had built the exquisitely carved amber panels that Peter the Great had received from the King of Prussia had completely disappeared, and no one knows to this day where the carvings went. Nothing remained of the Great Hall of the Palace but a blackened shell.

A few days later, Govorov's armies took Mga, the key to the German's siege. On the evening of January 27, he and Zhdanov announced to the accompaniment of twenty-four salvos from 324 guns that "the city of Leningrad has been entirely liberated from the enemy's blockade and his barbaric artillery bombardment."[92] The longest siege ever endured by a modern city was over. "Now we can walk on the street wherever we choose," Luknitskii rejoiced. No more listening for the scream of shells, no more worrying about whether a shell would land on the streetcar one had chosen to ride in, no more always keeping one eye peeled for every sign of danger.[93]

Most of all, people noticed how peaceful the city had become. "In Leningrad, it is quiet," Olga Berggolts wrote. "Children now can walk on the sunny side—'the most dangerous side'—of the Nevskii," she went on. "The children of our city now can walk peacefully on the sunny side! And they can live peacefully in rooms that look out on the sunny side. They can even sleep peacefully and soundly at night, knowing that they won't be killed." The October movie theater—on the sunny side of the Nevskii—reopened. And in a few more days the Germans marched through the Narva Triumphal Gates, just as Hitler had promised. Only they did so under guard, as prisoners of war.[94] Vera Inber, with whom Berggolts had sometimes worked at Radio Leningrad, simply could not find the words she needed. "It's the greatest event in the life of Leningrad, its complete liberation from the blockade," she wrote in her diary. "And here I am, a professional writer, and I simply can't find the words for it. All I can say is that Leningrad is free. And that's all."[95]

For the time being, that seemed to be enough. No one asked what it would take to put Leningrad back together, repair the forty-five billion rubles' worth of damage the Germans had inflicted, bring back the population (there were barely more than half a million now), and rebuild the factories, the apartments, the streets. All that lay in the future. For the time being, Leningraders wanted only to be at peace—even though the war still raged—and to keep close to their hearts memories of the torments that had bound them together. But would memories of torments endured at the hands of the Nazis bring to mind memories of torments suffered at the hands of their rulers themselves? Could Leningraders remember only the terror of the siege without being reminded of the terrors they had suffered in the decade that had come before? Those questions, too, remained in the future, although the answers would come sooner than anyone imagined.

That spring and summer the war went on. The Red Army stormed west, across the Don, the Dnepr, the Bug, and the Dnester into Poland and Rumania. It drove the Germans from Kiev, from Tallinn, from Lwow, from Warsaw, and from Budapest, and then continued on to Berlin. In Leningrad, people thought about the war and about the siege. They thought about rebuilding and they thought about remembering. On April 30, 1944, they opened an exhibition dedicated to the siege in the city's eighteenth-century salt warehouse, which, not long before the Revolution of 1917, had been converted to hold the Imperial Museum of Education, the Museum of the Imperial Technical Society, the Museum of Home Crafts, and the Imperial Museum of Agriculture. Nearly every house around the building had been hit by German shells and bombs. Now the Party and the Leningrad Front Military Council turned what remained of the salt warehouse into a museum—fourteen rooms, sixty thousand exhibits, twenty-four thousand square feet of floor space. Outside stood captured siege guns, Tiger tanks, and heavy field guns, all the weapons the Germans had brought to bear against the city.

People walked through the rooms in groups, in pairs, or alone, but everyone was alone with the memories the exhibit brought to life. Luknitskii stayed for four hours. Vera Inber saw the same blue bomb with yellow spots that had landed next to the hospital, where she and her husband had worked in the fall of 1941. Then it had been an object of terror. Now it was just a statistic: "Weight 1,000 kilograms. Diameter 660 millimeters. Length 990 millimeters."[96] Everyone looked at the model of a siege bread shop that had been fixed up so that the window was covered with ice and one could just make out a scale with its 125 grams of bread on the counter. In true Soviet fashion, the contents of the bread were posted above the scale: "50% defective rye flour, 10% salt, 10% cottonseed cake, 15% cellulose, 5% soya flour, 5% reclaimed flour dust, and 5% sawdust."[97] That brought to each person's mind images of a past they all shared and now treasured. But what of the future? By the spring of 1944, Leningraders were thinking about that, too.

Everything that had been taken out of the city had to be brought back, and everything that had been destroyed rebuilt. Well over three million square meters of housing, more than five hundred schools, two-thirds of the eighteenth-century buildings that had been preserved as monuments, more than eight hundred factories had to be rebuilt or repaired, and so did seventy-five kilometers of sewer lines, forty-four kilometers of water lines, more than seventy bridges, and nearly two hundred kilometers of streets. And the city had to be expanded so that it could hold at least a million more people than before the war.[98] Then there was the Hermitage. Deliberately targeted by the Germans throughout the siege, it had been hit by thirty-two artillery shells and two bombs. It needed to be repaired and restored, and to have its incomparable collection of art treasures returned. Told to compile a list of the materials needed for that task, director Iosif Orbeli requested sixty-five tons of gypsum plaster, eighty tons of alabaster, a hundred tons of cement, two tons of joiner's glue, forty tons of chalk plaster, thirty tons of chipped chalk, and a hundred tons of asphalt mastic. That was just the beginning. Orbeli's list also included thirty tons of ground pigments, twenty tons of dry pigments, ten tons of white lead, twenty tons of linseed oil, two tons of casting bronze, two tons of sheet bronze, eighty kilograms of powdered bronze, six kilograms of gold, and thousands upon thousands of square meters of glass, canvas, and decorative fabrics.[99]

All the treasures had to be packed up in far-away Sverdlovsk and brought back. When the two trains reached Leningrad on October 10, 1945, the scenes from the summer of 1941 were replayed in reverse. A huge convoy of trucks loaded more than a thousand crates now headed down the Nevskii Prospekt from the Moscow Railway Station to return the treasures of Peter and Catherine the Great and some of Russia's greatest nobles to the Hermitage. Right after that, the curators of the Hermitage started to unpack. Rembrandt's *Portrait of an Old Man in Red*, his *Portrait of a Young Man with a Lace Collar*, and the *Descent from the Cross* all were returned to their frames and rehung. So were the Tintorettos, the Titians, and the Giorgiones. The Scythian gold treasures and the jewelry of Russia's empresses were returned to their special vaults, and Houdon's statue of Voltaire, seated and arrogant as always, was put back in its proper place. On the morning of Sunday, November 4, sixty-eight of the Hermitage's 345 exhibition rooms were opened to visitors. The eagle-eyed little old ladies who watched each room were back at their posts that day, along with Orbeli and all the Hermitage workers who had survived the siege. Like Leningrad, the Hermitage was about to embark on a new era of its history, and a strong sense of optimism prevailed. Orbeli and his staff looked forward to new opportunities and new acquisitions that would make their museum even greater than it had been before the war.[100]

Known only to Orbeli and a very few others, thousands of priceless new treasures already lay in the Hermitage's storerooms that day. Just six days after the much-heralded last trainload of treasures reached Leningrad from Sverdlovsk, another train had arrived from Berlin. Twice as long as the ones from the East, this one came with no fanfare, and even today we do not know the full extent of its contents. But on the bottom of each of its forty cars lay one or two of the priceless marble panels that had decorated the altar of Zeus at Pergamum. Carved in high relief in the second century B.C., these depicted the battle of the gods and giants in a frieze that stretched for more than 390 feet. "A giant, crying, screaming in torture, and the proud, victorious Athena are in front of me," the Russian art specialist who found the Nazis' hiding place for these treasures wrote in his diary. Here carved brilliantly in stone was "the eternal subject—the fight of life and death, of light and darkness . . . victory and catastrophe, destruction and the passionate, ecstatic success of life."[101] The Pergamum Museum in Berlin had been built especially to display these friezes, and they were one of the first things that the Red Army sent back to Russia as part payment for the damage the Germans had caused.

Other treasures had been piled on top of the panels as the train made its way East, and enough more were collected over the next couple of years to fill three more trains. Among other things, these included paintings and sculptures taken from Berlin's Kaiser Friedrich Museum, Munich's Alte Pinakothek, scores of paintings from the collection of Old Masters in Dresden, and hundreds more from private collections, especially that of Otto Krebs, a German industrialist, who, although he died of cancer of 1941, was said to have profited mightily from the Nazis' rearmament. The works of art that filled the four trains the Russians sent to the Hermitage went on and on: paintings by Cézanne, Renoir, Pissarro, Gauguin, Degas, and Goya, and others by Raphael, Van Dyck, Dürer, and Lucas Cranach. There were Egyptian stone carvings, Persian miniatures, Greek marbles, and Roman bronzes, the head of Nefertiti, Botticelli's drawings for the *Divine Comedy*, and treasures that Heinrich von Schliemann had taken from his excavations at Troy. All the gold Trojan jewelry that von Schliemann had given to the German nation in the 1880s had already been airlifted to the Pushkin Museum in Moscow, but his hoard of Trojan ceramics and bronzes, many of them perfectly preserved and unscarred, had come to the Hermitage. For many years, their existence in the Soviet Union was a closely guarded secret. Only in the 1980s did that curtain of secrecy begin to tear apart.

These treasures were taken from Germany, not by random looting but as part of a carefully designed undertaking that had been authorized by the Central Committee of the Communist Party and Stalin personally. Furious over the Nazis' willful destruction of hundreds of churches and palaces in Russia, and equally angry about their wholesale looting of treasures from the museums of Kiev, Novgorod, Pskov, and the suburban palaces around Leningrad, the Russians vowed to collect compensation as their armies stormed through Germany and the lands of its allies. Their rationale was straightforward and unambiguously stated. "The German-Fascist barbarians, who tried to annihilate Russian culture and destroyed many famous examples of Russian art, must be held responsible for all their crimes," the director of Moscow's Pushkin Museum wrote to the Council of People's Commissars in 1944. "The museums of the Axis countries are full of wonderful masterpieces," he went on. "[These] must be given to the Soviet Union as compensation."[102]

That opinion was widely held in Leningrad. "People who deliberately destroy works of art have no right to own any," a number of Leningraders told the British correspondent Alexander Werth. "They cannot have any real love of art," they continued. "So why, then, should the Huns own the European treasures of Dresden, Munich, and Berlin?"[103] As the war entered its final year, that became the view of the Central Committee of the Communist Party of the Soviet Union, which gave temporary military rank to scores of art historians and curators and sent them to Germany with the Red Army.[104] These were by no means Party hacks or mean-spirited ideologues. The three key figures involved in the planning of the Soviet expropriation of German art treasures were the dean of Soviet art historians, Igor Grabar, Sergei Troinitskii (one of Orbeli's predecessors as director of the Hermitage), and Viktor Lazarev, former curator of paintings at the Pushkin Museum and one of Russia's greatest experts. These men knew the art of the West and where to find it. Their agents went to Germany with detailed lists of paintings and their locations, all part of a clear plan that specified what they would take to compensate for the damage the Germans had inflicted on the art treasures of the Soviet Union between 1941 and 1944.

Seizing art from the museums of Germany and its allies was only part of a huge effort to transform the postwar Soviet Union into a living monument to the achievements of Communism. With its shattered buildings and bombed-out factories, some planners thought, Leningrad could show the world what people working as a collective could accomplish. The sacrifices that Leningraders had made between 1941 and 1944 already had demonstrated what men and women dedicated to a higher purpose could achieve. Could the common purpose that had driven them to such feats in wartime be carried over into an era of peace? Could Leningrad be made whole again? How long would it take? And could the city, as Party Secretary Andrei Zhdanov told the assembled delegates of the Leningrad City and Regional Party apparatus in the spring of 1944, be made "even more comfortable than it was"? Many thought that the devastation inflicted on the imperial palaces at Pushkin, Peterhof, Gatchina, and Pavlovsk could never be repaired, and some insisted that their ruins ought to be left as monuments to Nazi barbarity. But no one disputed that Leningrad itself must be rebuilt. "Our task," Zhdanov insisted as the Soviet armies entered Poland and stormed westward, "is not just reconstruction but restoration of the city."[105] Old buildings were to be returned to their former grandeur, and new ones were to be built. The city of Peter the Great was to be fully transformed into the city of Lenin. While standing as a monument to Russia's past, it was also to become a symbol of its present and future, a city of unmatched architectural wonders and of unmatched suffering.

That was the vision of the men and women who drafted plans for Leningrad's future as the Allied armies closed in on Berlin. But there was another side to the city's past, present, and future that had to be taken into account. In the eighteenth century it had been the center of Russian shipbuilding, and in the nineteenth century it had become the core of Russia's heavy industry. The city had continued to play that role in Soviet times, and although the years between 1928 and 1944 had seen many factories and plants built east of the Ural Mountains, Soviet planners had no intention of allowing Leningrad's tradition of precision machine building to slip away. Leningrad must be restored as an industrial center, and some of the workers skilled in tool and die making, weapons manufacture, and shipbuilding brought back. When the siege was entirely lifted in January 1944, the city held just under six hundred thousand people. Twenty months later, that number had more than doubled. Yet the budget for housing construction was no larger than it had been in 1940, even though the Nazi siege had destroyed more than fifteen million square feet of housing space.[106]

As early as 1945, Leningrad's planners and builders had to start chipping away the corners from their vision of the city as a great cultural metropolis that would blend its imperial past with a grandiose Soviet future. Ordinary housing and rebuilt factories took precedence over the grandiose vistas that the planners of 1943 and 1944 had hoped to create. Imagination and vision gave way to pragmatism in shaping Leningrad's revival, and by 1948 virtually all of the verve and daring that the city's starving planners had displayed in the final months of the siege had slipped away. This was in part due to financial constraints, but not entirely. Political infighting in the Kremlin had a major impact on Leningrad's future, and that had a direct connection to the rapid fading of any hope for a huge renaissance as the 1940s drew to an end.

Even during the darkest days of the war, Kremlin politics had continued at their vicious, murderous worst. As the fighting in Germany neared its end, the rivalry for first place in Stalin's inner circle had become a battle between Leningrad's Party Chief Zhdanov and Georgii Malenkov, both of whom had used the purges of the 1930s as stepping stones to high positions in the Kremlin. Zhdanov's stock had plummeted during the early days of the war, and it seems virtually certain that he would have been shot had the city fallen. But Leningrad's stubborn resistance gave Zhdanov a much-needed reprieve. By 1944, the pendulum had started to swing back in his favor, and he returned to Moscow, leaving his close ally Aleksei Kuznetsov to run the Party machinery in Leningrad. With his power second only to Stalin's, Zhdanov set out to become the Soviet Union's special arbiter of culture, and in doing so he launched a reign of terror that still bears his name. *Zhdanovshchina*—the era of Zhdanov's greatest influence—continues to be remembered for its obscurantism, rigidity, and ideological blindness in the arts. In Leningrad it ended all dreams of greatness and brought forth the persecution of some of the city's greatest writers starting with Anna Akhmatova, who had spent much of the war in Central Asia, in Tashkent.

Before she left Leningrad at the end of September 1941, Akhmatova had vowed that the steadfast women of Leningrad would save their city, and she held to that belief throughout the siege. In Tashkent, she lived among the best of the Russian intelligentsia, reading and writing poetry, talking, pondering, and composing. The city's steep, narrow alleys, its Eastern flavor, its exotic reminders of being a world apart from the place she had left behind fascinated her, and she spoke of Tashkent often in her poems. She had come down with typhus and scarlet fever there, recovered, and looked ahead. But her main thoughts continued to be of Leningrad, its suffering, its people's courage, and its future. She returned to the city in 1944, depressed by the devastation she found but hopeful that life would become better for writers and artists. She hoped that her own work could be published once again, and that Leningrad would resume its rightful place as Russia's window on the West.[107]

Akhmatova found in Leningrad what Joseph Brodsky called "a lean, hard face with the abstract glitter of its river reflected in the eyes of its hollow windows . . . behind which—among old pianos, worn-out rugs, [and] dusty paintings in heavy bronze frames . . . a faint life was beginning to glimmer."[108] As the greatest of all Leningrad poets to survive the purges and the siege, she enjoyed immense popularity, saw her poems printed and reprinted, and quickly became the grande dame of the city's postwar intelligentsia. Now in her fifties, she still made a stunning impression, just as she had in the days of her youth at Ivanov's Tower and Pronin's Stray Dog. Isaiah Berlin, whose postwar writings about the Russian intelligentsia would establish him as one of the West's leading experts, found her "immensely dignified, with unhurried gestures, a noble head, beautiful, somewhat severe features, and an expression of immense sadness."[109] That sense of "immense sadness" stayed with Berlin for the rest of his life. "Leningrad after the war was for her nothing but a vast cemetery, the graveyard of her friends," he remembered more than forty years afterward. "Her sustenance," he went on, "came . . . from literature and images of the past: Pushkin's St. Petersburg; Byron's, Pushkin's, Mozart's, Moliere's Don Juan; and the great panorama of the Italian Renaissance."[110]

Akhmatova's sustenance may have come from the past, but she still had to contend with a present in which Stalin wanted no rivals to Moscow and no challenges to his power. Throughout 1945 and the first two-thirds of 1946, the acclaim for Akhmatova continued. Then, as Stalin's alter ego, Zhdanov struck. At his urging, the Central Committee of the Communist Party condemned Akhmatova and Leningrad's brilliant master of satire Mikhail Zoshchenko as decadent relics of the past and strongly censured the Leningrad literary journals that had published their work.

Three weeks later, Zhdanov called a special meeting of the Leningrad branch of the Union of Soviet Writers, read them the Central Committee's Resolution, and demanded that they expel Akhmatova and Zoshchenko from their ranks. "Leningrad should not be a haven for all kinds of slimy literary rogues who want to exploit Leningrad for their own goals," he told his stunned listeners.[111] Akhmatova's poetry, he went on in a meeting that lasted for seven hours, undermined the morals of Russia's youth and was hopelessly decadent in that it could only "sow despondency, spiritual depression, and the desire to walk away from the urgent questions of public life."[112] For this, he announced, Akhmatova must be condemned, and her work no longer published.

Once expelled from the Writer's Union, Akhmatova received no pay and no ration coupons. For too many years, this woman whose poetry so intimately told of life and suffering in Leningrad had to live on the charity of friends, condemned to obscurity and silence. "I was famous, then I was very infamous," she remarked to a friend. "I am convinced that essentially it's one and the same thing."[113]

Having silenced Leningrad's greatest poet, Zhdanov then turned on the city's greatest composer. He declared that any music which did not have "a melody that could be hummed" was degenerate,[114] and for transforming music into "a chaotic conglomeration of sounds" that reflected the decadent "spirit of American and European music," he condemned Shostakovich to silence as well.[115] The acclaim that had greeted Shostakovich's *Leningrad* Symphony faded in an instant. From Akhmatova, Zoshchenko, and Shostakovich, the condemnations spread to others, particularly to Olga Berggolts, whose daily readings on Radio Leningrad had done so much to give heart to Leningraders during the worst days of the siege. No one in the Kremlin wanted to be reminded of that suffering now. Officially it was transformed into willing work for a higher purpose. That people had died from hunger by the hundreds of thousands was now to be forgotten (it would be remembered again after Stalin's death), and the Museum of the Defense of Leningrad was suddenly closed. One day, all the blue and white signs that had warned citizens which side of the street was the most dangerous during the Germans' shelling disappeared. Accounts of the siege that contained anything in any way "gloomy," "terrible," "negative," "frightening," "demoralizing," or "disquieting" could not be published.[116] Olga Berggolts collected them all in her apartment, and every month, the pile of papers marked

"N. O." for "*ne opublikovano*"—"not published"—grew larger. This was the manner in which Zhdanov (and through him Stalin) chose to make it clear that all contacts between Russia and the West—and especially the contacts between Western-oriented Leningrad and the West—must end. Once again, the culture of the West had become decadent, degenerate, and very dangerous.

But there was more to the new wave of persecutions in Leningrad than an effort to cut the city off from the West. As always in the Soviet Union artists and writers were only the first victims of political warfare, and Zhdanov's death in 1948 marked the beginning of a savage effort by Malenkov to obliterate his lieutenants and the thousands of minor officials who had served him. Not only was the Museum of the Defense of Leningrad closed, but its director was sent to Siberia, and all the documents relating to the siege were locked away where no historian was allowed to see them for more than a quarter of a century. Zhdanov's speeches disappeared, and none of his papers were published. The volume of materials about the siege that he had ordered collected in 1944 was never published during the Soviet era, nor were several others to which some of the city's leading writers and artists had contributed. History was to be changed, and so was memory insofar as was humanly possible.

Dreams that Leningrad would become Russia's new gateway to the West were shattered and buried, and it was decided that the Soviet Union would have no gateway to the West at all. War damage in Moscow was repaired. So was the destruction in Kiev, Odessa, Minsk, and Stalingrad. Leningrad came last in line, as if no one in the Kremlin wanted to remember that it existed at all. Although the official burying place for all who died in the siege starting in February 1942 was the Piskarevskoe Cemetery, its memorials were not put in place until 1960. That was when each of the huge hecatombs was marked, and when Olga Berggolts's final tribute to the Leningraders who died in the siege was carved there in stone:

> Here lie Leningraders,
> The men, women, and children of the city,
> Alongside the fighting men of the Red Army.
> All gave their lives
> In defending you, O Leningrad,
> Cradle of the revolution.

We cannot list the names
Of the noble ones who lie beneath this eternal granite.
But of those honored by this stone
Let no one forget, let nothing be forgotten.[117]

Whatever the policies of their leaders, Leningraders' memories of those nine hundred days would never fade, for that was when their city had been redefined and had taken on a new identity. "St. Petersburg, Petrograd had gone forever," the Russian-born British correspondent Alexander Werth wrote after he had visited the city in wartime. "One no more felt like calling Leningrad 'St. Petersburg' or 'Petrograd,'" he added, "than one felt like calling Stalingrad 'Tsaritsyn'."[118] The siege had fixed the city and its name in people's minds for all time. The city of Peter was the home of the Bronze Horseman, the Admiralty, St. Isaac's, the Kazan Cathedral, and the Winter Palace. People remembered it as the cradle of the Revolution, the city of Pushkin, Gogol, Dostoevskii, and Aleksandr Blok. Leningrad was the city of Shostakovich, of Akhmatova, of Olga Berggolts, and the siege of nine hundred days, and no one who had lived through that terrible yet exhilarating time would ever think of it in any other way. When they met in 1945, Akhmatova told Isaiah Berlin quite emphatically that she had been formed in St. Petersburg. But the city that had endured the siege was in her mind Leningrad, not St. Petersburg. "My life has been spared to mourn," she wrote to the nameless heroes of the nine hundred days. "Everyone down on your knees!" she continued. "A crimson light pours! And Leningraders come through the smoke in even rows—the living and the dead: for glory never dies."[119]

Thanks to its defenders between 1941 and 1944, Leningrad had not been occupied by a hostile army. It was the only major city on the European continent that could make that claim. But what was its fate to be? And where was it headed? Akhmatova once had written that "just as the future ripens in the past, so the past smolders in the future."[120] How past and future would come together in Leningrad no one knew when Stalin died in 1953, nor did they know the answer when Khrushchev gave his famous secret speech condemning Stalin to the XX Party Congress in 1956. The answers to those questions lay in the way events unfolded in the 1960s, 1970s, and 1980s, when Leningraders would march together in step as they worked to fulfill a vision that time would never make entirely clear.

# ELEVEN

# TOGETHER
# IN STEP

"COLLECTIVES" OF INDIVIDUALS working together to achieve common goals stood at the very heart of the Soviet vision of a Communist society. In factories, on farms, in schools, and in government offices all across the Soviet Union, Bolsheviks envisioned "collectives" of dedicated men and women working to bring the greatest good to the greatest number at the same time as each member realized his or her greatest potential as an individual. In October 1917, Lenin's victorious Bolsheviks had thought that such a utopia could be created almost overnight, and that world revolution would follow within a few months or years at most. But when hopes for utopia and world revolution faded, Stalin adopted a course that envisioned the more gradual realization of Socialism in the Soviet Union before moving on to Communism. Socialism in one country was possible, Stalin had insisted. So long as war with the capitalist West could be postponed, dedicated proletarians could use the unlimited natural resources of the fallen Russian Empire to create first Socialism and then Communism. What the Bolsheviks had hoped to accomplish between 1917 and 1921 would eventually come to pass, Stalin had promised. But it would require more time, effort, and patience than had previously been thought.

In the history of Leningrad, the 1920s and 1930s thus became known as the "era of the construction of Socialism,"[1] in which socialist competition between "collectives" of all sorts worked to build the society of opportunity and social justice that the Bolsheviks envisioned. Because World War II and the Nazi siege had interrupted that process, the two decades after 1945 became "the time of completing the construction of Socialism and the gradual transition to Communism" (the subtitle of the sixth volume of the huge *Essays on the History of Leningrad* that the Soviet Academy of Sciences published in 1970).[2] But by 1989, when the seventh and final volume of the *Essays* appeared, any idea of a transition to Communism had fallen by the wayside. Well before the 1960s ended, the work of Leningrad's "collectives" had degenerated into a deadening process of marching together in step toward goals that were more propagandistic than real. The "transition to Communism" had proved to be little more than a farcical era of slogans. By then, the vision and ideals for which so many dedicated Bolsheviks had given their lives in the 1920s had long since faded into oblivion.

But forces other than the socialist competitions so esteemed by the Bolsheviks did make "collectives" work on some occasions. Patriotism helped, and so did a feeling of being tied to Leningrad's history. During the siege, being part of a "collective" had been important to Orbeli and the heroes of the Hermitage, to Olga Berggolts and the heroes of Radio Leningrad, and to those thousands of men and women who had chosen to live at their places of work between 1941 and 1944. Postwar Leningrad was destined to live differently. With barely six hundred thousand people remaining alive when the first link in the German siege was broken in January 1943, the city would not regain its prewar population until 1965. And because so many Leningraders had been killed or left in the places to which they had been evacuated, the city's postwar population would be made up largely of newcomers who had to be absorbed into the fabric of its daily life.

Unlike the men and women who had lived through the siege, Leningrad's new citizens of the late 1940s, 1950s, and 1960s had to find ways to fit themselves into the city's traditions. With no previous ties to the city to which they had come, many had almost no knowledge of their adopted city's history, and even less understanding of the part it had played in Russia's transformation from a medieval kingdom to the nation that had destroyed the armies of Nazi Germany on the Eastern Front. It took time for them to acquire that special arrogance that had distinguished the many generations who had identified with the city's past and present since the days of Catherine the Great. How they would understand their new heritage and what they would do with it did much to shape the destiny of Leningrad for the rest of the twentieth century.

The fact that World War II transformed Leningrad from a city of men into a city of women meant that its newcomers would define their relationship to it differently than had those who came before. As the command center of the Russian army and the imperial bureaucracy since the days of Peter the Great, Romanov St. Petersburg had always drawn large numbers of men to it, and its rise as the center of Russia's heavy industry in the middle of the nineteenth century had attracted even more. At the beginning of the twentieth century, peasant women had moved to St. Petersburg to work in its textile mills, and for a while they outnumbered the city's men. But the first Five-Year plans had attracted more men than women until war had shifted the tide. The Russo-Finnish War and World War II had slaughtered Leningrad's men at an appalling rate, and when the city's population started to increase again in 1944, it was women who filled the places left vacant by the men who had gone to war.[3] Leningrad's new women came from villages whose names few had ever heard. Many had ended their schooling after just a few years, and they often had almost no training in the jobs for which they were hired. These were not people who read in their leisure hours, and their view of the world was correspondingly narrower than that of the workers whose places they filled. But the difficulties of daily life in postwar Leningrad compounded by the extra training their jobs demanded left them little time for leisure in any case. For many of them daily life continued to be focused mainly on survival.[4]

Between March 1943 and September 1945, this tidal wave of young women doubled Leningrad's population to one and a quarter million. By 1948, scarcely one worker in eight in the city's textile mills, and barely more than one in three in its machine-building plants, could claim to have had any connection with Leningrad before the war. More than six out of every ten were under thirty, and one in four had not yet reached twenty. Women held three out of every five jobs in Leningrad's steel mills and machine-building plants, and nine out of every ten in the factories that produced textiles and consumer goods. They had little experience with the political processes in which Leningrad had always played such a major part, and they were hesitant to enter the arena of local and national politics too quickly. Between 1940 and 1945, Communist Party membership in Leningrad fell by nearly a half. While one out of every ten national Party members had come from Leningrad at the time of Kirov's murder in 1934, only one in fifty did so just ten years later.[5]

Weakened by such reduced numbers, the Leningrad Party found itself tossed and heaved in the treacherous eddies of Soviet politics during the decade after the war, and that caused its visions of the city's future to shift dramatically. As the Red Army marched West, Zhdanov had begun to speak of an entirely transformed city, much larger than before, with its great architectural monuments rebuilt and whole new sections added. In Zhdanov's plan for a Leningrad Renaissance, huge squares were to be created and grandiose new buildings built. Central gas heat would replace old wood stoves and furnaces, and an even larger network of public transportation would move millions of workers back and forth across the city. The new Leningrad would claim much more than its fair share of the Soviet reconstruction budget, would produce far more consumer goods than before, and would trade extensively with the West. But the planners of 1944 and 1945 had no doubt that money used for restoration and construction would be well spent. No other modern city had ever proved so enduring as Leningrad, and many thought it had come to stand during the siege as a true monument to the soul and will of Russia itself. Rebuilt and transformed, Leningrad would become the new "heart of Europe,"[6] the novelist and international correspondent Ilia Ehrenburg promised. There was even talk that it would once again replace dowdy, peasant Moscow as the Soviet capital.

The chauvinist campaign against art and culture that Zhdanov launched at Stalin's urging in 1946 changed Leningrad's fate overnight. Men and women were sent to Siberia just as readily between 1946 and 1953 as they had been between 1934 and 1940, and the reasons for the tragedies that befell them were no more clear or less whimsical. Many of the people who had led the Leningrad Party during the war were shot before 1950, the dean of Leningrad University was driven out of office, and the city's innovative film studios were practically shut down. Art, poetry, fiction, history, and music all became dangerous pursuits, but work on restoring the physical remains of the city's past seemed more safe. Leningraders therefore drew closer to the great buildings of Trezzini, Rastrelli, Quarenghi, Vallin de la Mothe, Rossi, and any number of others that could be rebuilt as monuments to Russia's national achievement. These now were thought to be as much a part of the city of Lenin as they were of the city of Peter the Great.

It was in this way that women from Rybinsk and Kostroma, men from Orel, teenagers from Ukraine, and new graduates from specialized schools and technological institutes in faraway Irkutsk, Kiev, and Kazan began to become Leningraders during the decade after the war. Whether peasant, worker, or intellectual, whether a Party member or not, and whether Russian, Jew, Tatar, or any of a score of other nationalities who made up the city's population, no one who came to postwar Leningrad could escape the feeling of being in a place that was different from every other in the Soviet Union. People who had never seen a building higher than two stories and whose sense of a town was a group of buildings laid out along a single paved street could not help being awed by the Winter Palace, the General Staff Headquarters, the Peter and Paul Fortress, the Cathedrals of Our Lady of Kazan and St. Isaac, Smolnyi, and a score of other significant eighteenth- and early-nineteenth-century buildings, shattered though they might be. Nor could they fail to be impressed by the massive blocks of workers' apartments that had taken shape along International Prospekt (renamed after Stalin at the end of the war) in the 1930s. Newcomers thus began to acquire a sense of pride of place, especially as the city came back to life. Some found more grandeur in Leningrad than in Moscow, but they also found more gloom, especially during the years that separated the death of Zhdanov in 1948 from that of Stalin in 1953.

All through these years the Leningrad Affair hung like a dark cloud over the city. For the better part of a century, St. Petersburg's intellectuals had remembered the time between 1848 and 1855 as the "dark and dismal seven-year era," and now, exactly a hundred years later, another dismal seven-year era came upon them. It began, as its predecessor had, with the persecution of the city's intellectuals. Then—and again as had happened a century before, the focus shifted from the arts to politics. This time, its roots lay in the conflict between Zhdanov and Georgii Malenkov, one of the chief perpetrators of the Great Purges of 1936–1938, and a rival for a place in Stalin's inner circle. When Zhdanov died in 1948,

Malenkov, with the support of secret police chief Lavrentii Beria, declared war on his supporters and launched a reign of terror against the city that had served as Zhdanov's power base. Almost certainly due to Malenkov's efforts, both of Zhdanov's successors as First Secretary of the Leningrad Party organization—Aleksei Kuznetsov and Petr Popkov— were shot, and one of Malenkov's creatures put in their place. But the purge reached much further. It affected not only politics in Leningrad and the Kremlin, but also the course that the city's life would follow for several decades to come.

During 1949 and 1950, Malenkov and Beria drove Leningrad's high officials from office, along with another two thousand lesser officeholders. These people had begun their careers under Kirov in the early 1930s and had worked together to build the industrial base called for in the First Five-Year plans. They had helped to lead Leningrad through the terrors of the siege, and many were still in their forties when the war came to an end. In the words of the Yugoslav Communist Milovan Djilas, they were "educated, hardworking people who had taken on their shoulders . . . the tragic greatness of the city."[7] Bound together by the experiences they had shared, they threatened to become a powerful voice that might one day speak out on behalf of Leningrad. Fearful of any political force that did not depend directly on him, Stalin therefore seems to have allowed Malenkov and Beria to manufacture false evidence against Leningrad's officials in order to get them out of the way. As expected, their fall weakened the city's influence in the highest Soviet policy-making circles. And it effectively took away any chance there might have been for Zhdanov's grandiose plan for the city's recovery from the destruction of World War II to be put into practice.[8] For Zhdanov's plan stood in conflict with the further development of heavy industry that Stalin saw as the cornerstone of the Soviet Union's recovery after World War II. As in the rest of the Soviet Union, the development in Leningrad of factories capable of maintaining the nation's new dominance in international affairs took precedence over everything else.

When World War II ended in Europe, Stalin's planners had taken stock of the devastation that Hitler's armies had inflicted upon the Soviet land and people. Some 1,700 towns and 70,000 villages had been destroyed wholly or in part, along with 6 million buildings, 84,000 schools, 31,000 factories, and 1,300 bridges. The war had cost the Soviet Union 7 million horses, 17 million head of cattle, 20 million hogs, and 27 million sheep and goats, not to mention 137,000 tractors, 49,000 combine-harvesters, 15,000 locomotives, 400,000 railway cars, 100,000 collective farms, and tens of millions of people.[9] Anxious to repair these terrible losses and preserve the status that their country had gained in the international arena during the war, Stalin and his associates put heavy industry first in planning their nation's recovery. Leningrad received the capital needed to rebuild its factories, but all dreams of a greater renaissance had to be canceled. The city had lost three million square meters of housing space during the war, but the funds allocated for housing in 1945 were scarcely more than they had been in 1940.[10] With an average of more than three families still living in each apartment in 1951, Leningraders would be obliged to share communal facilities for at least another generation, and it would not be until the very late 1970s that a Leningrad family of four could expect to have housing space equal to a modest one-bedroom apartment in New York City.[11]

Leningrad's postwar reconstruction was therefore tied to heavy industry hand and foot. As a key Soviet producer of precision instruments and high-quality industrial goods starting in the 1950s, Leningrad developed a larger scientific research community to add to its industrial capacity as the years went by. Home to almost a million specialists with higher or specialized secondary educations by the early 1980s, Leningrad produced a tenth of all Soviet export machinery, more than a half of all its turbines and generators, and more than a quarter of all its printing facilities, even though it encompassed less than a thirtieth of the nation's total industrial capacity. As its planners began to build gigantic housing blocks in nearby vacant lands, Leningrad sprawled first to the south and then to the north so that by 1980 it covered thirteen times as much ground as it had in 1917. Still many of its people continued to prefer the congestion of the city's center to the openness of its suburbs, and the early 1980s still found a quarter of all Leningraders crowded into a center that covered a mere seven-tenths of a single percent of its territory.[12]

In the late 1950s, half of all Leningraders lived in the center of the city, but by 1980, three-quarters of them lived outside it, with their numbers being almost evenly divided between the intermediate and outer regions.[13] As postwar Leningrad expanded outward into its new Krasnoselskii, Zhdanovskii, Vyborgskii, Kalinskii, and Krasnogvardeiskii districts, its people relied on public transportation more than ever, for the days of walking from one side of the city to the other in an hour or less had long since passed. In 1953, some 1,250 kilometers of public transport routes moved nearly 1.4 billion passengers across the city. Thirty years later, Leningrad's bus, streetcar, and subway lines had increased two and a half times, and they carried 3.25 billion riders every year. By that time, Leningraders were traveling over five kilometers each time they bought a ticket, often wearily transferring from subway, to streetcar, to bus as they went to and from work, tried to buy food for the family dinner, or did errands on their days off.[14]

In the 1970s and 1980s, the city subway—officially known as the Metropolitan Named After V. I. Lenin—moved the most Leningraders over the longest distances. After the stunning success that the Moscow subway had enjoyed from the moment it opened in the mid-1930s, Soviet planners had begun to lay out a subway system for Leningrad only to have its construction delayed by the outbreak of World War II. Leningrad's first subway line therefore did not open until the thirty-eighth anniversary of the Bolshevik Revolution, on November 7, 1955. After that, new subway lines moved with the city's expansion deeper into the surrounding countryside until, by 1990, four lines with forty-nine stations reached from the far southern suburbs of Dachnoe and Aleksandrovskoe to their northern counterparts beyond Ozerki and Murino. Designed to move people from the outer districts of Leningrad to its railroad stations, key factories, and central shopping districts, these lines intersected with bus and streetcar routes that funneled riders to and from the subway. At the end of its first decade, the Leningrad subway was moving a third of a billion passengers every year. By its twenty-fifth anniversary that number had risen to nearly three-quarters of a billion, many of them coming from the still sparsely populated suburbs.[15]

Like their counterparts in Moscow, Leningrad's architects designed its subway stations to be People's Palaces, to which each and every citizen who could pay the five-kopek fare (which equaled the cost of half an ounce of beef or a third of a pound of bread) had equal access. Especially in the suburbs, men and women lived gray lives in massive blocks of apartment buildings that grew more nondescript with each decade that passed, yet sixty to ninety seconds spent on an escalator could bring any of these people into a subterranean realm of bright light, marble, crystal, and bronze. Here shining inlaid marble floors replaced dirty streets and sidewalks, and heroic statues vied with huge murals to portray the glorious future into which Communism would lead them. In Leningrad's subway

*Leningrad's first metro station, Narvskaia. (Courtesy of the Central State Archive of Kino-Photo-Phono Documents, St. Petersburg)*

stations, every citizen became a prince or princess of the future. They rode not in grimy, graffiti-smeared cars like those found in New York City and London, but in shining steel coaches that arrived quickly and left quietly to speed them on their way.

During the 1950s, the city's grandiose subterranean subway stations were the only reminders of Zhdanov's wartime vision of a Leningrad Renaissance. In 1960, that began to change with the installation of the powerful Mother-Homeland statue at the Piskarevskoe Cemetery and the completion of the huge ensemble of hecatombs and granite walls that went with it. As it became possible for Leningrad to celebrate the heroes of its defense against the Nazis once again, this was followed by other gigantic war monuments. Between 1975 and 1977, the city's artists and architects placed a towering Monument to the Heroic Defenders of Leningrad in the center of Victory Square, near the far southern end of Moscow Prospekt (the former Stalin Prospekt) in the vicinity of Dachnoe and Kupchino. Here clusters of heroic fighting men and women cast in bronze stood atop two granite platforms, from the very center of which rose a huge polished granite monolith.[16]

Huge hotels, concert halls, office buildings, and sports complexes, each set in the center of a vast empty square, showed that Leningrad was

*The subway platform—one of Leningrad's "People's Palaces"—in the Avtovo station.*
*(Courtesy of the Central State Archive of Kino-Photo-Phono Documents, St. Petersburg)*

spreading out into regions that Peter and Catherine the Great could never have imagined would ever have come within the boundaries of their capital. In all this there was a certain grandeur, but an emptiness, too, for these monumental new constructions lacked the integrity and brilliance that had marked the work of the great builders who had served Russia's emperors and empresses. There was too much space, too little talent displayed in its use, and too little connection with the surrounding environment for most of the monuments created in Soviet Leningrad during the 1960s, 1970s, and 1980s to match the work of Rastrelli, de Thomon, or Rossi. Nor could they equal the brilliance of the creations of Montferrand, Zakharov, Voronikhin, or half a dozen other of the Soviets' imperial predecessors. To that generalization, perhaps, the deeply emotional monuments of the Piskarevskoe Cemetery remained a striking exception. Nothing from the imperial era ever matched their ability to

*The burial mounds in Piskarevskoe Memorial Cemetery each hold some twenty thou-
sand victims of the nine-hundred-day siege. (Photo by M. Shirman. Courtesy of the Central
State Archive of Kino-Photo-Phono Documents, St. Petersburg)*

wrench those chords that responded to the deepest of human emotions
in the hearts of natives and visitors alike. Grief, sadness, and deep, enduring hatred for the enemies who had inflicted such devastation upon
millions of innocents all flowed from the cemetery's monuments.
Nowhere else did stone, bronze, and simple mounds of earth stir the
viewer's feelings so deeply.

Leningrad's memorials and monuments to World War II inevitably
posed a disturbing question, the irony of which could only be extracted
from the pages of the city's, and Russia's, history. During the reign of
Nicholas I between 1825 and 1855—almost exactly a hundred years before Stalin's reign of terror—St. Petersburg's intellectuals had struggled to
understand the meaning of history, art, truth, and faith so as to determine
what place they had in the politically repressive world that surrounded
them. Called "cursed questions" in those earlier times, these were all an-

swered by Stalin's interpretations of Marxist-Leninist dogma, which placed each person firmly within the "collective" and set the meaning of history, art, and truth within the sure and certain framework of the dialectic Marx and Lenin had embraced. Yet as the 1960s shaded into the 1970s, Leningrad's postwar monuments persistently confronted thoughtful people with new "cursed questions" more dangerous than any that had confronted the intellectuals of the Nicholas era. Did the brutality of Hitler's Nazi invaders differ from that of Stalin, the NKVD, and its postwar successor, the KGB? And, how did the repressions of the present compare with the tyranny of the past?

Dmitrii Shostakovich seems to have felt all along that Hitler and Stalin represented two forms of tyranny that were similarly oppressive and equally cruel, and others came to the same conclusion. But the contrast between the persecutions of the Stalin era and those of the regime of Nicholas I was even more striking. With every Soviet schoolchild being taught the stories of the Decembrists and others who had been condemned to Siberian exile for criticizing the government of Nicholas I, who in Leningrad could not draw parallels between them and the victims of Stalin's time? Nicholas I's victims had numbered in the hundreds, but Stalin's had soared into the millions. Especially after Khrushchev's not-so-secret speech to the XX Party Congress in 1956, Leningraders knew that the tyranny of Stalin had surpassed anything in their history many times over.

Despite the many stories of tsarist oppression highlighted in Soviet books and films, the fact remained that only five men had been executed during Nicholas I's thirty-year reign. But each and every one of Leningrad's intellectuals knew of dozens who had been shot and of hundreds more who had disappeared. In those earlier times, the Tsar himself had proclaimed that the state must care for the widows, orphans, and families of people punished for political transgressions. But who among the intellectuals of Soviet Leningrad had not known the gut-wrenching fear of being found guilty by association when a relative or friend had been arrested? Wives had been condemned to penal servitude for the supposed sins of their husbands, and children for the transgressions of their parents or grandparents. It took very little imagination and almost no knowledge of history to know that the so-called tyranny of Nicholas I and the emperors who had come before and after him was very mild compared to the war that Stalin had waged against the Russians between 1928 and 1953.

Every Leningrad schoolchild also had read about the long years of confinement endured by Russia's nineteenth-century revolutionaries. Again and again, the hagiographies of Soviet revolutionary heroes told of young men and women imprisoned under harsh conditions that had permitted them to read only a few books at a time, allowed only limited access to writing materials, and authorized visits from loved ones only rarely. But who could fail to compare these experiences with those of the millions of victims who had languished in Stalin's forced labor camps and the millions more who had endured the agonies of NKVD prisons, where prisoners starved to death, and where books and writing materials were almost never seen? Especially as these victims returned home after 1956 and their memoir accounts of life in Stalin's camps and prisons—meticulously transcribed by hand or typed on carbons filched from government offices—began to circulate in the Leningrad underground (there was a time when carbon paper and typewriter ribbons could be bought only on the black market), it became clear how vicious the oppressions of the Stalin era had been and how little hope there was that the system that had spawned them would change.

Zhdanov's condemnation of Akhmatova as "either a nun or a whore" continued to be repeated in the Soviet press well into the 1960s, and so did his charge that Mikhail Zoshchenko was a "literary hooligan." All of the men and women who had fled the Bolshevik Revolution to win fame in the West continued to be branded as traitors to the Soviet homeland—writers such as Vladimir Nabokov and Ivan Bunin, painters such as Marc Chagall and Vasilii Kandinskii, composers such as Igor Stravinskii, dancers and choreographers such as George Balanchine, and scores of others. Yet, as pressures from within and without opened small fissures in the wall with which Stalin had surrounded Russia, Leningraders began to discover the brilliant cultural achievements from which they had been separated for more than a quarter of a century. There was much in the West, and much that Russians had accomplished in the West, that had been concealed from them for too long. Was there a way to bring these treasures back to Leningrad? And how great was the risk in doing so?

A sense of gloom that all too often shaded into hopelessness hung over Leningrad after the brief "thaw" of 1956–1962 ended. As their forebears had done when they had sought liberation through alcohol during the Nicholaevan era, so Leningrad's intellectuals again turned to drink as the last traces of their earlier idealism vanished. "We drank fantastic amounts," the poet Lev Loseff remembered. "I owe everything good in my life to vodka," he added. "Vodka was the catalyst of spiritual emancipation, opening doors into interesting cellars of the subconscious and at the same time teaching me not to be afraid—of people or the authorities."[17] For some, perhaps, that was true, but for most Leningraders life simply became unbearably boring as the long twilight of the Brezhnev years settled upon their city and Russia.

In part because of boredom but mainly because they wanted to become a part of the vibrant, pulsating postwar world that lay just beyond the Finnish frontier, Leningraders struggled to expand their contacts with the West even as Zhdanov and Stalin began their war against its culture. Jazz, which continued to project a sense of modernity, youthfulness, and energy, offered one way to maintain contact with the outside world despite the dangers it posed for the musicians who played it and the audiences who listened. Starting with the arrest of the Polish-Soviet jazz hero Eddie Rosner late in 1946, most Soviet jazzmen were imprisoned or silenced, with saxophonists taking the brunt of the assault, since they were particularly associated in the minds of the authorities with music that was "hot."[18]

Since saxophones had never been produced in the Soviet Union, they had been made available to jazz bands by the government, which, in 1949, required every instrument to be turned in and its user's work papers to be changed to show that he played some other instrument. But jazz survived, sometimes in the most unexpected places. Sentenced to penal servitude in the terrible Kolyma death camps of Siberia's Northeast, Eddie Rosner fell in with a camp commandant who arranged for him to put together a quartet made up of the best musicians to be found in the region's camps. Rosner's ensemble ended up playing for Panteleimon Derevenko, head of the entire Dalstroi prison camp network, and his elephantine wife Galina. Following in the footsteps of their predecessor Ivan Nikishov and his wife Maria Gridasova (whom the U.S. Vice President Henry Wallace once called charming "pioneers of the machine age [and] builders of cities"),[19] the Derevenkos maintained a theater at the Magadan forced labor camp, and Rosner's musicians became one of its chief attractions.[20]

By the time Rosner became a regular feature at gatherings the Derevenkos sponsored at the Magadan House of Culture, his quartet had grown into an orchestra that featured several musicians from what had been Moscow's leading jazz bands. Elsewhere in the Soviet Union, jazz flourished in such out-of-the-way provincial cities as Kazan, where Oleg

Lundstrem, a third-generation Russian from Siberia, managed to play arrangements by Fletcher Henderson, Duke Ellington, and Glenn Miller all through the years of the *Zhdanovshchina*. Some of Lundstrem's broadcasts were picked up in the wee morning hours by fans of hot music in Moscow. "These were the sounds of heaven coming not from New York or Paris but from Kazan," one young musician remembered.[21] During those years, the sounds of jazz also echoed from the capital cities of the Baltic Republics—from Riga, Vilnius, and most of all Tallinn, where a Swing Club of young musicians began experiments with jazz that led them to the music of Stan Kenton, Charlie Parker, and Dizzy Gillespie.[22]

Like so many other forms of art, jazz returned to Leningrad slowly during the 1950s, 1960s, and 1970s. As larger groups of Europeans visited the city for weekends and holidays, Western recordings began to slip past Soviet customs agents in greater numbers. Enterprising Leningraders turned these treasures from the West into bootleg recordings made on used X-ray plates (hence the nickname "bone music"),[23] and from them new groups drew inspiration that they started to display in a handful of the city's restaurants in the late 1950s and early 1960s. Once again, Iosif Weinstein's orchestra (famous two decades earlier as the Kronstadt District Navy Jazz Orchestra) began to play the classics of Glenn Miller, Harry James, and Duke Ellington, to which it soon added arrangements by Count Basie and Buddy Rich. With a singer who sounded like Frank Sinatra and rare skill in negotiating with ham-handed bureaucrats, Weinstein made his band into the premier performer of jazz in the USSR between 1955 and 1965, although others could lay ready claim to being more "modern." Two of Weinstein's leading bandsmen, trumpeter Konstantin Nosov and saxophonist Gennadi Golstein (the latter played an instrument that his uncle had somehow managed to smuggle to him from New York City) both had a large following in post-Stalin Leningrad, and by the late 1950s the city had at least ten other Dixieland bands playing in public places. Jazz really seemed to be coming back. Although their musicians were paid far less than they could have earned in orchestras that the Establishment thought more desirable, some of the new groups started to perform at the White Nights Cafe and the Neva Restaurant in the heart of the city.

The first club of jazz fans in the Soviet Union was founded in Leningrad in 1958, and it was quickly followed by a second formed among the students at Leningrad State University. The term "swinging"

*Iosif Weinstein's jazz orchestra, 1967. (Courtesy of the Central State Archive of Kino-Photo-Phono Documents, St. Petersburg)*

*(svingovanie)* came into the Russian language just in time for Benny Goodman's tour of the USSR in 1962. Goodman's stay in Leningrad, which included an all-night jam session at the Astoria Hotel at which Golstein and several other top musicians played with the Americans, brought jazz even more prominently into the public eye. But a few months later, Khrushchev unleashed his tirade against modern art at Ilia Beliutin's exhibit in Moscow. When, in the Kremlin leader's earthy language, the government declared war on all such producers of "dog shit,"[24] jazz was included along with modern art. Two years of nervous waiting followed. Only after Khrushchev was driven from the Kremlin in 1964 could the fans of Western music breath a momentary sigh of relief. During the early years of the Brezhnev era, the Leningrad Jazz Club played a prominent part of the city's musical life. Then the forces that worked against influences from the West started to pile up once again.[25]

　　At the beginning of 1967, several dissidents were put on trial in the Soviet Union. In May, Stalin's daughter fled to the West, and a few months after that the client states supported by the Soviet Union in the Middle

East lost the Six-Day War to Israel. Less than a year later, Andrei Sakharov, who had fathered the Soviet hydrogen bomb at the age of thirty-two, challenged the authorities by publishing his *Thoughts on Progress, Peaceful Coexistence, and Intellectual Freedom* in the West. Then the Czech crisis, which had been brewing for several months, burst into a full-fledged confrontation late in the summer of 1968, when Brezhnev sent the Red Army into Prague in force. Jazz became dangerous once again. A few years later, a critic lamented that the period from 1968 to 1970 "appears to have been the most stagnant years for jazz in our country."[26] But the truth was that interest had shifted, as the Beatles and the Rolling Stones swept aside the older loyalties that had been formed during Russia's modern jazz revolution of the 1950s.[27]

In the late 1960s, rock bands began to spring up all across the USSR, multiplying "like rabbits," as one cult figure said.[28] Among them in Leningrad was the group formed by Georgii Ordanovskii, while another combo called the Argonauts was not far behind. But the real trailblazer in the early 1970s was Vladimir Rekshan's band, which called itself Sankt-Petersburg and rebelled against the boredom and inertia of the times. Soon, almost every factory and institute had at least one rock band, and among Soviet youth, who in 1965 spent as much time on the dance floor as on the athletic field and in the gymnasium, no dance was complete without one. Unable to stem the tide, the authorities turned to officially sponsored bands, the best known of which in Leningrad was the Singing Guitars, headed by a thirty-one-year-old saxophone player by the name of Anatolii Vasiliev, who had graduated from the Leningrad Conservatory. In 1974, this group collaborated with Aleksandr Shurbin to create *Orpheus and Eurydice*, the first official Soviet rock opera, which a number of critics called "brilliant."[29]

But such officially approved groups did nothing to stop the spread of renegade combos, whose music resounded from courtyards in the old parts of Leningrad and blared across the empty spaces that separated the massive blocks of new apartments in its outskirts. Before the end of the decade, even the Party faithful who had embraced Khrushchev's condemnation of modern popular art as "dog shit" had to accept the inevitable. With its pirated magnetic tapes, homemade guitars whose necks had been sawn out of bedroom headboards, and amplifiers made out of everything from parts stolen out of public telephones to electronics pirated from the Soviet space program, rock had become impossible to stamp out.

In 1979 Elton John performed for an audience of properly frenzied Leningrad fans. Three years later, a Moscow rock group called the Time Machine filled Leningrad's Jubilee Sports Arena with hysterical fans who created such a mob scene that the vans carrying the band had to detour and drive to the arena by a different route.

From time to time the authorities tried to dictate what could and could not be played, as they did when they forbade the Western rock group that called itself Boney M to play the new hit "Rah Rah Rasputin, Russia's Greatest Love Machine." But the prohibition only spread the infection. Within weeks, even bands in the remote Siberian city of Iakutsk were playing the song.[30] Once again, the Party had failed to define popular values and tastes. Leningraders—and young people from all parts of the Soviet Union for that matter—had insisted on having their way in defining the culture they would embrace.

By the early 1980s, the Leningrad Rock Club, having talked its way into being sponsored by the Center for Individual Amateur Performance at No. 13 Rubinshtein Street, just off the Nevskii Prospekt, took command of the city's popular music scene. At first the Club's mainstay was a band called the Aquarium, which Boris Grebenshchikov had formed several years earlier. Grebenshchikov played the guitar and wrote poetry, and his lyrics showed the influence of the turn-of-the-century Acmeists, of whom Akhmatova's first husband Nikolai Gumilev had been one of the leading figures. The authorities were quick to condemn Grebenshchikov's lyrics as "Akhmatovism," and when they banned the Aquarium from playing in the city, the audiences at the Rock Club were treated to performances by bands calling themselves Kino (Cinema), Zoopark (Zoo), and Televizor (Television). Grebenshchikov and the Aquarium continued to perform underground in places outside Leningrad, becoming something like cult figures for the city's rock fans.

In 1987, when Mikhail Gorbachev's efforts toward *perestroika* were gathering steam and a calculating Kremlin was trying to win back alienated and cynical Soviet youth, the Aquarium managed to release a record under the well-known Soviet Melodiya label. Conservatives continued to rail at music they considered "mentally and morally damaging,"[31] but in Leningrad and all across the Soviet Union rock music had become a fact of life that could no longer be eradicated by irate editorials and churlish complaints. By then, more than a year had passed since a recording of four Leningrad rock bands, including the Aquarium, had been released in

California. Like blue jeans, expensive running shoes, and VCRs brought in by Finnish weekend tourists to trade for vodka, rock music had come to Leningrad to stay.[32]

Just as Leningraders took control of their popular culture bit by bit, so they reclaimed those treasures of the fine arts that the Party had tried to smother during the Stalin era. During the second half of the nineteenth century, St. Petersburg's Mariinskii Ballet had been the most brilliant in Russia and its school, which surpassed any in the West, in large part due to the emperor's annual subsidy of two million gold rubles, trained a collection of stars that lit stages all across Europe. Elena Andreanova, Matilda Kshesinskaia, Tamara Karsavina, Vatslav Nizhinskii, and the legendary Anna Pavlova all had studied at the cloister-like Imperial Ballet School on the city's famed Theater Street. There they lived the lives of recluses while the great teachers Johannson and Cecchetti worked to shape talents that needed only to be polished to become perfect. Together these stars and teachers had brought a languishing art form back to life. Then, thanks to the genius of Diagilev, they had taken the ballet from St. Petersburg back to Paris and London in productions that left their audiences and critics stunned.

Still dedicated to perfection, the school and the ballet had lived through the Revolutions of 1917, the purges of the 1930s, and the horrors of the Nazi siege. But like everything else in Russia, the ballet (renamed the Kirov after 1934) did not emerge from the Stalin era unscathed. Stalin's paranoia cut Leningrad's teachers and dancers off from the daring experiments that Ballet School expatriates led by Diagilev and his famed Ballets Russes were developing in the West. The artists Lev Bakst and Aleksandr Benois had left Russia by then to work on Diagilev's sets, and so had Natalia Goncharova and Marc Chagall. Anna Pavlova, marooned in the West by the outbreak of World War I, now danced Fokin's *Dying Swan* on stages all around the world. And Georgii Balanchivadze, soon to win fame as the New York City Ballet's George Balanchine, was in Paris by then, as was his life-long collaborator Igor Stravinskii.

Balanchine's experiments with increasingly "plotless" ballets won acclaim from aesthetes who were seeking to embrace both modernism and classicism in the arts, but in Leningrad, where ideological considerations muddied the debate about technique, modernism, and classical ballet, different problems demanded different solutions. The first problem, of course, was to find dancers. Some of the leading performers of the Imperial Mariinskii Ballet had fled to the West during the first few weeks after the Bolsheviks seized power, and others had joined them as soon as it became clear that the Revolution might not produce as much artistic freedom as they had been led to believe. The bitter, painful months of the Civil War added to the ballet's difficulties, because the dancers at the Mariinskii found it no easier to eat and stay warm during the freezing winters of 1918 and 1919 than did anyone else. Under the stern, exacting eye of the irascible Agrippina Vaganova, whose relentless pursuit of precision transformed native genius into artistic perfection, the Mariinskii Ballet School produced its first class of post-Revolution graduates in 1925.[33] Only then did the Soviet ballet begin to come to life.

The Mariinskii's dancers and choreographers needed to find ways to make the fundamentally aristocratic medium of ballet accessible to the masses, who now sat in the places of the ladies and lords overthrown by the Revolution. Some believed that only natural movements could capture the flavor of the new age and create visions of life that would be meaningful in a modernizing, industrializing, revolutionary society. Vaganova thought otherwise, and continued to demand clarity and precision as the only keys to perfect performance. Then in 1925, one of her first students, Marina Semenova, made her Leningrad debut in *The Brook*, and her performance is still remembered as a symbolic triumph of the classical ballet in Soviet Russia. Semenova's dancing convinced all but the most stubborn modernists that the classicists were right in the debate about technique, but it still left unanswered the larger question about how to bind the audience more closely to the performance. The new challenge, one critic explained, was "to renovate [the classical ballet and] bring its washed and lustrous surface close to the people so that the power of their imagination could create newer and richer pictures in its mirror."[34] Easily said, that turned out to be much more difficult to do. Neither ideology nor classical training could provide the insight needed to make the connection the Leningrad ballet sought to establish.

In trying to come closer to the people, Leningrad's choreographers tried blending classic and acrobatic dances in new works that reflected the world they believed was taking shape around them. Yet a number of failures soon made it clear that contemporary themes and traditional dance did not mix, and it was not until 1932, when Vasilii Vainonen's *Flames of Paris* premiered at the Mariinskii, that the proper new form was discovered. This turned out to be "choreodramas," which focused more on plot

*The Baltiskii Shipbuilding and Machine Factory, 1910. (Courtesy of the Central State Archive of Kino-Photo-Phono Documents, St. Petersburg)*

*The Putilov Factory, 1915. (Courtesy of the Central State Archive of Kino-Photo-Phono Documents, St. Petersburg)*

*Sorting cloth at a state paper factory. (Courtesy of the Central State Archive of Kino-Photo-Phono Documents, St. Petersburg)*

*Maxim Gorkii*

*Sunday afternoon on the Palace Embankment, 1913. (Courtesy of the Central State Archive of Kino-Photo-Phono Documents, St. Petersburg)*

*Electric trams at the Baltiiskii Station. (Courtesy of the Central State Archive of Kino-Photo-Phono Documents, St. Petersburg)*

*A dance lesson at the Smolnyi Institute for Young Noblewomen, 1914. (Courtesy of the Central State Archive of Kino-Photo-Phono Documents, St. Petersburg)*

*Richard Strauss directs the Court Orchestra in a benefit concert, 1913. (Courtesy of the Central State Archive of Kino–Photo–Phono Documents, St. Petersburg)*

*Restaurant in the Hotel Europa. (Courtesy of the Central State Archive of Kino-Photo-Phono Documents, St. Petersburg)*

*Rising food prices often drove St. Petersburg's poor to seek free meals, 1908. (Courtesy of the Central State Archive of Kino-Photo-Phono Documents, St. Petersburg)*

*Donon's Restaurant, 1912. (Courtesy of the Central State Archive of Kino–Photo–Phono Documents, St. Petersburg)*

*Workers' dormitory, 1909, built by the St. Petersburg Temperance Society. (Photo by K. Bulla. Courtesy of the Central State Archive of Kino–Photo–Phono Documents, St. Petersburg)*

*Workers' apartment. (Courtesy of the Central State Archive of Kino-Photo-Phono Documents, St. Petersburg)*

*Russian Headquarters of the Singer Sewing Machine Company, at 28 Nevskii Prospekt. (Courtesy of the Central State Archive of Kino-Photo-Phono Documents, St. Petersburg)*

*Leningraders lie dead after a shelling on the Nevskii Prospekt, October 1941. (Photo by D. Trakhtenberg. Courtesy of the Central State Archive of Kino-Photo-Phono Documents, St. Petersburg)*

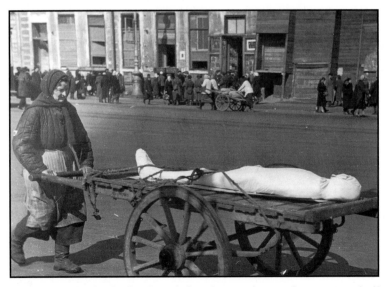

*A woman takes her husband, a victim of starvation, to the cemetery, April 1942. (Photo by R. Mazelev. Courtesy of the Central State Archive of Kino-Photo-Phono Documents, St. Petersburg)*

*A young victim of the 900-day siege of Leningrad, May 1942. (Photo by Taviavich. Courtesy of the Central State Archive of Kino-Photo-Phono Documents, St. Petersburg)*

*"A horse for food!" 1942. (Photo by D. Trakhtenberg. Courtesy of the Central State Archive of Kino-Photo-Phono Documents, St. Petersburg)*

*An emaciated Leningrader with his daily ration of bread, 1942. (Courtesy of the Central State Archive of Kino-Photo-Phono Documents, St. Petersburg)*

*A "well" on Decembrist Street. (Photo by V. Kapustin. Courtesy of the Central State Archive of Kino-Photo-Phono Documents, St. Petersburg)*

*Washing clothes after bombs destroyed the city's water towers, March 1942. (Photo by B. Losin. Courtesy of the Central State Archive of Kino-Photo-Phono Documents, St. Petersburg)*

*Dmitrii Shostakovich, composer and member of a voluntary fire brigade made up of professors and instructors from Leningrad's conservatory, 1941. (Photo by R. Mazelev. Courtesy of the Central State Archive of Kino-Photo-Phono Documents, St. Petersburg)*

*Evacuees crossing Lake Lagoda's "Ice Road," April 1942. (Photo by R. Mazelev. Courtesy of the Central State Archive of Kino-Photo-Phono Documents, St. Petersburg)*

*Cleanup on Ostrovskii Square in front of the Pushkin Drama Theater, 1943. (Photo by V. Fe-doseev. Courtesy of the Central State Archive of Kino-Photo-Phono Documents, St. Petersburg)*

*"We defended Leningrad. We will rebuild it!" Poster, 1944. (Courtesy of the Central State Archive of Kino-Photo-Phono Documents, St. Petersburg)*

development and dramatic expressiveness than on the dancers' abilities to perform dazzling movements and complicated steps. Yet the majesty of human labor in Soviet Georgia (a theme in the choreodrama *Maltavka*) and the heroism of members of the Komsomol living in the forest and fighting foreign agents (the subject of *Svetlana*, which was first performed at the Bolshoi in Moscow) proved not to provide the best vehicles for ballet. Proletarian audiences remained unmoved and unimpressed, and even Soviet critics called *Svetlana* a "pompous and naive allegory."[35]

Such failings were not to be found in *Romeo and Juliet*, the last big production of the Kirov Ballet before World War II. Pressing beyond the established principles of the form, Prokofiev structured his ballet symphonically, with laconic "musical portraits" that combined images and drama to create dynamic action.[36] At the Kirov, Leonid Lavroskii's masterful choreography supported the lyricism of the music, while Konstantin Sergeev and Galina Ulanova, who represented Leningrad's ballet tradition at its best, eloquently expressed the forces leading Romeo and Juliet to their doom. "Ulanova," one critic observed, "has discovered in Juliet a theme of deep universal appeal and a kindred spirit."[37] Ulanov's wraithlike brilliance in this role lifted her onto the exalted plane of her great prerevolutionary rivals.

Traditionalists continued to complain about not enough dancing, but a succession of much better choreodramas that stretched from *Flames of Paris* and *The Fountains of Bakhchisarai* in the early 1930s to *Romeo and Juliet* and *The Bronze Horseman* in the 1940s drew cheers from Leningrad's audiences. Some of the most accomplished ballerinas and *danseurs* of the Soviet period created their most vivid roles in these productions. Semenova, Galina Ulanova, and Natalia Dudinskaia all danced in them, and so did Vakhtang Chabukhiani and Aleksei Ermolaev, whose stunning leaps and dramatic posturing paved the way for Rudolf Nureyev and Mikhail Baryshnikov in the postwar generation.

Both Nureyev and Baryshnikov owed much of their early successes to Aleksei Pushkin, Vaganova's counterpart in teaching the male dancers at the Kirov. Convinced that Nureyev bore the stamp of genius, Pushkin took him into his class when he was about to be expelled, invited him to live in his home, and became something of a second father to him. Carefully and with great dedication, Pushkin honed Nureyev's talent so that, at his graduation concert in 1958, the young rebel from Siberia, who could hardly bear the constraints that Soviet life imposed, astounded the audience. Yet Nureyev's hunger to be free of the shackles of bureaucracy and ideology proved stronger than the deep sense of obligation he felt toward his mentor. In a sudden desperate moment as he was passing through Paris's Le Bourget Airport in 1961, he fought off his two Soviet "bodyguards" and fled to freedom in the West, where Margot Fonteyn became his new protector.[38]

Nureyev's flight made it clear that the Kirov dancers had grown tired of the straitjacket in which Stalinist bureaucrats tried to encase their art. First performed at the Kirov in 1949, *The Bronze Horseman* was the last effective choreodrama, after which the genre rapidly degenerated into a series of crude Socialist Realist stereotypes. Feeling cut off from everything new and challenging, talented dancers hungered for the chance to experiment with different interpretations and techniques. Then in 1962, just a year after Nureyev's dash to freedom, George Balanchine brought the New York City Ballet to Leningrad. After leaving the Soviet Union in 1924, Balanchine had had no desire to return. Everything about Soviet Leningrad—the transformation of the beautiful Kazan Cathedral into the Museum of the History of Religion and Atheism and even the name of the city itself—he found offensive, and he only agreed to a tour after repeated requests from the State Department. His visit to Leningrad in 1962 and his return ten years later made a powerful mark on the Kirov that led to the defection of two more of its leading dancers.[39]

For the young dancers of the Kirov, one observer wrote, Balanchine's productions made it seem "as if a gigantic sponge had washed off the dusty scenery" of the world in which they lived.[40] Especially Leonid Iakobson, who had been a student with Balanchine in the early 1920s and had remained in Leningrad when his friend had gone to the West, used the visit as a means to reclaim a few more fragments of the heritage that Stalin's agents had tried to take away. Soon afterwards, Iakobson choreographed a special role for Natalia Makarova (who defected to the West in 1970) and then created the cameo ballet *Vestris* for Mikhail Baryshnikov, another of Pushkin's students who blended stunning talent with insatiable curiosity and defected in 1974.

Dancers of such genius as Nureyev, Makarova, and Baryshnikov had to be recognized as artists of the first order who had defected to find the freedom they needed to express and develop their talent. That unarguable fact posed an awkward dilemma for liberal and radical intellectuals in the West, who since the 1920s had dismissed Russian émigrés as monarchists and political reactionaries. More urgently, these defections posed a problem for those Soviet authorities who were growing more sensitive to the political winds that blew from the United States and Europe. By the time Baryshnikov defected, the rude rhetoric of Russia's Stalinist bureaucrats had repeatedly tarnished the Soviet Union's image by condemning Boris Pasternak's and Aleksandr Solzhenitsyn's Nobel Prizes, by trying to muzzle Andrei Sakharov, and by expelling the young poet Joseph Brodsky. For writers, too, were trying to recapture the literary heritage that the Stalinists had attempted to wipe out. By 1953, many of the writings of Dostoevskii and all of the works of the Silver Age poets and such later émigrés as Ivan Bunin and Vladimir Nabokov had been officially eradicated from the world of Soviet literature. But within half a decade of Stalin's death, Leningrad's intelligentsia started a long, slow campaign to reclaim them.

They began with Fedor Dostoevskii, in many ways the most tormented writer Russia ever produced and certainly one of the greatest chroniclers of life among St. Petersburg's "insulted and injured," as he once called the men and women who crowded the festering slums near the Haymarket. Unlike Tolstoi, Dostoevskii had suffered rough treatment on several occasions at the hands of Soviet critics. "It clarifies nothing," Maksim Gorkii concluded after reading some of Dostoevskii's work. "[It] does not exalt the positive in life [and] always depicts [man] as helpless amid the chaos of dark forces."[41] Although in the 1920s there were literary critics still writing in Russia who insisted that "all contemporary literature is following in Dostoevskii's footsteps,"[42] Gorkii's view prevailed. Dostoevskii was seen as an arch-reactionary and a mystic, whose view of humankind was shaped by the brutal capitalist world that the Bolsheviks had vowed to destroy. He was, a Soviet critic explained in the early 1930s, a "chronicler . . . of the history of bourgeois renegadism," who was "most profoundly hostile to those who . . . are at present laying the foundation of Socialist society." Others dismissed him as a "complete obscurantist, the standard bearer of reactionary social groups [and] the ideologist of the enemies of socialism."[43]

Stalin's cynical efforts to stir the cauldron of Russian national sentiment during World War II rehabilitated Dostoevskii briefly. Critics lauded his many gibes at German arrogance and smugness, and acclaimed "the Russian nature of his writing." For the 125th anniversary of his birth in November 1946, long-awaited new editions of his writings appeared, and one critic even acclaimed him as "the gigantic emotional inspiration of the Russian soul." In the famous speech that Dostoevskii had delivered in Moscow at the unveiling of a monument to the poet Pushkin in 1880, critics even found a prophecy that the Soviet Union would lead the world to victory over Fascism. Dostoevskii, a leading Soviet literary scholar concluded 1947, had "a vague presentiment of the fact that the center of gravity in the struggle for socialism would be transferred to [Russia]."[44]

Exactly one year later all that changed. At Zhdanov's instigation, Dostoevskii became an "enemy of the Soviet people and the working class," the "spiritual father" of "double dealers and traitors" who had set out "to poison Russian youth with ideological venom." Critics now placed Dostoevskii "in the vanguard of reaction," and even claimed to have found evidence that tied his ideas to "the ideological lackeys of Wall Street." Almost overnight, his view of the world became a "trite, sanctimoniously witless crotchet of lifeless Christian morality." Here, the critics concluded, was an "active ideologist of reaction" who had used "the prospect of the proletarian revolution to frighten his readers." No entry on Dostoevskii appeared in a volume for children and teenagers entitled *Classics of Russian Literature* that was published in 1952. Nor was his name added to a second edition that appeared in 1954, more than a year after Stalin died.[45]

Efforts to restore Dostoevskii to Russia's literary pantheon began in 1955, when the literary scholars at Leningrad's Institute of Russian Literature and the Academy of Sciences began to make plans to celebrate the 75th anniversary of the writer's death the following year. As part of that effort, the director of Leningrad's Gorkii Dramatic Theater, Georgii Tovstonogov, began to lay plans for a stage production of Dostoevskii's novel, *The Idiot*, which presented a rare opportunity for commenting on the pain and torment of Soviet life. Both the novel and the play open with the hero Prince Myshkin coming back to St. Petersburg after a long absence, just as the "rehabilitated" victims of Stalin's purges were returning to the same city. But to bring that scene onto the Leningrad stage, Tovstonogov had to tread as if walking on eggs filled with dynamite. In the role of Prince Myshkin there was the potential to make the most dramatic statement about the pain of exile ever to be seen in Russia since the great nineteenth-century realist Ilia Repin had shown his painting *They Did Not Expect Him* in 1884. For, like Stalin's returning victims, Myshkin could be made to look at the city with amazement, his thirst to speak again with people he had thought about during his long isolation in a European hospital almost painful to see and hear.

But, as Tovstonogov knew all too well, the connection between past and present could be made only in the minds of the audience, not as the result of anything the actors did on stage. There could be nothing overt in the performance, just the suggestion of a connection that could be noticed only by people who had lived through the terrors of Stalin's time. To accomplish that feat required nothing less than genius from the actor who would play Myshkin and the director who would teach him the part. For that key role, Tovstonogov chose the young and little-known actor Innokentii Smoktunovskii. He could not have made a better choice, for Smoktunovskii had not only the talent but the discipline for the role he would have to play. "We rehearsed for the play for three months," he remembered, "[and] I lived the whole time with the vision and moods of Prince Myshkin."[46] On stage Smoktunovskii's success was astounding and his genius for projecting an image of Prince Myshkin bewitched the audience with its easy naturalness and sincerity. Even physically, though with no obvious gestures or comments, he transformed the image of Myshkin into a prison camp returnee. "His figure is narrow, with elongated arms and legs," a critic explained. It was "not so much a human body," he wrote, "as an outline of a body, a poor diagram for life in the flesh."[47]

On the heels of Tovstonogov's stunning production of *The Idiot* came the first edition of Dostoevskii's collected works ever to be published in Soviet Russia. Prepared by a series of leading Dostoievskii scholars, its ten volumes included most of the master's greatest works. The first two volumes appeared in 1956 in a huge printing of 300,000 copies, and others followed on schedule. But that did not mean that the barriers surrounding Dostoevskii had been entirely pulled down, or that his Leningrad editors were free of the ideological overseers who watched their every move from the Kremlin. In 1967, in fact, the secretary of the Dostoevskii editorial committee was arrested on the patently absurd charge of plotting terrorism against the Soviet state.[48] The time when art and politics could be kept apart was still very far away indeed.

The arrest of Dostoevskii's Leningrad editor came at the tail end of a movement to crack down on dissent in literature and the arts that had begun when Khrushchev's brief thaw ended. In Leningrad, the key victim was Joseph Brodsky, a thin, red-headed twenty-three year-old Jewish school dropout who would later become America's first foreign-born poet laureate. Born in 1940, Brodsky lived through the first winter of the siege of Leningrad with his mother before being evacuated and saw his naval officer father only once during the first eight years of his life. Some of his earliest memories were of nights spent in the bomb-shelter basement of a cathedral that had once been the regimental church of the Preobrazhenskii Imperial Guards, and of the corned beef from America that his mother brought home during the last days of the war. "Its flavor was less memorable than the cans themselves," he remembered. "Tall, square-shaped, with an opening key attached to the side, they heralded different mechanical principles, a different sensibility altogether."[49]

Empty corned beef cans used as flower pots and household decorations, and the odds and ends of Western technology that ended up in Leningrad's flea markets, in friends' apartments, and on the school play-ground led Brodsky to suspect early in life that a very different world lay beyond the borders of the Soviet Union. Soon he started to explore it, first through Hollywood movies (always identified when shown as military trophies "[captured] in the course of the great war for our mother-land"), and then in books.[50] Robert Taylor, Vivien Leigh, Errol Flynn, American Studebakers and Packards left over from the Lend Lease of World War II, and dozens of American records that his father brought back from China marked the beginnings of an odyssey that would even-tually carry Brodsky from Leningrad to a state farm in Russia's far north to Greenwich Village to Mount Holyoke College in the hills of central Massachusetts, where he taught poetry for the last fifteen years of his life. "I believe that my first English utterance was indeed 'His Master's Voice,'" he once wrote in recalling the RCA Victor recordings in his fa-ther's collection.[51] Acquired hit or miss, these tangible bits and pieces of an alluring new world formed the true beginnings of Brodsky's education.

Brodsky's postwar childhood centered around school, the one-and-a-half-room communal apartment in which he and his parents lived, and a Philips short-wave radio on which he continued his tour of the world. By pure chance, his family lived at No. 24 Liteinyi Prospekt, apartment 28, the very one from which Zinaida Gippius and Dmitrii Merezhkovskii had ruled Petersburg's turn-of-the century avant-garde during the golden days of the Silver Age. Complete with parquet floor, the Brodskys' room and a half (the Gippius-Merezhkovskii apartment had been partitioned to accommodate four families in the early 1920s), included the balcony on which Gippius had often stood. With only eleven people (instead of the usual twenty-five to fifty) to share a single kitchen, tub, and toilet, the Brodskys thought themselves fortunate. Even better, their neighbors were people with whom they could get along. The feuds and conflicts that led communal dwellers to dump soap into their neighbors' pots of soup and trample their drying linen in the hallway do not seem to have been part of the Brodskys' daily life. Still, living at No. 24 Liteinyi Prospekt had a rawness that allowed for few secrets. "By the volume of the fart," Brodsky explained, "you can tell who occupies the toilet, you know what he/she had for supper as well as for breakfast. You know the sounds they make in bed and when the women have their periods. . . . There is something tribal about this dimly lit cave," he concluded, "something primordial—evolutionary, if you will."[52]

Brodsky grew up in a world dominated by images of Stalin and Lenin. The names and likenesses of the two men were everywhere, carved in marble and concrete, cast in bronze, printed on posters and in the newspapers, and continually quoted on radio, TV, and at school. Brodsky disdained it all, including the tears that everyone shed when Stalin died. (He remembered one hysterical teacher crying out wildly: "On your knees! On your knees!" when the students first heard of the Great Leader's death.)[53] By then, Brodsky was thirteen and had become enthralled by the jazz he heard on Voice of America. "Something began to happen . . . even to our walk," he wrote in recalling himself and his school friends in those days. "The joints of our highly inhibited Russian frames harkened to 'swing.'" Louis Armstrong, Sidney Bechet, Duke Ellington, Ella Fitzgerald, Charlie Parker—they all had become a part of Brodsky's life well before the day he walked out of school at the age of fifteen and never went back.[54]

In 1956, Brodsky went to work in the part of the Arsenal defense plant that had been converted to make farm machinery after the war, and for a time he lived in the mainstream of Leningrad's working class. This was a world into which Russia's intellectuals almost never ventured, where gross crudity and real meanness reigned, and where violence and misery coexisted with boring monotony. Here everyone lived crammed together, Brodsky remembered, "sleeping in shifts, drinking like sharks, . . . beating their women with moribund determination, crying openly when Stalin dropped dead or at the movies, and cursing with such frequency that a normal word like 'airplane' would strike a passerby as something elaborately obscene."[55] Many elements of life in a Leningrad workers' dormitory mirrored the world of Petersburg's Haymarket in the nineteenth century, where people made few friends and many alliances, all of them based on greed and self-interest. Here everyone lived for the moment.

Most of the men with whom Brodsky lived searched in vain for the future in the bottoms of bottle after bottle of vodka, the main pastime in a city where it was easier to find a drunk at nine o'clock in the morning than a taxi. But the future just wouldn't come into focus. No one believed the government's propaganda, or the visions of life that Russia's Socialist Realist writers and painters created. But they had no idea what to expect instead or where to start looking for it.

Everything at the Arsenal—"a whole cast-iron zoo full of exotic creatures bearing the names Cincinnati, Karlton, Fritz Werner, Siemens & Schuckert [all taken from the Germans as reparations]," Brodsky recalled—was out of date. Every day was a crisis, and every moment chaos. Machines broke down, but there were no spare parts. Raw materials turned out to be fourth or fifth rate. "Semi-drunk tinkers" tried to hold things together, patching, taping, soldering, tying things up with wire. Almost no one tried to work and few even cared. "Virtually everyone would have a hangover on Mondays, not to mention the mornings after paydays," Brodsky wrote. "[And] production would decline sharply the day after a loss by the city or national soccer team."[56] Almost everyone's standard of living was low, and the wages workers received every payday were all but worthless because there was so little to buy anyway. In a sense, it was a fair exchange—almost no work for virtually no compensation, and everybody knew it. "The government makes believe that it pays us," people said at the time. "And we make believe that we're working."

Not uncommonly for young men whose childhoods had embraced the war, the death of Stalin, and the uncertainty of life as the Soviet Union struggled to take up its role as a superpower, Brodsky drifted from job to job. From operating a milling machine at the Arsenal, he moved next door to a hospital morgue, where he dissected corpses. That was in 1957, and after that he changed jobs eleven times in the next five years. He thought of becoming a doctor, a pilot, or a geologist. Then one day when he was working with a geological expedition in Siberia, he picked up an odd volume of Russian Romantic poetry at a book kiosk in faraway Iakutsk. The poems seized his imagination and held it fast. "When I read this book," he confessed many years later, "I knew . . . that poetry was the only thing I understood."[57] For Brodsky, poetry was truth, the very antithesis of the life he saw and lived. "The people of my generation," he once remarked, "couldn't be shocked by anything. We knew about the lies, the duplicity, the callousness all around us. We lied ourselves."[58] But a writer—not a Party hack but a true writer—had to tell the truth. Among Brodsky and his friends, it became the writer's moral duty to tell about life as it really was, not as it ought to be or as the Party wanted it to be.

As a leading figure in the group of young poets whom the aging Akhmatova dubbed her "magic choir," Brodsky represented the best of the postwar generation of Leningrad's artists and intellectuals, many of whom, he later noted, ended up doing odd jobs or "something mindless" because they fell victim to the scruples imposed by literature. "Nobody knew literature and history better than these people, nobody could write in Russian better than they, nobody despised our times more profoundly," he explained. "This wasn't, as it might seem, another lost generation," he went on. "This was the only generation of Russians that had found itself, for whom Giotto and Mandelshtam were more imperative than their own personal destinies." They believed that ideas truly made a difference. "Books became [for them] the first and only reality," Brodsky wrote. "Reality itself," he added, "was regarded as either nonsense or nuisance."[59]

These were the people who spent their nights copying out poetry from the past and present—from the long-forbidden-but-somehow-still-preserved first editions of Osip Mandelshtam, Velimir Khlebnikov, Marina Tsvetaeva, and Boris Pasternak, and from the dog-eared manuscripts of the young poets who made up Akhmatova's "magic choir." Along with the bitter, accusing memoirs of Lidiia Chukovskaia, Nadezhda Mandelshtam, and Evgeniia Ginzburg, these copyings formed the beginnings of *samizdat,* the forbidden manuscript literature that circulated underground in Leningrad and many other Russian cities. Here in the late 1950s and early 1960s, Brodsky discovered what treasures Russian poetry really contained despite the authorities' efforts to bury them under mountains of regulations, prohibitions, and verbal garbage. Aside from the handful of Silver Age poets who survived into the Soviet era (the last two were Akhmatova and Pasternak), Russian poetry had by then become dangerously infected with provincialism as it looked more and more away from the world in which St. Petersburg's turn-of-the-century avant garde had played such a vital part. As the 1950s moved into the 1960s, forbidden *samizdat* writings helped Brodsky to connect his art to the heritage of the Silver Age, at the same time as he drew upon the cosmopolitanism that had evolved from his passion for the culture of the West.

In 1959, Brodsky had his first encounter with the police. He was arrested again in 1961 and for a third time in 1963, when he was confined briefly to a psychiatric hospital in Moscow. He worked occasionally during these years (but not enough to prevent the authorities from later charging him with "parasitism") and wrote tens of thousands of lines of poetry, much of which circulated in *samizdat*. In the summer of 1961, he met Akhmatova, and they began to talk regularly. One winter he even rented a cottage near hers in the country and saw her every day. She called him her "cat and a half" and included him in her "magic choir." He called her "the keening muse" and absorbed her poetry like a sponge. She shared with him her still unpublished "Requiem" and "Poem Without a Hero," challenging him, cajoling him, threatening him as poetry flooded from his pen.[60] "Akhmatova transformed you into *Homo Sapiens* with just the tone of her voice or the turn of her head," he remembered many years later. "Every meeting with Akhmatova was an exceptional experience for me," he added. "Nothing like it ever happened to me before or, I think, after."[61]

Then in 1964, the KGB closed in. January found Brodsky on the run, moving from town to town, staying with friends, sleeping at cottages they had in the country, and trying to keep out of sight. But the moment he slipped into Leningrad on February 11, he was taken to jail, and his trial took place three days later, the case against him having been put together beforehand. Like the case itself, the trial and verdict were prepared in advance, just like tens—even hundreds—of thousands of other trials of the Soviet era. But Brodsky's trial was different. One brave woman managed to compile a transcript of the trial despite the judge's order for her to cease writing, and that document undercut the official lies with which the authorities tried to surround their verdict. Compiled without censorship, Frida Vigdorova's account circulated in *samizdat* and then made its way to the West, where it appeared in *Encounter* and *The New Leader* to reveal the perverse tyranny of the Soviet system.

In the past, many Western intellectuals had turned a blind eye to Soviet tyranny—as, for example, when such literary giants as Theodore Dreiser, George Bernard Shaw, Romain Rolland, and André Gide had applauded the "humanity" of the Soviet system in the 1930s, and a number of prominent American intellectuals had sent an angry letter to protest the Book-of-the-Month Club's selection of a novel by the émigré Mark Aldanov in 1943. But this time there were protests, and even so staunch a defender of the Soviet system as Jean-Paul Sartre wrote a letter to Chairman of the Presidium of the Supreme Soviet Anastas Mikoian. Later these would have an impact, but not before Brodsky had been tried and punished.

Brodsky's trial began on February 14, 1964, in a grimy courtroom at No. 36 Uprising Street in Leningrad's Dzerzhinskii district. Brodsky slouched against the wall, facing a blank-looking female judge, who proved to be completely ignorant about art and literature. "Legally speaking, it was absolutely grotesque," he remembered, "and I tried to divorce myself as much as possible from what was happening. . . . For me," he went on, "it was psychologically somehow already out of date—like something one reads in books, books already written like Kafka's *Trial.*"[62]

"Who has said you're a poet?" the judge asked. "Who ranked you as a poet?"

"No one," Brodsky replied. "And who ranked me as a human being?"

"Have you studied this?" the judge went on, refusing to be diverted. "Have you tried to do a course where you are prepared . . . where you are taught [to write poetry]?"

"I didn't think that came through education," Brodsky answered.

"Well, how [does it come] then?"

"I think," he said, "that it comes from God."[63]

The judge ordered Brodsky committed to a psychiatric clinic, where a favorite "treatment" was to wrap him tightly in a sheet, toss him into a tub of water, and then put him next to a hot radiator, where the sheet, as it dried, would pull off pieces of his skin.[64] After three weeks, the psychiatrists declared him fit for hard labor, and he was sentenced to serve a five-year sentence in the far north, where he did menial jobs on a state farm. It was a grim, poverty-stricken world, where time had stopped decades earlier and where farmers worked from dawn to dark for a few kopeks a day. People became formless, clad in rags and canvas boots against the cold. In every direction, there was only gray emptiness—fields filled with stubble over which clouds hung low and dark. "[Here] it is physiologically unpleasant to write, to talk, to dip my pen in the ink-well," Brodsky confided to a friend.[65]

Yet the poetry still took shape. "Buried alive here. . . . Frozen hands pressed to my hips. . . . Feeling almost no pain. . . . The frost reaches out for the slit of my mouth. . . . My laugh is twisted; it brings terror to the brushwood path." Over time such phrases formed themselves into Brodsky's "New Stanzas to Augusta,"[66] in which, along with "Autumn in Norenskaia," he told of men and women aged before their time, their spirits deadened by hard work, malnutrition, chronic fatigue, and boredom. "There's nothing to do there, either as a moving body in the landscape or as a spectator," he later explained. Even the White Nights, so marvelous in Leningrad, brought no lessening of the monotony in the lands of Brodsky's exile. "They introduced an element of total absurdity," Brodsky concluded. "They shed too much light on what absolutely did not merit illumination."[67]

In November 1965, Brodsky's persecutors set him free. Word of what he had suffered had made his poetry known worldwide, but the chiefs of Russia's literary establishment learned no lessons from that. The next year, they put Andrei Siniavskii and Iulii Daniel on trial for writing novels and essays critical of the Soviet Union, and their case became a new *cause célèbre* in the West. Then Aleksandr Ginzburg, who followed Vigdorova's example and kept notes at their trial, was arrested, as was Iurii Galanskov for publishing what Ginzburg had recorded. Those persecutions drew still more unfavorable attention. The year 1968 saw the Union of Soviet Writers expel Solzhenitsyn. After that, the police sent Natalia Gorbanevskaia to a psychiatric hospital for protesting against the Soviet invasion of Prague.

In ranting against the men and women they branded as betrayers of the Soviet dream, the authorities made few changes in the crude rhetoric they had used in earlier times. In the late 1940s, Zhdanov had condemned the compositions of Prokofiev and Shostakovich as "chaotic conglomerations of sounds" that reflected the decadent "spirit of American and European music."[68] In the 1960s, his successors dismissed Pasternak's poetry as "the most blatant example of rotten decadence," and the Soviet press greeted *Doctor Zhivago* as being "the life story of a malicious philistine" that had been "fished out of a decadent heap." Zhivago, they insisted, was "an infuriated moral freak," and Pasternak nothing more than a "tool of bourgeois propaganda."[69] A decade later, propagandists described the writers of Brodsky's generation as "little people reaching for their toady's hunk of meat" whose "bombastic bleatings" could "elicit nothing but revulsion." Brodsky himself, they announced in the mid-1970s, had become "a sponger off Western secret services."[70] Even as late as 1987, the KGB referred to Brodsky's Nobel Prize as "a provocative political act by reactionary circles in the West."[71] As these crude persecutions brought more criticism from the Western intellectuals who had supported the Soviet Union for so long, the authorities finally tried a new tack. Just as Brodsky had been the first poet to be brought to trial by Khrushchev, so in 1972 he became the first in a long line of brilliant writers to be deported from the Soviet Union by Brezhnev.

The Soviet establishment sought to counterbalance dynamic creativity with mediocre conformity. But in doing so they admitted that it was becoming all but impossible to cut Russians off from their past and from the West, for the growing numbers of visiting academics, performing artists, and tourists provided too many sources of new information. More in the 1970s than in the 1960s, and still more in the 1980s than in the 1970s, the door to the West, innovation, and the illicit treasures of Russia's past creaked opened. *Samizdat* became a rising flood, circulating political commentary, novels, essays, and poetry from hand to hand on the principle that the reader was obliged to make more copies and to pass them on. Eventually realizing that censorship was driving more and more material into the channels of *samizdat*, from which it flowed all too easily to the West, the authorities started to ease their grip. One of the first indications came when the sesquicentennial of Dostoevskii's birth in 1971 was celebrated in Leningrad with volumes of literary criticism of a quality that far surpassed anything that had been published on the 75th anniversary of his death just fifteen years earlier.

No longer did the work of such brilliant formalists as Viktor Shklovskii or the sensitive modernist studies of Iurii Lotman have to be ignored, and even the pressure on Akhmatova eased in the years before she died of a heart attack in 1966. In fact the Silver Age tradition out of which she, Brodsky, and his friends all had drawn so much inspiration was slowly being pulled back into focus by Leningrad's intellectuals, who saw it as another major landmark in their culture that needed to be reclaimed. In 1946, Zhdanov had called the Silver Age "the most shameful and most mediocre decade in the history of the Russian intelligentsia." Now as the forces of reclamation grew stronger and moved faster, the arts and poetry of the Silver Age moved into the open more quickly than had the ballet or even the works of Dostoevskii. Barely two decades after they celebrated the 150th anniversary of Dostoevskii's birth, Leningraders would be calling the Silver Age "the key to the treasure box of the twentieth century."[72]

Throughout the 1960s, Akhmatova and her followers had laid the groundwork for Leningraders to reclaim the art and literature of the Silver Age, but so had rawer elements among the city's bohemians, who turned more readily to Olga Berggolts and to friendships with a handful of avant-gardist survivors from the 1910s and 1920s. These people looked on the deadening boredom of the Brezhnev era with despair and insisted that life had to be connected to art in meaningful ways. Because they thought human existence transcended the limits of time, political ideologies, and geographical boundaries, they saw themselves as part of a movement that embraced both Russia's past and the modern West. For some of them, the world turned around black market trade in Western art books, literature, and music. Others dressed in traditional Russian shirts and blackened knee-high boots in the manner of Maksim Gorkii and sought inspiration in the Futurist poetry of Velimir Khlebnikov, who had long ago aspired to raise the arts above the plane of reason to a realm in which the contradictions of earthly life could be reconciled. Like Brodsky, these young rebels responded to the inertia of the times by taking menial jobs as dock workers, janitors, and stokers. Some lived by collecting bottles and turning them in for deposits, and nearly all of them drank too much. They read the poets of the Silver Age and argued passionately about the vision they shared. Eventually, they shaded into the Leningrad "hippies" of the 1980s.

Because the Silver Age remained officially off limits throughout the 1970s and most of the 1980s, Leningrad's intellectuals maintained contact with its masterpieces only through underground exchanges of dog-eared pre-Revolutionary editions and smuggled volumes published by such Western publishers as Ardis and the YMCA Press. Yet during those years their contacts broadened, with more restless men and women gaining a sense of the brilliance that had illuminated their city at the beginning of the century. The advent of the electronic age under Gorbachev destroyed the government's monopoly on information at the very moment when Leningraders were gaining access to computers. Long-forbidden materials thus came quickly within easy reach, and as the authorities lost control, the wall that had cut Leningraders off from their artistic past started to crumble. Books began to appear and names began to change. Leningrad State University lost the stigma of being "named after Andrei Zhdanov," and in 1988 the Party's Central Committee rescinded its forty-two-year-old condemnation of Akhmatova and Zoshchenko.

In the spring of 1987, Akhmatova's poetic memorial to the terrible years when "innocent Russia writhed . . . under the tires of the Black Marias" and "the ones who smiled were the dead," was finally published in Russia.[73] The next year, a collection of her first husband Nikolai Gumilev's Acmeist verses appeared, and the year after that the Leningrad authorities opened an Akhmatova Museum in the Sheremetiev Palace apartment in which she had lived so many years of her life. A flood of works that had not been republished for more than sixty years began, with editions of the poetry of Andrei Belyi, Mikhail Kuzmin, Osip Mandelshtam, and Zinaida Gippius all pouring from the very presses that had disdained them for so long. Leningrad orchestras started to play the works of Stravinskii, and the Kirov added the ballets of George Balanchine to its repertoire. Then came other treasures of which Russians had barely known: the paintings of Marc Chagall and Vasilii Kandinskii, the poetry of Joseph Brodsky, and, as one critic wrote, "all of [Vladimir] Nabokov's gigantic legacy, the whole baker's dozen of his novels and all that comes with them."[74] Like a flood the long forbidden art came in a rush. "The effect of this 'submersion in material,'" one reader remarked, "is like having the bends."[75]

Everywhere, Leningraders were reclaiming their past, taking back the hoard of treasures that their Soviet masters had kept hidden for so long. At the Hermitage and the Russian Museum, paintings by Picasso, Matisse, Modigliani, Natan Altman, and Iurii Annenkov started to reappear, bringing new light and vibrancy to a city that seemed tired and tattered after its seventy-year Soviet occupation. Then, on October 1, 1991, when Leningrad officially became Sankt-Peterburg once again, its people reclaimed the name of their city itself. Once again, as Mayor Anatolii Sobchak pointed out, the city had become "the only Russian door to Europe,"[76] the center of the three-hundred-year-old debate about Russia's relationship to itself, to modernity, and to the West.

But what did that mean? Looked at over the 288 years that separated the first crude shelters built by Menshikov's soldiers from the tattered city that saw the Soviet Union fall apart, St. Petersburg was in some ways a living monument to Russia's past at the same time as it hinted at what the future might become. For whether it was called Sankt-Peterburg, Petrograd, or Leningrad, the city remained "Piter" to the people who lived there—not Petr as it would have been had its name been taken directly from that of its founder, but an intimate, Hollandicized version that suggested both alienation and affection. This was still the city of Pushkin, of Dostoevskii, of Peter and Catherine the Great, of Aleksandr Blok, of Shostakovich, Akhmatova, and Brodsky. As such it was lonely, intimate, grandiose, beautiful, oppressive, romantic, ephemeral, isolationist, and apocalyptic. It was a place of wealth and poverty, of crime and punishment, of damnation and redemption. Once freed from the shackles of its

Soviet past, St. Petersburg could stand again as a guidepost for all of Russia, blending past and present to create a vision of the future. How that could be understood was the dilemma Petersburgers faced when their city shed its Leninist alias in 1991, for its story seemed once again to have become that of all Russia itself. To understand them both required rediscovering the long-hidden past. From a plethora of visions of the city and its founder, an amalgam had to be shaped, for only then could the people of "Piter" begin to sense what lay ahead.

# TWELVE

# PAST
# AND PRESENT

 

*E*VER SINCE THE TSARS OF OLD MUSCOVY first began to gather the lands of Eurasia into a state, the Russians have struggled to determine whether their destiny pointed East or West. Powerful enemies came from each direction, sometimes from both at once, as in the thirteenth century, when the Mongols overran Russia from the East, and the Swedes, Poles, Livonian Knights, and Lithuanians attacked from the West. The Mongols demanded tribute, but the conquerors from the West took land, including the territory around the Neva River's mouth. In the centuries that followed, horsemen from the East burned Moscow. Then, Poland's armies seized the Kremlin, while the Swedes built fortresses along the Baltic coast and took the great trading center of Novgorod. Even after they succeeded in throwing off the Mongol yoke in the 1480s, the Grand Prince of Moscow still had not the means to stand against the armies they faced in the West.

But gradually Russia had grown stronger. Between the 1580s and the 1650s Russian Cossacks and trappers crossed the five thousand miles of wilderness that separated the Urals from the Pacific and took command of Siberia to give Russia's tsars control over the world's richest supply of furs and other natural resources whose variety and value could not even be guessed at the time. Siberia's furs alone gave Russia's tsars a new source of wealth to support the larger and more modern armies they needed to stand against their enemies from the West. When they drove the Poles from Russia's western lands and the Swedes from the Baltic coast during the second half of the seventeenth century, the Russians showed the new strength that would soon allow them to overwhelm their traditional enemies. By the time Napoleon's Grande Armée was driven out at the end of 1812, all of Russia's former adversaries had grown too weak to stand against it, and so had China and the once powerful khanates of Central Asia. By then the Tsar ruled more than a sixth of the earth's lands, from the Vistula River in Poland to Northern California's Bodega Bay. But the question of whether the nation's future lay in the East or West still remained unresolved.

Like war and politics, commerce also pulled the Russians toward East and West. Furs flowing from Siberia across China's remote northwestern frontier in return for silks, spices, and tea drew the Russians toward the East, but the British and Dutch merchants who came to the new White Sea port of Arkhangelsk in search of furs, timber, hemp, and tar pulled them West. Goods from all parts of the world were flowing steadily across Russia's borders by the time Peter the Great seized the throne from his half-sister Sofiia in 1689. But the country still had no real window on either East or West. History, religion, and the vastness of Eurasia continued to make Russia an enigma, the secrets of which had yet to be deciphered.

Peter the Great's decision to build St. Petersburg and to move his capital there opened Russia's first true window on a world that was more technologically advanced and modern than anything within its borders. Through the St. Petersburg window, Peter brought in modern weapons, ships, fashions, architecture, institutions of government, and learning. He brought in a new calendar and a new alphabet, books on manners, and new ways of everyday life. After vacillating for hundreds of years, it seemed that Russia had finally decided to look westward, although, when Peter died in 1725, most Russians still thought St. Petersburg too remote, its way of life too expensive, and its demeanor too foreign. To many it represented a kind of world they wished not to enter, and it was no accident that they thought of Peter as the Antichrist, sent into their midst by mysterious forces whose identity remained unknown. Even those men and women willing to embrace the modern ways that St. Petersburg represented preferred to live elsewhere. And it was no mere whim that convinced Peter's grandson, Peter II, to move Russia's capital back to Moscow in 1728. That this incident coincided with the opening of Russia's first window to the East, the trading center of Kiakhta on the Siberian-Chinese frontier, may not have been pure chance. During the centuries that lay ahead, the Russians almost never turned away from the West without launching new probes in the East as they searched for the means to balance themselves astride the continents of Europe and Asia.

Many regarded the Empress Anna's decision to return her capital to St. Petersburg in 1732 as a definitive statement that Russia's rulers had decided to seek their nation's future in the West, although it was immediately followed by Russian expeditions that explored Siberia and crossed the Bering Strait to Alaska. By then, some of Russia's churchmen had embraced the city as the "new Jerusalem,"[1] the regularity of its center being divided by a great river as foretold in the Book of Revelation (21:10–23, 22:1–2). St. Petersburg the New Jerusalem now took precedence over Moscow the Third Rome, and Russia's church drew closer to the West in terms of its architecture and art. Following the examples of Byzantium and Kiev, Moscow's medieval churches had evolved from the East. Now built with soaring spires, domes, and columns, the churches of St. Petersburg resembled those in the West.

Having lived most of her adult life in the West before she became Russia's sovereign, the Empress Anna expected Petersburgers to embrace European manners and fashions as a matter of course. For her leading courtiers, this meant building Western-style townhouses and palaces, but everyone who hoped to get ahead at her court or in government had to learn European ways. For the first time, an awareness of civility began to appear in Russia, and the Empress's court in St. Petersburg led the way. What civility meant and how it should be practiced was not yet clearly understood. To some extent, the Europeans in Anna's entourage served as models for Petersburgers, and the handful of Russians who had visited the West did likewise. Beyond that, to school Petersburgers in the art of courtly behavior Anna established the Aristocratic Infantry Cadet Corps, where young lords learned to dance, fence, and ride horseback, while they studied the languages and ways of the West. With a student body of something over two hundred, the influence of the Cadet Corps did not reach much beyond St. Petersburg during the first half of the eighteenth century, but it created the beginnings of the Europeanized society that would flourish in the city and spread deeper into Russia later on.[2]

Even as Anna called upon Petersburgers to imitate the West, she remained enough of a Russian at heart to demand that they act from time to time in ways that recalled their non-Western past. Each year, she dedicated the anniversary of her accession to Bacchus and insisted that every courtier get thoroughly drunk to celebrate. Like her giant uncle, she reveled in the antics of dwarfs and jesters, even though such amusements had long since disappeared from European courts. One midwinter day, she summoned her courtiers to a small palace built entirely of ice in the middle of the Neva River to attend the wedding of her jester Prince Golitsyn to a peasant woman she had chosen for his bride. On her instructions, the guests arrived in sleighs pulled by hogs, goats, reindeer, and oxen, and they looked on in amazement while the couple were wedded and locked in their icy nuptial chamber for the night. As Russia's window on Europe, St. Petersburg was not the East, but such celebrations made it clear that it was not yet entirely part of the West either.

That began to change during the reign of Elizabeth, who did not share her father's and cousin's taste for crudity. Elizabeth set Russia firmly on the Western path, and it was she who transformed St. Petersburg from a Europeanized riverfront backed by thousands of native hovels into a Western metropolis. Under Elizabeth, the various parts of Russia's capital became integrated so that they no longer resembled the heap of linked villages that visitors had noted in Peter's time.[3] St. Petersburg became a city of wide avenues and broad perspectives formed by canals and riverfront vistas that highlighted the stunning baroque palaces that were taking shape under the supervision of Rastrelli and his students, rivals, and followers. By the middle of Elizabeth's reign, St. Petersburg had become everything Peter the Great had envisioned: a fortress, a bustling port, a window on the West, a center of government, and a model for everything Russia might be (or ought to become).

Nowhere was the Western character of St. Petersburg portrayed more vividly at mid-century than in the engravings of Mikhail Makhaev, an artist who learned in his thirties to work in the best manner of eighteenth-century Italy and France. Using huge optical cameras that permitted him to project detailed images onto large sheets of paper, Makhaev traced St. Petersburg's panoramas in detail, adding boats, carriages, and people as they suited his designs. From these drawings, Makhaev produced engravings that became famous for their precision and detail the moment they appeared. First published in large albums in the early 1750s, these showed the emergence of St. Petersburg as a true Western oasis in Russia. Described as "remarkable documents of their time,"[4] Makhaev's engravings portrayed a world of Western buildings, carriages, boats, and people that contained almost no hint of the Old Russia that had been left behind. These engravings were copied endlessly by Russian and foreign artists to show the details of St. Petersburg life. Until they were displaced by the popular lithographs of Vasilii Sadovnikov in the 1830s, redrawn versions of them appeared on everything from huge oil canvases to tiny snuffboxes, not to mention illustrations in dozens of foreign works about Russia and its capital.[5]

The fact that Makhaev projected his perspectives from rooftops allowed him to conceal the empty spaces that still separated some parts of the city, but those filled in quickly during the second half of the eighteenth century to make St. Petersburg more European in the density of its buildings. As the city developed, artists began to look at it up close, treating it as a landscape, not an architectural perspective. Now not the overall impression of the city but the intimate details of its bridges, monuments, individual buildings, people's clothing, and all the varied aspects of daily life came into focus. Still an opening through which the Russians could see the West, Russia's capital was starting to become too Western for Europeans to see through it the real Russia. St. Petersburg was about to become the model for what the rest of Russia wanted to be, but to see the rest of Russia Europeans now had to look beyond its capital.

Early in her reign, Catherine the Great had insisted that Russia was in every sense "a European power,"[6] and everything she undertook in her capital had been calculated to highlight that belief. Yet the dichotomy that had made it possible for St. Petersburg to take shape in the beginning remained, and that added another dimension to the riddle of East and West. For in contrast to Western capitals, St. Petersburg owed its rise to the ability of Russia's sovereigns to impose servitude upon their people. In that it had more in common with Peking than with Paris, even though its urban landscape resembled more closely that of the West than the East.

Peter the Great's success in founding a city on a swamp, the ease with which Catherine II had ordered the fifteen-hundred-ton rock on which Falconet wanted to mount his famed Bronze Horseman to be moved from a bog to the city center, the ability of Nicholas I's chief adjutant to rebuild the entire Winter Palace in less than two years after fire destroyed it at the end of 1837, and the transformation of Russia's constitutional monarchy into the Stalinist tyranny all reflect the ways despotism and servitude have shaped St. Petersburg's (and Russia's) history. Even the city's most heroic moment—its refusal to surrender during the siege of nine hundred days in World War II—was defined by those forces. For without a long history of demanding that the masses accept whatever sacrifices their masters asked for, no government could have expected Leningrad's people to bear the torments that the siege forced upon them. St. Petersburg thus still stands as a monument to the forces that have shaped Russia's history and the vision of its builders. How those should be balanced is a dilemma that has confronted every Russian ruler, statesman, writer, and thinker since the time of Peter the Great.

For the better part of three hundred years the question of how to blend a preference for East or West with the forces of despotism and servitude has dominated an ongoing conversation that Russia has carried on with itself. So often the model of what Russia wanted to become (although sometimes a reflection of what it wanted not to be), St. Petersburg has stood at the very center of that conversation, and its physical and human development have reflected that fact. In Peter's time, the conversation focused on despotism, the West, and how Russia needed to enter the modern world. The means by which despotism could conquer nature, change the tempo at which the nation moved, and restructure the mores of an entire society all figured into St. Petersburg's beginnings, and the speed with which Russia's rulers accomplished those ends accounted for the city's spectacular rise. In less than a single human lifetime, St. Petersburg evolved from a desolate wasteland that hosted a few lonely fishermen to Russia's busiest Baltic port. In terms of the races and nationalities to be found on its streets and waterfronts, it became the most cosmopolitan city in Europe at the same time as it became the nerve center of the world's largest contiguous empire. Palaces by the dozens, townhouses by the scores, wharves, warehouses, shipyards, cathedrals, government offices, and housing for a hundred thousand people all appeared during St. Petersburg's first half century, and that marked only a beginning. Nowhere in Europe did rulers build with such speed and on such a scale. Only the treasure and labor of an entire nation—and a form of despotism more stern than any to be found in the West—could bring that about. No sovereign in Europe used those instruments more energetically than did Peter the Great. And none used his power more boldly to alter his nation's destiny.

Incomplete, growing in several directions at once, a masterpiece whose final form was neither certain nor clear, St. Petersburg at the time of Peter's death was, like the new Russian Empire, very much a work in progress. During the reigns of the empresses Anna and Elizabeth, Russia's ongoing conversation started to shift from how it needed to enter the modern world to how it fitted into Europe, and the shape of St. Petersburg changed accordingly. Because the empresses Anna and Elizabeth were less concerned with the technology of the West than with its trappings, they were less interested in St. Petersburg's development as a trading center, shipyard, and fortress than as a city that could stand proudly among the capitals of the Western world of which Russia was becoming a part. It was to that end that Anna instructed architects to lay out plans for the city's overall development, and the same motivation underlay Elizabeth's passion for building on a scale never before seen in Russia. With all of Europe enthralled by Versailles, Elizabeth built in and around St. Petersburg not one such palace but four in barely more than a decade. The palaces at Peterhof and Tsarskoe Selo in addition to the summer and winter palaces in St. Petersburg showed again the dramatic results that despotism and servitude could achieve.

Yet there was more to the rise of St. Petersburg than its buildings. During Elizabeth's reign Russia's ladies transformed themselves into artistic monuments by means of complex structures built of whalebone, steel joints, and other devices, upon which they shaped the latest styles of clothing and coiffures.[7] Such living artistic creations found a proper setting in St. Petersburg's theater, opera, and high society balls, all of which flourished during the 1740s and 1750s. Begun by Anna, these entertainments became more sophisticated during the reign of Elizabeth, who thought festivals, formal dinners, and grand balls were essential to a proper royal setting. European haute cuisine became a part of St. Petersburg high society then. Vodka, mead, and the crude cooking of Old Russia continued to be staples of life in the countryside, but in St. Petersburg champagnes, clarets, pâtés from Périgord, and scores of other delicacies became the fare of the nobility.

By the time Catherine the Great seized the throne in 1762, the focus of Russia's conversation had begun to shift from duplicating the physical trappings of the West to embracing the ideas and feelings that lay beneath them. Having become accustomed to acting like Europeans, a few aristocratic Petersburgers now began to think like them, and the last third of the century saw literature and poetry rise to the level of the Western examples that the Russians had so recently imitated. The Russian theater came into its own in the reign of Catherine the Great, and so did painting, as the great Petersburg portraitists Dmitrii Levitskii and Vladimir Borovikovskii began to challenge the preeminence of Thomas Gainsborough and Sir Joshua Reynolds. For the first time, the city's aristocrats began to feel truly comfortable with the new cultural world around them, and by the end of the century they were as much at ease in Paris, London, or Vienna as they were at home. After setting out to imitate the ways of eighteenth-century France, they had become so much a part of the Old Regime that some preferred French to Russian, a fact made especially clear by the dialogue in Tolstoi's *War and Peace* and the memoirs of French royalists who sought refuge in St. Petersburg after the Revolution of 1789.

Yet there was more to St. Petersburg politics, society, and culture under Catherine the Great than re-creating the lifestyle of *ancien régime* France. At least in a physical sense, the Empress's passion for neoclassicism began to bind Russia more closely to the heritage of Ancient Greece and Rome, and St. Petersburg's architectural models shifted during those years from Baroque Italy and France to the temples at the Eternal City, the Near East, and Paestum. Poets glorified Catherine as the sovereign who would make Russia into a "flourishing Rome" and envisioned her atop Mount Olympus, in the clouds, among the gods. Likening their sovereign to a triumphal goddess, Petersburgers made the simple majesty and elegant taste attributed to the ancients the goal of life and art. "Statues on the banks of the Aegean and the Tiber," one observer wrote, became the ideals of men and women who aspired to live among the "poetry of columns" that signified wealth and elegance.[9] "What a city! What a river!" the poet Konstantin Batiushkov exclaimed in 1814. By then, St. Petersburg had become a city of "marvelous buildings, gilded by the morning sun ... reflected in the clean mirror of the Neva."[10]

When Batiushkov wrote his paeans to St. Petersburg's beauty, Russia had assumed a new role in relationship to the West, and the place of St. Petersburg in the scheme of universal history had shifted. In 1789, the French Revolution had left Russia standing as the strongest example of the Old Regime society that the Parisian crowd wanted to eradicate. With a rich and powerful nobility, and a ruler in command of the vast resources of Eurasia, Russia had became a bastion of stability in a tumultuous world, with St. Petersburg at the very center of the elegant way of life that the forces of history had so suddenly transported from the banks of the Seine to the embankments of the Neva. Here the aristocratic salons and soirées rivaled those that had flourished in Paris during the age that France's revolutionary turmoil had swept away. And while agents of the mob fed the guillotines of Paris, St. Petersburg remained peaceful and calm. Hardly a ripple disturbed the tranquility of the city during the last years of Catherine's reign, for vigilant censors and diligent police made certain that dissent stayed out of sight. On the continent of Europe, Russia soon challenged Napoleon's new Imperial visions. Both the Emperor Alexander and Napoleon embraced the heritage of Ancient Rome, but each saw the other differently. For the Russians, Napoleon was an upstart seeking legitimacy by manipulating history. To Napoleon, Russia stood not only as an imperial rival but as a bulwark of the Eastern Orthodox piety that had always opposed the forces of reason.

In 1812, Napoleon led his Grande Armée into Russia. As if to ignore St. Petersburg as the center of a rival imperial vision, he marched directly on Moscow. From the Russians' point of view, the invasion signaled a direct attack by the world order they had worked for so long to emulate, and the psychological impact of that assault soon drove East and West apart. The victorious Russian Empire that emerged from its wars with Napoleon was clearly the most powerful on the European continent. To the men who ruled it, this made Russia indisputably the new Rome, spread onto three continents, with St. Petersburg as an imperial center that had to equal Rome in every way. Buildings that dwarfed the Pantheon, cathedrals that rivaled St. Peter's, and parade grounds that surpassed any in Paris, Vienna, London, or even ancient Rome itself all reflected the imperial vision of Catherine's grandsons. Tens of tons of bronze, tens of thousands of tons of granite, semiprecious stones, gold, and silver all helped to shape the new imperial buildings of nineteenth-century St. Petersburg. No sovereigns had built on such a scale before, for the capital of the Romanovs had to reflect the greatness of an empire that stretched almost halfway around the world.

The accession of the Emperor Nicholas I in December 1825 marked another dramatic shift in Russia's relationship to the West and an expansion of its role in the East. Unlike his grandmother and older brother, Nicholas did not see Russia as essentially a part of Europe, and he insisted that it stand separately as a bastion of order in an increasingly uncertain world. More than ever before, the St. Petersburg of Nicholas I became the center of a Eurasian empire, for the Russians now had a new sense of uniqueness stemming from their growing belief that their nation's mission no longer lay mainly in Europe. The 1840s and 1850s saw the greatest explorations of Russia's Asian lands in nearly a century, as trappers, traders, ethnographers, and military commanders pursued dreams that carried them across Siberia and the Aleutian Islands to Bodega Bay on the North California coast. To-bolsk, Krasnoiarsk, and Irkutsk no longer seemed so distant, even though the coming of the Trans-Siberian Railroad still lay half a century away. Georgia, Azerbaidjan, and the mountains of Tien Shan all entered the Russian realm then, and so did huge parts of the Amur River valley.

In St. Petersburg, Russia's new Eastern focus brought the Imperial Geographical Society into being along with societies that studied the relics of the past. Now Petersburgers began to seek the roots of their history in Asia and the long-ago events that set them apart from the West. Russia's great poets Pushkin and Lermontov and a young army officer by the name of Lev Tolstoi wrote of the Caucasus and the impact of the Russians on the simple purity of native life. The wealth of Asia now began to play a greater part in Russian life than ever before. In 1824, Alexander I had opened all of Siberia's watercourses and river valleys to exploration by prospectors, and in less than thirty years more than sixty thousand men were moving four million tons of dirt a year to mine gold from Eurasia's alluvial sands.[11] The first of those huge nineteenth-century discoveries that were destined to increase the world's gold supply many times over, the Siberian gold rush of the 1830s and 1840s poured new wealth into the Imperial Treasury, and it was no mere whim that allowed Nicholas to spend huge sums on building in the imperial style. In 1811, his brother had spent some four million rubles to build St. Petersburg's Kazan Cathedral. Over the three decades between 1825 and his death in 1855 (which coincided with the first flood of Siberian gold), Nicholas I spent more than six times that sum on the Cathedral of St. Isaac.[12]

Elegant, opulent, overbearing, and imperial in every sense of the word, St. Petersburg during the reign of Nicholas I became detached and cold. In a sense it was working out its own true identity, centered in neither East nor West but self-sufficient like the empire it served. Its sovereigns and statesmen now envisioned an imperial future in which order would reign supreme, while the law remained what the rich and powerful made it. "You need a superior mercy so as to soften the law, and this can only come to us in the form of absolute monarchy," the writer Nikolai Gogol explained in those days. "Without an absolute monarch, a state is like an automaton," he added. "A state without an absolute ruler is like an orchestra without a conductor."[13]

Such a view permeated Petersburg life, making influence and the rank that reflected it count for even more than wealth. People caught up in this chameleon world could never be counted upon to be the same from one day to the next, or to deal with different people in the same way. "Depending on whom he was speaking to," one Petersburger wrote of a high official he knew, "he resembled either the awe-inspiring countenance of Jupiter or the fawning figure of an enchantress trying to curry favor."[14] No wonder that Gogol described St. Petersburg as a city in which the mind and eye played constant tricks. It was foggy and phantasmagoric, with sunlight at midnight turning into darkness at noon. "There was something irresistibly attractive about it," one writer explained in the mid-1860s. "Something hideously beautiful."[15]

Wealth, poverty, despotism, servitude, palaces, hovels, clear vistas, fog-clogged streets—almost everything in St. Petersburg seemed to generate an opposite, and those contrasts sharpened as time passed. No one captured them more dramatically than Dostoevskii, for whom the capital was "a sumptuous picture . . . [that was] deaf-mute in spirit," and it drew people's imaginations not to its "splendid panoramas" but to its dark alleys and hidden corners.[16] Yet Dostoevskii did more than create a vivid chronicle of the suffering that St. Petersburg's back streets revealed, for he expanded the Russians' ongoing conversation about past, present, and future to embrace the ways in which suffering might lead to redemption. Good and evil, generosity of means and meanness of spirit, the chance to tempt fate and the opportunity to surrender to it—all these were a part of life in Dostoevskii's St. Petersburg, where people lived with or without hope depending on circumstances and their willingness to challenge the hard hand of Fate. Far from seeing in St. Petersburg a model for Russia to follow, Dostoevskii thought it a "half-mad city"[17] that was drawing Russia away from its destiny. To him it seemed that Russia ought not to re-create the West but to provide instead "an outlet for the anguish of Europe in the All-Human and All-Uniting Russian soul,"[18] of which St. Petersburg was the chief negation.

If salvation could not be found in St. Petersburg, did the city still have meaning, or had it simply become a window on a world that the Russians were beginning to turn away from? During the waning years of the nineteenth century, writers wrote less about their capital's dramatic vistas and promise of success. A darkening of St. Petersburg's image in Russian literature and art had begun, and shades, fog, and the watery light of streetlamps replaced the hopeful brilliance of earlier times. Later to become famous for his huge historical canvases about Old Russia's history, the Siberian artist Vasilii Surikov was perhaps the first to portray St. Petersburg darkly on canvas by emphasizing the gloominess that reigned as the fog rolled in or when darkness fell. Beginning in the 1870s, St. Petersburg, the city of leaden skies—often painted at twilight or after nightfall—became a favorite subject as artists embroidered on the verbal images that Gogol and Dostoevskii had created. Broad panoramas disappeared. Painters looked instead at the city as if through a glass darkly, concentrating on the shadows and silhouettes that nighttime brought forth.

Such darkened images did not mean that Russians rejected their capital, or even that they had lost contact with the soul that so many generations had embraced. Yet the image was no longer as bright and unambiguous as it had been in the days of the poet Pushkin, Catherine the Great, or the men who had shaped the imperial metropolis over which Nicholas I had reigned. By the 1880s, St. Petersburg was completely in the grip of the Industrial Revolution, its center ringed by a forest of tall chimneys that spewed smoke and soot and wrapped the city in a blanket of grimy fog. To this forbidding wilderness of brick and concrete Petersburg's masses flowed each morning, and then, like the tide, ebbed homeward in the evening. All were pale and worn from work, and most lived from hand to mouth. As it had not done since the days when tens of thousands of Peter's workmen had died in its swamps, St. Petersburg was starting to devour people en masse. That fact alone added a note of uncertainty to a way of life that had been so certain in earlier times.

In this new realm of mist and smog, thoughtful Petersburgers began to see otherworldly forces moving in a direction that could never be clearly described. An ominous and exhilarating sense of where things were heading began to emerge only in the early twentieth century, especially in the work of Mstislav Dobuzhinskii, the law-student-turned-artist, whose illustrations of Dostoevskii's *White Nights* favored darkness over light. In Dobuzhinskii's St. Petersburg, the works of man blotted out the creations of Nature and God to project an ominous vision. City scenes of shades and shadows illuminated by tiny points of light, nondescript buildings that cast long shadows, machines that replaced people, and a sense that people no longer mattered—all these were a part of the scenes painted by Dobuzhinskii and his friends between 1900 and 1922.

Shades of an angry Apocalypse were descending upon St. Petersburg as the twentieth century moved toward its rendezvous with World War I and the Russian Revolution, and not even the music of Chaikovskii and the passion with which some of Dobuzhinskii's friends embraced the spirit of the past in the pages of *The World of Art* could slow its approach. St. Petersburg was becoming a city of "langorous and bitter poetry," Dobuzhinskii once wrote,[19] and a sense that evil powers were gathering over it began to dominate its artists' work. To some it seemed that the foundations of St. Petersburg were starting to crumble. In 1909, the discovery that more than 300 gallons of water had somehow collected *inside* Falconet's Bronze Horseman[20] seemed to indicate that the very element that eighteenth-century builders had been obliged to harness before the city could flourish had now found a way to attack it from within, while legions of hungry proletarians continued to threaten it from without.

On the eve of World War I, the Moscow symbolist Andrei Belyi saw fearsome shadows in Russia's capital whose meaning could not yet be fully understood. A powerful sense of Apocalypse in which the city cast a dark shadow across Russia's present dominated his novel *Petersburg*, which portrayed Russia's capital as being "ashy and indistinct" and entirely superfluous to its future. The "blackish-grayish cubes" of city buildings, Belyi wrote, were barely visible through the "greenish murk" and "greenish yellow fog" that permeated its streets. And its people—"not quite people and not quite shadows"—comprised a "human swarm" tinged with yellow and green and "utterly permeated with smoke." Convinced that it would "go to pieces" in the upheavals he saw ahead, Belyi promised that St. Petersburg would sink from sight and that Russia would take a new course. Yet neither he nor anyone else sensed exactly what lay beyond the horizon. Awash in the paraphernalia of progress, St. Petersburg stood no longer for the grandeur of empire but for things that many thoughtful Russians found troubling in the West. After almost two centuries of trying to make the city more European, they now complained that it was too "non-Russian."²¹ Its clanging machines represented "an evil power in the soul of objects," one of Belyi's friends remarked.²² To such people, the time had come for the conversation about the present and future to shift away from Europe and to concentrate on those forces in Eurasia that seemed to have shaped Russia's destiny for more than a millennium.

But what exactly were those forces and how might they affect Russia's future? In seeking to unravel the riddle of Eurasia, the poet Aleksandr Blok saw a vision that blended East and West into a new revolutionary future. Hopeful that revolution could "organize things so that . . . our false, filthy, boring, hideous life should become a just, pure, merry, and beautiful life," Blok looked on in dismay in late 1917 as violence became a way of life. Yet from the "flames of enmity, barbarism, Tatarism, anger, humiliation, oppression, [and] revenge" that were sweeping Russia, he extracted a poetic icon that foretold a brave new world that promised to transform humankind.²³ Like so many before him, Blok's vision centered on St. Petersburg, where he hoped that the "swelling music" of the Revolution could be shaped into "ungovernable freedom."²⁴ In the poem that he titled *The Twelve*, the figure of Christ Himself wearing a crown of white roses—the symbolic color of the Apocalypse—emerged to lead the way. "Forward, Forward working men and women," Blok urged his readers. "Keep in step with the Revolution!"²⁵

Blok quickly discovered that Russia's Communist future lay in Moscow, for St. Petersburg's Western heritage fit poorly with the Bolsheviks' Eurasian vision. After Lenin moved the capital back to Moscow in 1918, St. Petersburg became the Soviets' "second city," uncertainly proud of being the "cradle of the Russian Revolution" but ill at ease with the name of Leningrad that Lenin's political heirs bestowed upon it. All through the Soviet era it continued to look west and remained a haven for independent artists, writers, and musicians who refused to embrace the collectivist teachings of the Soviet system. For half a century the city's Westernized soul stayed alive in the poetry of Akhmatova, Mandelshtam, and Brodsky, the music of Shostakovich, and the creations of a host of only slightly lesser lights who would not yield to the demands for conformity that Stalin and his successors sought to impose. Only rarely after 1918 could something innovative and modern not be found somewhere in Leningrad's theaters, literary circles, private concerts, or cabarets. In that way its people lived through the terror of the 1930s, the siege of 1941–1944, and the boredom of the Khrushchev and Brezhnev years, when such brilliant poets as Joseph Brodsky and Lev Loseff were driven into exile for refusing to create art that reflected the Soviet creed and stagnation lay so heavily upon the friends they left behind.

By that time, the Cold War was taking a heavy toll. Military needs swallowed up the capital that was supposed to have financed increases in consumer goods and public services, and everyone suffered as a result. Once in the vanguard of Russian industry, Leningrad could not compete with the tidal wave of microchip processors and high technology that poured from the Western world during the 1970s and 1980s. Even by the 1960s, many of the city's factories were out of date, and more became antiquated as time went on. For a time, scientists at the Institute of Theoretical Nuclear Physics were obliged to fly their data to Belgrade to be encoded and processed because the Leningrad branch of the Academy of Sciences could not make modern computers available. When word processors started to replace typewriters in the West, typewriter ribbons were still hard to come by in Leningrad, and when hand-held calculators became so commonplace in the West that some people threw them away rather than bother to replace the batteries, cashiers in Leningrad's shops and offices still toted up sums on abacuses. Automobiles made in the early 1980s looked like those seen on the streets of London and New York twenty years earlier. (Indeed, they looked suspiciously as though they had been produced from the same dies.) Except for cheap cameras, few things manufactured in the Soviet Union could find any market in the West, and that hit Leningrad, once the center of high-quality production, especially hard.

Shortages in the 1970s became more common than they had been a decade earlier, and they disrupted life in absurd ways. One winter, there were no dinner plates for sale anywhere in Leningrad. Another time there was a four-month drought of fresh eggs, and for several months people could buy bread, rusks, and cakes, but no flour. For a while, mayonnaise couldn't be found. Neither could mustard. In the second city of one of the world's two superpowers, it was a hundred times easier to buy vodka than toilet paper, and a prescription often meant not the start of a cure but the beginning of a long, often futile search for the medication that had been prescribed. During the 1960s, the bounty from the waters of the Eastern Baltic had still fed the city, but by the late 1970s, most of it had run out, depleted by desperate overfishing. A canned mixture of ground-up fish parts and pieces called "A Tourist's Lunch" replaced the finer mackerel and haddock of earlier times. The cans' contents looked and smelled like cheap cat food.

A joke that made the rounds soon after the Soviet Union started to let Jews emigrate in the late 1970s focused on Leningrad's many shortages. "Why do you want to leave?" an official at the visa office asked a Jew who was applying for permission to go to Israel. "Because there's too much happiness here," he said flatly. "I can't stand it." "What do you mean, 'too much happiness'?" the puzzled official replied. "How can there be too much happiness?" "Well, when my wife needs a pair of winter boots, we look and look for weeks," the applicant explained. "Finally we hear about a shop that is selling boots 'under the counter,' as it were. So we buy them, even though they cost us more than a month's pay. And we're so happy. Then we want to buy a goose to celebrate the New Year. After days of looking, my wife finally finds a scrawny chicken. It's not exactly what we wanted, but we're happy to have found something. Then our son needs medicine. We can't find it anywhere here, so I go to Moscow and I finally find some on the black market there. Again, we're so happy. I can't stand any more of this happiness," he concluded. "That's why I want to emigrate!"

"We consistently depleted the country's human, social, natural, and moral resources," Leningrad's future mayor Anatolii Sobchak once said in looking back. "Without exception," he concluded, "the 'successes' of the Communist doctrine—from the victory over Hitler to space flights, from ballet to literature—were all taken out of the pocket of Russian history."[26] By definition what always had value during the Soviet era was anything that had been made before it began. Leningraders had headed for the city's antique shops when World War II began in the hope of turning their cash savings into something with lasting value for just that reason. And that was why the Soviet government levied a huge export tax on things made before 1917 that did not apply to anything made afterwards. Paintings, jewelry, icons, books—even odd encyclopedia volumes and paperbound history books published before the Revolution—all were subject to heavy export taxes. So were tsarist stamps, copper kopeks, and even picture postcards made before 1918.

Starting in the 1980s, *glasnost* showed how stale the vision that had shaped the Soviet system had become. The future was uncertain for all of Russia, and for Leningrad, perhaps, most of all, because no one knew whether it would be able to follow its natural inclination to the West. Everything was changing: the names of streets, squares, bridges, the Kirov ballet, the great university that once had been home to Pavlov and Mendeleev, and finally the name of the city itself. Could Leningrad ever truly be St. Petersburg again? Or was it true, as the British correspondent Alexander Werth had written near the end of the Nazi siege, that St. Petersburg was "gone forever," and that Leningrad had taken its place.[27] Even Akhmatova had spoken of Leningrad when she talked about the siege and the victims of Stalin's purges.[28] But would she have changed her mind if she had lived to see the Soviet Union fall apart like great hunks of wet mud during the summer and fall of 1991? Perhaps she would have been drawn to Brodsky's idea that it was better for future generations to "live in a city that bears the name of a saint than a devil."[29] Or maybe she would have remembered the tragedies that had scarred her lifetime. The millions of deaths and millions more ruined lives that the Soviet experience had inflicted were all a part of her native city's life as Leningrad, not St. Petersburg. "Let no one forget, let nothing be forgotten," Olga Berggolts had written after the war.[30] The memories of so much sacrifice and so many heroes could not be tossed aside. Could they remain alive in a reborn St. Petersburg?

What had the loss of so many lives really accomplished? How different was the city that became St. Petersburg again in 1991 from the one that had been given Lenin's name sixty-seven years earlier? Certainly it had more people, covered more ground, and had a public transportation system that no one could have imagined in earlier times. It had more schools, more university graduates, more factories, more apartment buildings. But the Soviet heritage was mainly a dead weight because it brought problems that no city wanted to inherit, ones that St. Petersburg could not afford to solve. City streets, water mains, and sewers were crumbling, and thousands of shoddy buildings erected after World War II were falling apart. As it made its way through the city's outskirts, the main road to Oranienbaum passed blocks of apartment buildings that listed precariously to one side, like leaning towers set in military formation.

*The 1990s brought street repairs and Western-style advertising to Liteinyi Prospekt, where Sergei Diagilev and the Nevskii Pickwickians, Zinaida Gippius and Dmitrii Merezhkovskii, and Joseph Brodsky once lived. (Photo courtesy of Jack Kollmann)*

Bricks fell out of walls, facings and facades peeled off, windows and doors didn't fit, sometimes leaving gaps of several inches. Plumbing and heating didn't work. And some subway lines had been dug so close to the foundations of nearby buildings that a few were beginning to collapse. There was more truth than anyone wanted to admit in the remark that the only way to tell when a new building was finished was when the construction crew moved out and the repair crew moved in. Many buildings were so badly built that proper repairs would cost more than complete reconstruction. Yet, St. Petersburg entered its new life poor as the proverbial church mouse.

The city's brilliant eighteenth- and nineteenth-century architectural heritage was falling apart, too. Rotting stucco and crumbling brick had almost never been properly repaired, and decades of neglect had taken a serious toll. In the Soviet push for modernization, plumbing and heating installations had been haphazard and too often undertaken more with an eye to supporting propaganda claims than to making lasting improvements. City water continued to be unsafe to drink, just as it had been in 1703 and in 1914. Except for a handful of monumental reconstructions such as those undertaken at Tsarskoe Selo's Catherine Palace and the palace at Peterhof, repairs done after the Nazi siege had started to crumble even before the Soviet Union. Medical facilities simply could not support St. Petersburg's population, and such diagnostic devices as CAT scans, MRIs, and other forms of electronic imaging were available to only the tiniest fraction of the population. Even EKGs were hard to come by, and in the early 1990s there were stories of people who needed injections being told to bring their own syringes and needles to clinics. Prescription medicines became even harder to find than in Soviet times.

On the brighter side, daily life in St. Petersburg lost some of the gray drabness of the Soviet era. The crowds on Nevskii Prospekt dressed more colorfully, and the styles of clothing were less monotonous. Shops soon acquired all the material richness of the West and offered a variety that even privileged Soviets could not have imagined a few years before. By the mid-1990s, Burberry raincoats, Ferragamo scarves, Florentine leather coats and shoes, and French cosmetics all had moved from back-alley black markets into shops on the city's main thoroughfares. But their prices put them so far beyond the reach of almost everyone that St. Petersburg's best shops quickly became museums to display the wealth of the West, in which the masses could look but only a tiny handful could hope to buy.

Many Petersburgers had to live on the equivalent of fifty dollars a month, and some had even less as middle-class professionals from the Soviet era found that their skills had no place in the new world taking shape around them. Even more than in tsarist times, St. Petersburg in 1990s became a city with a handful of haves and a horde of have-nots. During the Soviet era, it had not been a shortage of wealth that had kept people out of the best hotels and restaurants but simply the lack of the connections needed to be admitted. Now, money ruled all aspects of life, but it stayed in the hands of an arrogant handful who patronized fine restaurants and luxury hotels, where breakfast cost the better part of a fortnight's wages for the men and women who thronged the streets outside. People trying to sell the few treasures they had gathered in Soviet times replaced the black marketeers in St. Petersburg's side streets. Beggars reappeared, and so did an army of petty thieves.

*Eliseev's food emporium at 56 Nevskii Prospekt, designed by Gavriil Baranovskii in 1904, again offers delicacies. (Photo courtesy of Jack Kollmann)*

With the approach of St. Petersburg's tercentennial, the weight of these many problems leaves observers wondering about the city's future. Can St. Petersburg recover from the trauma of the Soviet experience and regain its equilibrium? If so, where will it be heading? Can the city that Peter built really become Russia's window on the West once again as its mayor promised in 1991? Or will it, at the beginning of the twenty-first century, turn toward the East as so many of the intellectuals who watched it enter the twentieth century urged it to do? How Petersburgers respond to these questions holds a key to their fate. But the history of this remarkable city has shown that facts and figures alone will never determine its future because Petersburgers are different. They use language differently, and they are more inclined to reach out, to take chances, to embrace the unsolvable. They see the past differently, too.

Some three-quarters of the way through the boring Brezhnev years, the Leningrad artist Evgenii Ukhnalev painted *The Road to Nowhere*, which showed a Leningrad entryway leading into pitch darkness. "It is dark as the cave in Leonardo da Vinci's well-known parable, capable of concealing within itself numberless new and unknown images," the Petersburg writer Grigorii Kaganov commented when looking at Ukhnalev's work in 1995. "Among [these images]," he went on, "there might well be the most unforgettably eerie as well as the most unforgettably beautiful things."[31] It was impossible to tell, and as had happened so many times before, there was no way to guess which would emerge or in what order. Beauty, ugliness, brilliance of speech, prolixity, and a hundred other opposites all have been part of St. Petersburg's experience from the very beginning. That they continue to be so now makes the future even harder to discern.

The "impenetrable profundity" that Kaganov sensed in the inner recesses of Ukhnalev's painting applies directly to what lies ahead. For the burdens that St. Petersburg must bear are immense, and practical solutions far from easy. But history has shown that it is a city of remarkable and resilient people capable of huge sacrifices and stunning achievements. Surely the men and women whose ancestors raised a national capital from the Neva's muddy delta, made it the Venice of the North, protected its treasures from the depredations of Soviet "progress," and stood with it against overwhelming odds during the Nazis' siege will meet the challenges that lie ahead in some remarkable way. "The notion of freedom—perhaps phantasmagorical, but very powerful—inevitably arises in the consciousness of anyone living there," Joseph Brodsky once told a friend about St. Petersburg. "In this city," he added, "the individual is always going to strive to reach beyond."[32] In that, Brodsky may have identified the key to St. Petersburg's future. For in politics, in their relations with the outside world, and in the arts, the people of St. Petersburg have always striven to reach beyond the limits of normal human experience. No doubt they will do so again, but only time can reveal what form their efforts will take.

# NOTES

## Prologue

1. Quoted in O. N. Zakharov, *Arkhitekturnye panoramy nevskikh beregov* (Leningrad, 1984), p. 155.

2. Quoted in Solomon Volkov, *St. Petersburg: A Cultural History*, translated by Antonina W. Bouis (New York, 1995), p. 10.

3. N. V. Gogol', "Nevskii prospekt," in *Sobranie sochinenii N. V. Gogolia* (Moscow, 1959), III, p. 42.

4. Friedrich Christian Weber, *The Present State of Russia* (Reprint, New York, 1968), I, p. 4.

5. Quoted in Harrison E. Salisbury, *The 900 Days: The Siege of Leningrad* (New York, 1970), p. 432.

6. G. F. Petrov, *Piskarevskoe kladbishche* (Leningrad, 1975), p. 36.

7. M. E. Saltykov-Shchedrin, *Sobranie sochinenii* (Moscow, 1970), X, p. 271.

8. Quoted in Volkov, *St. Petersburg*, p. 545.

9. A. S. Pushkin, "Mednyi vsadnik," in *Polnoe sobranie sochinenii v desiati tomakh* (Moscow, 1963), IV, pp. 396, 395.

## Chapter 1: The Builders

1. *Sanktpeterburg: Izsledovaniia po istorii, topografii i statistike stolitsy* (St. Petersburg, 1870), II, pp. 5–28. In 1870, the number of islands in the Neva delta was sixty-five. See also Dmitri Shvidkovsky, *St. Petersburg: Architecture of the Tsars*, with photographs by Alexander Orloff, translated from the French by Jane Goodman (New York, London, Paris, 1996), p. 20.

2. Henry Storch, *The Picture of Petersburg*, translated from the German (London, 1801), p. 10.

3. P. N. Petrov, *Istoriia Sankt-Peterburga s osnovaniia goroda, do vvedeniia v deistvie vybornago gorodskago upravleniia, po uchrezhdeniiam o guberniiakh, 1703–1782* (St. Petersburg, 1884), I, pp. 30–38; K. N. Serbina, "Istoriko-geograficheskii ocherk raiona Peterburga do osnovaniia goroda," in M. P. Viatkin, ed., *Ocherki istorii Leningrada* (Moscow-Leningrad, 1955), I, pp. 11–27.

4. Zakharov, *Arkhitekturnye panoramy nevskikh beregov*, pp. 84–85.

5. S. P. Luppov, *Istoriia stroitel'stva Peterburga v pervoi polovine XVIII veka* (Moscow, 1957), p. 23.

6. See, for example, *Pis'ma i bumagi Imperatora Petra Velikago*, IV (St. Petersburg, 1887), p. 445 (19 November 1706); VI (St. Petersburg, 1912), pp. 160–161 (20 November 1707); IX (Moscow-Leningrad, 1950), p. 55 (27 January 1709), p. 472 (29 November 1709). In addition, see James Cracraft, *The Petrine Revolution in Russian Architecture* (Chicago and London, 1988), p. 175; Luppov, *Istoriia stroitel'stva Peterburga*, pp. 15–17, 80–83; G. E. Kochin, "Naselenie Peterburga do 60-kh godov XVIII v.," in M. P. Viatkin, ed., *Ocherki istorii Leningrada* (Moscow-Leningrad, 1955), I, pp. 94–95; Weber, *The Present State of Russia*, I, p. 300; A. V. Predtechenskii, "Osnovanie Peterburga," in A. V. Predtechenskii, ed., *Peterburg petrovskogo vremeni* (Leningrad, 1948); P. N. Stolpianskii, *Peterburg: Kak voznik, osnovalsia i ros Sankt-Piterburkh* (Petrograd, 1918), pp. 7–9.

7. V. O. Kliuchevskii, *Sochineniia v vos'mi tomakh* (Moscow, 1958), IV, p. 125.

8. Quoted in Predtechenskii, "Osnovanie Peterburga," p. 24.

9. Quoted in Cracraft, *Petrine Revolution in Russian Architecture*, p. 218.

10. Pushkin, "Mednyi vsadnik," p. 395. Zakharov, *Arkhitekturnye panoramy nevskikh beregov*, p. 85.

11. Peter first applied this description to St. Petersburg in a letter to Menshikov in 1706. "Pis'mo Petra Alekseevicha k A. D. Menshikovu," 11 sentiabria 1706, *Pis'ma i bumagi Imperatora Petra Velikago* (St. Petersburg, 1900), IV, pt. 1, no. 1349.

12. Quoted in Lindsey Hughes, *Russia in the Age of Peter the Great* (New Haven and London, 1998), p. 213.

13. V. N. Bernadskii and A. E. Sukhnovalov, *Istoricheskoe proshloe Leningrada* (Leningrad, 1958), pp. 53–56; Weber, *The Present State of Russia*, I, pp. 314–320.

14. Quoted in Hughes, *Russia in the Age of Peter the Great*, p. 215.

15. Zakharov, *Arkhitekturnye panoramy nevskikh beregov*, p. 69.

16. Quoted in N. V. Kaliazina, L. P. Dorofeeva, and G. V. Mikhailov, *Dvorets Menshikova: Khudozhestvennaia kul'tura epokhi, istoriia i liudi, arkhitekturnaia khronika pamiatnika* (Moscow, 1986), p. 11.

17. Quoted in Shvidkovsky, *St. Petersburg*, p. 257.

18. Cracraft, *The Petrine Revolution in Russian Architecture*, pp. 148–154, 179; Luppov, *Istoriia stroitel'stva Peterburga*, p. 45; Kochin, "Naselenie Peterburga do 60-kh godov XVIII v.," pp. 94–102; I. Grabar', *O russkoi arkhitekture* (Moscow, 1969), p. 282; Weber, *The Present State of Russia*, I, p. 323; William Brumfield, *A History of Russian Architecture* (Cambridge and New York, 1993), pp. 271–272; Shvidkovsky, *St. Petersburg*, pp. 246–270.

19. W. Bruce Lincoln, *Between Heaven and Hell: The Story of a Thousand Years of Artistic Life in Russia* (New York, 1998), p. 58; Ivan Zabelin, *Domashnii byt*

*russkikh tsarei v XVI i XVII st.*, vol. 1 of *Domashnii byt russkago naroda v XVI i XVII st.* (Moscow, 1895), pp. 444–486; Ia. Reitenfel's, "Skazaniia svetleishemu gertsogu Toskanskomu Kos'me Tret'emu o Moskovii," *Chtenie v obshchestve istorii i drevnostei rossiiskikh pri Imperatorskom Moskovskom universitete*, no. 3 (1905), pp. 92–94.

20. Christopher Marsden, *Palmyra of the North: The First Days of St. Petersburg* (London, 1943), p. 65.

21. Brumfield, *History*, pp. 201–208. See also M. V. Iogansen, "Ob avtore general'nogo plana Peterburga petrovskogo vremeni," in T. V. Alekseeva, ed., *Ot srednevekov'ia k novomu vremeni* (Moscow, 1984), pp. 50–72; Cracraft, *Petrine Revolution in Russian Architecture*, pp. 150–157; V. F. Shilkov, "Arkhitektory-inostrantsy pri Petre I," in I. E. Grabar', ed., *Istoriia russkogo iskusstva* (Moscow, 1960) V, pp. 84–115.

22. I. Lisaevich, *Pervyi arkhitektor Peterburga* (Leningrad, 1971), pp. 39–40; I. E. Grabar', "Osnovanie i nachalo zastroiki Peterburga," in Grabar', *Istoriia russkogo iskusstva*, V, pp. 71–73, 86; Cracraft, *Petrine Revolution in Russian Architecture*, pp. 155–158; and T. T. Rice, "The Conflux of Influences in Eighteenth-Century Russian Art and Architecture: A Journey from the Spiritual to the Realistic," in J. G. Garrard, ed., *The Eighteenth Century in Russia* (Oxford, 1973), pp. 270–271; "Domeniko Trezini," in I. Grabar', *Peterburgskaia arkhitektura v XVIII i XIX vekakh*, vol. 3 of *Istoriia russkago iskusstva* (Moscow, 1910), pp. 45–64.

23. Luppov, *Istoriia stroitel'stva Peterburga*, pp. 15–17, 80–83; Kochin, "Naselenie Peterburga do 60-kh godov XVIII v.," pp. 94–95.

24. Quoted in Cracraft, *Petrine Revolution in Russian Architecture*, p. 213.

25. Quoted in ibid., pp. 211–212.

26. Weber, *The Present State of Russia*, I, p. 151.

27. Mrs. William Vigor, *Letters from a Lady who Resided some Years in Russia*, 2d ed. (London, 1777), pp. 3, 6.

28. I am indebted to Herbert H. Kaplan for the data that show that goods and commodities imported and exported by the British from St. Petersburg during these years increased by nearly a third.

29. S. S. Bronshtein, "Peterburgskaia arkhitektura 20–30-kh godov XVIII veka," in Grabar', *Istoriia russkogo iskusstva*, V, p. 150.

30. Ibid., pp. 122–130; Grabar', *Peterburgskaia arkhitektura v XVIII i XIX vekakh*, pp. 155–161; M. V. Iogansen, *Mikhail Zemtsov* (Leningrad, 1975), *passim*.

31. Grabar', *Peterburgskaia arkhitektura v XVIII i XIX vekakh*, pp. 170–172; Bronshtein, "Peterburgskaia arkhitektura 20–30-kh godov XVIII veka," pp. 144–148.

32. Iogansen, *Mikhail Zemtsov*, pp. 105–106.

33. N. A. Evsina, *Arkhitekturnaia teoriia v Rossii XVIII v.* (Moscow, 1975), pp. 77–93; Iurii Alekseevich Egorov, *The Architectural Planning of St. Petersburg*, translated by Eric Dluhosch (Athens, Ohio, 1969), pp. 27–40.

34. Petrov, *Istoriia Sankt-Peterburga*, I, pp. 324–342.

35. Shvidkovsky, *St. Petersburg*, pp. 56–61.

36. Ibid., p. 61. An abbreviated version of the remarks that follow about Rastrelli first appeared in W. Bruce Lincoln, *Between Heaven and Hell*, pp. 70–75.

37. Marsden, *Palmyra of the North*, p. 108.

38. Vigor, *Letters from a Lady*, pp. 94–95.

39. Iu. Ovsiannikov, *Franchesko Bartolomeo Rastrelli* (Leningrad, 1982), pp. 5–60; D. Arkin, *Rastrelli* (Moscow, 1954), pp. 10–16; George Heard Hamilton, *The Art and Architecture of Russia*, 3d ed. (New Haven and London, 1983), pp. 276–278; B. R. Vipper, "V. V. Rastrelli," in I. E. Grabar', ed., *Istoriia russkogo iskusstva* (Moscow, 1955), V, pp. 174–179. N. Kostomarov, *Russkaia istoriia v zhizneopisaniiakh eia glavneishikh deiatelei* (St. Petersburg, 1893), VII, p. 143; Iogansen, *Mikhail Zemtsov*, pp. 126–133; Grabar', *Peterburgskaia arkhitektura v XVIII i XIX vekakh*, p. 180.

40. Anthony Cross, ed., *Russia under Western Eyes, 1517–1825* (New York, 1971), pp. 192–194.

41. Arkin, *Rastrelli*, pp. 36–38; Ovsiannikov, *Franchesko Bartolomeo Rastrelli*, pp. 72–75; Brumfield, *History*, pp. 236–242.

42. B. R. Vipper, *Arkhitektura russkogo barokko* (Moscow, 1978), p. 80.

43. Quoted in ibid., p. 81. See also Grabar', *Peterburgskaia arkhitektura v XVIII i XIX vekakh*, pp. 206–212; Brumfield, *History*, pp. 250–253; Lincoln, *Between Heaven and Hell*, pp. 73–75.

44. Ovsiannikov, *Franchesko Bartolomeo Rastrelli*, pp. 156, 160.

45. Iu. M. Denisov, "Ischeznuvshie dvortsy," and "Zimnyi dvorets Rastrelli," in V. I. Piliavskii and V. F. Levinson-Lessing, eds., *Ermitazh: Istoriia i arkhitektura zdanii* (Leningrad, 1974), pp. 32–37, 39–47; Marsden, *Palmyra of the North*, pp. 246–248; Brumfield, *History*, pp. 246–247.

46. Hamilton, *The Art and Architecture of Russia*, p. 288.

47. Kaliazina, Dorofeeva, and Mikhailov, *Dvorets Menshikova*, pp. 11–13.

48. A. E. Sukhnovalov, "Ekonomicheskaia zhizn' Peterburga do 60-kh godov XVIII v.," in Viatkin, *Ocherki istorii Leningrada*, pp. 52–93; William Coxe, *Travels in Poland, Russia, Sweden, and Denmark*, 5th ed. (London, 1802), II, pp. 102–103.

49. Zakharov, *Arkhitekturnye panoramy nevskikh beregov*, pp. 128–129.

50. Petrov, *Istoriia Sankt-Peterburga*, II, pp. 206–246.

51. Kochin, "Naselenie Peterburga do 60-kh godov XVIII v.," in Viatkin, *Ocherki istorii Leningrada*, pp. 94–114.

52. Louis-Guillaume, vicomte de Puibusque, *Lettres sur la guerre de Russie en 1812, sur la ville de Saint-Petersbourg, les moeurs et les usages des habitans de la Russie et de la Pologne* (Paris, 1817), p. 189.

53. Quoted in Volkov, *St. Petersburg*, p. 17.

54. Pis'mo Imperatritsy Ekateriny II k Mel'khioru Grimmu, 23 avgusta 1779 g., in Ia. Grot, ed., *Pis'ma Imperatritsy Ekateriny II k Grimmu (1774–1796), Sbornik Imperatorskago russkago istoricheskago obshchestva,* hereafter *SIRIO* (St. Petersburg, 1878), p. 157.

55. V. G. Lisovskii, *Akademiia khudozhestv: Istoriko-iskusstvovedcheskii ocherk* (Leningrad, 1982), pp. 18–26.

56. Grabar', *Peterburgskaia arkhitektura v XVIII i XIX vekakh,* p. 312.

57. Ibid., pp. 312–315; M. F. Korshunova, *Iurii Fel'ten* (Leningrad, 1988), pp. 39–44.

58. Brumfield, *History,* p. 275.

59. F. F. Vigel', *Zapiski,* edited by S. A. Shtraikh (Moscow, 1928), I, p. 181.

60. Quoted in Shvidkovsky, *St. Petersburg,* p. 100.

61. Quoted in Hamilton, *The Art and Architecture of Russia,* pp. 309–310.

62. Ibid., p. 310.

63. A. N. Voronikhina, M. F. Korshunova, and A. M. Pavelkina, eds., *Arkhitekturnye proekty i risunki Dzhakomo Kvarengi iz muzeev i khranilishch SSSR* (Leningrad, 1967), pp. 17–34.

64. Pis'mo imperatritsy Ekateriny II k Mel'khioru Grimmu, 28 oktiabria 1785 g., *SIRIO* (St. Petersburg, 1878), p. 365; M. F. Korshunova, *Dzhakomo Kvarengi* (Leningrad, 1977), pp. 28–110.

65. Korshunova, *Dzhakomo Kvarengi,* pp. 111–137.

66. N. N. Belekhov and A. N. Petrov, *Ivan Starov: Materialy k izucheniiu tvorchestva* (Moscow, 1950); D. A. Kiuchariants, *Ivan Starov* (Leningrad, 1982); A. I. Kudriavtsev and G. N. Shkoda, *Aleksandro-Nevskaia lavra: Arkhitekturnyi ansambl' i pamiatniki nekropolei* (Leningrad, 1986), pp. 25–30; Hamilton, *The Art and Architecture of Russia,* pp. 300–304; Shvidkovsky, *St. Petersburg,* pp. 102–107.

67. Hamilton, *The Art and Architecture of Russia,* p. 302.

68. Shvidkovsky, *St. Petersburg,* p. 104.

69. Quoted in Hamilton, *The Art and Architecture of Russia,* p. 303.

70. G. E. Kochin, "Naselenie Peterburga 60–90-kh godakh XVIII v.," in Viatkin, *Ocherki istorii Leningrada,* I, pp. 294–295.

71. V. I. Makarov, "Ekonomicheskaia zhizn' Peterburga 60–90-kh godov XVIII v.," in Viatkin, *Ocherki istorii Leningrada,* I, pp. 288–289; Storch, *Picture of Petersburg,* pp. 264–268.

72. Storch, *Picture of Petersburg,* p. 119.

73. Makarov, "Ekonomicheskaia zhizn' Peterburga 60–90-kh godov XVIII v.," pp. 292–293.

## Chapter 2: Lords of the Realm

1. Quoted in Nicholas V. Riasanovskii, *A History of Russia,* 3d ed. (New York, 1977), p. 241.

2. Kliuchevskii, *Kurs russkoi istorii* (Moscow, 1937), V, pp. 235–236.

3. Richard S. Wortman, *Scenarios of Power: Myth and Ceremony in Russian Monarchy from Peter the Great to the Death of Nicholas I* (Princeton, 1995), pp. 43–61.

4. Among many examples, see *Pis'ma i bumagi Imperatora Petra Velikago* (St. Petersburg, 1900), IV, pp. 183–184; VII (Petrograd, 1918), pp. 90–91; M. I. Semevskii, "Petr I kak iumorist'," in *Slovo i delo: Ocherki i razskazy iz russkoi istorii XVIII veka* (St. Petersburg, 1885), pp. 285, 296–297, 314–315, 319–320; and Johann Georg Korb, *Diary of an Austrian Secretary of Legation at the Court of Czar Peter the Great*, translated from the original Latin and edited by Count MacDonnell (London, 1863), I, p. 256.

5. Iu. Lotman, "The Poetics of Everyday Behavior in Russian Eighteenth Century Culture," in A. Shukman, ed., *The Semiotics of Russian Culture* (Ann Arbor, 1984), pp. 232–234.

6. P. N. Miliukov, *Ocherki po istorii russkoi kul'tury* (Moscow, 1995), III, p. 208; W. Bruce Lincoln, *The Romanovs: Autocrats of All the Russias* (New York, 1981), pp. 251–252; Hughes, *Russia in the Age of Peter the Great*, pp. 193, 289, 322.

7. Quoted in Hughes, *Russia in the Age of Peter the Great*, p. 430.

8. Weber, *The Present State of Russia*, pp. 187–188.

9. Peter Henry Bruce, *The Memoirs of Peter Henry Bruce, Esq. A Military Officer in the Service of Prussia, Russia, and Great Britain* (London, 1782), pp. 85–86.

10. Quoted in Wortman, *Scenarios of Power*, pp. 54–55.

11. Quoted in Hughes, *Russia in the Age of Peter the Great*, p. 284.

12. Quoted in Miliukov, *Ocherki*, p. 235. See also Wortman, *Scenarios of Power*, pp. 55–60; E. P. Karnovich, "Assamblei pri Petre Velikom," *Drevniaia i novaia Rossiia* (1887), no. 1, pp. 81–82.

13. Quoted in Hughes, *Russia in the Age of Peter the Great*, p. 273.

14. Grigory Kaganov, *Images of Space: St. Petersburg in the Visual and Verbal Arts*, translated from the Russian by Sidney Monas (Stanford, 1997), p. 4. See also E. E. Libtal' and S. P. Luppov, "Opisanie ... stolichnogo goroda Sankt-Peterburga," in M. K. Anikushin, ed., *Belye nochi* (Leningrad, 1974), IV, pp. 197–247.

15. Kochin, "Naselenie Peterburga do 60-kh godov XVIII v.," pp. 112–114.

16. Ibid., pp. 98–114.

17. E. V. Anisimov, "Anna Ivanovna," in Donald J. Raleigh, ed., and A. A. Iskenderov, comp., *The Emperors and Empresses of Russia: Rediscovering the Romanovs* (Armonk and London, 1996), p. 52.

18. I. G. (Johann Gottlieb) Georgi, *Opisanie rossiisko-imperatorskogo stolichnogo goroda Sankt-Peterburga i dostopamiatnostei v okrestnostiakh onogo, c planom* (1794; rpt. St. Petersburg, 1996), pp. 459–460.

19. Quoted in Anthony Cross, *By the Banks of the Neva: Chapters from the Lives and Careers of the British in Eighteenth-Century Russia* (Cambridge, 1997), p. 21. See also pp. 19–20.

20. Storch, *Picture of Petersburg*, p. 574.

21. Herbert H. Kaplan, *Russian Overseas Commerce with Great Britain During the Reign of Catherine II* (Philadelphia, 1995), pp. 269–270. See also pp. 211–268.

22. For this particular insight I am indebted to Professor Herbert H. Kaplan.

23. Quoted in Anthony G. Cross, "The British in Catherine's Russia: A Preliminary Survey," in J. G. Garrard, ed., *The Eighteenth Century in Russia* (Oxford, 1973), pp. 242–243. See also Kaplan, *Russian Overseas Commerce*, pp. 243–244.

24. Quoted in Cross, *By the Banks of the Neva*, p. 334.

25. See Storch, *Picture of Petersburg*, and Georgi, *Opisanie*, pp. 459–460.

26. This is William Richardson's account, quoted in Cross, *By the Banks of the Neva*, p. 348.

27. Quoted in ibid., pp. 389–390.

28. W. Bruce Lincoln, "The Russian State and Its Cities: A Search for Effective Municipal Government, 1786–1842," *Jahrbücher für Geschichte Osteuropas*, XVII, no. 4 (December 1969), pp. 531–541.

29. Georgi, *Opisanie*, pp. 60–63; Storch, *Picture of Petersburg*, pp. 23–24.

30. G. Komelova, G. Printseva, and I. Kotel'nikova, *Peterburg v proizvedeniiakh Patersena* (Moscow, 1978).

31. Georgi, *Opisanie*, pp. 148–149.

32. Makarov, "Ekomomicheskaia zhizn' Peterburga 60–90-kh godov XVIII v.," pp. 284–285.

33. Storch, *Picture of Petersburg*, p. 115.

34. Karl Baedeker, *Russia with Teheran, Port Arthur, and Peking: Handbook for Travellers* (Leipzig, 1914), p. 102.

35. John T. Alexander, "Catherine the Great and Public Health," *Journal of the History of Medicine and Allied Sciences*, XXXVI (1981), pp. 184–204; John T. Alexander, *Catherine the Great: Life and Legend* (New York and Oxford, 1989), pp. 145–147. See also S. P. Luppov, "Gorodskoe upravlenie i gorodskoe khoziaistvo Peterburga v 60–90-kh godakh XVIII v.," in Viatkin, ed., *Ocherki istorii Leningrada*, I, pp. 376–377.

36. A. A. Eliseev and G. E. Pavlova, "Estestvoznanie i tekhnika v Peterburge ot kontsa XVIII v. do 1861 g.," in Viatkin, *Ocherki istorii Leningrada*, pp. 846–848.

37. Georgi, *Opisanie*, pp. 277–313; Storch, *Picture of Petersburg*, pp. 214–246.

38. A. I. Khodnev, *Istoriia Imperatorskago vol'nago ekonomicheskago obshchestva* (St. Petersburg, 1865), pp. 1–35.

39. Kochin, "Naselenie Peterburga v 60–90kh godakh XVIII v.," pp. 294, 301.

40. Ibid., p. 409. See also pp. 205, 194–213.

41. Coxe, *Travels*, II, p. 75.

42. Storch, *Picture of Petersburg*, p. 411.

43. Coxe, *Travels*, II, pp. 124–125.

44. Peter Putman, ed., *Seven Britons in Imperial Russia, 1689–1812* (Princeton, 1952), p. 171.

45. Storch, *Picture of Petersburg*, p. 417.

46. Ibid., pp. 408–409.

47. Ibid., p. 453.

48. Coxe, *Travels*, II, pp. 134–135.

49. William Tooke, *View of the Russian Empire during the Reign of Catherine the Second and to the Close of the Eighteenth Century* (London, 1800), II, p. 233.

50. Ibid., pp. 233–234.

51. S. M. Troitskii, *Finansovaia politika russkogo absoliutizma* (Moscow, 1966), pp. 311, 316; Georgi, *Opisanie*, pp. 158–159; Kochin, "Naselenie Peterburga v 60–90-kh godakh XVIII v.," pp. 310–311.

52. Alexander, *Catherine the Great*, p. 323; Storch, *Picture of Petersburg*, pp. 465–467.

53. Storch, *Picture of Petersburg*, pp. 461–462.

54. Alexander, *Catherine the Great*, pp. 321–324.

55. S. M. Troitskii, *Russkii absoliutizm i dvorianstvo v XVIII v.: Formirovanie biurokratii* (Moscow, 1974), pp. 171–173, 181.

56. *Sanktpeterburg*, III, pp. 106–107.

57. Kaganov, *Images of Space*, p. 76.

## Chapter 3: The Shadow of the Winter Palace

1. Isabel de Madariaga, *Russia in the Age of Catherine the Great* (London, 1981), p. 327.

2. Volkov, *St. Petersburg*, p. 15.

3. Quoted in K. Waliszewski, *The Romance of an Empress: Catherine II of Russia* (New York, 1894), p. 346.

4. Quoted in ibid., p. 341.

5. Geraldine Norman, *The Hermitage: The Biography of a Great Museum* (New York, 1998), pp. 29–35.

6. Quoted in Waliszewski, *The Romance of an Empress*, pp. 344–345.

7. Ibid., p. 344. See also Norman, *The Hermitage*, pp. 21–46.

8. Quoted in Waliszewski, *The Romance of an Empress*, p. 344.

9. Quotes from ibid., pp. 346–348.

10. Quoted in ibid., p. 346. See also Norman, *The Hermitage*, pp. 328–329.

11. Baedeker, *Russia*, pp. 144–145.

12. Madariaga, *Russia in the Age of Catherine the Great*, p. 151.

13. Storch, *Picture of Petersburg*, pp. 33, 30.

14. Coxe, *Travels*, II, p. 154.

15. *Secret Memoirs of the Court of St. Petersburg, Particularly Towards the End of the Reign of Catherine II and the Commencement of that of Paul I* (London, 1895), p. 38.

16. Quoted in Fitzgerald Molloy, *The Russian Court in the Eighteenth Century* (New York, 1905), II, pp. 447, 455.

17. Quoted in Wortman, *Scenarios of Power*, p. 131.

18. V. N. Golovine, *Memoirs of Countess Golovine* (London, 1910), p. 38.

19. N. M. Gershenzon-Chegodaeva, *Dmitrii Grigor'evich Levitskii* (Moscow, 1964), pp. 39–162; N. M. Chegodaeva, "D. G. Levitskii," in Grabar', *Istoriia russkogo iskusstva*, VII, pp. 40–48.

20. Quoted in Hans Rogger, *National Consciousness in Eighteenth-Century Russia* (Cambridge, Mass.: 1960), pp. 202–203.

21. Quoted in Wortman, *Scenarios of Power*, p. 137.

22. Quoted in ibid., pp. 110, 124.

23. Ibid., pp. 138–139.

24. Quoted in ibid., p. 145.

25. Quoted in ibid., pp. 143–144.

26. Quoted in D. Arkin, *Mednyi vsadnik: Pamiatnik Petru I v Leningrade* (Leningrad, 1958), p. 11. See also pp. 8–10.

27. Quoted in A. Kaganovich, *"Mednyi vsadnik": Istoriia sozdaniia monumenta* (Leningrad, 1975), p. 53. See also pp. 16–18.

28. "Donesenie kniazia Golitsyna N. I. Paninu ot 31 avgusta 1766 goda, s prilozheniem kontrakta, zakliuchennago s Fal'konetom i spiska veshcham ego," *SIRIO*, XVII (St. Petersburg, 1876), pp. 372–377; P. M. Maikov, *Ivan Ivanovich Betskoi: Opyt ego biografii* (St. Petersburg, 1904), pp. 344–345.

29. Louis Reau, *Etienne-Maurice Falconet* (Paris, 1922), II, pp. 334–335.

30. Maikov, *Ivan Ivanovich Betskoi*, pp. 348–349; Reau, *Etienne-Maurice Falconet*, I, pp. 96–100; "Kopiia Vsepoddanneishago doklada Pravitel'stvuiushchago Senata ot 4 marta 1776 g.," in *SIRIO*, XVII, pp. 406–408.

31. Etienne-Maurice Falconet, *Oeuvres d'Etienne Falconet* (Lausanne, 1781), I, pp. 181–182, 191.

32. Quoted in Kaganovich, *"Mednyi vsadnik,"* p. 92.

33. Quoted in ibid., pp. 62–63. See also "Pis'mo Falkoneta Imperatritse Ekaterine II, 25 marta 1773 g.," in *SIRIO* XVII (1876), pp. 186–187; Reau, *Etienne-Maurice Falconet*, II, pp. 367–368.

34. Kaganovich, *"Mednyi vsadnik,"* pp. 161–166.

35. Quoted in Arkin, *Mednyi vsadnik*, p. 11. See also pp. 8–10.

36. Quoted in Kaganovich, *"Mednyi vsadnik,"* p. 53. See also pp. 16–18.

37. Quoted in Arkin, *Mednyi vsadnik*, pp. 13, 16. See also Charboures (Carburi), Marinos Komis, *Monument élève à la gloire de Pierre-le-Grand* (Paris, 1777); Reau, *Etienne-Maurice Falconet*, II, p. 361; Kaganovich, *"Mednyi vsadnik,"* p. 42.

38. Kaganovich, *"Mednyi vsadnik,"* pp. 161–166.

39. N. I. Novikov, "Otryvok puteshestviia v*** I*** T***," in I. V. Malyshev, ed., *N. I. Novikov i ego sovremenniki: Izbrannye sochineniia* (Moscow, 1961), p. 100.

40. "Smertnyi prigovor A. N. Radishchevu," in D. A. Babkin, ed., *Protsess A. N. Radishcheva* (Moscow, 1952), p. 244.

41. Ibid.

42. "Pis'mo Ekateriny II k D'Alemberu s predlozhdeniem priekhat' v Peterburg i zaniat'sia vospitaniem Velikago Kniazia Pavla Petrovicha, 13 noiabria 1762 g.," *SIRIO*, VII (1871), p. 179.

43. Quoted in A. Startsev, *Radishchev v gody "Puteshestviia"* (Moscow, 1960), p. 21.

### Chapter 4: The Hub of Empire

1. Lincoln, *The Romanovs*, pp. 461–462; Wortman, *Scenarios of Power*, pp.170, 210.

2. Quoted in Wortman, *Scenarios of Power*, p. 311.

3. V. N. Petrov, "M. I. Kozlovskii," in Grabar', *Istoriia russkogo iskusstva*, VI, pp. 420–433. See also V. A. Evseev, A. G. Raskin, and L. P. Shaposhnikova, *Monumental'naia i dekorativnaia skul'ptura Leningrada* (Leningrad, 1991), pp. 24–25.

4. Petrov, "M. I. Kozlovskii," p. 433; Wortman, *Scenarios of Power*, pp.211–212.

5. Vigel', *Zapiski*, I, pp. 179, 177–178.

6. G. Vilinbakhov, "Sankt-Peterburg—voennaia stolitsa," *Nashe nasledie*, no. 1 (1989), pp. 16–17.

7. Lincoln, *Between Heaven and Hell*, pp. 110–111; M. A. Il'in, "A. D. Zakharov," in Grabar', *Istoriia russkogo iskusstva*, VIII, bk. 1, pp. 86–104; G. G. Grimm, *Arkhitektor Andreian Zakharov* (Moscow, 1940), pp. 7–62; V. I. Piliavskii and N. Ia. Leiboshits, *Zodchii Zakharov* (Leningrad, 1963); Brumfield, *History*, pp. 356–358; Hamilton, *Art and Architecture of Russia*, pp. 321–322.

8. Théophile Gautier, *The Complete Works of Théophile Gautier*, translated and edited by F. C. DeSumichrast (New York, 1910), VII, p. 110.

9. Quoted in Shvidkovsky, *St. Petersburg*, p. 144.

10. Lincoln, *Between Heaven and Hell*, p. 114; I. E. Grabar', "T. Tomon," in Grabar', *Istoriia russkogo iskusstva*, VII, bk. 1, pp. 111–112; P. Svin'in, *Dostopamiatnosti Sanktpeterburga* (St. Petersburg, 1816), II, pp. 98–109.

11. S. V. Bezsonov, *Krepostnye arkhitektory* (Moscow, 1938), pp. 39–54; V. Panov, *Arkhitektor A. N. Voronikhin* (Moscow, 1937), pp. 25–30; M. A. Il'in, "A. N. Voronikhin," in Grabar', *Istoriia russkogo iskusstva*, VIII, bk. 1, pp. 62–80; Ia. I. Shurygin, *Kazanskii Sobor* (Leningrad, 1987), pp. 7–41; G. G. Grimm, *Arkhitektor Voronikhin* (Leningrad, 1963), pp. 33–58; Svin'in, *Dostopamiatnosti Sanktpeterburga*, II, pp. 52–57; Lincoln, *Between Heaven and Hell*, pp. 114–115, 118–119; Brumfield, *History*, pp. 348–348.

12. Quoted in Brumfield, *History*, p. 359. See also pp. 400–403; Egorov, *Architectural Planning*, pp. 157–166; N. F. Khomutetskii and N. A. Evskina, "Arkhitektura", in Grabar', *Istoriia russkogo iskusstva*, VIII, bk. 2, pp. 463–467; Lincoln, *Between Heaven and Hell*, pp. 111–112.

13. Gautier, *Complete Works*, VII, pp. 240–241.

14. Ibid., pp. 250–251, 268, 267.

15. Quoted in Brumfield, *History*, p. 359.

16. Quoted in Hamilton, *Art and Architecture of Russia*, p. 327.

17. M. Z. Taranovskaia, *Karl Rossi—arkhitektor, gradostroitel', khudozhnik* (Leningrad, 1980), pp. 9–18; Brumfield, *History*, pp. 358–360.

18. G. G. Grimm, M. A. Il'in, and Iu. A. Egorov, "K. I. Rossi," in Grabar', *Istoriia russkogo iskusstva*, VIII, bk. 1, pp. 132–138.

19. Ibid., pp. 151–157; N. Veinert, *Rossi* (Moscow-Leningrad, 1939), pp. 99–130; Taranovskaia, *Karl Rossi*, pp. 96–156; Lincoln, *Between Heaven and Hell*, pp. 112–113.

20. Veinert, *Rossi*, pp. 57–85; Egorov, *Architectural Planning*, pp. 137–154; Taranovskaia, *Karl Rossi*, pp. 71–85; Lincoln, *Between Heaven and Hell*, p. 113; V. I. Piliavskii, *Zodchii Rossi* (Moscow, 1951), pp. 83–94; Brumfield, *History*, pp. 361–364, 402–403.

21. Grimm, Il'in, and Egorov, "K. I. Rossi," pp. 158–161; Lincoln, *The Romanovs*, pp. 466–467; Piliavskii, *Zodchii Rossii*, p. 95–98; Veinert, *Rossi*, pp. 131–141; Egorov, *Architectural Planning*, pp. 166–182.

22. S. Frederick Starr, *Decentralization and Self-Government in Russia, 1830–1870* (Princeton, 1972), pp. 27–28.

23. Quoted in Michael Florinsky, *Russia: A History and An Interpretation* (New York, 1968), II, pp. 896–897.

24. W. Bruce Lincoln, *In the Vanguard of Reform: Russia's Enlightened Bureaucrats, 1825–1861* (DeKalb, 1982), pp. 12–13; P. A. Zaionchkovskii, *Pravitel'stvennyi apparat samoderzhavnoi Rossii v XIX v.* (Moscow, 1978), p. 69.

25. L. V. Tengoborskii, "Extraits du Mémoire secret du Conseiller Privé Actuel Tengoborski (janvier 1857)," Rossiiskii gosudarstvennyi istoricheskii arkhiv v Sanktpeterburge (RGIA), fond 851, opis' 1, delo no. 289–290.

26. A. P. Zablotskii-Desiatovskii, "Statisticheskoe obozrenie gosudarstvennykh i obshchestvennykh povinnostei, dokhodov i raskhodov v Kievskoi gubernii, 1850–1851 gg.," RGIA, fond 940, opis' 1, delo no. 69/3.

27. A. I. Artem'ev, "Dnevnik, 1 iiulia–31 dekabria 1856 g.," Otdel rukopisei, Rossiiskaia natsional'naia biblioteka (ORRNB), fond 37, delo no. 159/138.

28. M. P. Veselovskii, "Zapiski M. P. Veselovskago s 1828 po 1882," ORRNB, fond 550.F.IV.861/420.

29. L. A. Perovskii, "O prichinakh umnozheniia deloproizvodstva," RGIA, fond 1287, opis' 36, delo no. 137/15.

30. P. A. Valuev, "Duma russkago vo vtoroi polovine 1855 g.," *Russkaia starina*, LXX, no. 5 (May 1891), p. 355.

31. Saltykov-Shchedrin, *Sobranie sochinenii*, X, p. 271.

32. A. I. Artem'ev, "Dnevnik, 1 ianvaria–31 iiulia 1856 g.," Entry for January 11, 1856, ORRNB, fond 37, delo no. 158/8.

33. Lincoln, *In the Vanguard of Reform*, pp. 91–100.

34. I. D. Iakushkin, *Zapiski, stat'i, pis'ma dekabrista I. D. Iakushkina*, edited by S. Ia. Shtraikh (Moscow, 1951), pp. 41–42.

35. W. Bruce Lincoln, *Nicholas I: Emperor and Autocrat of All the Russias* (London, 1978), pp. 31–47.

36. Quoted in Volkov, *St. Petersburg*, p. 23.

37. Pushkin, "Mednyi vsadnik," in *Polnoe sobranie sochinenii*, IV, pp. 389, 395.

38. N. K. Shil'der, *Imperator Nikolai Pervyi: Ego zhizn' i tsarstvovanie* (St. Petersburg, 1903), II, p. 362; A. V. Predtechenskii, "Politicheskaia i obshchestvennaia zhizn' Peterburga 30–50-kh godov XIX v.," in Viatkin, ed., *Ocherki istorii Leningrada*, I, pp. 680–681.

39. A. V. Nikitenko, *Dnevnik* (Moscow, 1955), I, p. 312.

40. V. P. Bykova, *Zapiski staroi smolianki* (St. Petersburg, 1898), p. 180.

41. "Obozrenie khoda i deistvii kholernoi epidemii v Rossii v techenie 1848 goda," *Zhurnal Ministerstva vnutrennikh del*, XXVII, no. 9 (September 1849), pp. 314–328.

42. Pushkin, "Mednyi Vsadnik," p. 383.

43. Lincoln, *Between Heaven and Hell*, p. 137.

44. Quoted in A. S. Pushkin, "Evgenii Onegin," in *Polnoe sobranie sochinenii*, V, p. 140.

45. Quoted in Volkov, *St. Petersburg*, p. 26.

46. Vladimir Nabokov, *Nikolai Gogol* (New York, 1944), p. 8.

47. "Pis'mo N. V. Gogolia k P. P. Kosiarovskomu, 3-go oktiabria 1827 g.," in Gogol', *Sobranie sochinenii* (1959), VI, p. 273.

48. Volkov, *St. Petersburg*, p. 31.

49. Nabokov, *Nikolai Gogol*, p. 12.

50. N. V. Gogol', "Nevskii Prospekt," in Gogol', *Sobranie sochinenii* (1959), III, p. 43.

51. Victor Erlich, *Gogol* (New Haven and London, 1969), p. 79.

52. Lincoln, *Between Heaven and Hell*, p. 286.

53. Nabokov, *Nikolai Gogol*, p. 12.

54. Andrei Belyi, *Peterburg* (Munich, 1967), II, p. 12.

55. Gogol', "Nevskii Prospekt," p. 42.

56. Ibid., pp. 7–8.

## Chapter 5: The Nevskii Prospekt

1. Gogol', "Nevskii Prospekt," p. 8.

2. Ibid., pp. 8–9.

3. I. G. Kotel'nikova, *Vidy Peterburga: Akvareli V. Sadovnikova* (Leningrad, 1970), pp. 1–3; Kaganov, *Images of Space*, p. 81.

4. Quoted in Kaganov, *Images of Space*, p. 107.

5. Gogol', "Nevskii Prospekt," p. 8.

6. Ibid., pp. 10–11.

7. Ibid., p. 12.

8. A. I. Kopanev, *Naselenie Peterburga v pervoi polovine XIX veka* (Moscow-Leningrad, 1957), pp. 17, 27, 54, 58; A. I. Kopanev, "Naselenie Peterburga ot kontsa XVIII v. do 1861," in Viatkin, ed., *Ocherki istorii Leningrada*, I, pp. 527–528.

9. Kopanev, "Naselenie Peterburga ot kontsa XVIII v. do 1861," p. 532.

10. Ibid., pp. 542–544.

11. Quoted in Kaganov, *Images of Space*, p. 109.

12. Lincoln, *Vanguard of Reform*, pp. 12–25; W. Bruce Lincoln, "The Daily Life of St. Petersburg Officials in the Mid-Nineteenth Century," *Oxford Slavonic Papers*, VIII (1975), pp. 82–100.

13. "O polozhenii chernorabochikh v S.-Peterburge," RGIA, fond 869, opis' 1, delo no. 350/1–16.

14. Reginald E. Zelnik, *Labor and Society in Tsarist Russia: The Factory Workers of St. Petersburg, 1855–1870* (Stanford, 1971), pp. 241–244.

15. Nikitenko, *Dnevnik*, II, pp. 393, 454.

16. Quoted in Volkov, *St. Petersburg*, p. 44.

17. Richard Stites, *The Women's Liberation Movement in Russia: Feminism, Nihilism, and Bolshevism, 1860–1930* (Princeton, 1991), pp. 60–63.

18. A. A. Bakhtiarov, *Briukho Peterburga: Ocherki stolichnoi zhizni* (Sankt-Peterburg, 1994), p. 140.

19. Théophile Gautier, *Travels in Russia*, translated and edited by F. C. de Sumichrast (New York, 1902), p. 231.

20. Bakhtiarov, *Briukho Peterburga*, pp. 140–141.

21. Ibid., pp. 53–76; Kopanev, *Naselenie Peterburga*, pp. 32–48.

22. Nikitenko, *Dnevnik*, I, p. 79.

23. William L. Blackwell, *The Beginnings of Russian Industrialization, 1800–1860* (Princeton, 1968), pp. 274–278.

24. Ibid., pp. 279–302; S. P. Luppov and N. N. Petrov, "Gorodskoe upravlenie i gorodskoe khoziaistvo Peterburga ot kontsa XVIII v. do 1861," in Viatkin, *Ocherki istorii Leningrada*, pp. 622–624.

25. M. A. Pylaev, *Staryi Peterburg* (Leningrad, 1990), pp. 108–119.

26. Quoted in ibid., p. 120.

27. Ibid., pp. 123–126.

28. Quoted in Volkov, *St. Petersburg*, pp. 61–63. See also Lincoln, *Between Heaven and Hell*, pp. 147–149.

29. Pylaev, *Staryi Peterburg*, pp. 89–94; Gautier, *Travels in Russia*, p. 231.

30. Quoted in I. N. Bozherianov, *Zhizneopisanie Imperatritsy Aleksandry Fedorovny* (St. Petersburg, 1898), I, p. 37.

31. Quoted in Pylaev, *Staryi Peterburg*, p. 104.

32. Quoted in ibid., p. 104.

33. Quoted in Blackwell, *Beginnings of Russian Industrialization*, p. 295.

34. Norman, *The Hermitage*, pp. 71–76.

35. P. Kropotkin, *Memoirs of a Revolutionist* (Boston and New York, 1899), pp. 157–158.

36. Quoted in Abbott Gleason, *Young Russia: The Genesis of Russian Radicalism in the 1860s* (Chicago and London, 1983), p. 169.

37. Quoted in Franco Venturi, *Roots of Revolution: A History of the Populist and Socialist Movements in Nineteenth-Century Russia*, translated from the Italian by Francis Haskell, with an introduction by Isaiah Berlin (Chicago and London, 1983), pp. 293, 292, 296.

38. Quoted in Starr, *Decentralization and Self-Government*, p. 53.

39. D. G. Kutsentov, "Naselenie Peterburga: Polozhenie peterburgskikh rabochikh," in B. M. Kochakov, ed., *Ocherki istorii Leningrada* (Moscow-Leningrad, 1957), II, pp. 172–174, 182–183, 206–207.

40. Quoted in N. Antsiferov, *Dusha Peterburga* (Peterburg, 1922), p. 141.

## Chapter 6: Modernity's Challenge

1. James H. Bater, *St. Petersburg: Industrialization and Change* (Montreal, 1976), pp. 192, 203, 206–208.

2. Ibid., pp. 177–178, 182–183.

3. Quoted in ibid., p. 184.

4. G. Dobson, *St. Petersburg* (London, 1910), pp. 110–111.

5. Bater, *St. Petersburg*, pp. 349–352.

6. S. M. Lapitskaia, *Byt rabochikh Trekhgornoi manufaktury* (Moscow, 1935), p. 63.

7. P. N. Stolpianskii, *Zhizn' i byt peterburgskoi fabriki za 210 let ee sushchestvovaniia, 1704–1914 gg.* (Leningrad, 1925), pp. 120–121.

8. Kopanev, "Naselenie Peterburga ot kontsa XVIII v. do 1861," pp. 627–628; Kutsentov, "Naselenie Peterburga. Polozhenie peterburgskikh rabochikh," p. 216.

9. Ibid., p. 174; Stolpianskii, *Zhizn' i byt peterburgskoi fabriki*, pp. 120–121.

10. M. I. Gil'bert, "Dvizhenie zarabotkov rabochikh v kontse XIX v.," in M. V. Nechkina et al., eds., *Iz istorii rabochego klassa i revoliutsionnogo dvizheniia* (Moscow, 1958), pp. 319–332.

11. Bater, *St. Petersburg*, pp. 335–336, 345–347; Kutsentov, "Naselenie Peterburga," pp. 202–203.

12. Quoted in I. A. Baklanova, "Formirovanie i polozhenie promyshlennogo proletariata. Rabochee dvizhenie: 60-e gody—nachalo 90-kh godov," in V. S. Diakin et al., eds., *Istoriia rabochikh Leningrada* (Leningrad, 1972), p. 143.

13. Bater, *St. Petersburg*, pp. 337–342.

14. Ibid., p. 393.

15. N. V. Kireev, "Promyshlennost'," in Kocharov, *Ocherki istorii Leningrada*, II, pp. 94–101.

16. Bater, *St. Petersburg*, pp. 222–227.

17. M. Mitel'man, B. Glebov, and A. Ul'ianskii, *Istoriia Putilovskogo zavoda* (Moscow-Leningrad, 1939), pp. 21–38; René Girault, "Finances internationales et relations internationales (à propos des usines Poutiloff)," *Revue d'histoire moderne et contemporaine*, no. 3, XIII (juillet-septembre 1966), p. 220.

18. Quoted in *The Modern Encyclopedia of Russian and Soviet History* (Gulf Breeze, Fla.), p. xxx, 106.

19. Ibid., pp. 106–108; Mitel'man, Glebov, and Ul'ianskii, *Istoriia Putilovskogo zavoda*, pp. 163–170, 361–371; Girault, "Finances internationales et relations internationales," pp. 219–221.

20. N. V. Kireev, "Transport, torgovlia, kredit," in Kocharov, *Ocherki istorii Leningrada*, II, pp. 156–168; Olga Crisp, *Studies in the Russian Economy before 1914* (New York, 1976), pp. 123–127; I. I. Levin, *Aktsionernye kommercheskie banki v Rossii* (Petrograd, 1917), pp. 176–177, 194–196, 289–301; I. F. Gindin, *Russkie kommercheskie banki* (Moscow, 1948).

21. Bater, *St. Petersburg*, pp. 128–139, 275–284, 308–309.

22. Quoted in William Craft Brumfield, *The Origins of Modernism in Russian Architecture* (Berkeley and Los Angeles, 1991), pp. 17–18.

23. Quoted in ibid., p. 4.

24. Ibid.

25. Quoted in ibid., pp. 7–8.

26. V. G. Isachenko, "Fedor Lidval," in V. G. Isachenko, comp., *Zodchie Sankt-Peterburga: XIX-nachalo XX veka* (St. Petersburg, 1998), pp. 705–722; Brumfield, *The Origins of Modernism*, pp. 174–177.

27. Brumfield, *The Origins of Modernism*, pp. 181–192.

28. Ibid., p. 212.

29. See Henry Charles Bainbridge, *Peter Carl Fabergé: Goldsmith and Jeweller to the Russian Imperial Court and the Principal Crowned Heads of Europe* (London, 1949), pp. 9–12; Gerald Hill, ed., *Fabergé and the Russian Master Goldsmiths* (New York, 1989).

30. I. G. Tokareva, "V poiskakh 'novogo stilia'," *Leningradskaia panorama*, no. 6 (1986), p. 33.

31. V. S. Gorniunov, N. V. Isachenko, and O. V. Taratynova, "Gavriil Baranovskii," in Isachenko, comp., *Zodchie Sankt-Peterburga*, pp. 609–627.

32. Brumfield, *Origins of Modernism*, pp. 212–220; V. G. Isachenko et al., *Arkhitektory stroiteli Peterburga-Petrograda nachala XX veka* (Leningrad, 1982), pp. 117–127; V. G. Isachenko, "Pavel Siuzor," in Isachenko, comp., *Zodchie Sankt-Peterburga*, pp. 501–517.

33. Quoted in Brumfield, *Origins of Modernism*, p. 459.

34. Ibid., pp. 220–246; Brumfield, *History*, pp. 458–464; Georgii Lukomskii, "Neo-klasitsizm v arkhitekture Peterburga," *Apollon*, no. 5 (1914), pp. 10–19.

35. Quoted in Brumfield, *Origins of Modernism*, pp. 258, 238, 265.

36. Ibid., pp. 265–273; V. E. Zhukov, "Ivan Fomin," in Isachenko, comp., *Zodchie Sankt-Peterburga*, pp. 786–815; I. E. Gostev, "Marian Peretiatkovich," in ibid., pp. 746–760; B. M. Kirikov, "Marian Lialevich," in ibid., pp. 912–924.

37. E. E. Kruze and D. G. Kutsentov, "Naselenie Peterburga," in Kochakov, *Ocherki istorii Leningrada*, III, p. 105; S. S. Volk, "Prosveshchenie i shkola v Peterburge," in ibid., p. 536.

38. *Russkaia periodicheskaia pechat': Spravochnik*, 2 vols. (Moscow, 1957–1959); vol. 1, *1702–1894*, ed. A. G. Dement'ev, A. V. Zapadov, and M. S. Cherepakhov; vol. 2, *1895-oktiabr' 1917*, ed. M. S. Cherepakhov and E. M. Fingerit.

39. N. G. Chernyshevskii, "The Aesthetic Relation of Art to Reality," in N. G. Chernyshevskii, *Selected Philosophical Essays* (Moscow, 1953), pp. 379–381.

40. Quoted in Venturi, *Roots of Revolution*, p. 174.

41. Adam B. Ulam, *In the Name of the People: Prophets and Conspirators in Pre-Revolutionary Russia* (New York, 1977), pp. 135–137; William F. Woehrlin, *Chernyshevskii: The Man and the Journalist* (Cambridge, Mass., 1971), pp. 313–319.

42. Gleason, *Young Russia*, pp. 308–309, 324–326; E. S. Vilenskaia, *Revoliutsionnoe podpol'e v Rossii (60-e gody XIX v.)* (Moscow, 1965), pp. 394–414; Venturi, *Roots of Revolution*, pp. 334–345.

43. Vilenskaia, *Revoliutsionnoe podpol'e v Rossii*, pp. 102–109; Gleason, *Young Russia*, pp. 126–127, 330–331.

## Chapter 7: The Peter and Paul Fortress

1. A. V. Predtechenskii, "Osnovanie Peterburga. Politicheskaia i obshchestvennaia zhizn' goroda 1703–1725 gg.," in Viatkin, *Ocherki istorii Leningrada*, I, pp. 34–35, 48–49; A. I. Gegello and V. D. Shilkov, "Arkhitektura i planirovka Peterburga do 60-kh godov XVIII v.," in ibid., pp. 117–120, 130–132; A. N. Petrov et al., *Pamiatniki arkhitektury Leningrada* (Leningrad, 1972), pp. 28–30; M. N. Gernet, *Istoriia tsarskoi tiur'my* (Moscow, 1960), I, pp. 161–165.

2. Gernet, *Istoriia tsarskoi tiur'my*, I, pp. 165–168.

3. Hughes, *Russia in the Age of Peter the Great*, pp. 409–411; V. Ulanov, "Oppozitsiia Petru Velikomu," in *Tri veka* (Moscow, 1912), pp. 79–82.

4. Gernet, *Istoriia tsarskoi tiur'my*, I, pp. 185–195.

5. Iakuskhin, *Zapiski, stat'i, pis'ma dekabrista I. D. Iakushkina*, pp. 65–67; M. V. Nechkina, *Dvizhenie dekabristov* (Moscow, 1955), II, pp. 392–400.

6. Quoted in Gernet, *Istoriia tsarskoi tiur'my*, III, p. 121.

7. Vera Figner, *Memoirs of a Revolutionist* (New York, 1927), p. 152.

8. Lincoln, *Nicholas I*, pp. 303–310; J. H. Seddon, *The Petrashevtsy: A Study of the Russian Revolutionaries of 1848* (Manchester, 1985), pp. 14–15, 24–31.

9. Quoted in Gernet, *Istoriia tsarskoi tiur'my*, III, p. 222.

10. F. M. Dostoevskii, *Pis'ma* (Moscow-Leningrad, 1928), I, p. 128. See also W. Bruce Lincoln, *The Conquest of A Continent: Siberia and the Russians* (New York, 1994), pp. 177–178.

11. Quoted in Leonid Grossman, *Dostoevskii* (Moscow, 1965), p. 154.

12. Quoted in ibid., p. 157.

13. Quoted in Gernet, *Istoriia tsarskoi tiur'my*, III, p. 343.

14. Kropotkin, *Memoirs of a Revolutionist*, p. 343.

15. Ibid., p. 342.

16. Ibid., pp. 352, 345–346.

17. Ibid., p. 353.

18. Ibid., p. 351.

19. Stepniak [Sergei Kravchinskii], *Russia under the Tzars*, translated into English by William Westall (New York, 1885), pp. 148, 154.

20. Quoted in David Footman, *Red Prelude: The Life of the Russian Terrorist Zhelyabov* (New Haven, 1945), pp. 107, 110.

21. Quoted in the introduction to A. F. Koni, "Vospominaniia o dele Very Zasulich," in *Sobranie sochinenii* (Moscow, 1966), p. 19. See also W. Bruce Lincoln, *In War's Dark Shadow: The Russians before the Great War* (New York, 1983), pp. 158–160.

22. Vera Figner, *Zapechatlennyi trud: Vospominaniia* (Moscow, 1964), I, pp. 219–227; S. S. Volk, *Narodnaia volia, 1879–1882* (Moscow-Leningrad, 1966), pp. 102–104; Footman, *Red Prelude*, pp. 130–139; Lincoln, *The Romanovs*, pp. 441–443; Lincoln, *In War's Dark Shadow*, pp. 164–165.

23. Quoted in Footman, *Red Prelude*, p. 167.

24. Lincoln, *In War's Dark Shadow*, pp. 165–166.

25. Quoted in Footman, *Red Prelude*, p. 106.

26. Lincoln, *In War's Dark Shadow*, pp. 165–166.

27. Ibid., pp. 167–169; Footman, *Red Prelude*, pp. 171–185; Figner, *Zapechatlennyi trud*, pp. 258–267.

28. Quoted in Footman, *Red Prelude*, p. 236. See also pp. 218–235, 248, and Gernet, *Istoriia tsarskoi tiur'my*, III, pp. 156–158.

29. Footman, *Red Prelude*, pp. 236–243.

30. Figner, *Memoirs of a Revolutionist*, p. 152.

31. Ibid., p. 188.

32. Quoted in Samuel H. Baron, *Plekhanov: The Father of Russian Marxism* (Stanford, 1963), p. 55.

33. G. V. Plekhanov, "Pervye shagi sotsial-demokraticheskogo dvizheniia v Rossii," in *Sochineniia*, edited by D. Riazanov (Moscow-Leningrad, 1923), XXIV, pp. 178–179.

34. S. I. Mitskevich, *Revoliutsionnaia Moskva, 1888–1905* (Moscow, 1940), p. 143.

35. Iu. Martov, *Zapiski sotsial-demokrata* (Berlin-Petersburg-Moscow, 1922), p. 19.

36. Lincoln, *In War's Dark Shadow*, pp. 178–182.

37. Quoted in Gerald D. Suhr, *1905 in St. Petersburg: Labor, Society, and Revolution* (Stanford, 1989), p. 54.

38. Ibid., pp. 53–56.

39. Quoted in K. M. Takhtarev, *Rabochee dvizhenie v Peterburge (1893–1901 gg.)* (Leningrad, 1924), pp. 56–58.

40. Ibid., pp. 79–83; Allan K. Wildman, *The Making of A Workers' Revolution: Russian Social Democracy, 1891–1903* (Chicago, 1967), pp. 64–80; Richard Pipes, *Social Democracy and the St. Petersburg Labor Movement, 1885–1897* (Cambridge, Mass., 1963), pp. 94–98.

41. Quoted in Takhtarev, *Rabochee dvizhenie v Peterburge*, p. 66.

42. Quoted in Suhr, *1905 in St. Petersburg*, p. 90.

43. Ibid., pp. 87–95.

44. Quoted in Harrison E. Salisbury, *Black Night, White Snow: Russia's Revolutions, 1905–1917* (New York, 1977), p. 93.

45. Quoted in Walter Sablinsky, *The Road to Bloody Sunday: Father Gapon and the St. Petersburg Massacre of 1905* (Princeton, 1976), p. 43.

46. G. A. Gapon, *Zapiski Georgiia Gapona* (Moscow, 1918), pp. 27–28. See also pp. 11–27.

47. Quoted in Sablinsky, *The Road to Bloody Sunday*, p. 85.

48. Quoted in Gerald D. Suhr, "Petersburg's First Mass Labor Organization: The Assembly of Russian Workers and Father Gapon," *Russian Review*, XL, no. 3 (July 1981), p. 259.

49. A. E. Karelin, "Deviatoe ianvaria i Gapon," *Krasnaia letopis'*, no. 1 (1922), p. 107.

50. Quoted in Sablinsky, *The Road to Bloody Sunday*, pp. 88–89.

51. Ibid., pp. 142–144.

52. Quoted in ibid., p. 158.

53. Quoted in Suhr, *1905 in St. Petersburg*, p. 161.

54. Quoted in Sablinsky, *The Road to Bloody Sunday*, p. 198.

55. Quoted in Salisbury, *Black Night, White Snow*, p. 123.

56. L. Gurevich, "Narodnoe dvizhenie v Peterburge 9-go ianvaria 1905 goda," *Byloe*, no. 1 (January 1906), p. 204.

57. Quoted in A. El'nitskii, *Tysiacha deviat'sot piatyi god* (Kursk, 1925), p. 34. See also Lincoln, *In War's Dark Shadow*, pp. 285–289.

58. S. N. Semanov, *Krovavoe voskresen'e* (Leningrad, 1965), pp. 72–73.

59. Gurevich, "Narodnoe dvizhenie," p. 213.

60. Quoted in Salisbury, *Black Night, White Snow*, p. 124.

61. P. M. Rutenberg, "Delo Gapona," *Byloe*, Nos. 11–12 (July-August 1909), p. 33. See also Semanov, *Krovavoe voskresen'e*, p. 86.

62. M. Gor'kii, "9-e ianvaria," in I. P. Donkov, I. M. Mishakova, and N. V. Senichkina, *Pervaia russkaia . . . Sbornik vospominanii aktivnykh uchastnikov revoliutsii 1905–1907 gg.* (Moscow, 1975), p. 10.

63. Sablinsky, *The Road to Bloody Sunday*, pp. 229–261; Salisbury, *Black Night, White Snow*, pp.123–131; Lincoln, *In War's Dark Shadow*, pp. 288–291.

64. Quoted in Sablinsky, *The Road to Bloody Sunday*, p. 269.

65. Edward J. Bing, ed., *The Letters of Tsar Nicholas and Empress Marie* (London, 1937), p. 139.

66. P. I. Klimov, *Revoliutsionnaia deiatel'nost' rabochikh v derevne v 1905–1907 gg.* (Moscow, 1960), pp. 107–108; N. Karpukhin, ed., *1905 god v Riazanskoi gubernii* (Riazan, 1925), p. 18; Lincoln, *In War's Dark Shadow*, pp. 290–298; Bertram Wolfe, *Three Who Made A Revolution: A Biographical History* (New York, 1948), pp. 320–321; Leon Trotsky, *1905*, translated by Anna Bostock (New York, 1971), pp. 92–94.

67. L. M. Ivanov, ed., *Vserossiiskaia politicheskaia stachka* (Moscow-Leningrad, 1955), I, p. 354.

68. My translation of Mintslov's diary entries first appeared in *In War's Dark Shadow*, pp. 298–299. The original is in S. R. Mintslov, *Peterburg v 1903–1910 godakh* (Riga, 1931), pp. 161–164.

69. Quoted in Salisbury, *Black Night, White Snow*, p. 159.

70. Quoted in ibid., p. 162.

71. Trotsky, *1905*, p. 111.

72. Quoted in Suhr, *1905 in St. Petersburg*, pp. 332, 334.

73. Mintslov, *Peterburg v 1903–1910 godakh*, p. 166.

74. Quoted in Wolfe, *Three Who Made A Revolution*, p. 323.

75. Quoted in Florinsky, *Russia*, II, p. 1183.

76. E. E. Kruze, "Gody novogo revoliutsionnogo pod"ema v Peterburge," in Kochakov et al., eds., *Ocherki istorii Leningrada*, III, pp., 462–463.

77. Ibid., pp. 502, 512–513.

78. Ibid., pp. 526–529; K. Sidorov, ed., "Bor'ba so stachechnym dvizheniem nakanune mirovoi voiny," *Krasnyi arkhiv*, XXXIV (1929), pp. 96–97.

79. A. V. Liverovskii, "Poslednie chasy Vremennogo pravitel'stva. Dnevnik ministra Liverovskogo," *Istoricheskii arkhiv*, no. 6 (1960), p. 47.

## Chapter 8: On the Eve

1. Antsiferov, *Dusha Peterburga*, p. 219.

2. Belyi, *Peterburg*, p. 13.

3. M. D. Calvocoressi and Gerald Abraham, *Masters of Russian Music* (New York, 1976), p. 332.

4. Lawrence and Elizabeth Hanson, *Tchaikovsky: The Man Behind the Music* (New York, 1966), p. 363.

5. Quoted in Volkov, *St. Petersburg*, p. 111.

6. Quoted in Iuri Keldysh, "Tchaikovsky: The Man and His Outlook," in Dmitrii Shostakovich et al., *Russian Symphony: Thoughts About Tchaikovsky* (Freeport, N.Y., 1969), p. 22.

7. Volkov, *St. Petersburg*, pp. 69–70, 111–112.

8. Ibid., p. 121.

9. Quoted in ibid., pp. 151, 144.

10. Aleksandr Benua (Alexandre Benois), *Moi vospominaniia,* 5 vols. in 2 (I–III, IV–V) (Moscow, 1980), I–III, p. 11.

11. Quoted in I. N. Pruzhan, *Lev Samoilovich Bakst* (Leningrad, 1975), p.35.

12. Camilla Gray, *The Great Experiment: Russian Art, 1863–1922* (New York, 1962), p. 44. See also Zinaida Gippius-Merezhkovskaia, *Dmitrii Merezhkovskii* (Paris, 1951), pp. 79–81; John E. Bowlt, *The Silver Age: Russian Art of the Early Twentieth Century and the "World of Art" Group* (Newtonville, Mass., 1979), p.60.

13. Benua, *Moi vospominaniia,* I–III, p. 654.

14. Ibid., p. 603.

15. Ibid., p. 654. In her pathbreaking study, Katerina Clark calls this Preservationism. See Katerina Clark, *Petersburg: Crucible of Cultural Revolution* (Cambridge, Mass., 1995), pp. 57–60.

16. Benua, *Moi vospominaniia,* IV–V, p. 189.

17. Quoted in John E. Bowlt, "The World of Art," *Russian Literature Triquarterly* (1972), p. 191.

18. Aleksandr Benua, *Vozniknovenie "Mira iskusstva"* (Leningrad, 1928), pp. 5–19.

19. Quoted in Janet Kennedy, *The "Mir Iskusstva" Group and Russian Art, 1989–1912* (New York and London, 1977), p. 1.

20. Benua, *Moi vospominaniia,* I–III, p. 642.

21. Ibid., p. 644.

22. Quoted in Arnold L. Haskell, in collaboration with Walter Nouvel, *Diaghileff: His Artistic and Private Life* (New York, 1935), p. 60.

23. Benua, *Moi vospominaniia,* I–III, p. 645.

24. Benua, *Vozniknovenie,* p. 27.

25. Quoted in Haskell, *Diaghileff,* p. 87.

26. Quoted in Benua, *Vozniknovenie,* p. 42.

27. Quoted in Volkov, *St. Petersburg,* pp. 135–136.

28. Quoted in O. A. Liaskovskaia, *Il'ia Efimovich Repin* (Moscow, 1982), p. 244. See also pp. 245–262.

29. Lincoln, *Between Heaven and Hell,* pp. 195–197.

30. Quoted in Volkov, *St. Petersburg,* p. 131.

31. Lincoln, *Between Heaven and Hell,* pp. 269–270.

32. James H. Billington, *The Icon and the Axe: An Interpretive History of Russian Culture* (London, 1966), pp. 476–478; W. Bruce Lincoln, *Passage Through Armageddon: The Russians in War and Revolution, 1914–1918* (New York, 1986), pp. 262, 272.

33. Quoted in C. Harold Bedford, *The Seeker: D. S. Merezhkovsky* (Lawrence, Kans., 1975), 66–67.

34. Quoted in Bernice Glatzer Rosenthal, *Merezhkovskii* (The Hague, 1975), p. 104. See also Lincoln, *Between Heaven and Hell*, pp. 270–271.

35. Andrei Belyi, *Nachalo veka* (Moscow-Leningrad, 1933), pp. 173–174.

36. Ibid., p. 434.

37. Ibid., pp. 173–174.

38. Olga Matich, *Paradox in the Religious Poetry of Zinaida Gippius* (Munich, 1972), p. 49.

39. Quoted in Marc Slonim, *From Chekhov to the Revolution: Russian Literature, 1900–1917* (New York, 1962), p. 101.

40. Quoted in Volkov, *St. Petersburg*, p. 168.

41. Andrei Belyi, *Lug zelenyi* (New York and London, 1967), pp. 200, 178; Martin P. Rice, *Valery Bryusov and the Riddle of Russian Decadence* (Berkeley and Los Angeles, 1985), pp. 104–110.

42. Quotes from K. V. Mochul'skii, *Aleksandr Blok* (Paris, 1948), p. 57.

43. Quoted in ibid., p. 64.

44. V. Zlobin, "Z. N. Gippius: Ee sud'ba," *Novyi zhurnal*, XXXI (1952), p.153.

45. K. V. Mochul'skii, *Andrei Belyi* (Paris, 1955), p. 43. See also Belyi, *Nachalo veka*, pp. 189–192, 418–426; Andrei Belyi, "Vospominaniia o Bloke," *Epopeia*, no. 1 (1922), pp. 181–189.

46. Quoted in Volkov, *St. Petersburg*, p. 169.

47. Nicholas Berdyaev, *Dream and Reality* (New York, 1951), p. 145.

48. Belyi, *Nachalo veka*, pp. 173–174.

49. Lincoln, *Between Heaven and Hell*, pp. 271–272.

50. Quoted in Mochul'skii, *Andei Belyi*, p. 76.

51. Belyi, *Nachalo veka*, p. 422; Lincoln, *In War's Dark Shadow*, pp. 355–360; Lincoln, *Between Heaven and Hell*, p. 271.

52. Quotes from Mochul'skii, *Andrei Belyi*, p. 42, and Oleg A. Maslennikov, *The Frenzied Poets: Andrey Biely and the Russian Symbolists* (Berkeley and Los Angeles, 1952), p. 106.

53. Quoted in Avril Pyman, *The Life of Aleksandr Blok: The Distant Thunder, 1880–1908* (Oxford, 1979), p. 241.

54. Lincoln, *Between Heaven and Hell*, pp. 274–278; Pyman, *Distant Thunder*, pp. 27–155; Belyi, *Nachalo veka*, pp. 270–279.

55. Kornei Chukovskii, *Iz vospominanii* (Moscow, 1958), p. 371.

56. Quoted in Volkov, *St. Petersburg*, p. 159.

57. Ibid.

58. Quoted in Pyman, *Distant Thunder*, p. 156.

59. Quoted in ibid., p. 205.

60. Quoted in M. A. Beketova, *Aleksandr Blok* (Petersburg, 1922), p. 102.

61. Quoted in Pyman, *Distant Thunder*, p. 171.

62. Quoted in Bernice Glatzer Rosenthal, "Eschatology and the Appeal of Revolution: Merezhkovsky, Belyi, Blok," *California Slavic Studies*, XI (1980), p. 111.

63. Beketova, *Aleksandr Blok*, p. 101.

64. Kornei Chukovskii, "Nat Pinkerton," in *Sobranie sochinenii* (Moscow, 1969), VI, pp. 122, 124.

65. Volkov, *St. Petersburg*, p. 151.

66. Renato Poggioli, *The Poets of Russia, 1890–1930* (Cambridge, Mass., 1960), p. 161.

67. Salisbury, *Black Night, White Snow*, p. 181.

68. Belyi, *Nachalo veka*, pp. 321–323.

69. Ibid., p. 323.

70. Lincoln, *Between Heaven and Hell*, pp. 281–283.

71. E. Iu. Kuz'mina-Karavaeva, "Vstrechi s Blokom," in V. E. Vatsuro et al., eds., *Aleksandr Blok v vospominaniiakh sovremennikov* (Moscow, 1980), II, pp. 62–63.

72. Viacheslav Ivanov, *Po zvezdam: Stat'i i aforizmy* (St. Petersburg, 1909), p. 372; Mochul'skii, *Andrei Belyi*, p. 91.

73. A. Blok, *Zapisnye knizhki*, edited by P. N. Medvedev (Leningrad, 1930), pp. 55–57.

74. V. F. Khodasevich, *Nekropol': Vospominaniia* (Brussels, 1939), p. 14.

75. Quoted in Volkov, *St. Petersburg*, p. 257.

76. Quoted in Neil Tierney, *The Unknown Country: A Life of Igor Stravinsky* (London, 1977), p. 47. See also pp. 39–43.

77. Ibid., p. 50.

78. Quoted in Volkov, *St. Petersburg*, p. 256.

79. Igor Stravinsky, *Stravinsky: An Autobiography* (New York, 1936), p.48.

80. Gippius-Merezhkovskaia, *Dmitrii Merezhkovskii*, p. 208.

81. Quoted in Avril Pyman, *The Life of Aleksandr Blok: The Release of Harmony, 1908–1921* (Oxford, 1980), p. 140.

82. Quoted in ibid., p. 119.

83. Aleksandr Blok, introduction to "Vozmezdie," in *Sobranie sochinenii v shesti tomakh* (Moscow, 1971), IV, p. 148.

84. Blok to Belyi, 3 March 1911, in V. I. Orlov, ed., *Aleksandr Blok i Andrei Belyi* (Moscow, 1940), p. 249.

85. Quoted in Billington, *The Icon and the Axe*, p. 507.

86. Quoted in Volkov, *St. Petersburg*, p. 218.

87. Andrei Bely, *Petersburg*, translated, annotated, and introduced by Robert A. Maguire and John E. Malmstad (Bloomington, Ind., 1978), p. vii.

88. Volkov, *St. Petersburg*, p. 215.

89. Bely, *Petersburg*, p. xi.

90. Quotes from Lincoln, *Between Heaven and Hell*, p. 287; Lincoln, *In War's Dark Shadow*, p. 387.

91. Quotes from Lincoln, *Between Heaven and Hell*, pp. 286–287.

92. Kruze and Kutsentov, "Naselenie Peterburg," pp. 115–120, 142–144; Lincoln, *In War's Dark Shadow*, pp. 377–378; Stites, *The Women's Liberation Movement in Russia*, p. 183.

93. Volkov, *St. Petersburg*, p. 143.

94. S. S. Volk, "Prosveshchenie i shkola v Peterburge," in Kochakov, *Ocherki istorii Leningrada*, III, p. 585.

95. S. Frederick Starr, *Red and Hot: The Fate of Jazz in the Soviet Union, 1917–1980* (New York, 1983), pp. 11, 27.

96. D. G. Ivaneev, "Zarozhdenie i pervye shagi kino," in Kochakov, *Ocherki istorii Leningrada*, III, pp. 837–845.

97. Mathilde Kschessinska, *Dancing in Petersburg* (New York, 1961), p. 146.

98. Ibid., p. 252; Zinaida Gippius, *Siniaia kniga: Peterburgskii dnevnik* (Belgrade, 1929), pp. 12–14.

99. Maurice Paléologue, *La Russie des Tsars pendant la Grande Guerre* (Paris, 1921), I, p. 44.

100. S. D. Sazonov, *Vospominaniia* (Paris, 1927), p. 151.

101. Grand Duchess Maria Pavlovna, *Education of a Princess: A Memoir*, translated from the French and Russian (New York, 1931), p. 162.

102. Quoted in Mikhail Lemke, *250 dnei v tsarskoi stavke (25 sentiabria 1915–2 iiulia 1916)* (Petersburg, 1920), p. 7.

103. Sir Bernard Pares, *The Fall of the Russian Monarchy: A Study of the Evidence* (New York, 1961), pp. 187–188. See also Lincoln, *Passage through Armageddon*, pp. 41–43.

104. Paléologue, *La Russie des Tsars*, I, pp. 51–52.

105. Ibid., I, p. 106.

106. A. I. Spiridovich, *Velikaia voina i Fevral'skaia revoliutsiia* (New York, 1960), I, pp. 13–14; Lincoln, *Passage through Armageddon*, p. 43.

107. Pares, *Fall of the Russian Monarchy*, p. 237.

108. Gippius, *Merezhkovskii*, p. 208.

109. Ilya Ehrenburg, *People and Life: Memoirs of 1891–1917*, translated by Anna Bostock and Yvonne Kapp (London, 1961), p. 173.

110. Harold B. Segal, *Turn-of-the-Century Cabaret: Paris, Barcelona, Berlin, Munich, Vienna, Cracow, Moscow, St. Petersburg* (New York, 1987), p. 305.

111. This is Benedikt Livshits's account, excerpted in Wiktor Woroszylski, *Life of Mayakovsky*, translated from the Polish by Boleslaw Taborski (New York, 1970), p. 138. See also Lincoln, *Between Heaven and Hell*, pp. 308–310.

112. Quoted in Segal, *Cabaret*, pp. 307–308.

113. Quoted in Roberta Reeder, *Anna Akhmatova: Poet and Prophet* (New York, 1994), p. 44.

114. Quoted in Lincoln, *Between Heaven and Hell*, p. 311.

115. I. V. Odoevtseva, *Na beregakh Nevy* (Washington, D.C., 1967), p. 144.

116. Georgy Adamovich, "Meetings with Anna Akhmatova," in Konstantin Polivanov, ed., *Anna Akhmatova and Her Circle*, translated from the Russian by Patricia Beriozkina (Fayetteville, 1994), p. 64.

117. Anna Akhmatova, *Stikhi* (Moscow, 1988), p. 50.

118. Quoted in Reeder, *Akhmatova*, p. 79. See also Lincoln, *Between Heaven and Hell*, pp. 311–312.

119. Quoted in Reeder, *Akhmatova*, p. 36.

120. Volkov, *St. Petersburg*, p. 185.

121. V. V. Shul'gin, *Dni* (Belgrade, 1925), p. 76.

122. Lincoln, *Between Heaven and Hell*, p. 312.

123. Quoted in ibid., p. 296.

124. This is the recollection of Benedikt Livshits, excerpted in Woroszylski, *Life of Mayakovsky*, p. 139.

125. Quoted in Lincoln, *Between Heaven and Hell*, pp. 312–313.

126. Paléologue, *La Russie des Tsars*, III, p. 24.

127. "Doklad Petrogradskogo okhrannogo otdeleniia osobomu otdelu departamenta politsii, oktiabr' 1916 g.," in M. N. Pokrovskii, ed., "Politicheskoe polozhenie Rossii nakanune Fevral'skoi revoliutsii v zhandarmskom osveshchenii," *Krasnyi arkhiv*, XVII (1926), pp. 10–12.

128. Tsuyoshi Hasegawa, *The February Revolution: Petrograd, 1917* (Seattle and London, 1981), p. 200.

129. M. N. Pokrovskii, "Ekonomicheskoe polozhenie Rossii pered revoliutsii," *Krasnyi arkhiv*, X (1925), p. 67.

130. Quoted in Hasegawa, *The February Revolution*, p. 201.

131. Pokrovskii, "Politicheskoe polozhenie Rossii," p. 15.

132. Quoted in Hasegawa, *The February Revolution*, pp. 183–184.

133. Quoted in E. D. Chermenskii, *Chetvertaia Gosudarstvennaia duma i sverzhenie tsarizma v Rossii* (Moscow, 1976), p. 277.

134. Paléologue, *La Russie des Tsars*, III, p. 92.

135. "Zapiski otdeleniia po okhranenniu obshchestvennoi bezopastnosti i poriadka v stolitse, 14 fevralia 1917 g.," RGIA, 1405, opis' 530, delo no. 953; "Vedomost' predpriiatiiam goroda Petrograda, rabotaiushchim na Gosudarstvennuiu oboronu, masterovye koikh prekratili raboty 14-go fevralia 1917 goda," RGIA,

fond 1405, opis' 530, delo no. 953/40–41. E. N. Burdzhalov, *Vtoraia russkaia revoliutsiia: Vosstanie v Petrograde* (Moscow, 1967), I, pp. 85–93; I. P. Leiberov, *Na shturm samoderzhaviia: Petrogradskii proletariat v gody pervoi mirovoi voiny i Fevral'skoi revoliutsii* (Moscow, 1979), pp. 108–115; I. I. Mints, *Istoriia Velikogo Oktiabria* (Moscow, 1967), I, pp. 470–476.

136. Gippius, *Siniaia kniga*, p. 72; Paléologue, *La Russie des Tsars*, III, pp. 214–215.

137. Hasegawa, *The February Revolution*, pp. 233–247; A. A. Blok, *Poslednie dni imperatorskoi vlasti* (Petrograd, 1921), p. 53; Lincoln, *Passage through Armageddon*, pp. 318–326.

138. Letters of Nicholas to Aleksandra, February 25 and 26, 1917, in Nicholas II, *Letters of the Tsar to the Tsaritsa, 1914–1917*, translated by A. L. Hynes (London, 1929), pp. 315–316; Nicholas II, *Journal intime de Nicolas II (juillet 1914–juillet 1918)* (Paris, 1934), p. 92; D. N. Dubenskii, "Kak proizoshel perevorot v Rossii," in P. E. Shchegolev, ed., *Otrechenie Nikolaia II: Vospominaniia ochevidtsev, dokumenty* (Leningrad, 1927), pp. 36–39.

139. "Dopros generala S. S. Khabalova, 22 marta 1917 g.," in P. E. Shchegolev, ed., *Padenie tsarskogo rezhima* (Moscow-Leningrad, 1924), I, p. 190.

140. A. B. Rodzianko, "Pis'mo kn. Zin. N. Iusupovoi grafine Sumarokovoi-El'ston, 12 fevralia 1917 g., in P. Sadikov, ed., "K istorii poslednikh dnei tsarskogo rezhima (1916–1917 gg.)," *Krasnyi arkhiv*, XIV (1926), p. 246.

### Chapter 9: Comrades

1. The lines from *Masquerade* are quoted from V. A. Manuilov, "Lermontov," in B. P. Gorodetskii, *Istoriia russkoi literatury* (Moscow-Leningrad, 1955), VII, p. 307. The censor's opinion of it is quoted in Marc Slonim, *The Epic of Russian Literature from Its Origins through Tolstoi* (New York, 1964), p. 114.

2. Quoted in Volkov, *St. Petersburg*, p. 200. See also Lincoln, *Passage through Armageddon*, pp. 318–320.

3. Quoted in Volkov, *St. Petersburg*, p. 201.

4. Gippius, *Siniaia kniga*, p. 76.

5. Lincoln, *Passage through Armageddon*, pp. 328–329. I have dealt with the events of Russia's 1917 revolutions in much greater detail in this volume, pp. 315–476.

6. "Dopros Generala S. S. Khabalova," p. 191.

7. Quoted in Marc Ferro, *La Révolution de 1917* (Paris, 1967), I, p. 69.

8. I. P. Leiberov, "Petrogradskii proletariat v Fevral'skoi revoliutsii 1917 g.," in Diakin et al., eds., *Istoriia rabochikh Leningrada*, I, pp. 528–529.

9. "Telegramma generala S. S. Khabalova tsariu, 27 fevralia 1917 g.," RGIA, fond 1282, opis' 1, delo no. 737/70.

10. "Dopros grafa Frederiksa, 2 iiunia 1917 g.," in Shchegolev, *Padenie tsarskogo rezhima*, V, p. 38.

11. Nicholas II, *Journal intime*, p. 93. See also Lincoln, *Passage through Armageddon*, pp. 328–345; Hasegawa, *The February Revolution*, pp. 265–512; Shul'gin, *Dni*, pp. 178–307.

12. V. V. Maiakovskii, "Revoliutsiia: Poetokhronika," in V. V. Maiakovskii, *Sobranie sochinenii v vos'mi tomakh* (Moscow, 1968), I, pp. 224–225.

13. Quoted in Pyman, *Release of Harmony*, pp. 268–269.

14. Maxim Gorky, *Untimely Thoughts: Essays on Revolution, Culture, and the Bolsheviks, 1917–1918*, translated from the Russian with an introduction and notes by Herman Ermolaev (New York, 1968), p. 83.

15. V. I. Lenin, *Collected Works* (Moscow, 1960–1970), XXVI, p. 20.

16. Lenin, *Collected Works*, XXVI, p. 77.

17. L. Trotskii, *The History of the Russian Revolution*, translated by Max Eastman (Ann Arbor, 1960), III, p. 155.

18. N. N. Sukhanov, *Zapiski o revoliutsii* (Berlin-Petersburg-Moscow, 1921), VII, p. 76.

19. John Reed, *Ten Days That Shook the World* (New York, 1919. Reprinted 1960), pp. 49–50.

20. Trotskii, *History of the Russian Revolution*, III, pp. 167–173.

21. Reed, *Ten Days that Shook the World*, p. 41.

22. Sukhanov, *Zapiski o revoliutsii*, VII, pp. 91–92.

23. Quoted in Alexander Rabinowitch, *The Bolsheviks Come to Power: The Revolution of 1917 in Petrograd* (New York, 1976), p. 245.

24. Quoted in Rex A. Wade, *Red Guards and Workers' Militias in the Russian Revolution* (Stanford, 1984), p. 167. See also Mitel'man et al., *Istoriia putilovskogo zavoda*, I, p. 569.

25. Quoted in Reed, *Ten Days that Shook the World*, p. 89.

26. Lenin, *Collected Works*, XXVI, pp. 235, 234. See also M. V. Fofanova, "Poslednee podpol'e," in *Ob Il'iche* (Leningrad, 1970), p. 348.

27. Lenin, *Collected Works*, XXVI, pp. 234–235.

28. Quoted in Rabinowitch, *The Bolsheviks Come to Power*, p. 269.

29. Lincoln, *Passage Through Armageddon*, pp. 434–447.

30. Sukhanov, *Zapiski o revoliutsii*, VII, p. 160.

31. Quoted in S. P. Melgunov, *Kak bol'sheviki zakhvatili vlast'* (Paris, 1953), p. 108.

32. Gippius, *Siniaia kniga*, pp. 210–212.

33. Reed, *Ten Days that Shook the World*, p. 102. N. K. Krupskaia, *Vospominaniia o Lenine* (Moscow, 1968), p. 332.

34. Albert Rhys Williams, *Journey into Revolution: Petrograd, 1917–1918*, edited by Lucita Williams (Chicago, 1969), p. 111.

35. P. N. Maliantovich, "V Zimnem Dvortse, 25–26 oktiabria 1917 goda. Iz vospominanii," *Byloe*, XII, no. 6 (June 1918), pp. 123–124.

36. Lincoln, *Passage Through Armageddon*, pp. 447–451.

37. Maliantovich, "V Zimnem Dvortse," p. 130.

38. V. A. Antonov-Ovseenko, *Zapiski o grazhdanskoi voine* (Moscow, 1924), I, pp. 19–20.

39. Comte Louis de Robien, *The Diary of a Diplomat in Russia, 1917–1918*, translated from the French by Camilla Sykes (London, 1969), pp. 164, 175–176, 225. See also Ariadna Tyrkova-Williams, *From Liberty to Brest-Litovsk: The First Year of the Russian Revolution* (London, 1919), p. 440.

40. Quoted in L. Trotskii, *Moia zhizn'* (Berlin, 1930), II, p. 59.

41. De Robien, *The Diary of a Diplomat in Russia*, pp. 165–166.

42. R. H. Bruce Lockhart, *British Agent* (New York and London, 1933), p. 239.

43. Lenin, *Collected Works*, XXVII, p. 106; L. Trotskii, *Kak vooruzhalas' revoliutsiia (na voennoi rabote)* (Moscow, 1923), I, pp. 29–30.

44. *Iz istorii Vserossiiskoi Chrezvychainoi Komissii 1917–1921 gg.: Sbornik statei* (Moscow, 1958), p. 79.

45. Lockhart, *British Agent*, p. 254.

46. Quoted in George Leggett, *The Cheka: Lenin's Political Police* (Oxford, 1981), pp. 250–251.

47. A. N. Tolstoi, *Izbrannye sochineniia v shesti tomakh* (Moscow, 1956), III, p. 298.

48. Iu. V. Got'e, *Time of Troubles: The Diary of Iurii Vladimirovich Got'e*, translated, edited, and introduced by Terence Emmons (Princeton, 1988), p. 453.

49. Tyrkova-Williams, *From Liberty to Brest-Litovsk*, p. 433.

50. De Robien, *The Diary of a Diplomat in Russia*, p. 222.

51. Trotskii, *Kak vooruzhalas' revoliutsiia*, I, p. 310.

52. A. L. Fraiman, *Forpost sotsialisticheskoi revoliutsii: Petrograd v pervye mesiatsy sovetskoi vlasti* (Leningrad, 1969), pp. 289, 295, 306, 321–322; *God raboty Moskovskogo gorodskogo prodovol'stvennogo komiteta (mart 1917 g.–mart 1918 g.)* (Moscow, 1918), pp. 43–45; N. Orlov, *Prodovol'stvennaia rabota sovetskoi vlasti* (Moscow, 1918), p. 354.

53. G. I. Il'ina, "Chislennost', sostav i material'noe polozhenie rabochikh Petrograda v 1918–1920 gg.," in Fraiman, *Forpost*, pp. 89–90.

54. Tolstoi, *Izbrannye sochineniia*, III, pp. 297, 300.

55. Pitirim Sorokin, *Leaves from a Russian Diary* (New York, 1924), pp. 227–228.

56. Viktor Shklovsky, *A Sentimental Journey: Memoirs, 1917–1922*, translated by Richard Sheldon (Ithaca and London, 1970), pp. 174–176, 235.

57. Iu. Annenkov, *Dnevnik moikh vstrech: Tsikl tragedii* (New York, 1966), I, pp. 34–35.

58. Sorokin, *Leaves from a Russian Diary*, p. 218.

59. N. V. Afanas'ev, "Petrograd v 1920 g.," in S. I. Avvakumov et al., eds., *Ocherki istorii Leningrada*, IV, p. 211.

60. S. N. Semanov, *Likvidatsiia antisovetskogo kronshtadskogo miatezha 1921 goda* (Moscow, 1973), p. 25; Henry Noel Brailsford, *The Russian Workers' Republic* (London, 1921), p. 23.

61. Annenkov, *Dnevnik moikh vstrech*, I, p. 78.

62. Trotskii, *Kak vooruzhalas' revoliutsiia*, II, pp. 399, 383.

63. Ibid., pp. 441–442.

64. Ibid., p. 399; W. Bruce Lincoln, *Red Victory: A History of the Russian Civil War* (New York, 1989), pp. 289–299.

65. Quoted in Pyman, *Release of Harmony*, pp. 243, 249, 268–269, 281–282.

66. Lincoln, *Between Heaven and Hell*, pp. 316–317.

67. Quoted in Nikolai A. Gorchakov, *The Theater in Soviet Russia*, translated by Edgar Lehrman (New York, 1958), p. 109.

68. Quoted in Marc Slonim, *Russian Theater: From the Empire to the Soviets* (Cleveland and New York, 1961), p. 241.

69. Volkov, *St. Petersburg*, pp. 295–296.

70. Quoted in Marjorie L. Hoover, *Meyerhold: The Art of Conscious Theater* (Amherst, Mass., 1974), p. 112.

71. Quoted in James von Geldern, *Bolshevik Festivals, 1917–1920* (Berkeley and Los Angeles, 1993), p. 71. See also pp. 62–70, and Lincoln, *Between Heaven and Hell*, pp. 320–321.

72. Quoted in Volkov, *St. Petersburg*, p. 274.

73. Von Geldern, *Bolshevik Festivals*, pp. 199–207; Clark, *Petersburg*, pp. 122–124.

74. Semanov, *Likvidatsiia antisovetskogo kronshtadskogo miatezha*, pp. 27–31.

75. A. S. Pukhov, *Kronshtadtskii miatezh* (Moscow, 1931), pp. 11–12, 23–24; Got'e, *Time of Troubles*, pp. 422, 435, 452.

76. Emma Goldman, *Living My Life* (New York, 1931), p. 874.

77. Quoted in Paul Avrich, *Kronstadt 1921* (Princeton, 1970), p. 72.

78. Quoted in ibid., p. 64.

79. Ibid., pp. 51–63; Lincoln, *Red Victory*, pp. 489–491; Israel Getzler, *Kronstadt, 1917–1921: The Fate of Soviet Democracy* (Cambridge, 1983), pp. 19–183; P. Z. Sivkov, *Kronstadt: Stranitsy revoliutsionnoi istorii* (Leningrad, 1972), pp. 7–46, 83–336.

80. Avrich, *Kronstadt 1921*, p. 67.

81. *Izvestiia vremennogo revoliutsionnogo komiteta matrosov, krasnoarmeitsev, i rabochikh goroda Kronshtadta*, nos. 1–14, March 3–16, 1921. Reprinted in *Pravda o Kronshtadte: Ocherk geroicheskoi bor'by kronshtadtsev protiv diktatury Kommunisticheskoi partii* (Prague, 1921), p. 45.

82. Ibid., p. 128.

83. Goldman, *Living My Life*, pp. 884–885.

84. Alexander Berkman, *The Kronstadt Rebellion* (Berlin, 1922), p. 304.

85. Lenin, *Collected Works*, XXXII, p. 185.

86. Goldman, *Living My Life*, p. 886.

87. *Izvestiia vremennogo revoliutsionnogo komiteta*, p. 128.

88. Blair A. Ruble, *Leningrad: Shaping a Soviet City* (Berkeley and Los Angeles, 1990), p. 27; E. E. Kruze, "Petrograd v nachale 1921 g.," in Avvakumov et al., *Ocherki istorii Leningrada*, IV, p. 222.

89. M. V. Dobuzhinskii, *Vospominaniia* (Moscow, 1987), p. 23.

90. Volkov, *St. Petersburg*, p. 213.

91. Quoted in Annenkov, *Dnevnik moikh vstrech*, I, p. 74.

92. Iu. N. Zhukov, *Operatsiia Ermitazh: Opyt istoriko-arkhivnogo rassledovaniia* (Moscow, 1993), pp. 7–28; Robert C. Williams, *Russian Art and American Money, 1900–1940* (Cambridge, Mass., 1980), pp. 18–28; Norman, *The Hermitage*, pp. 179–186.

93. Norman, *The Hermitage*, pp. 192–195; Zhukov, *Operatsiia Ermitazh*, pp. 98–102; Williams, *Russian Art and American Money*, pp. 158–162.

94. Williams, *Russian Art and American Money*, pp. 173–179; Zhukov, *Operatsiia Ermitazh*, pp. 103–107.

95. S. Frederick Starr, *Red and Hot*, pp. 39–129; Clark, *Petersburg*, pp. 162–163.

96. Ibid., p. 27; Richard Taylor, *The Politics of the Soviet Cinema, 1917–1929* (Cambridge, 1979), p. 75; Clark, *Petersburg*, pp. 163–164.

97. Lincoln, *Between Heaven and Hell*, pp. 327–330. For additional material on early Soviet film, see Jay Leda, *Kino: A History of Russian and Soviet Film*, 3d ed. (Princeton, 1983); Denise J. Youngblood, *Soviet Cinema in the Silent Era, 1918–1930* (Ann Arbor, 1985); Taylor, *The Politics of the Soviet Cinema*; James Goodwin, *Eisenstein, Cinema, and History* (Urbana, Ill., and Chicago, 1993).

98. Clark, *Petersburg*, pp. 175–176.

99. Quoted in ibid., p. 178. See also p. 177.

100. Antsiferov, *Dusha Peterburga*, pp. 27, 219.

101. Ibid., pp. 127–128, 135.

102. Ibid., p. 219.

103. Quoted in Volkov, *St. Petersburg*, p. 418.

104. Ruble, *Leningrad*, pp. 43–46; V. V. Popov, "Stroitel'stvo i arkhitektura," in Avvakumov et al., *Ocherki istorii Leningrada*, IV, pp. 475–481; N. E. Nosov and Iu. S. Tokarev, "Narodnoe obrazovanie," in ibid., pp. 559, 571.

105. E. E. Kruze, "Leningrad v period vosstanovleniia narodnogo khoziaistva (1921–1925)," in ibid., pp. 232–244; A. P. Dzeniskevich, "Izmenenie sostava leningradskikh rabochikh za gody piatiletki," in ibid., pp. 317–318; Ia. M.

Dakhia, "Itogi pervoi piatiletki po gorodu Leningradu," in ibid., pp. 338–342; E. V. Stepanov, "Leningrad v gody tret'ei piatiletki (1938–1941 gg.)," in ibid., pp. 398–399.

106. Robert Conquest, *The Great Terror: A Reassessment* (New York and Oxford, 1990), pp. 37–52.

107. Ibid., pp. 485, 450.

108. Quoted in ibid., p. 214.

109. Quoted in ibid., p. 306.

110. Quoted in Reeder, *Anna Akhmatova*, p. 208.

111. Evgenii Shvarts, *Zhivu bespokoino: Iz dnevnikov* (Leningrad, 1990), pp. 629–630.

112. Quoted in Norman, *The Hermitage*, p. 234.

113. Ibid., pp. 230–240.

114. Quoted in Volkov, *St. Petersburg*, p. 496. See also pp. 494–497.

115. Shvarts, *Zhivu bespokoino*, p. 630.

116. Quoted in Volkov, *St. Petersburg*, p. 407.

117. Quoted in Reeder, *Anna Akhmatova*, p. 201.

118. Quoted in ibid., p. 217.

### Chapter 10: Nine Hundred Days

1. Elena Kochina, *Blockade Diary*, translated and introduced by Samuel C. Ramer (Ann Arbor, 1990), pp. 31, 37.

2. This comment comes from the late Tamara Rudzinska, who was living in Tallinn in the summer of 1941.

3. Quoted in Leon Gouré, *The Siege of Leningrad* (Stanford, 1962), p. 17. See also Salisbury, *The 900 Days*, pp. 148–157.

4. Ol'ga Berggol'ts, *Izbrannye proizvedeniia v dvukh tomakh* (Leningrad, 1967), I, pp. 105–106.

5. Gouré, *The Siege of Leningrad*, pp. 6–7; A. V. Karasev, *Leningradtsy v gody blokady* (Moscow, 1959), pp. 126–128; Dmitri V. Pavlov, *Leningrad 1941: The Blockade*, translated by John Clinton Adams, with a foreword by Harrison E. Salisbury (Chicago and London, 1965), p. 52.

6. Alexander Werth, *Russia at War, 1941–1945* (New York, 1964), p. 314.

7. Kochina, *Blockade Diary*, p. 34.

8. Quoted in Gouré, *The Siege of Leningrad*, p. 27.

9. Kochina, *Blockade Diary*, p. 34.

10. Werth, *Russia at War, 1941–1945*, p. 303.

11. I. I. Fediuninskii, *Podniatye po trevoge* (Moscow, 1961), pp. 58–59.

12. Quoted in Salisbury, *The 900 Days*, p. 199.

13. Gouré, *The Siege of Leningrad*, pp. 49–52.

14. Alexander Werth, *Leningrad* (New York, 1941), pp. 140–141.

15. Sergei Varshavskii and Boris Rast, *Saved for Humanity: The Hermitage during the Siege of Leningrad, 1941–1944*, translated from the Russian by Arthur Shkarovskii-Raffe (Leningrad, 1985), p. 82.

16. Quoted in Norman, *The Hermitage* p. 244. See also Varshavskii and Rast, *Saved for Humanity*, pp. 23–66.

17. Varshavskii and Rast, *Saved for Humanity*, pp. 60–68, 86–87, 99–101.

18. Kochina, *Blockade Diary*, p. 35.

19. Gouré, *The Siege of Leningrad*, pp. 52–57.

20. Quoted in Ales Adamovich and Daniil Granin, *A Book of the Blockade*, translated from the Russian by Hilda Perham (Moscow, 1983), p. 40.

21. Quoted in Salisbury, *The 900 Days*, p. 420.

22. Ibid., pp. 421–422; Pavel Luknitskii, *Skvoz' vsiu blokadu* (Leningrad, 1964), pp. 96–97.

23. Kochina, *Blockade Diary*, p. 33.

24. Quoted in Werth, *Russia at War, 1941–1945*, p. 297.

25. Salisbury, *The 900 Days*, pp. 380–382.

26. Trotskii, *Kak vooruzhalas' revoliutsiia*, II, p. 383.

27. Werth, *Leningrad*, p. 91.

28. Pavlov, *Leningrad 1941*, pp. xx, 43–44; Salisbury, *The 900 Days*, pp. 339–341.

29. Quoted in Gouré, *The Siege of Leningrad*, p. 128.

30. Quoted in Salisbury, *The 900 Days*, p. 339.

31. T. A. Zhdanova, *Krepost' na Neve* (Moscow, 1960), p. 28.

32. Werth, *Leningrad*, p. 77.

33. Pavlov, *Leningrad 1941*, p. 58.

34. Ibid., pp. 57–59.

35. Ibid., pp. 59–65.

36. Adamovich and Granin, *A Book of the Blockade*, p. 31.

37. Pavlov, *Leningrad 1941*, pp. 69–75. See also A. Skiliagin, V. Lesov, Iu. Pimenov, and I. Savichenko, *Dela i liudi leningradskoi militsii: Ocherki istorii* (Leningrad, 1967), pp. 289–290.

38. Quoted in Salisbury, *The 900 Days*, p. 550. See also pp. 549–552, and Adamovich and Granin, *A Book of the Blockade*, pp. 342–343.

39. Lidiya Ginzburg, *Blockade Diary*, translated from the Russian by Alan Myers (London, 1995), p. 28.

40. Quoted in Adamovich and Granin, *A Book of the Blockade*, p. 147.

41. Quoted in ibid., p. 90.

42. Karasev, *Leningradtsy v gody blokady*, pp. 134–138, 144–152; Salisbury, *The 900 Days*, p. 478; Gouré, *The Siege of Leningrad*, pp. 159–162.

43. Luknitskii, *Skvoz' vsiu blokadu*, p. 188.

44. Quoted in Salisbury, *The 900 Days*, p. 436.

45. Kochina, *Blockade Diary*, p. 64.

46. Ibid., p. 43.

47. Quoted in Adamovich and Granin, *A Book of the Blockade*, p. 363.

48. Kochina, *Blockade Diary*, p. 70.

49. Ibid., pp. 82–83.

50. Luknitskii, *Skvoz' vsiu blokadu*, pp. 204–207.

51. Ginzburg, *Blockade Diary*, pp. 38–39.

52. Pavlov, *Leningrad 1941*, pp. 134–135.

53. Elena Kochina's diary is full of instances in which she overlooked her husband's weaknesses, such as his inability to resist stealing part of the food ration when their daughter was at the brink of death and given special coupons for extra nourishment. See Kochina, *Blockade Diary*, *passim*. The same is true of Lidia Ginzburg's *Blockade Diary* and any number of other notes and diaries left by women who lived through the siege.

54. Pavlov, *Leningrad 1941*, pp. 140, 151, 153.

55. Ibid., pp. 136–147; Karasev, *Leningradtsy v gody blokady*, pp. 170–180; Gouré, *The Siege of Leningrad*, pp. 203–206.

56. Karasev, *Leningradtsy v gody blokady*, pp. 180–184; Pavlov, *Leningrad 1941*, pp. 150–160.

57. Pavlov, *Leningrad 1941*, p. 164.

58. Luknitskii, *Skvoz' vsiu blokadu*, pp. 217–223.

59. Kochina, *Blockade Diary*, p. 107; Salisbury, *The 900 Days*, pp. 578–579.

60. Pavlov, *Leningrad 1941*, p. 165.

61. Ginzburg, *Blockade Diary*, p. 3.

62. Volkov, *St. Petersburg*, p. 429.

63. Quoted in ibid., p. 430.

64. Berggol'ts, *Izbrannye proizvedenie*, II, pp. 161–162.

65. Quoted in Volkov, *St. Petersburg*, p. 440.

66. Salisbury, *The 900 Days*, pp. 590–591.

67. Quoted in Gouré, *The Siege of Leningrad*, p. 268. See also Skiliagin et al., *Dela i liudi leningradskoi militsii*, pp. 278–279.

68. Alexander Fadeev, *Leningrad in the Days of the Blockade*, translated by R. D. Charques (London and New York, n.d.), p. 9.

69. Gouré, *The Siege of Leningrad*, p. 268.

70. Ginzburg, *Blockade Diary*, pp. 30–32.

71. Quoted in Adamovich and Granin, *A Book of the Blockade*, pp. 89, 210.

72. Fadeev, *Leningrad in the Days of the Blockade*, p. 18.

73. Luknitskii, *Skvoz' vsiu blokadu*, pp. 317–319, 323–324.

74. Fadeev, *Leningrad in the Days of the Blockade*, pp. 39, 43–44.

75. Ibid., pp. 42, 36.

76. Luknitskii, *Skvoz' vsiu blokadu*, pp. 321–322.

77. Quoted in Volkov, *St. Petersburg*, p. 441.

78. Ibid., pp. 440–441; Salisbury, *The 900 Days*, pp. 618–619.

79. Karasev, *Leningradtsy v gody blokady*, pp. 260–262; Luknitskii, *Skvoz' vsiu blokadu*, pp. 329–330.

80. Salisbury, *The 900 Days*, p. 618.

81. Berggol'ts, *Izbrannye proizvedenie*, I, p. 137–138.

82. Ibid., II, pp. 192–193.

83. Ibid., II, pp. 194–195; Luknitskii, *Skvoz' vsiu blokadu*, pp. 341–380.

84. Vera Inber, *Stranitsy dnei perebiraia . . . (iz dnevnikov i zapisnykh knizhek)* (Moscow, 1967), p. 161. See also Salisbury, *The 900 Days*, pp. 628–631; Karasev, *Leningradtsy v gody blokady*, pp. 271–277.

85. Berggol'ts, *Izbrannye proizvedenie*, II, p. 233.

86. Karasev, *Leningradtsy v gody blokady*, pp. 295–297; Salisbury, *The 900 Days*, pp. 632–640.

87. Berggol'ts, *Izbrannye proizvedenie*, II, p. 241.

88. Quoted in Karasev, *Leningradtsy v gody blokady*, p. 304.

89. Quoted in Salisbury, *The 900 Days*, p. 646. See also pp. 643–645; Feduinskii, *Podniatye po trevoge*, pp. 174–177; Karasev, *Leningradtsy v gody blokady*, pp. 300–306.

90. Karasev, *Leningradtsy v gody blokady*, pp. 304–306; Luknitskii, *Skvoz' vsiu blokadu*, pp. 455–456.

91. Luknitskii, *Skvoz' vsiu blokadu*, pp. 456–457.

92. Quoted in Karasev, *Leningradtsy v gody blokady*, p. 309.

93. Luknitskii, *Skvoz' vsiu blokadu*, p. 498.

94. Berggol'ts, *Izbrannye proizvedenie*, II, p. 261.

95. Inber, *Stranitsy dnei perebiraia*, p. 209.

96. Quoted in Salisbury, *The 900 Days*, p. 656.

97. Quoted in ibid., p. 657.

98. Ibid., p. 659. See also Blair A. Ruble, "The Leningrad Affair and the Provincialization of Leningrad," *Russian Review*, XLII (1983), pp. 304–305.

99. Varshavskii and Rast, *Saved for Humanity*, pp. 253–254.

100. Ibid., pp. 264–270.

101. Quoted in Norman, *The Hermitage*, p. 268.

102. Quoted in ibid., p. 265.

103. Quoted in Werth, *Leningrad*, p. 188.

104. Norman, *The Hermitage*, pp. 261–281.

105. Quoted in Salisbury, *The 900 Days*, p. 658.

106. Ibid., pp. 659–661; Ruble, "The Leningrad Affair," p. 305.

107. Reeder, *Anna Akhmatova*, pp. 249–282.

108. Quoted in ibid., pp. 284–285.

109. Isaiah Berlin, "Anna Akhmatova: A Memoir," in *The Complete Poems of Anna Akhmatova*, translated by Judith Hemschemeyer, edited and with an introduction by Roberta Reeder (Somerville, Mass., 1990), II, p. 26.

110. Ibid., pp. 34–35.

111. Quoted in Volkov, *St. Petersburg*, p. 450.

112. Quoted in Reeder, *Anna Akhmatova*, p. 292.

113. Quoted in ibid., p. 324.

114. Quoted in Lincoln, *Between Heaven and Hell*, p. 413.

115. Quoted in Edward J. Brown, *Russian Literature Since the Revolution* (Cambridge, Mass., 1982), pp. 183–184.

116. Quoted in Salisbury, *The 900 Days*, p. 665.

117. Quoted in V. E. Mushtukov, A. A. Nashkevich, and B. K. Pukinskii, *Leningrad: Putevoditel'* (Leningrad, 1970), p. 401.

118. Werth, *Leningrad*, p. 18.

119. *The Complete Poems of Anna Akhmatova*, II, p. 191.

120. Quoted in Volkov, *St. Petersburg*, p. 476.

## Chapter 11: Together in Step

1. See S. I. Avvakumov et al., eds., *Ocherki istorii Leningrada: Period Velikoi Oktiabr'skoi sotsialisticheskoi revoliutsii i postroeniia sotsializma v SSSR, 1917–1941 gg.* (Leningrad, 1964), IV.

2. Z. V. Stepanov et al., *Ocherki istorii Leningrada: Leningrad v period zaversheniia stroitel'stva sotsializma i postepennogo perekhoda k kommunizmu, 1946–1965 gg.* (Leningrad, 1970), VI.

3. Ruble, "The Leningrad Affair," pp. 301–306.

4. V. A. Ezhov, "Izmeneniia v chislennosti i sostave rabochikh Leningrada v poslevoennyi period," *Vestnik Leningradskogo universiteta. Seriia istorii iazyka i literatury* (1966), no. 2, pp. 15–20.

5. Ruble, "The Leningrad Affair," pp. 306–309; V. A. Ezhov, *Rabochii klass— vedushchaia sila vosstanovleniia Leningrada v 1943–1950 gg.* (Leningrad, 1982), pp. 22–24; A. R. Dzeniskevich, "Leningrad v gody pervoi poslevoennoi piatiletki (1946–1950 gg.)," in Stepanov et al., *Ocherki istorii Leningrada*, VI, pp. 33–34.

6. Quoted in Salisbury, *The 900 Days*, p. 660.

7. Quoted in Ruble, "The Leningrad Affair," p. 318.

8. Ibid., pp. 310–320; Robert Conquest, *Power and Policy in the U.S.S.R.: The Study of Soviet Dynasties* (New York, 1961), pp. 95–111.

9. Riasanovsky, *A History of Russia*, p. 585; Paul Dukes, *A History of Russia: Medieval, Modern, Contemporary*, 2d ed. (Durham, N.C., 1990), p. 292.

10. Salisbury, *The 900 Days*, p. 661.

11. Ruble, *Leningrad*, p. 64.

12. Ibid., pp. 61–66, 82, 242.

13. Ibid., p. 70.

14. S. M. Semanov, "Gorodskoe khoziaistvo," in Stepanov et al., *Ocherki istorii Leningrada*, VI, pp. 259–261; A. P. Kitaigorodskaia, "Stroitel'stvo i arkhitektura," in A. Z. Vakser et al., *Ocherki istorii Leningrada*, VII, pp. 182–186.

15. V. I. Piliavskii, "Arkhitektura i stroitel'stvo," in Stepanov et al., *Ocherki istorii Leningrada*, VI, pp. 216–220; Kitaigorodskaia, "Stroitel'stvo i arkhitektura," pp. 185–186.

16. Kitaigorodskaia, "Stroitel'stvo i arkhitektura," pp. 156–157; I. A. Bashinskaia and E. A. Ivanova, "Izobrazitel'noe iskusstvo," in Stepanov et al., *Ocherki istorii Leningrada*, VI, pp. 383–385.

17. Quoted in Volkov, *St. Petersburg*, p. 520.

18. Starr, *Red and Hot*, pp. 216–218.

19. Quoted in Eleanor Lipper, *Eleven Years in Soviet Prison Camps* (Chicago, 1951), p. 112.

20. Lincoln, *The Conquest of a Continent*, pp. 345–346; Starr, *Red and Hot*, pp. 216, 224–225.

21. Quoted in Starr, *Red and Hot*, p. 228.

22. Ibid., pp. 224–234.

23. Joseph Brodsky, "Spoils of War," in Joseph Brodsky, *On Grief and Reason* (New York, 1995), p. 13.

24. Quoted in Priscilla Johnson, *Khrushchev and the Arts: The Politics of Soviet Culture, 1962–1964* (Cambridge, Mass., 1965), p. 121.

25. Starr, *Red and Hot*, pp. 251–275.

26. Quoted in ibid., p. 292.

27. Ibid., pp. 276–293.

28. Quoted in Volkov, *St. Petersburg*, p. 532.

29. Quoted in Timothy W. Ryback, *Rock Around the Bloc: A History of Rock Music in Eastern Europe and the Soviet Union* (New York, 1990), p. 151. See also pp. 151–155.

30. Volkov, *St. Petersburg*, pp. 531–534; Starr, *Red and Hot*, pp. 292–311.

31. Quoted in Ryback, *Rock Around the Bloc*, p. 230.

32. Ibid., pp. 156–166, 211–231.

33. Nikolai Volkov, "Agrippina Vaganova," in Juri Slonimsky et al., *The Soviet Ballet* (New York, 1947), pp. 45–47.

34. Iris Morley, *Soviet Ballet* (London, 1946), p. 16. See also pp. 14–15; Tim Scholl, *From Petipa to Balanchine: Classical Revival and the Modernization of Ballet* (London and New York, 1994), pp. 79–133.

35. Quoted in Morley, *Soviet Ballet*, p. 19.

36. A. Sokhor, "Kompozitor-dramaturg v balete," in *Muzyka sovetskogo baleta: sbornik statei*, edited by Lev Nikolaevich Raaben (Moscow, 1962), p. 101.

37. Juri Slonimsky et al., *The Soviet Ballet* (New York, 1947), pp. 31, 83.

38. Volkov, *St. Petersburg*, pp. 501–504.

39. Ibid., pp. 503–504.

40. Ibid., p. 505.

41. Quoted in Vladimir Seduro, *Dostoevskii in Russian Literary Criticism, 1846–1956* (New York, 1957), p. 83.

42. Quoted in Billington, *Icon and the Axe*, p. 415.

43. Quoted in Seduro, *Dostoevskii in Russian Literary Criticism*, p. 136.

44. Quoted in ibid., pp. 251, 258, 267.

45. Quoted in ibid., pp. 280, 278, 283, 285, 287–288.

46. Quoted in Vladimir Seduro, *Dostoevsky in Russian and World Theater* (North Quincy, Mass., 1977), p. 363. See also pp. 359–366.

47. Quoted in Volkov, *St. Petersburg*, p. 500.

48. Vladimir Seduro, *Dostoevski's Image in Russia Today* (Belmont, Mass., 1975), p. 165.

49. Brodsky, "Spoils of War," p. 3.

50. Ibid., p. 8.

51. Ibid., p. 16.

52. Joseph Brodsky, "In a Room and a Half," in Joseph Brodsky, *Less Than One: Selected Essays* (New York, 1985), pp. 455. See also pp. 447–454.

53. Quoted in Solomon Volkov, *Conversations with Joseph Brodsky: A Poet's Journey Through the Twentieth Century*, translated by Marian Schwartz (New York and London, 1998), p. 30.

54. Brodsky, "Spoils of War," p. 6.

55. Joseph Brodsky, "Less Than One," in *Less Than One*, p. 14.

56. Ibid., p. 15.

57. Quoted in Valentina Polukhina, *Joseph Brodsky: A Poet for Our Time* (Cambridge and New York, 1989), p. 9.

58. Quoted in ibid., p. 4.

59. Brodsky, "Less Than One," pp. 29, 28.

60. Polukhina, *Joseph Brodsky*, pp. 11–20; Volkov, *St. Petersburg*, pp. 478–482.

61. Quoted in Volkov, *Conversations with Joseph Brodsky*, p. 207.

62. Quoted in Polukhina, *Joseph Brodsky*, p. 23.

63. Quoted in ibid., p. 22.

64. Volkov, *St. Petersburg*, p. 477.

65. Quoted in Polukhina, *Joseph Brodsky*, p. 24.

66. Joseph Brodsky, "New Stanzas to Augusta," in Joseph Brodsky, *Selected Poems*, translated and introduced by George L. Kline, with a foreword by W. H. Auden (Harmondsworth, 1973), pp. 57–61.

67. Quoted in Volkov, *Conversations with Joseph Brodsky*, p. 77.

68. Quoted in Lazar Fleishman, *Boris Pasternak: The Poet and His Politics* (Cambridge, Mass., 1990), p. 254.

69. Quoted in Lincoln, *Between Heaven and Hell*, p. 416.

70. Quoted in Volkov, *St. Petersburg*, p. 514.

71. *Literaturnaia gazeta*, May 5, 1993.

72. Quoted in Volkov, *St. Petersburg*, p. 538.

73. *The Complete Poems of Anna Akhmatova*, II, pp. 98–99.

74. Lev Anninsky, "Returning to Nabokov," *Moscow News*, no. 18 (May 8–15, 1988), p. 10.

75. Ibid.

76. Quoted in Volkov, *St. Petersburg*, p. 545.

### Chapter 12: Past and Present

1. Quoted in Kaganov, *Images of Space*, p. 13.

2. P. N. Miliukov, *Ocherki po istorii russkoi kul'tury* (St. Petersburg, 1901), III, p. 207; M. M. Shtrange, *Demokraticheskaia intelligentsiia Rossii v XVIII veke* (Moscow, 1965), p. 11.

3. Weber, *The Present State of Russia*, I, p. 4.

4. John Milner, *A Dictionary of Russian and Soviet Artists* (Woodbridge, 1993), p. 272.

5. Kaganov, *Images of Space*, pp. 19–22.

6. N. D. Chechulin, ed., *Nakaz Imperatritsy Ekateriny II, dannyi Kommissii o sochinenii proekta novago ulozheniia* (St. Petersburg, 1907), pp. 1–2.

7. Kaganov, *Images of Space*, pp. 28–29.

8. Vigel', *Zapiski*, I, p. 179; Wortman, *Scenarios of Power*, p. 143.

9. Quoted in Volkov, *St. Petersburg*, p. 23.

10. V. V. Danilevskii, *Russkoe zoloto: Istoriia otkrytiia i dobychi do serediny XIX v.* (Moscow, 1959), pp. 253–255; A. P. Okladnikov et al., eds., *Istoriia Sibiri s drevneishikh vremen do nashikh dnei* (Leningrad, 1968), II, p. 399.

11. N. F. Khomutetskii and N. A. Evsina, "Arkhitektura," in Grabar', *Istoriia russkogo iskusstva*, VIII, pp. 463–467; V. M. Glinka and A. V. Pomarnatskii, *Otechestvennaia voina 1812 goda v khudozhestvennykh i istoricheskikh pamiatnikakh iz sobranii Ermitazha* (Leningrad, 1963), pp. 9–10; V. M. Glinka and A. V. Pomarnatskii, *Voennaia galereia Zimnego dvortsa* (Leningrad, 1981), pp. 7–28.

12. N. V. Gogol', *Polnoe sobranie sochinenii N. V. Gogolia* (Moscow, 1913), VIII, p. 41.

13. M. P. Veselovskii, "Zapiski M. P. Veselovskago s 1828 po 1882," GPB, fond 550.F.IV.861/389.

14. Quoted in Kaganov, *Images of Space*, p. 134.

15. Quoted in ibid., p. 130.

16. Quoted in Volkov, *St. Petersburg*, p. 49.

17. F. M. Dostoevskii, *Polnoe sobranie sochinenii* (Leningrad, 1979), XXVI, pp. 147–148.

18. Dobuzhinskii, *Vospominaniia*, p. 188.

19. Kaganov, *Images of Space*, p. 147.

20. Quoted in Lincoln, *Between Heaven and Hell*, p. 287.

21. Quoted in Kaganov, *Images of Space*, p. 150.

22. Quoted in Lincoln, *Between Heaven and Hell*, pp. 315–316.

23. Quoted in ibid., p. 315.

24. A. A. Blok, "Dvenadtsat'," in A. A. Blok, *Sobranie sochinenii* (Moscow, 1971), III, pp. 233–243.

25. Quoted in Volkov, *St. Petersburg*, p. 536.

26. Werth, *Leningrad*, p. 18.

27. *The Complete Poems of Anna Akhmatova*, II, p. 191.

28. Quoted in Volkov, *Conversations with Joseph Brodsky*, p. 271.

29. Quoted in Mushtukov, Nashkevich, Pukinskii, *Leningrad: Putevoditel'*, p. 401.

30. Kaganov, *Images of Space*, p. 182.

31. Quoted in Volkov, *Conversations with Joseph Brodsky*, p. 273.

# INDEX

# ABOUT THE AUTHOR

W. Bruce Lincoln, Distinguished Research Professor of History at Northern Illinois University, held appointments as a Senior Fellow at the Institutes of History at Moscow and Leningrad State Universities, a Research Fellow at the Academy of Sciences of the USSR, a Senior Research Fellow at Columbia University's Harriman Institute, a Fulbright Research Fellow, a Visiting Research Fellow at the Hoover Institute, and a John Simon Guggenheim Fellow. Among his many acclaimed books on Russia's past are *Nicholas I, The Romanovs, Red Victory*, and *Between Heaven and Hell. Sunlight at Midnight* is his twelfth and last book.